Employment Law

Blackwell HRM Series

Edited by Myron Roomkin
J. L. Kellogg Graduate School of Management

Employment Law

The Workplace Rights of Employees and Employers

Benjamin W. Wolkinson and Richard N. Block

School of Labor and Industrial Relations, Michigan State
University, East Lansing, Michigan, USA

Blackwell
Publishing

350 Main Street, Malden, MA 02148-5018, USA
108 Cowley Road, Oxford OX4 1JF, UK
550 Swanston Street, Carlton South, Melbourne, Victoria 3053, Australia
Kurfürstendamm 57, 10707 Berlin, Germany

First published 1996 by Blackwell Publishing Ltd
Reprinted 1998, 1999, 2000, 2001, 2002

Library of Congress Cataloging-in-Publication Data

Wolkinson, Benjamin W.
    Employment law: the workplace rights of employees and employers / Benjamin W. Wolkinson and Richard N. Block.
        p.   cm.
    Includes index.
    ISBN 1–55786–832–8 (pbk: alk. paper) — 1–55786–913–8 (hbk.)
    1. Employee rights—United States. 2. Labor contract—United States. 3. Discrimination in employment—Law and legislation—United States. I. Block, Richard N.
    KF3457.W65   1996
    344.73'01—dc20   95–12469
    [347.3041]   CIP

A catalogue record for this title is available from the British Library.

Set in 10 on 12pt Melior
by Graphicraft Typesetters Limited, Hong Kong
Printed and bound in the United States of America

For further information on
Blackwell Publishing, visit our website:
http://www.blackwellpublishing.com

Dedication

To Ruthie, Rachel, David, and Sarah;
Marcia, Talia and Jessica,
whose love is a faithful reminder of what is important in life.

Contents

Contents

Acknowledgments

In completing this work, the authors received considerable assistance from many sources. Terry Curry, Associate Director of the Personnel Management Program Services (PMPS) of the School of Labor and Industrial Relations, co-authored chapter 7. Scott Tobey of our school's Labor Program Service authored chapter 8, and Ed Welch of PMPS authored chapter 9.

We acknowledge and appreciate the assistance of our colleagues at the School of Labor and Industrial Relations, Karen Roberts and Catherine Lundy, who provided the authors with valuable reference materials on the Americans with Disabilities Act of 1990.

We thank the staff of the Labor and Industrial Relations Library at Michigan State University, its Director, Annie Cooper, and her assistants, Nancy Barkey-Young and Cynthia Bullock, who helped us immeasurably in accessing necessary judicial decisions and administrative regulations.

We have benefited from the helpful comments and suggestions of John Runyan, a partner in the law firm of Sachs, Waldman, O'Hare, Helveston, Hodges and Barnes, PC, of Detroit, Michigan, and David Sherwin, a partner in the law firm of Pinnisi, Wagner, Sherwyn, and Geldenhuys, PC, of Ithaca, New York.

Our typists Janet Grewe and Kathy Witte toiled long and hard over the manuscript and its completion reflects their dedication.

To Bernard D. Meltzer, Kurt Hanslowe and Frederic Freilicher, our teachers of labor law at the University of Chicago and at Cornell University's School of Labor and Industrial Relations, we owe a heavy debt of thanks. They inspired our interest in labor and employment law, and their scholarship remains a continuing source of critical insight and vitality.

Acknowledgments

Finally, we are most grateful for our wives Ruth and Marcia, whose love and support have always facilitated our work.

Benjamin Wolkinson and Richard Block
East Lansing, Michigan

Chapter 1
The Purpose of This Book

During the past sixty years, an enormous change has taken place in the law of the workplace. Between 1935 and 1965, the major employment relations law was the National Labor Relations Act (NLRA). Enacted in 1935, and amended in 1947 and 1959, the NLRA focused on the rights of employees to organize into unions and to bargain collectively. More generally, however, it was established to provide employees with collective or group rights. The premise underlying the passage of the NLRA was that workplace problems, if any, could be addressed by employees joining a union and bargaining collectively through that union to improve their terms and conditions of employment.

By the early 1960s, however, it had become clear that not all workplace problems could be addressed through providing employees with the right to organize and to bargain collectively. Not all employees wished to unionize and not all employees were covered by the NLRA. Unions did not have unlimited bargaining power and were unable to address all issues, and some problems could be exacerbated by unions. More generally, there was a sense that workplace protections should not be limited to those employees who chose union representation, or who happened to be covered by a collective agreement, perhaps as a result of taking a job at a previously unionized firm. Protection from unjust treatment, however defined, should be available to all workers.

The first important manifestation of this view was the passage of Title VII of the Civil Rights Act of 1964. It protected workers from discrimination in employment based on race, religion, gender, or national origin. Equally importantly, however, it established an important principle in the law of the workplace – that employees could exercise individual employment rights. Unlike the NLRA, which provided rights to employees only to the extent to which they acted in concert with other employees, and had limited coverage, Title VII provided legal rights to individual employees, and covered all employees, regardless of occupational status. Title VII, then, marked the beginning of a revolution in the law of the workplace in the United States, the development of law granting employees individual employment rights.

Prior to Title VII, laws covering individual employees had been narrowly focused. The Fair Labor Standards Act, enacted in 1939 and amended numerous times, provided for minimum wages and overtime for nonexempt employees who worked more than 40 hours per week. Most states also had laws providing for maximum hours for women and children. But as long as those minima were observed, the employer could deal with its employees in any way it wished. In addition, by the 1920s almost all states had enacted workers' compensation laws, providing employees with some level of benefits if they were injured on the job. But outside of these exceptions, there was no protection for employees.

The thirty years following the passage of Title VII were marked by a massive increase in protection for individual workers. To the prohibited discriminations in Title VII were added discrimination on the basis of age and disability, and the range of actions that constituted discrimination was considerably broadened. Several states and many localities also made discrimination on the basis of an employee's sexual preference unlawful. Legislation designed to provide safe working conditions was enacted in 1972 with the Occupational Safety Health Act (OSHA). Where workers' compensation laws were reactive, being triggered only after a worker was injured, the OSHA took the initiative to prevent occupational injuries or illnesses.

The 1980s marked the development of law to protect workers from unjust discharge under certain circumstances. Unlike the anti-discrimination and safety and health areas, however, this law was judge-made rather than legislatively enacted. It applied traditional notions of contract and tort law.

The late 1980s were also notable for an increasing interest in and concern over employee substance abuse. As a result, the government enacted legislation providing for drug and alcohol testing in regulated industries and among government contractors, and some employers began to test for drugs on their own initiative. Such efforts have raised serious issues regarding the accommodations of employer interests in productivity, safety, and health and employee needs to be free of unreasonable invasions of their privacy and person.

A different kind of privacy interest has been invoked in matters involving the personal relationships of employees. As it became clear to the legal profession that courts would seriously consider suits that alleged employer infringements on employee privacy rights, employees began to sue over their rights to engage in personal relationships without employer interference.

The result of this revolution in the law of the workplace is a burgeoning field of law called "employment law." Unlike labor law, the label used to indicate the law of union–management relations, employment law deals with individual employment rights. It is the purpose of this book to familiarize the reader with the basics of employment law. It is oriented both to the student taking a course in employment law and to the human resources professional, who must daily deal with matters that have legal significance and who must establish and apply human resources policies that are consistent with legal requirements.

To this end, the book examines the relevant statutes, judicial decisions, executive orders, and administrative policies that shape the respective rights of managers and workers at the workplace. This examination typically commences with an evaluation of factors generating the impetus for government (legislative or judicial) intervention, the specific legal requirements established, and their effect on an organization's policies and practices.

The book, then, goes beyond simply stating what is legal and what is illegal. While such statements are useful, the authors are aware that many employment situations do not so neatly categorize themselves as clearly legal or clearly illegal. As such, the book is based on the notion that the student and the professional in human resources need to understand the principles underlying the law, so that they can evaluate an organization's decisions against those principles. Consistent with this approach, the book borrows liberally from case material and administrative regulations, since it is the cases and the regulations that ultimately identify and explain the legal principles that are the major force influencing and shaping governmental policy.

Overview of the Book

The book is divided into three parts, and consists of twelve chapters. Part I, composed of chapters 2 through 7, addresses various aspects of equal employment opportunity law. Chapter 2 outlines the basic objectives and administrative mechanisms of Title VII of the Civil Rights Act of 1964, which is at the heart of the federal civil rights enforcement effort. It takes into consideration recent amendments that were incorporated into the 1991 Civil Rights Act.

Chapter 3 examines the various evidentiary models for proving or disproving charges of employment discrimination. This examination is critical, as managers who are sensitive about considerations of evidence and proof will be aware of those practices that are vulnerable to challenge and will have then the understanding to modify them.

Chapter 4 examines governmental policies under Title VII and the Equal Pay Act requiring gender equality in selection, pay, and working conditions. Recognizing the serious costs of sexual harassment claims for both workers and the organizations, the authors address behaviors that constitute sexual harassment, the scope and nature of an employer's liability, as well as the policies organizations should put in place to remedy and deter workplace abuses. Also covered in this chapter is the Family Leave Act, which substantially expands upon the rights of all workers, male and female, to take leaves because of individual or family health care needs.

Chapter 5 presents an overview of public policy protecting other classes of employees: workers aged over 40, religious minorities, and workers of different nationalities or ethnic backgrounds. With regard to problems of age discrimination, we will examine Equal Employment Opportunity Commission (EEOC) policies and judicial decisions under the Age Discrimination Employment Act (ADEA) and the Older Workers Benefit and Protection Act (OWBPA). Issues involving religious discrimination bring into play Title VII and introduce the reader to the difficult issue of employer workplace accommodation, e.g. to what extent must an employer or labor organization adjust pre-existing employment practices to accommodate the religious beliefs of its workforce. Under the due process clause of the Fourteenth Amendment, Title VII, and the Immigration Reform Control Act (IRCA), we will focus upon the employment rights of American citizens born outside the United States and of noncitizens who reside here lawfully.

Chapter 6 identifies the effort to protect and promote the employment rights of the handicapped or disabled worker under the Rehabilitation Act of 1973 and the Americans with Disabilities Act of 1990. Critical issues include defining the handicapped, evaluating the scope and nature of an organization's duty to accommodate, and identifying the employer's capacity to engage in pre- and post-employment medical inquiries and examinations including drug and alcohol testing.

Chapter 7 is divided into two parts. The first part focuses on a federal contractor's responsibility to develop written affirmative action programs under the federal executive order. Within this section, we will examine key ingredients of an affirmative action plan, how employers determine goals and timetables to increase the employment of underutilized groups and policies of the Office of Federal Contract Compliance (OFCCP) to enforce compliance. The second half will examine the legal status of policies of preferential treatment under both Title VII and the Fourteenth Amendment of the United States Constitution. This treatment will highlight the parameters within which valid affirmative actions programs must operate.

Part II of the book focuses on health and safety issues. The United States has chosen two different methods for encouraging employers to create a safe and healthy workplace – legislation and incentives. The legislative model is discussed in chapter 8, on the Occupational Safety and Health Act (OSH Act). The Act uses rules, regulations, and fines to require employers to provide a safe workplace. Chapter 9 deals with the incentive model – workers' compensation in the United States.

Part III addresses key new developments in employment law. The part focuses on three emerging areas: unjust discharge, privacy, and drug testing. Chapter 10 deals with the issue that many commentators believe constituted the major change in employment law in the 1980s, court decisions modifying the century-old doctrine of employment-at-will, under which an employer could terminate an employee for good reason, poor reason, or no reason at all, as long as no law or written contract was violated. In the

1980s, courts carved out exceptions based on implicit contracts, employee handbooks, the covenant of good faith and fair dealing, and public policy.

Chapter 11 addresses issues of employee privacy. In the 1980s and early 1990s judge-made law began to address the extent to which employers could intrude upon the personal lives of current and prospective employees. These cases often involve conflicts between employer business interests and the asserted constitutional privacy rights of employees.

Drug testing, a special case of invasion of privacy, is analyzed in chapter 12. In the 1980s the federal government enacted legislation and adopted rules for drug testing in regulated industries. This government interest in drug testing spilled over into the nonregulated industries. The extent to which public and private employers can test for drugs is explored in chapter 11.

Overall, we believe that this treatment of the workplace rights of managers and workers will be of practical use to current and future human resource professionals, and to those who may advise them. Legally suspect policies and decisions are invitations to lawsuits, while policies that are found unlawful render the organization vulnerable to back pay liability and damage judgments that may run into the millions of dollars. Thus, the capacity of charging parties under Title VII to seek punitive and compensatory damages, the availability of such judgments under tort law, and the exponential increase in fines under OSHA compel organizations to become increasingly familiar with the public policy limitations on their personnel practices.

More importantly, however, and aside from the need to escape liability, we maintain that compliance with its legal responsibilities is compatible with an organization's best interest. As we approach the next century, employers will confront increased difficulties in satisfying their workforce needs. In meeting this challenge, companies will have to accept a more diverse workforce, one composed of increased numbers of women, minorities, immigrants, and older workers. An organization's capacity to maintain such diversity is contingent on its acceptance of its statutory responsibilities in the area of equal employment opportunity law. Similarly, the maintenance of a healthy and safe working environment, respect for the privacy rights of workers, and policies to protect against their arbitrary treatment are indispensable to ensuring good morale and high productivity.

Furthermore, we as citizens ought to take pride in the expansive protection afforded the individual worker at the workplace. Nearly all of us in some capacity or another will work as an employee and our self-esteem and individual security rest on our being treated on the basis of our individual abilities to perform and not on the basis of stereotypical characterizations, perceptions, and judgments. Our nation was founded on principles of individual freedom and security and the extension of governmental policy to achieve these objectives in the work area mirror fundamental values that most Americans willingly accept.

Part I
Equal Employment Opportunity Law

Chapter 2
The 1964 Civil Rights Act: the EEOC and the Mandate for Equal Employment Opportunity

Background

Prior to the passage of the 1964 Civil Rights Act, serious economic disparities existed between white and non-white workers. In the early 1960s only
17 percent of non-white workers were in white collar occupations, as compared with 47 percent of white employees. Nearly half the minorities
employed in the United States were concentrated in the laboring and service
occupations, which formed the bottom of the social level. These occupational
patterns helped to account for non-white families earning approximately
half the income of white families in 1961, and for black unemployment
rates that were double those of white families, 11 and 4.9 respectively in
1962.[1] These deficiencies were in part the result of historical inequities in
educational opportunities that were available to white and black students.
In addition, however, there was both evidence and recognition that employment discrimination against blacks contributed to and exacerbated the
economic inequality between white and black workers.[2] These problems
were particularly severe in the American south, where minorities were restricted to low paying menial jobs in the steel, rubber, textile, and tobacco
industries. In the operating crafts of the railroad and in the building trades
industry and printing crafts, unions excluded minorities from admission and
thereby denied them entrance into higher paying skilled craft positions.[3]
 By the time Title VII was passed, over one half of the states had enacted
some legislation to combat employment discrimination. These, however,
proved to be rather ineffective. Some states, like Nebraska, Oklahoma, and

Virginia, had enacted provisions which lacked any kind of enforcement sanction. Others, like Delaware and Illinois, did not provide any administrative agency to enforce the law. Yet even among the 21 states that provided for administrative hearing and judicial enforcement, experience suggested that complaints were rare and prosecution was almost unheard of.[4]

In addition to the state fair employment practice commissions, the federal government under Presidents Kennedy and Johnson had issued executive orders under which federal contractors were forbidden to discriminate on the basis of race and national origin. As a result, federal contractors were responsible for establishing recruitment programs to afford minorities equal opportunity for employment. Here, too, deficiencies existed. The basic thrust of this program was to effect compliance through cooperation, and many firms and organizations remained resistant to real change.[5] As a result, more positive and enduring steps were necessary in order to ensure equal employment opportunity.

Discrimination against minorities was not, however, limited to employment. Segregated schools, exclusion from public accommodations, and denial of voting opportunities spawned widespread civil rights demonstrations across the south. In 1963, civil rights leaders gathered close to one million persons in Washington, DC to protest racial discrimination. Following President Kennedy's assassination, the Congress sought to remedy the historical injustices to which to all American negroes had been subjected and passed the most far reaching civil rights statute in our nation's history. The 1964 Civil Rights Act is divided into 11 separate titles, which address the following areas:[6]

Title I: Prohibits discrimination in voting, and permits federal court intervention to hear voting rights cases.
Title II: Requires equal access to public accommodations (i.e. restaurants, motels, theaters).
Title III: Requires equal access to facilities owned and operated by state, local, and municipal governments.
Title IV: Desegregates public education.
Title V: Extends the life of the US Civil Rights Commission.
Title VI: Prohibits discrimination in federally financed programs.
Title VII: Equal Employment Opportunity.
Title VIII: Directs the Census Bureau to compile statistics on registration and voting.
Title IX: Declares procedures for judicial review in certain cases, and permits intervention of the Attorney General in provide suits filed under the Fourteenth Amendment.
Title X: Establishes Community Relations Service.
Title XI: Miscellaneous.

This book will focus heavily on Title VII of the 1964 Civil Rights Act, as it constituted then and remains today the most important piece of legislation ever enacted by Congress to guarantee American workers equal employment opportunity. Two principal themes emerged from Title VII:

economic justice and national well-being. Regarding the first, Congress noted that discrimination unfairly forced upon black employees conditions of marginal existence. Additionally, however, at the national level the failure to provide minorities with equal job opportunities deprived the nation of the talent, skills, and intelligence of all its people. As a result, the nation's own prosperity would be increased by eliminating discrimination. Finally Title VII also reflected not only political and economic considerations, but the notion that it represented "the right thing to do."

> Aside from the political and economic considerations, however, we believe in the creation of job equality because it is the right thing to do. We believe in the inherent dignity of man. He is born with certain inalienable rights. His uniqueness is such that we refuse to treat him as if his rights and well-being are bargainable. All vestiges of inequality based solely on race must be removed in order to preserve our democratic society, to maintain our country's leadership and to enhance mankind.[7]

Who is covered

The 1964 Civil Rights Act as amended applies to employers, labor unions, and employment agencies. These groups are broadly defined. All employers with at least 15 workers who have been employed for a period of 20 weeks in a calendar year are covered. Consequently, even the smallest employer is covered under the statute. Additionally, the term "employer" applies not only to private sector firms but also to governmental units, including local, city, and state units.[8] In *Dothard* v. *Rawlinson* the Supreme Court reaffirmed application of Title VII to these governmental units by declaring that a state is not entitled to any greater deference than is typically given private employers in judicial determination of the legality of job qualifications.[9]

The term "employee" covers all types of workers. Unlike in the NLRA, there is no exclusion of independent contractors, supervisors, professionals, or managerial personnel.[10] Applicants for employment are also protected by virtue of Title VII's prohibition against discrimination in hiring. In effect, nearly the entire workforce is covered.[11] Originally when enacted, Title VII did not apply to employees of the federal government. However, in 1972 Congress amended Title VII and provided most federal government employees and employees of the District of Columbia with protection from religion, sex, race, and national origin discrimination.[12]

In 1991 the Supreme Court in *EEOC* v. *Arabian American Oil Company*[13] held that Title VII did not apply outside the territorial borders of the United States. As a result, an employee working for an American corporation abroad was not protected from racial, sexual, religious, and ethnic bias. The 1991 Civil Rights Act extends the protection of Title VII to American employees working abroad for American companies. Additionally, foreign operations controlled by an American employer would also be barred from discriminating against American citizens. Whether or not an employer is viewed as controlling a foreign corporation will be based upon such factors as (a) the interrelationship of operations, (b) common management, (c) the centralized control of labor relations, and (d) the common ownership or financial control of the employer and the corporation.[14] At the same time, there is an exemption from coverage if compliance with Title VII would require the employer to violate the law of a foreign country in which the workplace was located.[15]

Employment agencies have been broadly defined to mean any organizations which undertake "regularly with or without compensation to procure employees for an employer."[16] There has been very little litigation under this section. Traditional employment agencies are obviously covered, as well as university placement offices. There are conflicting opinions as to whether newspapers that publish classified job listings fall within the definition of employment agency.[17]

A labor organization is covered if it is viewed as engaging in an industry affecting commerce. To meet the standard of "affecting commerce" a labor organization either must maintain or operate a hiring hall which provides workers for a particular employer or alternatively have 15 or more members and (a) be the certified representative of employees under the National Labor Relations Act, (b) although not certified be a national, international, or local union acting in the capacity of a collective bargaining representative, (c) have chartered a local labor organization which is representing or seeking to represent employees, (d) be a conference, general committee, board, or council subordinate to a national labor organization.[18] With regard to their own employees, unions are liable not as labor organizations but as employers.[19]

Exclusions from coverage

There are a number of narrowly drawn entities and parties that are exempt from Title VII. They are:

- Bona fide tax exempt private clubs.[20]
- Indian tribes.[21]
- Preferences afforded Indians in businesses operating on or near Indian reservations.[22]
- Individuals denied employment opportunities because of membership in the Communist Party or because of their inability to satisfy security clearance requirements.[23]
- Aliens employed by US employers in foreign countries.[24]
- Publicly elected officials and the members of their personal staff. The exemption does not apply to those covered by local and state civil service laws or regulations.[25]

Prohibited Acts of Discrimination

The 1964 Act identifies a range of activities which if engaged in by employers would constitute unlawful employment practices. These include a refusal to hire or the dismissal of any individual because of race, religion, sex, and national origin. Furthermore, employers are barred from discriminating on these bases with regard to compensation and all other "terms and conditions of employment."[26] The language "conditions of employment" thereby extends the principal of equal employment opportunity to all matters affecting an employee's job status, including promotion, benefits, and layoffs. Employment agencies are also prohibited from failing or refusing to refer individuals.[27] This proscription addresses the critical role that employment agencies play in finding millions of jobs annually and the consequential importance of affording minorities access to these institutions.

Labor unions are prohibited from excluding or expelling individuals because of considerations of race, national origin, religion, or sex.[28] While by 1965 all international unions had eliminated formal race restrictions, many unions in the building and printing trades and in the railroads still maintained *de facto* policies of exclusion at the local level.

Unions are also prohibited from discriminating against minorities in the administration of apprenticeship training programs. This provision was compelled by evidence that exclusionary practices in apprenticeship training programs had resulted in blacks comprising less than 2 percent of all apprentices in the United States prior to 1964.[29] Other prohibited acts include discrimination in the referral of workers from union hiring halls and actions to compel an employer to discriminate.[30]

Similar to protection afforded workers under the National Labor Relations Act, Title VII protects from discrimination workers who (a) have opposed any unlawful practice and (b) have made a charge, testified, assisted, or participated in an investigation, proceeding, or hearing under the Act.[31] Under these provisions, employees who have presented complaints of discrimination to their supervisors, wrote letters to civil rights organizations, or even participated in picketing and strike activity that was authorized by their bargaining representatives, would be protected from retaliation.[32] On the other hand, "opposition" that prevented other employees from working or otherwise disrupted the work site would not.[33]

Administration of Title VII and Enforcement

Title VII created the Equal Employment Opportunity Commission and vested it with responsibility to investigate charges of employment discrimination and remedy meritorious complaints. The process by which charges are handled by the EEOC is identified in figure 1.

Under the statute an individual who feels aggrieved has 180 days from the date of the alleged act of discrimination to file a charge.[34] This requirement is a standard component of most regulatory statutes and is designed to facilitate both the investigation and the resolution of charges. Thus, charges that have become stale because they have been sitting for a substantial time period are difficult to investigate, as people's memories of critical events fade, witnesses become unavailable and records lost. The 180 day

Figure 1 EEOC processing of charges of discrimination (in non-deferral states).

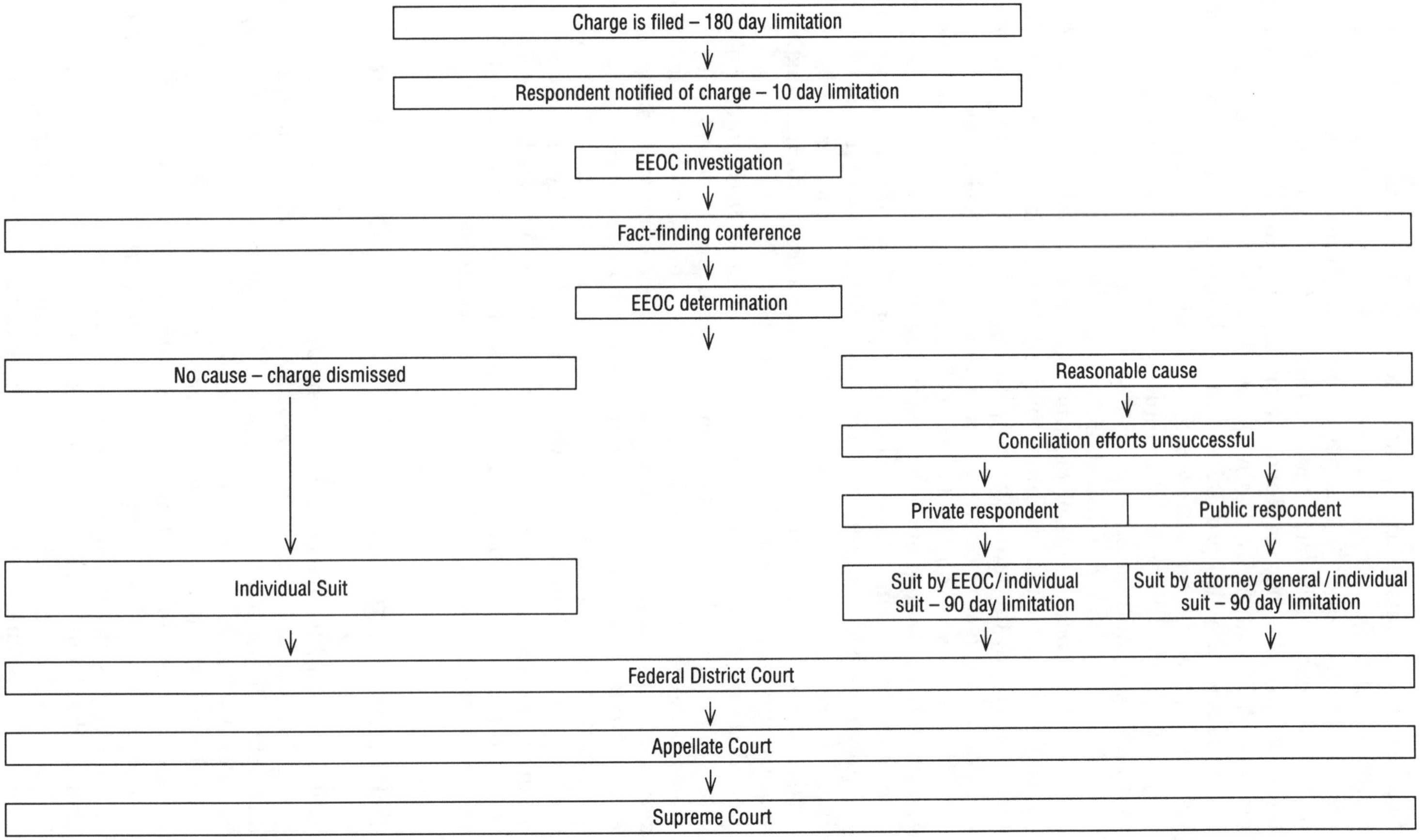

limitation is critical, for charges filed thereafter will be rejected as untimely. Interestingly, a unique feature of this statute is the capacity of the Commission itself to file a charge. The Commission may exercise this right where it believes that discrimination has occurred but no charges have been filed because workers are too fearful of initiating their own complaints.

Within ten days after a charge has been filed, the local EEOC office is required to inform the respondent (employer, union, employment agency against whom charges have been filed) of the time, place, and circumstances associated with the charge.[35] The EEOC will identify the person filing the charge unless it decides to withhold this information to protect charging parties from retaliation.[36] Receipt of this information affords the employer the opportunity to conduct its own investigation of the charge, to determine its merit and if feasible to resolve it informally.

Following its receipt of the charge the EEOC conducts an investigation. The EEOC possesses broad investigatory powers to determine the merits of the charge. These include subpoena powers to require the attendance and testimony of witnesses, the production of evidence including records and documents, and the right both to examine and to copy such evidence.[37] Respondents will usually cooperate with EEOC investigations as the EEOC's request for information and subpoenas are enforceable in federal courts. Even before an investigation has been completed and a determination made on the charge, the EEOC may invite the parties to attend a fact-finding conference. The purpose of this conference is normally to define the issues, to determine which elements are undisputed, to resolve issues, and to ascertain whether there is a basis for a negotiated settlement of the charge.

Where a fact-finding conference is not conducted or alternatively where it has failed to culminate in a resolution of the charge, the EEOC will conduct and complete its investigation. The EEOC's investigation will lead to a determination as to whether or not there is "a reasonable cause" to believe that an unlawful employment practice has occurred. The reasonable cause decision will be made either by the Commission or by the directors of local field offices to whom the EEOC has delegated authority to make these determinations.[38]

Note that a finding of no cause does not mean termination of the charge. Thus Title VII guarantees each individual his or her day in court. As a result, following the issuance of a no cause decision the charging party may request from the EEOC his or her right to sue. Once in receipt of a right to sue notice, the charging party then has 90 days within which to initiate a lawsuit against the defending organization.

On the other hand, where the EEOC finds reasonable cause to believe that employment discrimination has occurred or discriminatory employment practices are present, the EEOC will initiate conciliation efforts.[39] In conciliation the EEOC will attempt to execute a written settlement agreement, which has two primary objectives: to secure relief to the charging party and affected class members and to eliminate the discriminatory employment practice generating the complaint. Clearly these two objectives, while interrelated, are not coextensive. For example, providing for the hiring of a black worker who was refused employment does not prevent the employer from rejecting other black applicants by applying selection criteria that are discriminatory. In effect in many cases, a single charging party may represent a class of aggrieved workers who have not necessarily filed charges. Consequently, the conciliator will attempt to secure an agreement which will bring relief to the charging party and all similarly situated individuals, while simultaneously eradicating union or employer policies which generated the discriminatory situation.

If the conciliation effort fails, the charging party or the Commission may initiate a lawsuit in federal court against the defendant.[40] Note that if the respondent is a public employer, for example a state, country, or city municipality, the EEOC lacks authority to file suit. The authority to file suit is possessed by the attorney general.[41] In such cases suits would be brought by the civil rights division of the United States Department of Justice. Whether it is an individually initiated suit, a suit by the EEOC or one by the US Department of Justice, the suit is always first tried at the federal district court level. The decisions of the district court in turn are appealable to the US Courts of Appeal and ultimately to the United States Supreme Court.

This is the compliance process for investigating and remedying charges in so called non-deferral states. These are states which have not yet established their own state agencies with enforcement powers to investigate and remedy complaints of employment discrimination. The EEOC has identified those state agencies which have been recognized as acceptable deferral agencies.[42] In those states which have adopted civil rights agencies acceptable to the EEOC the process of compliance is somewhat different. An individual cannot file charges with the EEOC until the expiration of 60 days following commencement of a charge with the relevant state agency.[43] This requirement reflects the congressional purpose that an individual first attempt to resolve his or her charge of employment discrimination through the efforts of the local civil rights agency. The existence of a deferral agency will also affect the time period within which an individual may file a charge with the EEOC. An individual has up to 300 days to file an EEOC charge where that individual has previously commenced proceedings with the state or local agency.[44] Finally, under Title VII the Commission is obliged to accord "substantial weight to final findings and orders made by state or local authorities in proceedings commenced under state or local law."[45]

On review it is easy to conclude that the compliance process by which Title VII complaints are administered is both complex and time consuming. Charges are first screened and investigated by the EEOC, are then subject to conciliation efforts, and may be subject to judicial litigation. From the time of Title VII's inception tens of thousands of charges of employment discrimination have been annually filed. As a result, it takes many months for an EEOC field office to initiate a particular investigation. These delays hinder an investigator's ability to obtain relevant evidence, and impose constraints upon both the charging party and the defendant organization. While the person with a meritorious complaint is denied expeditious relief, the respondent must maintain operations despite the uncertainty of the scope and nature of its legal liabilities. While Title VII does provide that as far as practicable EEOC investigations will be completed within 120 days from the date a charge has been filed,[46] this limitation is rarely satisfied.

Adding to time delays and complexity is the EEOC's inability to hold hearings and issue binding determinations. Only the federal district courts, of which there are over 450, are authorized to conduct trials and to issue formal decisions as to whether or not discrimination has occurred. The multiplicity of federal court involvement in Title VII constantly leads to conflicting opinions, which ultimately have to be resolved at the appellate level. The federal district court decisions are appealable to 13 appellate courts. Yet ultimately it may only be after many years and a Supreme Court decision that the law of Title VII becomes finalized in a particular area. This has been the experience in the evolution of Title VII law involving the rights of racial and religious minorities, women, and older workers.

While the EEOC lacks the authority to issue binding rulings, it has vigorously exercised its administrative authority to promulgate guidelines interpreting employer responsibilities under Title VII. Over the years, the EEOC has issued guidelines in the areas of sex, religion, national origin, and age discrimination, as well as on employer selection procedures. The guidelines are significant because their violation may trigger the filing of charges and EEOC initiated lawsuits. Additionally, through subsequent congressional and Supreme Court acceptance, many of these guidelines have taken on the force of law and embody the legal obligations of employers.

Remedies

Under Title VII of the 1964 Civil Rights Act, the courts have the following remedial authority:

> If the court finds that the respondent has intentionally engaged in or is intentionally engaging in an unlawful employment practice charged in the complaint the court may enjoin the respondent from engaging in such unlawful employment practice and order such affirmative action as may be appropriate, which may include, but is not limited to, reinstatement or hiring of employees, with or without back pay . . . or any other equitable relief as the court deems appropriate.[47]

Essentially Title VII seeks to make whole charging parties for the losses they have sustained as a result of the discriminatory acts. Making whole typically includes providing workers with the jobs they were denied and with back pay for income they were unable to earn. Other relief available includes:

- Front pay. Where reinstatement may be denied because of extreme feelings of hostility between the parties, pay will be afforded the employee for a reasonable period of time to permit the discriminatee to gain other employment.

- Injunctions to preserve the status quo or to compel the termination of discriminatory practices.
- Attorney fees.
- Retroactive seniority.
- Affirmative action. The court is authorized to compel the organization to engage in affirmative conduct to remedy the effects of discrimination. This relief has at times been used to compel employers to utilize hiring quotas to rectify blatant discriminatory practices.[48]

Yet the relief available under Title VII has at times been inadequate. Where the employer's discriminatory conduct did not result in a person's loss of a job or a promotional possibility, there was no authority to compensate an individual for losses unrelated to income. For example, in cases of on-the-job harassment Title VII did not permit monetary damages to address a discriminatee's pain and suffering. When an employee required medical treatment because of the effect of discrimination, Title VII did not reimburse a discriminatee for such costs.[49]

These deficiencies were addressed in the 1991 Civil Rights Act, which permits complainants to recover compensatory and punitive damages against a respondent who has engaged "in unlawful intentional discrimination."[50] The damages are additional to other relief, such as back pay and reinstatement, that is otherwise recoverable under Title VII. They are, however, unavailable where the employee contests neutral practices, such as selection and referral criteria, that may have an adverse impact. The 1991 Act also places limitation on the amount of compensatory and punitive damages to be awarded. Section 102(b)(3) establishes a sliding scale of fines which increase with an organization's size.

15–100 employees	$50,000
101–200 employees	$100,000
201–500 employees	$200,000
501 or more	$300,000

Compensatory damages include compensation for job search, medical, psychiatric, physical therapy, and other quantifiable out-of-pocket expenses incurred as a result of the discriminatory conduct. They may also include compensation for intangible injuries, such as emotional pain, mental anguish, or loss of professional standing, that may be realized by a discriminatee. Punitive damages are designed to punish and to deter future discriminatory conduct. They may be levied where the defendant acted with "malice and with reckless indifference" to another's rights.[51]

In cases where damages are sought, it is the charging party's responsibility to demonstrate that losses were the result of the employer's discriminatory conduct. Additionally, employees are expected to mitigate their costs. For example, a discriminatorily discharged worker will be unable to recover his costs for relocating to another city if comparable jobs were available in the community where the defendant employer was located. At the same time, the expressed commitment of the EEOC to seek such damages and the capacity of complainants to seek jury trials, which are often more sympathetic to individual plaintiffs than corporate defendants, will significantly widen business exposure to liability.[52]

Summary

Title VII of the Civil Rights Act of 1964 is the cornerstone of the federal civil rights enforcement effort. While the process of compliance is bureaucratically cumbersome, those employers subject to EEOC litigation have substantially increased their employment of minority workers, particularly in professional and management positions.[53] Most significantly, through the threat of costly litigation and the establishment of sweeping legal precedents, employers throughout the United States have been compelled to eliminate discriminatory employment practices and to adopt personnel policies that broadly advance employment opportunities for minorities, women, and older workers.

However, the process by which charges are investigated and adjudicated merits substantial critical review. As of June 1994, the EEOC confronted a huge backlog of 90,000 cases pending investigation and decision. Clinton administration officials are examining proposals whose implementation is designed to structure and reduce EEOC's case load. Among the proposals being considered are:

- Dividing cases into four categories, from weak to strong. Cases in the first category are quickly dismissed; in the middle two, the EEOC pushes for a settlement; in the fourth, the agency conducts a full investigation.
- Using outside mediators to secure voluntary settlement of bias charges.
- Having hearing examiners settle cases. The major advantage of this option is that it keeps employment discrimination cases out of court.[54]

Initial results with the use of outside mediators have been good. Other changes, such as EEOC reliance on hearing examiners, an approach used by the National Labor Relations Board (NLRB), would require legislative approval. Such reforms, if implemented on a comprehensive basis, should reduce the litigation costs of both employers and charging parties, and by promoting more expedited relief, make Title VII a more effective mechanism for promoting equal employment opportunity.

Questions for discussion

1 Why did Congress permit employers to extend preferential treatment to American Indians? What type of employment practices should be encompassed by such preferences? See chapter 7.
2 The National Labor Relations board possesses cease and desist authority to enforce the National Labor Relations Act. What advantages or disadvantages would arise from applying the NLRA's enforcement model to Title VII.

3 What problems or issues may employers face by the application of Title VII to their operations abroad? Given such problems, what factors influenced Congress to amend Title VII in 1991 to permit its extra-territorial application?

4 Reflecting the continued persistence of employment discrimination in the United States, the EEOC in 1994 received 95,000 complaints of employment discrimination (*Wall Street Journal*, April 20, 1995, p. 2). Are problems of employment discrimination unique to this country or do other nations face similar issues? See, for example, Benjamin Wolkinson, "The recruitment and selection of workers in Israel, the question of disparate impact," *Journal of Racial and Ethnic Studies* (vol. 17, no. 2, 1994), pp. 260–82.

5 Jane Sparks believes that she was discriminatorily bypassed for promotion. Acting on the recommendation of a coworker, John Eager, she files charges with the EEOC. Upon discovering that Eager had advised Sparks to file charges, the company's labor relations director suspends him for instigating an EEOC investigation of the company's personnel practices. Is Eager's suspension lawful? See *Eichman* v. *Indiana State Board of Trustees*, 597 F.2d 1104, 19 FEP 979 (7th Circuit 1979).

NOTES

1 Lloyd Reynolds, *Labour Economics and Labor Relations* (Prentice-Hall, Englewood Cliffs, NJ, 1964), p. 401.

2 Arthur Ross, "The negro in the American economy," in *Employment, Race, and Poverty*, ed. Arthur Ross and Herbert Hill (Harcourt, Brace and World, New York, 1967), pp. 3–47.

3 Benjamin Wolkinson, *Black, Unions and the EEOC* (D.C. Heath, Boston, 1975), pp. 9–29.

4 Paul Norgren, "Government Fair Employment Practice Agencies," *Proceedings of the Fourteenth Annual Meetings of the IRRA* (1961), pp. 121–30.

5 *Civil Rights Act of 1964: Text, Analysis, Legislative History* (Bureau of National Affairs, Washington, DC, 1964), pp. 12–13.

6 Ibid., p. VII.

7 House Judiciary Committee Report, 88th Congress, Report 914, Part 2, Dec. 2, 1963, cited in BNA, *Civil Rights Act of 1964*, p. 285.

8 Section 701(b).

9 15 FEP 10, 433 US 321 (1977).

10 There is no express exception for independent contractors under Title VII. However, some courts have construed the term "employee" to exclude independent contractors from coverage. See, for example, *Cobb* v. *Sun Papers, Inc.*, 673 F.2d 337 (11th Cir.), cert denied 103 S. Ct 163 (1982); see also *Falls* v. *Sporting News*, 714 F. Supp. 843 (ED Mich), aff'd w/o opinion, 899 F.2d 1221 (6th Cir. 1990).

11 Section 703(a)(1).

12 Section 717, 42 USC section 2000e–16.

13 55 FEP 449 (1991).

14 Sections 109(a), 109(c)(1), and 109(c)(3).

15 Section 109(b).

16 Section 701(c).

17 *Brush* v. *San Francisco Newspaper Printing Co.*, 5 FEP 20, 469 F.2d 89 (9th Cir. 1972) and *Morrow* v. *Mississippi Publishers Corp.*, 5 FEP 287 (1972).
18 Section 701(c)(1–5).
19 *Abraham* v. *Graphic Arts International Union*, 26 FEP 818, 660 F.2d 811 (D.C. Cir. 1981).
20 Section 701(b).
21 Ibid.
22 701(i).
23 Section 706(f) and (g).
24 Section 702.
25 Section 701(f). Under Title III, section 302 of the 1991 Civil Rights Act, employees of the US Senate have been afforded protection from discrimination on the basis of race, religion, sex, national origin, age, or disability. Furthermore, under section 321, parallel protection was extended to individuals serving on the staff of elected state and local officials.
26 Section 703(a)(1).
27 Section 703(b).
28 Section 703(c)(1).
29 Paul Norgren and Samuel Hill, *Toward Fair Employment* (Columbia University Press, New York, 1964), p. 22.
30 Sections 702(c)(2) and (c)(3).
31 Section 704(a).
32 *Hicks* v. *ABT Associates*, 16 FEP 802, 572 F.2d 960 (3rd Cir. 1978); *Sias* v. *City Demonstration Agency*, 18 FEP 981, 588 F.2d 692 (9th Cir. 1978); *Payne* v. *McLemore*, 26 FEP 1500, 654 F.2d 1130 (5th Cir. 1981).
33 *Hochstadt* v. *Worcester Foundation for Environmental Biology*, 13 FEP 804, 545 F.2d 222 (5th Cir. 1976).
34 Section 706(e).
35 Sections 706(b) and 706(e).
36 29 CFR, section 1601.14, July 1, 1988.
37 29 CFR, section 1601.16, July 1, 1988.
38 29 CFR, sections 1601.19(5) and 1601.21(d), July 1, 1988.
39 29 CFR, section 1601.24, July 1, 1988.
40 Section 706(f), 1964 Civil Rights Act.
41 Ibid.
42 29 CFR, section 1601.70, July 1, 1988.
43 Section 706(c).
44 Section 706(e). In most deferral states, the EEOC has entered into a work sharing agreement with state FEP agencies, so that a charge filed with either agency is automatically filed with the other. The agencies will then decide which of the two will investigate and/or attempt to conciliate the charge. The Supreme Court has found that these procedures substantially comply with Title VII. See *Love* v. *Pullman*, 404 US 522 (1972); see also 29 CFR section 1601.13.
45 Section 706(b).
46 Section 706(h).
47 Section 706(g).
48 *US* v. *Paradise*, 43 FEP 1, 480 US 149 (1987).
49 *Report of the US Commission on Civil Rights on the Civil Rights Act of 1991*, July 1990, pp. 68–9.
50 Section 102(a)(1).
51 Section 102(b)(1).

52 EEOC Policy Guidance on Damage Provision of 1991 Act, July 7, 1992, BNA, *Daily Labor Report*, No. 131 (July 8, 1992), p. E-4.

53 Jonathan S. Leonard, "The impact of affirmative action regulation and equal employment law in black employment," *Journal of Economic Perspectives*, 4 (Fall 1990), pp. 57–60.

54 *Inside Labor Relations*, 2 (September 23, 1994), pp. 2–3.

Chapter 3
Evidence and Proof in Equal Employment Opportunity Cases

Title VII provided no operational definition to the term "discrimination." Consequently, the EEOC and the courts had to identify the circumstances when the Act had been violated. Over time two distinct evidentiary patterns of discrimination emerged, cases involving disparate treatment and those involving disparate impact.

Disparate Treatment Discrimination

As the Supreme Court has noted, disparate treatment is the most easily understood type of discrimination. In this situation, employers treat individuals less favorably than others because of their race, religion, sex, age, or national origin.[1] Proving discrimination thus hinges on a charging party demonstrating that the employer's conduct was intentionally discriminatory. Conceptually straightforward, disparate treatment cases vary greatly with the amount of evidence available to demonstrate employer or union prejudice. The following cases are illustrative.[2]

Example 1. Respondent (R) supervisor orally states that he did not hire charging party (CP) because she is a woman.

Example 2. CP (female) files a charge with the Commission alleging that R's dress code discriminates against women. Specifically, CP claims that R's policy of requiring females to wear mini skirts is discriminatory and also constitutes sexual harassment. Records indicate that R has no specific dress code policy for men in its employ. The Commission's investigation further reveals that R's dress policy for women does not have any relationship to its business.

Example 3. CP (female) files a charge alleging discriminatory discharge on the basis of sex. In her charge, CP states that she was told by one of R's supervisors that he did not think that women could or should perform construction work and he would never allow a woman to work for him. CP, however, did not work for this particular supervisor, and he had no authority over CP regarding her work with R. The supervisor admits that he made the biased statement to CP but asserts that the statement was his own opinion, expressed in a private conversation with CP. Evidence shows that CP was terminated because of excessive absenteeism and that she had been treated in the same manner as other male employees who had similar problems while working for R.

In the first case proving intentional discrimination is not difficult because the individual responsible for the discriminatory act verbally acknowledges his discriminatory motive. While situations of blatantly overt discriminatory behavior are relatively uncommon, they still may arise. For example, in *EEOC* v. *M.D. Pneumatics*, direct evidence of an employer's discriminatory intent was directly premised on the company president's statement, "It's going to be a cold day in hell before we really have women."[3] In the second example, direct evidence of discrimination is clearly manifested in the application of disparate grooming policies imposed on male and female employees. In the third example, the statement by R's supervisor is direct evidence of bias on his part. However, since it neither represented R's policy toward the charging party or women in general, nor had an adverse effect on CP's employment, it would not constitute direct evidence of discriminatory motive in her discharge.

Establishing liability through circumstantial evidence

In most cases there is no smoking gun providing direct evidence of disparate treatment. In such situations, courts have permitted the use of circumstantial evidence to prove inferentially that discrimination has occurred. In *McDonnell Douglas* v. *Green*,[4] the Supreme Court established the paradigm for proof in such situations. A complainant may establish a *prima facie* case by showing that: (a) he or she belongs to a racial minority; (b) he or she applied and was qualified for the job for which the employee was seeking applicants; (c) despite his or her qualifications the applicant was rejected; (d) after the person's rejection the position remained open and the employer continued to seek applicants from persons of the complainant's qualifications.

After these facts have been demonstrated, the burden of proof shifts to the employer "to articulate some legitimate non-discriminatory reason for the employee's rejection."[5] Where the employer justifies its rejection of the minority applicant, the courts leave open the possibility that the plaintiff could still prove his or her charge by demonstrating that the reasons advanced by the employer for the rejection were pretextual in nature.

This evidentiary model has been broadly applied in other disparate treatment situations, such as discipline and dismissal, promotion and layoffs.

For example, in a dismissal case the inference of discrimination can be drawn from the following facts:

1 Member of a minority group.
2 Was performing adequately.
3 Was dismissed.
4 Was replaced by non-minority or alternatively, if no replacement occurred, non-minorities with comparable work records were retained.[6]

While the charging party's initial evidentiary burden is relatively light, the defendants have a correspondingly broad array of defenses that can be used in rebuttal. To negate a *prima facie* case, the employer must articulate some legitimate non-discriminatory reason for the applicant's rejection. This may include:

1 Applicant's participation is unlawful conduct against the firm.[7]
2 Failure of charging party to possess requisite qualifications.[8]
3 Absence of vacancies at the time of charging party's application.[9]
4 Chosen candidate had more experience.[10]
5 Personality problems of charging party including the applicant's failure to work well with others.[11]
6 Poor attendance record.[12]
7 Considerations of personal patronage.[13]
8 Budgetary considerations.[14]
9 Application of seniority rights.[15]

Significantly, to successfully rebut a charge, an employer is not obligated to prove by objective evidence that the individual selected was better qualified than the minority candidate. As noted by the Supreme Court, the defendant's only responsibility is to identify reasons for its actions, and for these to be clear, specific, and reasonable. The employer having presented such evidence, the ultimate burden of persuasion remains on the charging party to demonstrate that he or she was a victim of intentional discrimination.[16] Intentional discrimination may be proven by evidence that the reasons advanced by the employer for the minority worker's rejection were pretextual in nature. In certain cases the employer's offered explanation is rejected because minority and non-minority employees have been shown to be treated differently. Other factors the courts will consider in determining whether a discriminatory factor influenced the employer's decision include the company's general policy and practices with regard to minority employment, and the company's treatment of the charging party during his or her employment with the firm.

For many years the EEOC and many appellate courts maintained that pretext can also be proven by demonstrating that the employer's articulated reason is unworthy of belief. Most recently, however, the Supreme Court has ruled that proof that an employer's explanation is false or lacking in credibility is by itself an inadequate basis for proving discrimination. In *St Mary's Honor Center* v. *Hicks*,[17] the Supreme Court dealt with a prison guard who was dismissed for violating various prison rules. In trial it was demonstrated that similar and more serious violations engaged in by other guards had been ignored by management or treated more leniently. Additionally, it was demonstrated that Hicks' supervisor had manufactured a verbal confrontation in order to provoke the charging party into threatening him. Nonetheless, the district court found that the charging party had failed to carry his ultimate burden of proving that his race was a determining factor in the employer's decision first to promote him and then to dismiss him. The district court concluded that "Although the charging party had proven the existence of a crusade to terminate him, he had not proven that the crusade was racially rather than personally motivated."[18]

The Court of Appeals overturned this decision, finding that, once a respondent proved all proper reasons for the adverse employment action to be pretextual, the charging party was entitled to judgment as a matter of law. The Court of Appeals reasoned:

> Because all of the defendants' proffered reasons were discredited defendants were in a position of having offered no legitimate reason for their action. In other words, defendants were in no better position than if they had remained silent offering no rebuttal to an established inference that they had unlawfully discriminated against the plaintiff on the basis of his race.[19]

This position was rejected by the Supreme Court, which noted:

> We have no authority to impose liability upon an employer for alleged discriminatory employment practice unless an appropriate fact finding determines according to proper procedure that the employer has unlawfully discriminated . . . Nothing in the law would permit us to substitute for the required finding that the employer's action was the product of unlawful discrimination, the much different (and much lesser) finding that the employer's explanation of its action was not believable.[20]

The Supreme Court with Justice Scalia writing for the majority has adopted what some commentators and the courts have called the "pretext plus" approach. Once an employer has articulated a legitimate business reason for its conduct, discrimination will be found only where the employee can show that (a) the employer's reasons were pretextual and (b) the reasons advanced were a pretext for discrimination. In effect, in order for an employer's reasons to be viewed as a pretext for discrimination, the plaintiff must show "both that the reasons were false, and that the discrimination was the real reason."

This determination has provoked widespread controversy both publicly and internally within the court.[21] In dissent, Justice Souter contended that a Title VII plaintiff should be able to prove that the reasons articulated by the employer are pre-textual and unlawful by showing either (a) that discriminatory factors influenced the employer's reasons or (b) that the employer's proffered reasons were unworthy of belief. He criticized the majority's approach as unfairly supportive of employers who have given false evidence and of ignoring the reality that an employer who lies is "simply trying to cover up the illegality alleged by the plaintiff."[22] Recognizing the difficulty of finding direct evidence of discrimination, he argued that the majority's approach will make it more difficult and costly to litigate Title VII claims by requiring more wide-ranging pre-trial discovery, longer trials and increased burdens on the judiciary.[23]

At the same time the gap between the positions of Justices Scalia and Souter may be significantly narrowed by the majority's recognition that there may be occasions where the reasons advanced by the employer are so unbelievable that they may be viewed as a cover for discriminatory motives.

> The fact finder's disbelief of the reasons put forth by the defendant (particularly if disbelief is accompanied by a suspicion of mendacity) may, together with the elements of a prima facie case, suffice to show intentional discrimination. Thus, rejection of the defendant's proffered reasons will permit the trier of fact to infer the ultimate fact of intentional discrimination, and the court of appeals was correct when it noted, upon such rejection, ["no additional proof of discrimination is required."][24]

Yet some preliminary evidence suggests that the Supreme Court's decision in Hicks has increased a complainant's evidentiary burden of proof in disparate treatment cases. At least two courts since Hicks have required complainants in ADEA cases to demonstrate that the charging parties articulated reasons were false and that age discrimination was the real reason for the employee's removal.[25] Similarly in *EEOC* v. *MCI Incorporated*[26] the District Court of New Jersey held that under the standard promulgated in Hicks the employee's evidence of pretext alone is not sufficient to defeat the employer's motion for summary judgment. The employee must also present evidence of a discriminatory motive.

Mixed motive situations

Certain cases will be characterized by evidence of a discriminatory motive and other evidence that the employer relied on nondiscriminatory considerations in rejecting the minority candidate. This is known as a mixed motive case. In 1989 the Supreme Court in *Hopkins* v. *Price Waterhouse*[27] developed the standard that once a charging party demonstrates through direct evidence that the employer's hiring or employer's employment decision was discriminatorily motivated then the employer, to escape liability, would have to demonstrate by a preponderance of the evidence that it would have made the same decision even absent consideration of the discriminatory factor. For example, an employer who refused to consider a female job applicant because of considerations of sex might be found innocent of discrimination if it could prove that the plaintiff would never have been hired because of her lack of qualifications. Yet this approach was criticized as inadequately protecting minority rights. It was noted that employers who engage in discriminatory behavior and escape liability might well be encouraged to engage in similar conduct in the future.

Responding in part to these concerns, Congress in the 1991 Civil Rights Act effectively overturned the *Price Waterhouse* decision. Currently an employment practice or decision is rendered unlawful where a motivating factor for its implementation is the employee's protected minority status.[28] Consequently, the presence of countervailing legitimate considerations will no longer provide a firm with immunity if the charging party can demonstrate that his or her status as a minority played some motivating factor in his or her rejection.

At the same time relief available to charging parties under the 1991 Civil Rights Act is still more restricted when the employer can demonstrate that the same decision would have been made absent considerations of illegal factors. In such situations the courts may only issue an injunction prohibiting the employer from considering the discriminatory factor in the future. They may also award the charging party attorney fees and costs.[29] These new remedies reflect congressional judgment that once injunctive or declaratory relief are granted to a charging party, the employer may well be deterred from future reliance on discriminatory factors. Yet, under the 1991 Act, the court is powerless to order reinstatement or force an employer to hire or promote or make any kind of monetary payments. This limitation reflected congressional opinion that inasmuch as the charging party would not have been afforded the job because of legitimate factors, the charging party was not a true victim entitled to compensatory benefits.

Disparate Impact

Griggs v. *Duke Power*[30] gave rise to the disparate impact paradigm for proving discrimination and in the process revolutionized the entire area of selection policies and procedures. The significance of this case merits a close review of its facts. In Griggs Power the plant was organized into five departments: labor, coal handling, operations, maintenance, and laboratory and tests. Minority employees were restricted to the labor departments, where the highest paid jobs paid less than the lowest paying jobs in the four other operating departments, in which only whites were employed. For candidates to qualify for selection in the operating departments, the company beginning in July 1965 began to require of them satisfactory scores on a Wonderlich personnel test and a Bennett mechanical comprehension test. In addition, individuals were required to possess a high school diploma. It is these selection criteria that minority workers challenged as discriminatory.

In evaluating the evidence the court found no evidence that the selection criteria were intended to discriminate. Indeed, the company's lack of any discriminatory intent was suggested by its willingness to provide financial assistance to employees willing to go to school to pursue their high school diploma. At the same time the court did find that these criteria would adversely affect the employment opportunities of minorities. Specifically, census data indicated that whereas 34 percent of all white males had graduated high school in North Carolina, only 12 percent of minorities had.

Moreover, EEOC records suggested that while 58 percent of whites passed these tests, only 6 percent of minorities did.

The court did not prohibit reliance on tests and selection devices. Yet it did find that reliance on selection criteria that exclude or screen out disproportionately greater number of minorities is unlawful unless these selection criteria properly measure a person's ability to perform. Thus the court noted:

> Nothing in the act precludes the use of testing or measuring procedures; obviously they are useful. What Congress has forbidden is giving these devices and mechanisms controlling force unless they are demonstrably a reasonable measure of job performance. Congress has not commanded that the less qualified be preferred over the better qualified simply because of minority origins. Far from disparaging job qualifications as such, Congress has made such qualifications the controlling factor so that race, religion, nationality, and sex becomes irrelevant. What Congress has commanded is that any test used must measure the person for the job and not the person in the abstract.[31]

Griggs is a seminal decision, as it clarified the critical components of a disparate impact case as well as the circumstances when tests may be used. Emerging from Griggs are the following principles. (a) Nothing in Title VII requires an employer to employ individuals who lack the requisite qualification to fill a job. The court noted that "The Act does not command that any person be hired simply because he was formerly the subject of discrimination or because he is a member of a minority group."[32] (b) Tests could be used and raise no Title VII issue as long as they had no disparate impact upon protected class workers. (c) Tests which have a disparate impact are subject to challenge, but might be used if they were proven to be job related. (d) To prove disparate impact, charging parties need not demonstrate that the employer was motivated by intent to discriminate. By focusing on the consequences of employer practices and not their motivation, the Court substantially reduced the evidentiary burden necessary to prove discrimination and thereby increased the capacity of applicants and employees to challenge and overturn employer selection policies. Griggs thus set the stage for further litigation contesting employers' use of arrest and conviction records, educational, testing, credit, experience, and grooming requirements. The process by which employers must screen their selection criteria as a result of the Griggs decision and subsequent EEOC guidelines is identified in figure 2. In the figure, we summarize the questions an organization must address under the EEOC's Uniform Guidelines on Employee Selection Procedures and judicial decisions when evaluating its selection decisions.

Yet the Griggs decision spawned other critical questions. For example: (1) What data base can be used to demonstrate adverse impact? (2) How much of a disparity between minority and non-minority satisfaction of a selection criteria will lead to the conclusion that adverse impact had been created? (3) What mechanisms would be employed to demonstrate that selection criteria are sufficiently related to job performance to justify reliance upon them regardless of their effect?

Figure 2   Employee selection procedures under the EEOC's uniform guidelines on employee selection.

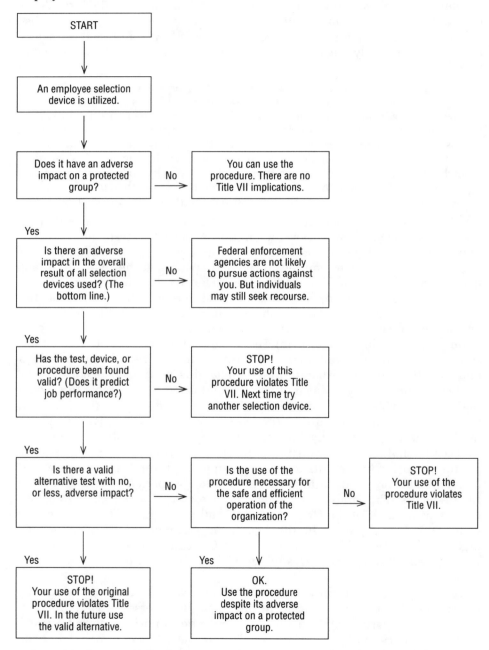

Source: Terry Curry, "A common-sense management approach to employee selection," *Personnel Administrator* (April 1981), p. 1. Reprinted with the permission of *HR Magazine*, published by the Society for Human Resource Management, Alexandria, VA.

Data sources demonstrating adverse impact

Perhaps the most easily understood data base and the one frequently relied upon by the courts to demonstrate adverse impact is applicant flow data. These data focus upon a comparison between the percentage of black and white job applicants that pass or fail the particular selection instrument. This mechanism has generally been used by the court as the preferred means for demonstrating adverse impact and should, therefore, operate as a focal point by the employer in evaluating its own selection criteria. The following case is illustrative. Assume the employer uses a mechanical aptitude test for selection. Two hundred minorities and two hundred white male job applicants take the test. Of the applicants, 150 white males and 100 minorities pass. Here the selection rate is 50 percent for minorities but 75 percent for white males. This difference raises the question of whether the test has an adverse impact, as the test seemingly screens out more minorities than whites.

A second data base for demonstrating adverse impact relies upon a comparison of the minority population that would pass or fail a selection instrument with the white population for a defined geographical area. This was the approach used in Griggs when the court cited census data for North Carolina, which demonstrated that only 12 percent of black males had completed high school as compared to 34 percent of white males. Similarly, in *Dothard* v. *Rawlinson*, in evaluating the potential exclusionary effect of a height requirement on women, the Supreme Court relied upon national statistics to demonstrate that a five feet two inch height requirement would exclude 32 percent of all women between the ages of 18 and 79 but only 1.28 percent of men within the same age group.[33] Population figures drawn from the census will be used to demonstrate adverse impact where there is concern that the application process will not accurately reflect the actual potential applicant pool. This condition frequently exists when the employer's reputation for excluding minorities discourages them from applying.

Courts also rely upon workforce availability data to examine racial discrimination claims. Thus, in *International Brotherhood of Teamsters* v. *US* the Court noted:

> absent explanation it is ordinarily to be expected that non-discriminatory hiring practices will in time result in a work force more or less representative of the racial and ethnic composition of the population in the community from which employees are hired. Evidence of long lasting and gross disparity between the composition of a work force and that of the general population thus may be significant even though section 703J makes clear that Title VII imposes no requirement that a work force mirror the general population.[34]

Here the Supreme Court, in finding that various trucking terminals had discriminated against blacks, relied upon the disparity between the heavy concentration of minority populations in the communities in which the terminals were located and the absence of minorities in the position of over-the-road truck drivers.

Teamsters was an example where the labor pool used to identify the availability of minorities for positions was defined as the proportion that minorities constitute of the population. There are, however, more narrowly drawn data bases that will be used by the courts to determine minority underrepresentation. These include (a) the percentage that minorities constitute of the labor force (labor force data) and (b) the percentage of minorities in the workforce possessing requisite skills. Obviously reliance on gross population data would make it easier to prove discrimination as the population for either whites or minorities will always exceed the number of persons in the workforce possessing specific skills.

Subsequent determinations by the United States Supreme Court in *Johnson v. Transportation Agency County of Santa Clara*[35] clearly indicate that the appropriate labor pool to be used in determining minority underrepresentation will depend upon the specific nature of the jobs involved. For entry level low skilled jobs, minority representation in the population or labor force can be used as it can be presumed that workers with no or minimum amounts of training can satisfactorily perform the required tasks. On the other hand, for more highly skilled professional jobs, the number of minorities qualified in the labor force will be the appropriate index of analysis. This more restrictive definition of what constitutes the available labor pool for skilled positions implicitly reflects judicial rejection of any notion that employers have either the capacity or the responsibility to provide minorities with sophisticated training necessary to qualify them for skilled jobs.

Identifying the appropriate geographical area from which the firm can recruit applicants is another issue that arises in the use of workforce data. For example, in *Hazelwood School District* v. *The United States*,[36] the government contended that the number of minority teachers employed by Hazelwood should be compared with the percentage of minority teachers within the City of St Louis, which was 15.5 percent. On the other hand, the school district claimed that the relevant labor pool was St Louis County, where minorities constituted only 5.7 percent of the teachers. Reliance on city data would have been sufficient to prove a *prima facie* case of discrimination against the school district, while reliance on county data would not have. While remanding the case for further inquiry, the Supreme Court did not provide any generalized set of criteria by which to identify the appropriate labor market.

One consideration relied upon by many courts is the geographical area from which the employer can reasonable recruit workers. This determination has to be made on a case-by-case basis depending upon the kinds of jobs to be filled, commuting pattern, available transportation, and cost of recruitment. For example, universities seeking personnel with highly specialized skills would typically engage in nationwide recruitment of faculty, while manufacturing plants employing production workers often restrict their focus to a more localized labor market.[37] If the firm is located in an outlying suburb of a large city, it may be economically feasible for inner city residents to apply if transportation is available to permit commuting from city to suburb. In such a situation the employer could be expected to extend its recruitment efforts to cover the metropolitan area. On the other hand, inadequate transportation may operate as an economic disincentive for inner city residents to commute to jobs in outlying suburbs. In such a situation, the scope of the employer's recruitment area may be limited to the community in which the plant is located.[38]

Another important consideration when examining workforce availability data is to select the appropriate time frame for the analysis. Comparisons between the actual number of minorities and whites selected should be for time periods after Title VII was enacted. Thus, the United States Supreme Court in *Hazelwood* emphasized that the employer is not liable for acts of discrimination that occur prior to passage of Title VII.[39] As a result courts will carefully evaluate workforce statistics, which merely show the make-up of the workforce and the applicant pool at a given time. For Title VII liability to be demonstrated one would have to clearly identify that disparate hiring and selection rates continued to occur after Title VII was enacted and were not primarily the result of pre-act policies of discrimination.

Measuring adverse impact: four-fifths rule

Whether utilizing actual applicant flow data or workforce data for a specific geographical area, courts must still examine whether disparate impact is sufficiently significant to render illegal the employer's selection policies. To address this problem when applicant flow data is used the EEOC has promulgated what has been called the four-fifths rule:

> A selection rate for any race, sex, or ethnic group which is less than four-fifths of the rate for the group with the highest rate will generally be regarded by federal enforcement agencies as evidence of adverse impact while a greater than four-fifths rate will generally not be regarded by federal agencies as evidence of adverse impact.[40]

Consequently, where, for example, 40 percent of minority applicants pass the test as compared with 80 percent of white males, adverse impact has been demonstrated, as the selection ratio for minorities versus whites is only 50 percent. In such a situation a *prima facie* case of discrimination has been demonstrated against the selection instrument.

At the same time the four-fifths rule is designed as a rule of thumb, and is not intended to be controlling in all circumstances. Commission guidelines provide that differences in selection rates of less than 20 percent might be significant where the data are drawn from a large sample and where differences in selection are large enough to be significant for both statistical and practical purposes.[41] For example, if demographic data for a region show that the use of a conviction rate would screen out 5 percent of whites but 10 percent of all Hispanics, the selection rate for the groups is 95 and 90 percent respectively. Here the four-fifths rule is satisfied. Yet since the information would be drawn from a national sample and the sample is large enough to yield statistically significant disparities (rejection rate of Hispanics is twice that of white males), the commission has indicated that it would find that the disqualification based on conviction rate here would also have an adverse effect.

On the other hand, differences of more than 20 percent in rates of selection would not, according to the EEOC, result in a finding of adverse impact if the number of persons selected is small.[42] For example, if the employer hired four males and one female from an applicant pool of 20 males and 10 females, the four-fifths rule would indicate adverse effect (selection rate for males equals 20 percent, for women 10 percent; 10 divided by 20 equals 50 percent, which is less than 80 percent). Yet given the small sample size even a slight change in the frequencies could produce totally different outcomes. For this reason adverse effect would not be presumed unless there was additional evidence that the differences in selection rates continued over a long period of time.

Standard deviation analysis

The four-fifths rule is just one statistical rule that helps to demonstrate the presence or absence of discrimination. The court has also recognized the validity of other forms of statistical analysis. One standard of statistical proof that has been specifically recognized by the Supreme Court is standard deviation analysis.[43] The standard deviation (SD) is a way to calculate the probability that chance is responsible for the difference between a predicted result and an actual result. For example, if we flip a penny 100 times we expect that 50 will be heads and 50 tails. If 51 flips out of 100 produce heads, we would chalk it up to chance, but if we get 85 or 90 flips producing heads we may begin to suspect the penny. Standard deviation analysis is the mathematical means for expressing how likely it is that the penny is suspect. Similarly, it may be used to determine whether hiring outcomes are suspect or biased by considerations of race and sex. If 100 flips yields 40 heads, the observed value falls two standard deviations below the expected value. The probability of this happening by chance is less than five times in 100. The probability of 100 flips yielding 35 heads or three standard deviations below the expected value is less than one in a 100. Statistics tends to discard chance as an explanation for a result when deviations from the expected value approach two standard deviations.

Similarly, take a case where an employer has 100 vacancies and both 100 black and 100 white applicants. Assuming that all applicants were equally qualified we would expect a hiring rate of 50 minorities and 50 whites. If, however, the hiring decisions results in only 35 minorities being employed, the probability of this happening by chance is less than one in 100. Thus, a hiring rate of 35 minorities is three standard deviations below the expected value and statisticians would suspect that the employer's hiring decisions have been biased.

The generic formula from the binomial distribution is:

$$SD = \sqrt{pqn}$$

where *p* is probability of success on any trial; $q = (1 - p)$; *n* is number of trials. This formula can be easily translated into one which is amenable to the analysis of selection, using a two-tail format:

$$SD = \sqrt{\left(\frac{\text{total black}}{\text{total applicants}} \times \frac{\text{total white}}{\text{total applicants}} \times \text{total selected} \right)}.$$

To illustrate the use of this statistic, suppose that 1,000 people applied for employment at a particular firm over time. Of these 1,000 applicants, 345 were black, 655 were white, and a total of 300 were selected; from the 300 employed, 70 were black and 230 were white. Applying the formula:

$$SD = \sqrt{\left(\frac{345}{1000} \times \frac{655}{1000} \times 300 \right)}$$

$$= 8.23.$$

The latter number, 8.23, represents one standard deviation from the mean or expected value. To determine whether the number of blacks selected falls within a probablistically acceptable range, the number of blacks expected to be hired is first computed by direct ratio: $(345/1000) \times 300 = 104$. This number, 104, suggests that without discrimination, on average roughly 34.5 percent of the employees hired should be black since 34.5 percent of the applicant pool was black. Finally, it is necessary to determine an acceptable range of black hirees. Hence, a 95 percent confidence interval (CI) can be constructed using $2 \times SD$, i.e. 2×8.23. Thus, the number of blacks expected to be hired is:

$$95 \text{ percent CI} = 104 \pm 16.46.$$

The interpretation of this result is straightforward. The probability of selecting between 88 and 120 (numbers rounded) black employees is 95 percent; in other words, the likelihoods of selecting fewer than 88 blacks or more than 120 black applicants are very small – about 2.5 percent each – suggesting that numbers outside the confidence interval did not occur by chance. In this case, with only 70 blacks chosen, it can be presumed that disparate impact accounted for the hiring outcome.

The decision in *Payne* v. *Travenol Laboratories Inc.*[44] reflects judicial application of the standard deviation analysis. The following list indicates the number of applicants referred, and the number of people hired by race and sex.

	Whites	Blacks	Total
Applicants for operative jobs	1,478	2,193	3,671
Hires	664	548	1,212

Note that although black males constituted 60 percent of the total applicants, they represented only 45 percent of those were hired. In contrast, while white males constituted 40 percent of all applicants referred, they composed 55 percent of those hired. The standard deviation analysis here revealed that the discrepancy between black and white hires was probative of discrimination. Thus, the court found that the observed number of black hires was 10.28 standard deviations fewer than the expected number, or an outcome that would be produced by chance in fewer than 1 in 1,000 cases.

From Wards Cove *to the 1991 Civil Rights Act*

In *Griggs* the US Supreme Court established the principle that selection criteria which adversely affected a disproportionately greater number of minorities were illegal unless they were justified by "business necessity." Under the business necessity standard, employers had to demonstrate that selection criteria were related to job performance. Essentially a job performance standard was imposed by the Supreme Court and applied by the lower courts. Thus, the court noted, "The touchstone is business necessity. If an employment practice which operates to exclude Negroes cannot be shown to be related to job performance, the practice is prohibited."[45]

Subsequent Supreme Court cases affirmed this approach. For example, in *Dothard* v. *Rawlinson* the court, citing *Griggs*, began its analysis by stating: "once it is shown that the employment standards are discriminatory in effect, the employer must meet the burden of showing that any given requirement has a manifest relationship to the employment in question."[46] In *Connecticut* v. *Teal* the court again reaffirmed this standard.

> Griggs and its progeny have established a three part analysis of disparate impact claims. To establish a prima facie case of discrimination, a plaintiff must show that . . . neutral employment practice had a significantly discriminatory impact. If this showing is made, the employer must then demonstrate that any given requirement has a manifest relationship to the employment in question in order to avoid a finding of discrimination.[47]

Even when the Supreme Court dismissed challenges to employer selection criteria it was because of a finding that the requirement was job related. In *New York City Transit Authority* v. *Beazer*[48] the court was concerned with the city's practice of refusing to hire applicants who were being treated with methadone. In dismissing the Title VII violation the court noted:

> the findings of the district court establish that the transit authority's legitimate employment goals of safety and efficiency require the exclusion of . . . a majority of all Methadone users. The district court also held that those goals require exclusion of all Methadone users from the 25 percent of its positions that are safety sensitive. Finally, the district court noted that those goals are significantly served by even if they do not require TA's rule as it applies to all Methadone users including those seeking employment in non-safety sensitive positions. The record thus demonstrates that TA's rule bears a manifest relationship to the employment in question.[49]

Similarly, a survey by the NAACP Legal Defense Fund showed that between 1971 and 1989 courts applied a job performance standard in 96 percent of cases in which selection criteria were challenged.[50]

In 1989 the Supreme Court issued its most controversial decision involving equal employment opportunity. In *Wards Cove Packing Company* v.

Antonio the court held that in disparate impact cases, charging parties had the burden of proving that a specific employment practice produced a disparate effect. Once this requirement was met, the employer could legitimize its practice by producing evidence of a business justification for the challenge practice. If the employer was successful then the charging party could still prevail if it could prove that illegal considerations of race or sex influenced the employer's use of a particular selection criteria, or that alternatively the employer refused to utilize other mechanisms that were equally cost effective.

This decision was roundly criticized as seriously eroding the balance of evidentiary requirements previously imposed on plaintiffs and defendants. Of great concern was the apparent removal of the employer obligation that selection criteria having a disparate effect satisfy a business necessity standard. Thus the court noted that there is "No requirement that the practice be essential or indispensable . . . for it to pass muster."[51] Additionally, the court potentially weakened the employer's evidentiary burden of rebuttal by noting that the employer, when producing evidence of the business justification, only has the burden of production and not one of persuasion. This reduced standard seemingly mirrored an organization's limited burden of rebuttal that the Supreme Court promulgated in disparate treatment cases in which employers could escape liability by only articulating a legitimate business reason, as opposed to proving its policies were job related. Yet this approach could well have undermined the integrity of the EEOC's guidelines on test validation. These guidelines imposed on employers the requirement to objectively prove and thereby persuade courts of the validity of selection instruments generating an adverse impact on minority workers.

The threat this decision posed to equal employment policies and practices long required by the EEOC and the courts alarmed civil rights groups. They responded by legislatively overturning the *Wards Cove* decision. Thus the 1991 Act resurrects the *Griggs* standard by specifically providing:

> an unlawful employment practice based on disparate impact is established under this title only if – (i) a complaining party demonstrates that a respondent uses a particular employment practice that causes a disparate impact on the basis of race, color, religion, sex, or national origin and the respondent fails to demonstrate that the challenged practice is job related for the position in question and consistent with business necessity.[52]

Additionally, the Interpretive Memorandum, which the Act indicates is the exclusive legislative history on business necessity,[53] states:

> The terms "business necessity" and "job related" are intended to reflect the concepts enunciated by the Supreme Court in Griggs v. Duke Power Co., 401 US 424 (1971), and in the other Supreme Court decisions prior to Wards Cove Packing Co. v. Antonio, 490 US 642 (1989).[54]

To drive home the point that employers may no longer justify employment practices on the basis of operational objectives that are unrelated to specific job performance, the legislative history to the 1991 Act indicates that:

Justifications such as customer preference, morale, corporate image, and convenience, while perhaps constituting "legitimate" goals of an employer, fall far short of the specific proof required under Griggs and this legislation to show that a challenged employment practice is closely tied to the requirements of performing the job in question and thus is "job related for the position in question."[55]

At the same time, the 1991 Act requires charging parties to identify the specific employment practice alleged to have the disparate effect. Section 105(B)(i) provides:

With respect to demonstrating that a particular employment practice causes a disparate impact as described in subparagraph 1(A)(i), the complaining party shall demonstrate that each particular challenged employment practice causes a disparate impact, except that if the complaining party can demonstrate to the court that the elements of a respondent's decision making process are not capable of separation for analysis, the decision making process may be analyzed as one employment practice.

In imposing this burden on plaintiffs, Congress was sensitive to employer concerns that a "bottom line" attack would subject firms to the nearly impossible task of defending and validating all their employment practices. This outcome is avoided by precluding charging parties from relying on the cumulative effects of a selection process as a basis for a disparate impact claim.[56] The Act does, however, provide for an exception when "the elements of a respondent's decision making process are not capable of separation from analysis."[57] This situation may arise when employers rely upon a functionally integrated process. For example, if a combination of height and weight requirements may be utilized to measure strength, then the charging party may challenge the overall results of utilizing a combination of height and weight as a screening device. Similarly, when an employer uses a 100-question examination, it is not necessary for the charging party to point out the five questions in the exam which might cause the disparate effect. The exam as a whole may be challenged.[58]

EEOC uniform guidelines on employee selection procedures

The resurrection of the business necessity standard revalidates EEOC guidelines imposing on firms the obligation to demonstrate that selection instruments having an adverse effect be job related. Under EEOC guidelines there are three generally accepted means for validating selection criteria: criterion related validity studies, content validity, and construct validity.

In criterion related validity, a selection procedure is justified by a showing of a statistical relationship between scores on the test and other selection procedures and measures of job performance. Critical to this validation is the performance of a full and accurate job analysis to ensure that measures of job performance are relevant to the jobs in question and represent critical or important job duties.[59] While supervisory ratings may be relied upon in part, they will be rejected if they are too subjective or if specific performance criteria have not been identified or provided the raters.[60] Certain criteria may be used without a full job analysis. These include production rates, error rates, tardiness, record of discipline, and absenteeism.[61] Some organizations will use satisfactory completion of a training program as a qualification of employments. EEOC guidelines permit such use but require that success in the training program be properly measured. Additionally, the employer must be able to document that the content of the training program reflects important job behaviors.[62]

In performing criterion validation employers may follow one of two approaches. One is to engage in a predictive study. Here all applicants are employed regardless of test results. Subsequently, after they have been on the job for a sufficient time period the record of employees' performance is measured against their test scores to determine whether or not there is any correlation between test scores and job performance. Alternatively, the employer may engage in a concurrent validation study. In this situation, only incumbent employees are tested and their test scores measured against the evaluation of their job performance.

In both types of studies, validity is expressed as a coefficient of correlation – the extent of the relationship between test scores and performance criteria. If applicants who achieve high test scores perform well and those who achieve low test scores perform poorly, the test is valid. But if those who achieve high test scores perform no better than those who have scored low, the test is not a good predictor of job performance and is not valid.[63]

Where there has been shown to be a substantial correlation between the selection criteria and job performance, the correlation must then be examined to ensure its statistical significance. EEOC guidelines provide that correlations will be accepted if measured to be statistically significant at the 0.05 level. This means that the probability is not more than one in twenty that the correlation between the selection instrument and job performance is due to chance.[64]

Concurrent validation may be less useful because the individuals take the test after being employed. As a result a person's test scores may be influenced by a person's familiarity with the job. On the other hand, a predictive validation study may not be possible where there are too few job applicants to permit a meaningful validation study. Additionally, the predictive validation study may impose some risk on the employer as workers must be employed regardless of their test scores, at least for a sufficient time period, in order to be able to obtain from them appropriate measures of job performance.

Content validation

In content validation there must be a job analysis of the important work behaviors required for successful job performance. A selection instrument is considered content valid if it measures a representative sample of behaviors of the job in question or the selection procedure provides a representative sample of the work product of the job. The closer the content and the context of the selection procedures are to work samples or work behavior, the stronger is the basis for showing content validity.[65] A typical example of a content validated test is a typing test. An employer may establish as a requirement for secretaries speeds of 70 words per minute. A typing test requiring 70 words per minute as the criterion for employment would be considered content valid if typing represents a secretary's key job duties. Similarly, tests for building trades craftsmen such as plumbers, electricians, welders, and carpenters consisting of representative work samples would also presumably be considered content valid.[66]

At the same time the guidelines warn employees that pencil and paper tests which provide abstract measures of mental abilities cannot be content validated. Thus, content validation is not appropriate for demonstrating the validity of selection procedures measuring such traits or constructs as intelligence, aptitude, judgment, or leadership abilities.[67]

In some cases courts have upheld as content valid pencil and paper tests which measure an applicant's knowledge of subject matter that must be used in the job. For example, the State of Carolina required successful completion of a written examination as a qualification for employment as a public school teacher. This requirement was implemented although the test had an adverse affect on minorities and was never proven to measure a teacher's ability within the classroom. Nonetheless, the Supreme Court found that the test was content valid because the test itself reflected subject matter the teachers would have to master as part of their training program.[68] Similarly, an entry level test for police officers testing their ability to fill out forms, to apply provisions of the law, and to identify precise criminal offenses was considered content valid as it measured significant aspects of police work.[69]

Construct validity

Construct validity involves identifying psychological traits (the construct) which are considered critical to successful job performance, and then devising a selection procedure that measures the presence and degree of these traits.[70] Examples of desired traits include interpersonal skills, intelligence, mechanical reasoning, and verbal fluency. As in other forms of validation, a thorough job analysis must be conducted of the constructs viewed as critical for successful job performance.[71] For an employer to select individuals on the basis of particular constructs, the selection instrument must be demonstrated as accurately measuring the required trait.[72] For example, in *Guardian Association* v. *Civil Service Commission*, while the court apparently acknowledged human relation skills as a significant aspect of police work, the court noted that the test itself did not accurately measure this trait.[73] Additionally, the employer must be able to demonstrate empirically the relationship between the construct and critical work behaviors. Thus, in the case of a salesperson who is selected on the basis of interpersonal skills, the employer must demonstrate the relationship between this skill and some specific performance measures such as sales.

Search for valid alternatives

Assume an employer has validated a test which has had an adverse effect. May the organization continue to rely upon it? EEOC guidelines suggest that an employer that has validated a selection criterion which has an adverse impact is under an obligation to investigate the availability and suitability of alternative selection procedures which may have a lesser adverse effect on minorities.[74] Employer concern over this requirement is understandable. The validation of a selection instrument is a time consuming and costly procedure and EEOC guidelines would impose on an organization a continuing obligation to engage in validation studies. The search for an alternative might be not only fruitless but costly as well. Furthermore, this obligation subjects an organization to a self-incriminating inquiry; if an employer identifies a second procedure with a lesser disparate effect, the evidence uncovered by the employer might be used against it by the charging party or by the EEOC.[75]

Significantly, the Supreme Court itself does not support this EEOC requirement. In *Albemarle* v. *Moody*,[76] the Supreme Court placed squarely on the shoulders of the charging party the obligation to demonstrate that an alternative exists once the employer has validated its selection criteria.

> If an employer does then meet the burden of proving that its tests are job related, it remains open to the complaining party to show that other tests or selection devices without a similarly undesirable racial effect, would also serve the employer's legitimate interests in efficient and trustworthy workmanship.[77]

This standard was reaffirmed in the 1991 Civil Rights Act when Congress provided that the demonstration of an alternative employment practice be consistent with legal concepts in existence on June 4, 1989.[78] Yet to date there has not been a single case where a charging party has met this evidentiary burden, and such an occurrence is most unlikely. Thus, charging parties may be unaware of alternatives. Additionally, they may not prove job related, or if validated may not have a lesser negative effect on minorities. Furthermore, because of differences in work behaviors, criterion measures, and other factors, a selection procedure proven valid in one organization may not be valid in other. As a result, while employers for affirmative action purposes may seek valid alternatives to eliminate adverse impact, those selection criteria that have proven to be job related on the basis of acceptable validation studies will normally withstand judicial scrutiny.

Bottom line analysis

An employer utilizes a selection instrument that screens out a disproportionately greater number of minorities. May the employer continue to rely on that selection instrument if, nonetheless, the overall results of the selection process are equally or more favorable to minorities than to others? This was the issue addressed by the Supreme Court in *Connecticut* v. *Teal*.[79]

In *Teal* all job applicants for the position of social worker had to pass a written examination. Those that passed the test were placed on an eligibility list. In choosing individuals from the eligibility list, the employer considered previous work performance, supervisory evaluation, seniority, and affirmative action considerations. The effect of the written examination was to screen out a disproportionately greater number of minorities than whites. Thus, whereas 54 percent of minorities passed the test, 79 percent of whites did. This result would lead to the conclusion that the four-fifths rule had been violated, as an adverse impact had been demonstrated. At the same time the overall results of the selection process were more favorable to minorities, as 22.9 percent of all minorities were selected and only 13.5 percent of whites were promoted to the position of social worker.

Minority applicants who had failed the test and who were thereby bypassed for promotion filed Title VII charges. They claimed that the test was discriminatory under the *Griggs* standard as it was never proven to be job related and simultaneously screened out a disproportionately greater number of minorities. In a five to four decision the United States Supreme Court rejected the notion that an employer's bottom line results in selection could immunize it from liability where it relied upon a non-validated test which screened out a disproportionately greater number of minorities. Justice Brennan writing for the majority noted:

> A non-job related test that has a disparate racial impact and is used to limit or classify employees is used to discriminate within the meaning of Title VII whether or not it was intended or designed to have this effect and despite an employer's effort to compensate for its discriminatory effect.[80]

From *Teal* we can make a number of observations. (a) All steps of the selection process are open to scrutiny. Inquiry into the final outcome of the selection hiring process is not sufficient, as each step of the hiring process must be evaluated to ensure there is no adverse effect. (b) Although the favorable bottom line result will not provide an organization with immunity from a suit filed by an individual plaintiff, such a suit would normally not be initiated by an administrative agency such as the EEOC or the United States Department of Justice in the case of a public sector employer. Thus, EEOC guidelines provide that as a matter of administrative and prosecutorial discretion, in the usual case agencies will not take enforcement action based upon the disparate impact of any component of a selection process if the total selection process results in no adverse impact.[81]

The dissent in *Teal* noted that there is another alternative by which employers may escape liability based on the adverse effect of any single component incorporated in their overall selection process. This would be achieved by ensuring that no single selection factor be used as a "knock out" or "threshold" selection factor. Instead each selection factor would be integrated and a composite score based upon an individual's performance on the entire set of criteria would be used when making selection decisions. According to the dissent such a hiring process would not result in a finding of discrimination unless the actual hiring decisions had a disparate impact on the minority group. At the same time employers should be very cautious in following this approach. Some courts since the *Teal* decision have not followed this approach and have ruled unlawful tests which had a disparate effect even when not used on a pass/fail basis and despite the fact that the overall selection process was not unfair to minorities.[82] The more prudent approach would be for the organization to carefully scrutinize each component of the selection process and eliminate those non-validated components which screen out a disproportionately greater number of minorities.

Adverse impact and race norming

One approach previously used to eliminate adverse impact is to use different cutoffs, with higher scores for majorities and lower ones for minorities, so that the desired number or percentage of each group is higher. For example, assume the minimum passing grade is 70 percent. If 50 percent of minorities scored 60 percent and 50 percent of whites attained the minimum score of 70, then the employer might either add points to the scores obtained by minorities to avoid adverse impact or alternatively have separate passing scores for the two groups. Previously courts had approved the establishment of differential passing grades to avoid adverse impact.[83]

This practice, however, is apparently illegal under the 1991 statute. Under section 106 of the 1991 Act it is unlawful for an organization to adjust the scores of or to use different cutoff scores or otherwise alter the results of employment related tests on the basis of race, religion, sex, or national origin. The requirements under the new statute that tests be job related and concurrent prohibitions against the adjustment of minority test scores to eliminate adverse impact will put further pressure on organizations to validate their selection criteria in accordance with the EEOC's validation guidelines. Alternatively, some organizations using tests may lower pass scores for all groups to avoid adverse impact. The State of Wisconsin recently lowered the pass score for the General Aptitude Test Battery, which is used for vocational counselling and job referral for a wide variety of public and private sector jobs.[84]

To help to improve minority performance on tests, human resource specialists and attorneys have suggested the following measures:[85]

- Test administration. Tests should be administered by those properly trained and skilled in the orientation and handling of people in test situations to ensure that members of minority groups are not subject to hostile or antagonistic comments that may affect their performance.
- Test retaking. Members of minority groups may regard tests as threatening and may as a result perform better as their experiences with test situations increase. Thus, an organization might improve minority test scores if workers are given the opportunity to take a test a second time.
- Changes in recruitment. Although not technically required by the guidelines, changes in recruitment might generate a greater number of

minorities with skills that are more compatible with the current selection process.

- Review of cutoff scores. At times qualified minority applicants may be screened out because the organization is using excessively high cutoffs.
- Review of job analysis. An accurate job analysis is critical to the validation process as it identifies behaviors essential to satisfactory performance. Jobs in question for which the test did not prove valid should be re-evaluated to assure that appropriate performance and selection criteria are being used.

Application of *Griggs* to Non-scored Selection Instruments

The *Griggs* standard has been applied by the courts to evaluate the legality of an entire range of selection instruments, including arrest and conviction records, garnishments, education, dress codes and experience requirement. Here is a short summary of the legal implications associated with the use of these selection criteria.

Arrest records

Arrest records are inherently suspect because statistical data will usually demonstrate that minorities in the aggregate are arrested with far greater frequency than non-minorities. Additionally, it is generally impossible for employers to validate this requirement as arrest records are inadequate to establish a person's guilt, because individuals are presumed innocent until convicted. Since *Litton* it has generally been recognized that employers violate Title VII if they rely upon arrest records which screen out a disproportionately greater number of minority applicants.[86] Furthermore, employers should eschew asking applicants whether they have a record of arrest, as such questions on an application or during the course of a personal interview might operate to discourage minority workers from applying.

Conviction records

In *Green* v. *Missouri Pacific Railroad*,[87] the court held illegal a sweeping personnel policy that excluded from employment all individuals who had been convicted of any crime with the exception of misdemeanors. Again the concern is that this policy will screen out more minorities than others. At the same time courts have noted that employers may have legitimate business reasons to identify whether applicants have been convicted of a particular crime. Whether or not a conviction should operate as an exclusionary factor is best determined on a case-by-case basis with due regard to such factors as relationship between the conviction and the job sought.

For example, an employer would be permitted not to employ a convicted felon for the position of bank teller as such an employee would be a security risk and might not satisfy insurance and bonding requirements imposed on the organization. The age at which the person was convicted of a crime is also a consideration. Crimes committed when an individual was a young adult might not be relevant in determining the suitability of employment of an individual who is currently 50 years old. The record of employment since the original conviction should also be weighed. A record of satisfactory employment from the date of the conviction might rebut the presumption of unsuitability created by the individual's original conviction.

Credit references

Individuals with poor credit records who have had their wages garnished are at times excluded from employment or dismissed because of the expense, time, and annoyance that may be involved in answering letters and phone calls from creditors and handling necessary paperwork. At the same time, because minorities are more likely to be below the poverty line than non-minorities, such a policy may have an adverse effect of excluding minorities from employment. Additionally, a record of wage garnishment in and of itself does not reflect on a person's ability to perform job tasks. As a result, some courts relying on general studies of minority poverty rates or other studies have found unlawful employer policies to penalize or discipline individuals because of a record of wage garnishments.[88]

Some courts, however, have rejected claims of adverse impact that are drawn exclusively on the basis of generalized census data. They have noted that although negroes may comprise a disproportionate large percentage of the poor, they do not necessarily comprise a disproportionately large percentage of the poor who do not pay their just debts.[89] Yet employers who do pursue policies against applicants or employees because of garnishments should carefully scrutinize such policies to ensure against any adverse impact. For example, in *Keenan* v. *American Cast Iron Pipe Company*[90] the Court found unlawful an employer's policy of disciplining employees because of poor credit records, as such a policy was demonstrated to have resulted in more minorities being reprimanded than non-minorities. The same consideration would apply to the practice of automatically rejecting any applicant with a record of a wage garnishment.

Educational criteria

High school diploma requirements have frequently been struck down by the courts for their disparate impact on minorities when used to screen individuals for unskilled or semi-skilled positions. Thus, the courts have held illegal the requirement of a high school diploma for such positions as factory production jobs, clerical employees, and apprentices entering craft training programs.[91] For the position of police officer, however, the courts have upheld a diploma requirement as a "bare minimum requirement" for the successful performance of a policeman's responsibility.[92] In reaching this conclusion the courts have focused upon general governmental studies emphasizing the importance of police officers having a good education in order to be able to perform with sufficient capability and sensitivity their public safety duties.

The validity of a degree requirement also depends upon the nature of the position for which it is being used as a selection criterion. For highly skilled positions such as airline pilots, the courts have upheld a college degree requirement even where it has had a disparate effect on minorities and where the requirement itself was never the subject of a formal validation study. Where jobs have an impact on public safety, courts have effectively reduced the employer's burden to validate selection criteria. Thus, in *Spurlock* v. *United Airlines*[93] the court noted:

> When a job requires a small amount of skill and training and the consequences of hiring an unqualified applicant are insignificant, the court should examine closely any pre-employment standard or criterion which discriminates against minorities. In such a case, the defendant should have a heavy burden to demonstrate to the court's satisfaction that his employment criteria are job related. On the other hand, when the job clearly requires a high degree of skill and the economic and human risk involved in hiring an unqualified applicant are great, the employer bears a correspondingly lighter burden to show that his employment criteria are job related.[94]

In *Spurlock* the court upheld the college degree requirement as reflecting applicants' ability to understand and retain concepts and information given in classes and in training programs. Where university training is a critical mechanism by which competence is achieved in various professions, such as law, medicine, university teaching, and nursing, courts will likely sustain such requirements when utilized as selection factors.[95]

Experience requirements

Experience requirements may have an adverse effect on minorities, particularly in such industries as the building trades, where minorities have previously been victims of employment discrimination. Nonetheless, where experience requirements are shown to be job related or required by public safety concerns, they will be upheld. For example, in *Chrisner* v. *Complete Auto Transit*[96] the employer required of all truck driver applicants either two years of experience or the completion of a truck driver training course. This requirement was shown to have an adverse impact on women. Nonetheless, the court upheld the requirement:

> An individual who possesses experience in driving large unwieldy vehicles is obviously a more rational choice for the job than is a person who does not have demonstrated ability to drive such vehicles. In this respect the

experience requirement accurately reflects the capacity of an applicant to do the job for which he is applying. There is some risk to the public safety as well as to the driver and truck in the employment of an unqualified yard employee. The important public interest in safety on the roads and highways is sufficiently weighty to convince us that the experience requirement manifestly related to the safe and efficient operation of its business of transporting automobiles over the public highways.[97]

On the other hand, courts have ruled discriminatory experience requirements having an adverse effect which have been established for unskilled positions or for entry level positions for which on-the-job training may be provided newly hired employees.[98] Employers should also be careful that the experience requirements are not set at too high a level, which would be deemed as excessive. For example, the Fifth Circuit declared illegal a requirement of 20 years of experience for management level positions.[99] At times experience in a lower level job is considered a requirement for performance in higher level jobs. Here, too, the employer must ensure that the residency requirement in the lower level job be the minimum amount necessary to provide that individual with the skills needed to perform higher level jobs.[100]

Grooming requirements

Grooming requirements applied to hair length and clothing styles have generally been upheld when reasonably related to the employer's effort to promote a favorable public image. In this, the courts have indicated that a Title VII violation only occurs where the employer is discriminating on the basis of an immutable characteristic. Since beards and hair styles can be changed at will by a person, the dismissal of an employee for failing to comply with the grooming standard is not covered by Title VII.[101] Courts have also permitted bans on the wearing of long sideburns by blacks.[102]

At the same time, minorities may have particular problems complying with a company policy prohibiting the wearing of beards. Because of a condition known as pseudofolliculitis barbae (PFB), blacks are at times unable to shave because of skin irritation. This is a condition unique to minorities and as a result a no-beard policy may have a disparate impact on them. Some early Title VII cases indicated that a no-beard policy was legal even when evidence suggested an adverse impact.[103] More recently, however, courts have been responsive to the problems that minorities would face from the application of a no-beard policy. Where studies have demonstrated that a substantial portion of a minority population is affected by PFB, courts have struck down such policies as discriminatory.[104] Yet, courts have been unwilling to extend protection of Title VII to minorities who insist on wearing beards, mustaches, or corn row hairdos as an expression of black cultural pride. Thus, for example, in *Rogers* v. *American Airlines* the court suggested that such expressions are an artifice and are not dictated by considerations of black ethnicity.[105]

Equal Employment Opportunities and Performance Evaluations

The major equal employment opportunity statutes are clear and consistent in providing a defense for employers who make seniority- or merit-based decisions. Despite the many challenges over many years to seniority-based decisions, such decisions still remain clear and uncomplicated when compared to merit-based decisions. Court review of an organization's performance appraisal system usually arises when the employer makes or defends decisions with the performance appraisal. For instance, a disgruntled employee says he or she was dismissed because of his or her race, sex, or age. The employer responds that race, sex, or age was not involved in the decision; the employee's performance, as documented in the performance appraisal, led to the decision. To the extent the performance appraisal is used as a basis for making human resources decisions, it is a "test" according to the Uniform Guidelines on Employee Selection Procedures. As such, if decisions based upon the performance appraisal result in an adverse impact on members of protected groups, then the appraisal must be job-related or valid. For example, if a performance appraisal based decision about who to retain during a company downsizing leads to a higher percentage of older employees being laid off, then the appraisal instrument must be job-related. By contrast, if an employer were simply using its performance review process for employee feedback, communications, and development, but not using it to make or defend human resources decisions, the employer has a lessened risk of judicial or EEOC review of its appraisal system.

The major factors which cause performance evaluation based decisions to fail upon judicial review are as follows.

1   The performance evaluation method is not job-related or valid. For example, if an organization uses one performance appraisal instrument with all of the items on it preprinted and uses it for everyone within the organization, then the chance that the instrument is really tailored to any specific job and will lead to decisions that are appropriate for that job is small.

2   Evaluations are based upon subjective or vague factors. Subjectivity cannot be eliminated from an effective performance review process in most jobs. However, when employers make decisions that are arbitrary, are not supported by a reasonable rationale, and are not backed by adequate documentation, employer actions are likely to be overturned. While it is true that factors like "initiative," "being a team player," and "leadership" may be important in some jobs, an employer needs to operationalize these criteria, i.e. what behaviors could one see and recognize?

3   Racial, sexual, age, etc., biases of evaluators may have influenced the appraisal. Obviously if there are any racial, sexual, age, disability, etc., biases in the evaluation that may have influenced it an employer's decision would be overturned.

Factors leading to defensible performance evaluations

A few factors are especially significant to organizations wishing to develop defensible performance appraisal programs.

1   Written instructions and training for evaluators are critical. Appraisers should not simply be given a form to complete, but should, at a minimum, be given instructions on: the program's purpose and objectives; communicating performance expectations to employees; providing on-going feedback to keep employees informed during the appraisal period; identifying and minimizing biases in the process; and completing the form and providing good performance feedback.
2   A results- or behavior-oriented system is easier to explain and defend. To the extent employers concentrate on measures of quality, quantity, timeliness, or cost/profit/budget, i.e. results, their decisions tend to be more defensible. Did the employee accomplish the expected outcomes or not? Sometimes, however, it is not possible or appropriate to focus only on results or outputs. To the extent employers concentrate on performance of the task and duties required of an employee, i.e. appropriate behaviors, the decisions tend also to be more defensible. In both cases, such decisions are usually less subjective and are easier for appraisers to explain to the employee.
3   The employee knows in advance what is expected. If one factor is more critical than any other in making defensible performance appraisal programs and decisions, that factor is that the employer did not use the performance appraisal as an after the fact process, but instead used it as a performance planning, communication, and feedback tool. The employee must have received forewarning about what was expected of him or her, and the employee should be given feedback throughout the year so that there are "no surprises" at the time of the review.

Additionally, an employer should have in place policies with regard to its performance appraisal system. There needs to be consistent application of the system, i.e. appraisers are required to complete reviews consistently and on time. There must be standardized methods and procedures for weighting and prioritizing appraisal factors so that one's appraisal depends upon one's performance, not one's supervisor, and so that there will be a consistent method for arriving at an overall rating. Finally, there needs to be a system of review and monitoring of appraisal results not only for possible illegal discrimination, but also for the identification of developmental needs, both in individuals and in the system.

Changes to the performance appraisal process

Many organizations looking at new work methods, including total quality management and team based work systems, have discarded traditional performance appraisal approaches. Many such organizations have instituted peer review processes and bottom-up appraisals (the so-called 360 degree feedback approaches). An underlying philosophy of these approaches is that feedback should be continuous and should have as its purpose helping an employee to grow and develop. Performance reviews should not be simply a once-a-year looking back over the shoulder at what has been accomplished. To the extent that such systems result in personnel decisions, they still must meet tests of defensibility.

The option of simply doing away with performance appraisals has been raised by some as a better approach. Some suggest that most variance in performance is more the product of system problems than it is a function of individual performance. Hence, individual performance reviews are not helpful and may be damaging in their effect on employee morale and motivation. However, without some consistent basis to defend personnel decisions when challenges are raised, the employer is left in a position of great potential liability. A good system of performance planning, feedback, and review, consistently used and in tune with organizational values, can provide the necessary defense for the employer and can contribute to effective human resources management.

Title VII and Seniority Systems

By seniority we generally mean a set of rules which give workers with longer years of continuous service a prior claim to a job over others with fewer years of service. The use of seniority to determine one's employment status in relation to others has been called "competitive status seniority." Competitive status seniority has normally been used to govern competition of employees for promotion, layoff and recall, transfer, and shift preferences.[106]

Seniority rules are also used to determine the benefits to which employees are entitled by virtue of their continuous service with the company. This is called benefit seniority. It is applied to such items as vacation time, sick leave, and pension benefits. These are benefits which employees accrue by virtue of the number of years they have worked for a company. Problems of employment discrimination usually involve the application of competitive status seniority. In applying competitive status seniority arrangements, companies differ as to the unit in which seniority operates. In some the department will be the unit for purposes of applying seniority, in others it will be the plant, and in others still it will be a group of functionally related jobs in a department which are organized into a separate progression line. Generally, the more homogeneous the work unit, the broader the seniority unit is likely to be.

It should be emphasized that a seniority system by itself is racially non-discriminatory. It applies equally to whites and blacks, allocating jobs on the basis of length of service in the unit within which seniority operates. Indeed, it is this nondiscriminatory feature of a seniority system that has given rise to its introduction. Yet seniority systems can become significant instruments for restricting minority employment opportunities. This can occur where they are superimposed upon restrictive hiring practices of companies. The legality of these seniority systems was first addressed in *Quarles* v. *Phillip Morris*.[107]

Here a tobacco processing plant had restricted minority workers into a leaf processing department where the work was seasonal in nature and low paying. Non-minority workers were concentrated in the fabrication department, occupying more skilled and higher paying jobs. The departmental seniority system reinforced the employer's hiring and placement pattern. Under it vacancies within the department were filled by workers with the most seniority in the department. As a result, minority workers had little opportunity to compete for jobs in the fabrication department. Furthermore, workers maintained their seniority only within the department where they worked. As a result, any minority employee who sought to transfer out of the leaf processing department would have to sacrifice his accrued seniority. Additionally, in transferring the black worker would even suffer a temporary loss in pay if the job he held paid more than the entry level job with the department to which he transferred. Consequently, even where the employer as in *Quarles* removed the bars formerly excluding minorities from the fabrication department, the system of departmental seniority operated to confine the black workers to the departments into which they were originally assigned.

Although the acts of hiring discrimination occurred before Title VII was enacted, the court nonetheless concluded that the seniority system was illegal because it continued to perpetuate into the present the effects of the company's previous policies of discrimination. Thus, the court noted: "Congress did not intend to freeze an entire generation of Negro employees into discriminatory patterns that existed before the Act."[108] The court also dismissed the notion that the seniority system was immune from challenge under section 703H of Title VII, which permits employees to make employment decisions pursuant to a bona fide seniority system. The court held that a departmental seniority system that has its genesis in racial discrimination could not be viewed as a bona fide seniority system. As a remedy, the court did not compel the employer to eliminate seniority as a concept, but ordered that minority employees be allowed to compete for job opportunities *vis-à-vis* non-minority employees on the basis of their total employment seniority with the firm. By being able to compete on the basis of their total work experience in the firm, minority workers would no longer be impeded from transferring into better placed departments if they possess the requisite qualifications.

The *Quarles* decision was endorsed by many courts, and applied to the paper, rubber, and steel industries.[109] The common thrust of the remedial orders issued by the courts in these cases was that minority workers restricted into inferior departments or lines of progression were permitted to compete for vacancies across the plant on the basis of their total employment seniority. This represented essentially a compromise approach from a remedial standpoint. Incumbent white employees were never bumped from jobs. At the same time, the job expectations of junior white employees who under the previous seniority arrangement may have been promoted to a job were not respected in the event a vacancy arose, and they competed against a minority employee who possessed greater plant-wide seniority.

This judicial approach was abandoned by the Supreme Court in *Teamsters* v. *United States.*[110] The company, a trucking terminal, had engaged prior to Title VII in a systematic pattern of hiring discrimination. Minority workers were frozen out of a more desirable over-the-road drivers unit. Instead minority employees were employed in the lower paying city driver position. Under the collective bargaining agreement, over-the-road driver and city positions were divided into two separate seniority units. As a result, employees only accrued seniority with reference to the seniority unit in which they were represented. As a practical matter, then, a minority city driver would only be considered for entry level positions in the over-the-road drivers unit, and if he were to transfer he would be required to forfeit all the competitive seniority he had accumulated in his previous bargaining unit. As in *Quarles*, this loss of seniority served as a major disincentive to the transfer of minority drivers out of departments in which they had originally been restricted.

The Court of Appeals had found the seniority system illegal as it had locked minority workers into inferior jobs by precluding their transfer from "the positions to which they are initially and discriminatorily assigned."[111] Nonetheless, the Supreme Court reversed. Reviewing the legislative history to Section 703H of the Act, the Court found that Congress did not intend to outlaw seniority systems that perpetuated the effect of prior acts of discrimination. Thus the court held:

> In sum, the unmistakable purpose of 703H was to make clear that the routine application of a bona fide seniority system would not be unlawful under Title VII. As the legislative history shows, this was the intended result even where the employer's pre-act discrimination resulted in whites having greater existing seniority rights than Negroes. Although a seniority system inevitably tends to perpetuate the effects of pre-act discrimination in such cases, the congressional judgment was that Title VII should not outlaw the use of existing seniority lists and thereby destroy or water down the vested seniority rights of employees simply because their employer had engaged in discrimination prior to the passage of the Act.[112]

This decision was reinforced by the Supreme Court's subsequent determination that employers and labor unions have wide latitude to negotiate and establish rules for the administration of seniority systems. In *California Brewers Association* v. *Bryant*,[113] the Court indicated that rules which define the beginning date of one's seniority, its forfeiture, or the employment decisions controlled by its use will generally be immune from challenge as they fall within the protected umbrella of Title VII's exemption to bona fide seniority systems. The mantle of legitimacy extended to seniority systems was completed by the Supreme Court when it ruled in *American Tobacco Corporation* v. *Patterson* that the seniority systems which were established after the effective date of Title VII would similarly be protected from challenge under section 703H.[114]

At the same time, the court will not permit seniority systems deliberately implemented to penalize minority workers. In making a determination whether a seniority system was so intended, courts will consider the following issues. (a) Does a seniority system only lock in and discourage minority workers from transferring, or does it equally lock in non-minority workers as well? (b) Are the seniority units that have been created rational and consistent with industry practice or NLRB precedent? (c) Did the seniority system have its genesis in racial discrimination and was it negotiated and implemented for illegal purposes?[115]

The 1991 Civil Rights Act reaffirmed the *Teamsters* and *Patterson* decisions by declaring unlawful seniority systems adopted for an "intentionally discriminatory purpose."[116] At the same time, the 1991 Act expands the time frame during which a complainant may challenge an allegedly discriminating system. Reversing the Supreme Court decision in *Lorance* v. *AT&T Technologies*,[117] the 1991 Act permits such challenges "When the seniority system is adopted, when an individual becomes subject to the seniority system, or when a person aggrieved is injured by the application of the seniority system or provision of the system."[118]

Teamsters and *Patterson* stand for the proposition that 703H of Title VII does not require employers to modify seniority systems to encourage or facilitate the movement of minorities from dead-end inferior departments into better paying positions in other departments within the employer's facility. Yet, where a qualified minority worker has been unlawfully denied employment, that worker is entitled to reinstatement, pay, and retroactive seniority back to the date of his or her original request for employment.[119] While recognizing that the granting of retroactive seniority may frustrate the job expectation of incumbent white employees, the Supreme Court had reasoned that the granting of retroactive seniority is necessary to restore to discriminatees the positions they would have occupied but for the unlawful discrimination.

Summary

With the enactment of Title VII, a new era in human resource management began. Previously, managers were free to rely on whatever recruitment, selection, and promotion criteria they desired. Following passage of Title VII and the evolution of equal employment opportunity case law, managers must not only eschew any overt discriminatory behavior, but must ensure that personnel practices, neutral on their face, not have a discriminatory effect unless such practices prove job related — essential to considerations of safety, efficiency, and productivity.

Such efforts have undoubtedly required the allocation and expenditure of considerable resources, as managers must collect and review demographic data, maintain personnel records on minority applications and employment, use more comprehensive job evaluation techniques, review their effect, and validate selection and promotion criteria. Yet the failure to engage in such efforts may impose even greater costs on organizations, which may confront the risk of adverse legal judgments. At the same time it ought to be remembered that nothing in Title VII requires an organization to offer employment to unqualified workers merely because they are members of a protected class. Title VII is only designed to eliminate discriminatory employment practices against qualified workers. Consequently, an organization's commitment to equal employment opportunity not only will promote the social and economic integration of minorities within our society, but by its emphasis on the implementation of job related personnel practices should help to facilitate the organization's critical goal of maintaining a qualified workforce.

Questions for discussion

1 What factors may influence a city to impose residency requirements on job applicants or employees? Are such requirements lawful? See, for example, *NAACP* v. *Township of Harrison, N.J.*, 56 FEP 680 (3rd Circuit, 1991).

2 Assume a minority worker has been discriminatorily dismissed. Subsequent to the worker's dismissal, the employer discovers that the worker had lied on his employment application. Under the company's policy, supplying false information on an employment application is automatic grounds for dismissal. Should the courts consider evidence of the employee's falsification in determining the merits of the worker's claim, or the remedy that may be implemented. See *McKennon* v. *Nashville Banner Publishing Corp.*, 66 FEP 1192 (Supreme Court, 1995).

3 At ABC, Incorporated, a successful job applicant has to complete a favorable interview and pass an aptitude test. Jane Good, a black female, fails the test and is not employed. Joseph Friend, a black male, is rejected because of his performance at an interview in which company officials determined that he lacked common sense and good judgment. Of 100 black and 200 white applicants, 20 blacks and 40 whites are hired. Of the 300 candidates, 40 blacks and 150 whites have passed the aptitude test and the personal interview. Following Good and Friend's rejection, they file Title VII charges. In response, the company attempts to promote minority employment by adding ten points to the interview and test scores of minority applicants. Examine the legality of the company's conduct under Title VII.

4 Collective bargaining agreements frequently contain provisions requiring an employer to afford employees equal employment opportunity. Breaches of this obligation may culminate in grievances that are taken to arbitration. Will courts defer to the grievance-arbitration process resolution of employment discrimination charges? Would workers and employers be better off litigating claims in arbitration or through the courts? See *Alexander* v. *Gardner-Denver*, 415 US 26 (1974) and *Gilmer* v. *Interstate Johnson Lane Corporation*, 500 US 20 (1991).

5 Seniority systems that reward workers on the basis of length of service in an organization are a common component of collective bargaining agreements in industrial settings. In a non-union setting, should employers make employment decisions based on length of service or seniority? Can they? See *Williams* v. *New Orleans S.S. Association*, 28 FEP 1092 (5th Circuit, 1982).

NOTES

1 *Teamsters* v. *US*, 14 FEP 1514, fn. 15, at 1519, 431 US 324 (1977).
2 EEOC Policy Guide on Damage Provisions of 1991 Civil Rights Act and Disparate Treatment Cases, July 7, 1992, BNA, *Daily Labor Report*, No. 131 (July 8, 1992), pp. E-10, E-11.
3 44 FEP 530 779 F.2d 21 (8th Cir. 1985).
4 *McDonnel Douglas* v. *Green*, 5 FEP 965, 411 US 792 (1973).
5 Ibid., at 969.
6 *Moore* v. *Charlotte*, 36 FEP 1582, 754 F.2d 1100 (4th Cir. 1985).
7 *McDonnel Douglas* v. *Green*, 5 FEP 965 (1973).
8 *Trotter* v. *Todd*, 33 FEP 19, 719 F.2d 346 (10th Cir. 1983).
9 *Daves* v. *Payless Cashways, Inc.*, 27 FEP 706, 661 F.2d 1022 (5th Cir. 1981).
10 *Colon-Sanchez* v. *March*, 34 FEP 1144, 733 F.2d 78 (10th Cir. 1984).
11 *Burrus* v. *United Tel. Co.*, 683 F.2d 339, 29 FEP 663 (10th Cir. 1982).
12 *Gilchrist* v. *Bolger*, 35 FEP 81, 733 F.2d 1551 (11th Cir. 1984).
13 *Lombard* v. *School District*, 19 FEP 72, 463 F.Supp. 566 (1978).
14 *Davis* v. *Weidner*, 19 FEP 668, 596 F.2d 726 (7th Cir. 1979).
15 *Kelly* v. *Atlantic Richfield*, 17 FEP 823, 468 F.Supp. 712 (1979).
16 *Texas Department of Community Affairs* v. *Burdine*, 25 FEP 113, 455 US 248 (1981).
17 62 FEP 96 (1993).
18 55 FEP 131, 756 F.Supp. 1244 (1991), at 137.
19 59 FEP 588, 970 F.2d 487 (1992), at 592.
20 Hicks, 62 FEP, at 102.
21 See for example, Victoria A. Condiff and Ann E. Chaitovitz, "St Mary's Honor Center v. Hick's. Lots of sound and fury but what does it signify?", *Employee Relations Law Journal* (vol. 19, no. 3, 1993–4).
22 Supra, note 20, at 111.
23 Ibid., at 112.
24 Ibid., at 100.
25 See *LeBlanc* v. *Great American Insurance Company*, 63 FEP 288, 1st Cir., 1993 and *Madden* v. *Cisneros*, 63 FEP 134 (E.D. Arkansas, 1993).
26 65 FEP 213 (1993).
27 49 FEP 954, 490 US 228 (1989).
28 Section 107(m).
29 Section 107(B)(i) and (ii).
30 3 FEP 175, 401 US 424 (1971).
31 Ibid., at 180.
32 Ibid., at 177.
33 *Dothard* v. *Rawlinson*, 15 FEP 10, 433 US 321 (1977).
34 14 FEP 1514, 431 US 324 (1977), fn. 20 at 1521.
35 43 FEP 411, 480 US 616 (1987).

36 15 FEP 1, 433 US 299 (1977).
37 Zachary Fasman and Michael Album, *Employment Law Compliance Handbook* (New York Executive Enterprises, 1988), pp. 108–10.
38 Walter B. Connolly, Jr and David W. Peterson, *Use of Statistics in EEO Litigation* (Law Journal Seminar Press, 1980), pp. 90–4.
39 15 FEP 1 (1977), at 5.
40 29 CFR section 1607.4(D) (1978).
41 "Questions and answers on the Uniform Guidelines," March 2, 1979, question 20, *BNA Fair Employment Practice Manual*, at section 403.437.
42 Ibid.
43 *Hazelwood School District* v. *US*, 433 US 299 (1977), 15 FEP 1, at fn. 17, p. 6.
44 28 FEP 1212, 673 F.2d 798 (1982).
45 *Griggs* v. *Duke Power*, supra, note 30, at 178.
46 15 FEP 10, 433 US 321 (1977), at 14.
47 29 FEP 1, 457 US 400 (1982), at 4.
48 19 FEP 149, 440 US 568 (1979).
49 Ibid., fn. 30, at 156.
50 NAACP Legal Defense and Educational Fund, Inc., *From Griggs to Wards Cove* (July 26, 1991), p. 2.
51 Ibid., at p. 1527.
52 Section 105(a)(i).
53 Section 105(b).
54 137 Congressional Record 9528, October 25, 1991.
55 137 Congressional Record 428 (Edwards Memorandum).
56 David Lathcart and Mark Snyderman, "The Civil Rights Act of 1991," 8 *Labor Lawyer* 849, 1992, pp. 862–9.
57 Section 105(B)(i).
58 137 Congressional Record 15,474.
59 29 CFR section 1607.5(B) (1978).
60 *Albemarle Paper Co.*, 10 FEP 1181, 422 US 405 (1975).
61 29 CFR section 1607.14B(3).
62 Ibid.
63 Jerome Siegel, *Personnel Testing under EEO* (AMACON, New York, 1980), p. 20.
64 29 CFR section 1607.14(B)(5).
65 29 CFR section 1607.14C(4).
66 *Lewis* v. *Bethlehem Steel*, 20 FEP 485, 440 F.Supp. 949 (1977).
67 29 CFR section 1607.14C(1).
68 *US* v. *South Carolina*, 15 FEP 1196, 445 F.Supp. 1094, aff. 126 FEP 501, 434 US 1026 (1978).
69 *Guardians Association* v. *Civil Service Commission*, 23 FEP 909, 630 F.2d 79 (1980).
70 Dale Yoder and Paul Staudham, "Testing and EEOC," *Personnel Administrator* (February 1984), p. 80.
71 29 CFR section 14D(2).
72 29 CFR section 1607.14D(3).
73 23 FEP 909, at 926.
74 29 CFR 1607.3B.
75 Arthur Larson and Lex Larson, *Employment Discrimination*, 3 (1989), Section 79.20.
76 10 FEP 1181, 422 US 405 (1975).

77 Ibid., at 1190.
78 Section 105(c).
79 29 FEP 1, 457 US 400 (1982).
80 Ibid., at 6–7.
81 29 CFR Section 1607.4(C).
82 *Wilmore* v. *City of Washington*, 31 FEP 2 (3rd Cir. 1983).
83 *Brown* v. *New Haven Civil Service Board*, 20 FEP 1377, 474 F.Supp. 1266 (1979) and *Kirkland* v. *New York Department of Correctional Services*, 23 FEP 1217, 628 F.2d 796 (2nd Cir. 1980).
84 *Milwaukee Sentinel* (August 2, 1994), p. 1.
85 Phyllis Wallace et al., "Testing of minority group applicants for employment," *Personnel Testing and Equal Employment Opportunity* (US Equal Employment Opportunity Commission, Washington, DC, 1970), pp. 9–10; Stephen Rosenfield and Michael Crino, "The Uniform Guidelines: a personnel decision-making perspective," *Employee Relations Law Journal*, 7 (Summer 1981), pp. 111–17.
86 *Gregory* v. *Litton Systems, Inc.*, 5 FEP 267, 472 F.2d 631 (9th Cir. 1972).
87 10 FEP 1409, 523 F.2d 1290 (1975).
88 *Wallace* v. *Debron*, 7 FEP 595, 494 F.2d 674 (8th Cir. 1974); *Johnson* v. *Pike*, 3 FEP 1021, 332 F.Supp. 490 (1971); *Robinson* v. *City of Dallas*, 10 FEP 1235, 514 F.2d 1271 (5th Cir. 1975).
89 *Robinson* v. *City of Dallas*, 10 FEP 1235, 514 F.2d 1271 (5th Cir. 1975); *EEOC* v. *Virginia Chemicals, Inc.*, 19 FEP 425 (1978).
90 32 FEP 142, 707 F.2d 1274 (11th Cir. 1983).
91 Arthur Larson and Lex Larson, *Employment Discrimination* (Mathew Bender, New York, 1989), section 76-20.
92 *Aguilera* v. *Cook County Police and Corrections Merit Board*, 37 FEP 1140, 760 F.2d 844 (7th Cir. 1985).
93 5 FEP 17, 475 F.2d 216 (1975).
94 Ibid., at 19.
95 See, for example, *EEOC* v. *Cleveland State University*, 28 FEP 1782 (1982); *Merwine* v. *Board of Trustees*, 37 FEP 340, 754 F.2d 631 (1985).
96 25 FEP 484, 645 F.2d 1251 (6th Cir. 1981).
97 Ibid., at 491–2.
98 Player, *Employment Discrimination Law*, p. 832.
99 *Fisher* v. *Proctor and Gamble Manufacturing Co.*, 22 FEP 356, 613 F.2d 527 (5th Cir. 1980).
100 *Local 189, United Papermakers*, 1 FEP 875, 416 F.2d 980 (5th Cir. 1969), at fn. 6, p. 879.
101 *Willingham* v. *Macon Telegraph Co.*, 9 FEP 189, 507 F.2d 1089 (5th Cir. 1975).
102 *Smith* v. *Delta Airlines*, 6 FEP 1102, 486 F.2d 512 (5th Cir. 1973).
103 *Woods* v. *Safeway Stores*, 17 FEP 1246, 579 F.2d 43 (4th Cir. 1978); *EEOC* v. *Greyhound*, 24 FEP 7, 635 F.2d (3rd Circ. 1980).
104 *EEOC* v. *Trailways*, 27 FEP 801, 530 F.Supp. 54 (1981); *Johnson* v. *Memphis Police Department*, 50 FEP 211, 1713 F.Supp. 244 (1989); *Bradley* v. *Pazacco of Nebraska*, 55 FEP 347, 926 F.2d 714 (8th Cir. 1991).
105 *Rogers* v. *American Air Lines*, 27 FEP 694, 527 F.Supp. 229 (1981); *Carlswell* v. *Peachford Hospital*, 27 FEP 698 (1981); *Brown* v. *D.C. Transit*, 10 FEP 841, 523 F.2d 725 (CADC 1975).
106 Benjamin W. Wolkinson, *Blacks, Unions, and the EEOC* (D.C. Heath, Boston, 1975), pp. 17–18.
107 1 FEP 260, 279 F.Supp. 505 (1968).

108 Ibid., at 269.
109 *US* v. *Bethlehem Steel Corp.*, 3 FEP 589, 446 F.2d 602 (2nd Cir. 1971); *Johnson* v. *Goodyear Tire and Rubber*, 7 FEP 627, 491 F.2d 1364 (5th Cir. 1974); *Rogers* v. *International Paper Co.*, 10 FEP 404, 510 F.2d 1340 (8th Cir. 1975).
110 14 FEP 1514, 431 US 324 (1977).
111 11 FEP 66, at 78.
112 Supra, note 110, at 1526.
113 22 FEP 1, 444 US 598 (1980).
114 28 FEP 713, 456 US 63 (1982).
115 *Teamsters* v. *US*, supra, note 110, at 1527.
116 Section 112(2).
117 49 FEP 1606, 490 US 900 (1989).
118 Section 112(2).
119 *Franks* v. *Bowman Transportation Co.*, 12 FEP 549, 424 US 747 (1976).

Chapter 4
Gender and Leave Issues in Employment

Background

The provision in Title VII prohibiting sex discrimination was introduced by Congressman Howard W. Smith of Virginia. In an ironic twist, Smith and other legislators who had opposed Title VII's prohibition against race discrimination supported the amendment prohibiting sex discrimination. They did so for fear that in its absence white women would be discriminated against in favor of minority women. While many supporters of civil rights were opposed because it shifted the focus of the bill away from the objective to end racial discrimination in employment, education, voting, and public accommodations, supporters of the amendment were able to achieve narrow victories in both the House and subsequently the Senate.[1]

While many in Congress in 1964 did not see sex discrimination as a major problem, even then women confronted major barriers to equal employment opportunity. In 1964 forty states and the District of Columbia still maintained restrictions on the number of hours women could work, either per day or per week, in one or more occupations. A dozen jurisdictions maintained limitations on the weight women workers could be required to lift or carry. Even in the absence of these governmental constraints, employers acting on the basis of stereotypical judgments excluded women from many jobs.[2] Such exclusion influenced the occupational segregation of women in the labor market, with women workers concentrated in a small number of occupations traditionally open to them: clerical, retail trade, waitressing, bookkeeping, teaching, and nursing.

This situation has changed dramatically, as women have made significant employment gains in predominantly male occupations. For example, whereas in 1966 the private sector employment participation rate of women was 9.3 percent in the job category of officials and managers, by 1990 it had increased to 29.3 percent. Similarly, the participation rate of women in professional positions increased from 20.5 percent in 1966 to 47.6 percent in 1990.[3] Currently, women constitute 22 percent of all lawyers, 26 percent of physicians, 35 percent of computer system analysts, 56 percent of personnel labor relations managers, and 30 percent of college and university teachers.[4] Their gains have been influenced by EEOC regulations, favorable judicial rulings, and employer implementation of affirmative action programs.

Bona fide occupational qualification (BFOQ) exemption

While Title VII does prohibit sex discrimination in employment, it also permits firms to consider an applicant's gender where "sex is a bona fide occupational qualification reasonably related to the performance of the job." In practice there will be only a small range of jobs in which the BFOQ exemption will be permitted, as the courts have imposed a very stringent evidentiary burden on organizations seeking to impose gender restrictions. In *Weeks* v. *Southern Bell Telephone Company*, the fifth circuit ruled that an employer could rely on the BFOQ exemption only by proving "a factual basis for believing that all or substantially all workers would be unable to perform safely and efficiently the duties of the job involved."[5] This same court subsequently ruled that discrimination based on sex is only valid when the "essence of the business operation would be undermined by not hiring members of one sex exclusively."[6] These determinations have been accepted by the Supreme Court[7] and as a result organizations are precluded from excluding men and women from jobs on the basis of stereotypical characterizations or assumptions more common to one sex or another. For example, the notion that women will be unable or unwilling to work at nights or in difficult or in dangerous circumstances and occupations cannot legally be the basis for excluding women from employment. Similarly, customer preferences have been rejected as a basis for establishing a BFOQ, as not to do so would afford employers the continued license to discriminate. In short, a person's qualifications and individual choice dictate the jobs an individual will seek to fill.

The EEOC has also narrowly construed the BFOQ exemption, citing it as possibly necessary for purposes of authenticity (e.g. actors or actresses).[8] The courts, however, have recognized that considerations of modesty and personal privacy may dictate a BFOQ limitation. For example, courts have permitted employers to consider gender when filling such jobs as guards with responsibility to strip-search inmates, bath house attendants and nurses providing patients with intimate physical care.[9]

In *Dothard* v. *Rawlinson*[10] the United States Supreme Court permitted the State of Alabama to establish a BFOQ exemption whereby women were excluded from the position of guard in a maximum security prison housing sex offenders. This decision reflected the dangerous conditions existing within the prison, which arose from the failure to segregate inmates according to their offenses and the threat they posed others. In this setting, the court concluded that women guards confronted a real risk of assault which justified the creation of a BFOQ for security purposes. At the same time, this decision probably has limited precedential value. In other states, when prisons have exercised more control over inmates, women guards have been used effectively in maximum security institutions.

Employers also violate Title VII if they screen out women because of factors or characteristics that are only considered when women compete for jobs. This is known as sex plus discrimination. For example, in *Philips* v. *Martin Marietta Corp.*[11] the US Supreme Court held unlawful a hiring policy that considered whether female applicants had pre-school age children, but ignored this factor when men applied. Similarly, both the EEOC and the courts have invalidated policies barring marriage or imposing sanctions for illicit affairs or for having children out of wedlock where such policies have been imposed only upon female applicants and employees.[12]

Pregnancy and Maternity Benefits

Many women who work do so out of economic necessity. They include women who are widows, divorced, single, and married to men who earn low incomes. Because of their financial constraints these women will not regard pregnancy or childbirth as a reason to leave their positions.[13] Other women in higher level jobs or in better financial situations will decide to work through their pregnancy for professional reasons. In these cases women will take a short break for childbirth and then return to their positions.

Historically, pregnant women in the United States have been subject to discrimination. Often, they have been denied employment. When employed they have been required to leave work far in advance of their period of disability and to stay away after their period of disability has ended. Additionally, while on maternity leave they have frequently been denied the fringe benefits allowed other workers otherwise unable to work because of illness or disability.

In 1972 the EEOC issued guidelines that required employers to treat pregnancy like any other illness or disability for purposes of the disability insurance program sick leave, and all other conditions of employment. In 1976 the Supreme Court effectively nullified the EEOC's guidelines in *Gilbert* v. *General Electric Corporation*.[14] Although General Electric employees were covered by a disability plan which provided weekly non-occupational sickness and accident benefits, women workers absent from work because of pregnancy were not covered. Nonetheless, the court found no violation because in its view pregnancy constituted an additional risk only to women, and a failure to compensate them for this condition did not undermine the parity in benefits otherwise accruing to both male and female employees. Justices Marshall and Brennan issued a strong dissent. They noted that while pregnancy was excluded from coverage, illnesses and medical conditions unique to men (prostate surgery, vasectomies) were covered. Additionally, they viewed the EEOC guidelines as a reasonable governmental response necessary to immunize women from the financial burdens and job insecurity that they frequently confronted because of pregnancy.

The Supreme Court's decision generated strong protests from labor unions, women's groups, and civil rights organizations. Responding to these pressures, Congress in 1978 amended Title VII by enacting the Pregnancy Discrimination Act, which in Section 701(K) essentially promulgated into law the original EEOC guidelines.

> Section 701K. The terms "because of sex" or "on the basis of sex" include but are not limited to because of or on the basis of pregnancy, childbirth or related medical conditions; and women affected by pregnancy, childbirth or related medical conditions shall be treated the same for all employment related purposes including receipt of benefits under fringe benefit programs as other persons not so affected but similar in their ability or inability to work. Nothing in section 703H shall be interpreted to permit otherwise.

Note that this particular provision does not confer on pregnant women any special set of rights. It merely provides that there shall be no discrimination against women on the basis of pregnancy. Additionally, pregnant women are entitled to the same set of benefits that other workers receive because of their inability to work. For example, if the employer allows stroke victims a six-month leave of absence, then a pregnant woman unable to work must be afforded the same amount of leave during periods of her recovery. Similarly, if all other employees on medical leave accrue seniority, and are reinstated to their original position, then pregnant women must be given the same benefits.

The new amendment also operates to bar under normal circumstances company policies which would compel pregnant women either to leave work upon the completion of a certain stage of their pregnancy or to remain home after childbirth for a predetermined period. Essentially a woman's ability to perform would determine her tenure on the job during and after pregnancy. Some limited exceptions have been permitted for safety reasons. For example, in the airline industry courts have permitted policies requiring women to cease flying during their last trimester of pregnancy, and to present a physician's certificate of fitness if pregnant personnel seek to fly during their second trimester.[15]

While the Pregnancy Discrimination Act and EEOC guidelines mandate that pregnancy be treated like any other illness or disability, the Supreme Court has held that the effect of the statute has been to establish a floor beneath which pregnancy disability benefits cannot drop. Under this approach, states are permitted to mandate special protection so that women will not be adversely affected because of their pregnancy. Thus, the Supreme Court upheld California's pregnancy disability leave statute, which required employers to reinstate women to their original jobs following completion of their pregnancy-related leave, although the state plan did not afford men equal protection if they required disability leave.[16]

At the same time, employers are not required to provide the same level of coverage for the pregnancy-related medical conditions of spouses of male employees that it might provide for female employees. Similarly, where an employer provides no coverage for dependants, the employer is not required to institute any such coverage even for pregnancy. Yet if an employer's insurance program covers the medical expenses of spouses of female employees, then it must equally cover the medical expenses of spouses of male workers, including those arising from pregnancy-related conditions.[17]

There is one expressed limitation that Congress permitted with regard to employer coverage of a women's pregnancy-related medical condition. Taking into consideration conservative religious sentiment, Congress in the Pregnancy Discrimination Act provided that health insurance need not be provided for abortions except where the life of the woman would be in danger if the fetus were carried to term or where medical complications arise from an abortion.[18] However, an employer cannot discriminate in employment against a woman because she has had an abortion.

Family and Medical Leave Act

As noted earlier, pregnant women under Title VII are not guaranteed any specific level of leave. Additionally, Title VII was not designed to address the many health-related problems that both men and women may confront for which leave may be necessary but unavailable under an employer's policies and practices. The Family and Medical Leave Act, which became effective on August 5, 1993, addresses these concerns. It is predicated on two key premises: (a) employees should not be forced to forfeit their jobs when required to take leave because of their own illness or a medical emergency involving their family members; (b) stability in the workplace and higher productivity can be promoted by offering workers reassurances that such leave will be granted.[19]

While approximately 12 pages in length, the law is quite complex and has already generated nearly 100 pages of rules issued by the Department of Labor, which administers it. We can summarize some of its key provisions.

Coverage, employee eligibility, and leave entitlement

The Act applies to all public agencies, including state, local, and federal employers. Furthermore, private sector firms which employ 50 or more workers and are engaged in an industry affecting commerce will be covered. To be eligible for benefits, an employee must (a) work for a covered employer, (b) have worked for that employer for at least 12 months, (c) have worked at least 1,250 hours over the previous 12 months, and (d) work at a location where at least 50 employees are employed by the employer within a 75-mile radius.[20]

A covered employer must grant an eligible worker up to 12 work weeks of unpaid leave during any 12-month period for one or more of the following reasons: (a) for the birth or placement of a child for adoption or foster care; (b) to care for an immediate family member such as a spouse, child, or parent with a serious health condition; or (c) to take medical leave when the employee is unable to work because of a serious health condition. Spouses employed by the same employer are jointly entitled to a combined total of 12 work weeks of family leave when required for the birth or placement of a child for adoption or foster care. Alternatively, they may be entitled to 12 weeks to care for a child or parent (but not parent-in-law) who has a serious health condition.[21]

A "serious health condition" means any period of incapacity or treatment: (a) connected with inpatient care (i.e. an overnight stay in a hospital, hospice or residential medical care facility); (b) requiring absence of more than three calendar days from work that involves continuing treatment by or under the supervision of a health care provider; (c) requiring continuing treatment by a health care provider for a chronic or long-term health condition that is incurable or so serious that if not treated it would likely result in a period of incapacity of more than three calendar days; or (d) for pre-natal care.[22]

According to congressional reports the term "serious health condition" is not intended to cover short-term conditions for which treatment and recovery are very brief, since such conditions would generally be covered by the employer's sick leave policy. Examples of a serious health condition include heart attacks, heart conditions, most cancers, back conditions requiring extensive therapy, strokes, severe respiratory conditions, appendicitis, pneumonia, emphysema, severe arthritis, injuries caused by serious accidents, ongoing pregnancy, the need for prenatal care, childbirth, and recovery from childbirth. It appears that voluntary or cosmetic treatments, such as most treatments for orthodonture or acne which are not medically necessary, are not included in the definition of serious health condition unless inpatient hospital care is required.[23]

Department of Labor guidelines address whether or not family leave has to be taken all at once or in parts. They indicate that family leave may be taken intermittently or result in a reduced leave schedule being afforded an employee. Intermittent leave is taken in separate blocks of time because of a single illness or injury rather than over a continuous time period. It may cover periods of just one hour or more to several weeks. Examples of intermittent leave include time taken off on an occasional basis for medical appointments or leave taken several days at a time spread over a period of six months, such as for chemotherapy. A reduced leave schedule involves an employee working a reduced work week or a reduced number of hours per day. This may represent a change in employee status from full to part time, and may occur when an employee following childbirth is unable to work a full schedule.[24]

Family leave may be taken intermittently whenever it is medically necessary to care for a serious ill family member or because the employee is seriously ill and unable to work. Where such leave is for birth or for place-ment of adoption or foster care, use of intermittent leave is subject to the employer's approval.[25]

Employees taking intermittent leave may cause production problems if necessary work assignments are not performed because of the employee's reduced work schedule. Addressing these concerns, the regulations permit the employer to temporarily transfer the employee on intermittent leave to an available alternative position to which the employee is qualified and which better accommodates recurring periods of leave. However, the new position must provide the transferred employee with the equivalent pay and benefits.[26]

Generally, family leave is unpaid; however, under certain circumstances paid leave may be substituted for a family leave. For example, paid vaca-tion or personal leave may be substituted at either the employee's or the employer's option for any qualified family leave that is covered by the employer's paid leave plan. Furthermore, paid leave provided under a plan covering temporary disabilities is counted towards family leave usage. For example, disability leave for the birth of a child would be considered fam-ily leave for a serious health condition and counted in the 12 weeks of leave permitted. At the same time, only with the employer's approval will an employee have the right to substitute paid medical sick leave for family leave to care for a seriously ill family member. Similarly, an employee cannot substitute paid medical sick leave for a serious health condition which is not covered by the employer's leave plan.[27]

Maintenance of health benefits and jobs

During any family leave an employer is required to maintain the employ-ee's coverage under any health group plan. Furthermore, the same health benefits provided to an employee prior to taking leave must be maintained. Thus, if an employee receives family member coverage prior to the leave, family member coverage must be maintained during the leave period.[28] At the same time, the employee may be required to pay his or her share of health benefit premiums during the leave on the same basis that they were paid prior to the leave being taken. If the premiums are raised or lowered, the employee would be required to pay the new premium rates. The em-ployer may recover premiums if paid to maintain health insurance cover-age for any employee who fails to return to work following the leave period unless the employee's failure to return is due to the continuation, recur-rence, or onset of a serious health condition or due to other circumstances beyond the employee's control.[29]

Once the employee returns from the leave, the employee is ordinarily entitled to be returned to the same position that he or she held prior to the leave. If that position is no longer available, then the employer has the responsibility to reinstate the employee to a parallel position which pro-vides that worker with equivalent pay, benefits, and other terms and con-ditions of employment.[30] At the same time the employee has no absolute right to reinstatement. An employee has no greater right to reinstatement than any other employee who has been continuously employed during the leave period. If the employee who had been granted leave would not otherwise have been employed at the time of his or her reinstatement, then reinstatement need not occur. For example, an employer might be able to demonstrate that the employee would have been laid off during the leave period because of production slowdowns, elimination of work shifts, or the closure of a particular department.[31]

Under certain limited circumstances reinstatement may be denied a "key employee."[32] A key employee is defined as a salaried employee who is among the highest paid 10 percent of all the employees employed by the organization within 75 miles of the employee's work site.[33] In order for the employer to deny reinstatement, the employer must (a) notify the employee of his or her status as a key employee following the worker's notice of intent to take leave, (b) explain to the worker the reasons for its decision, and (c) upon termination of the leave period, and at the employee's request, make a final determination as to whether reinstatement will be denied.[34]

The Department of Labor presumes that only in a limited number of circumstances will the employer be permitted to exercise such rights. Denial of reinstatement may only occur where the employer can determine that there will be "substantial and grievous economic injury" as a result of the reinstatement. This standard may be met if the reinstatement of the key employee would threaten the economic viability of the firm or the employee's reinstatement would cause substantial long-term economic injury. Minor inconveniences and costs that the employer would experience in the normal course of doing business would not constitute "substantial and grievous economic injury."[35]

Notice and certification

Employees seeking to use family leave may be required to provide 30-day advance notice of a need to take such leave when the need is foreseeable. When such 30-day notice is not practicable (for example, in the case of a medical emergency) notice must be given as soon as possible.[36] If an employee fails to give such notice, the employer may deny the taking of leave until at least 30 days after the date the employee provides notice to the employer of the need for such leave. At the same time, in all cases where leave is denied because of an employee's failure to afford appropriate notice, it must be clear that the employee had actual notice of the family leave notice requirement.[37] In this regard, covered employers are obliged to post a notice approved by the Secretary of Labor explaining rights and responsibilities under the statute. An employer that willfully violates this posting requirement may be subject to a fine of up to $100 for each separate offense.[38]

Additionally, an employer may require that an employee document through medical certification the need for leave due to a serious health condition affecting the employee or an immediate family member.[39] The

Department of Labor has developed an optional form for an employee's use in obtaining medical certification which reflects the appropriate medical information that must be provided (figure 3). While use of this form is optional no request for additional information may be required. Where an employer doubts the validity of a medical certification, it may at its own expense require that the employee obtain a second opinion. If the opinions of the employee's and the employer's designated health care providers differ, the employer may require the employee to obtain certification from a third health care provider, again at the employer's expense. This third opinion is final and binding.[40]

The employer may also require employees to report periodically on their status and their intent to return to work. Where the employee receives leave because of a serious health condition that affected his or her ability to perform a given job, an employer may require that the employee obtain certification testifying to his or her fitness to return to work.[41] At the same time the employer seeking a fitness for duty certification can do so only with regard to the particular health condition that caused the employee's need for leave. Furthermore, the imposition of a fitness for duty requirement must be pursuant to a uniformly applied policy that is based upon such factors as the nature of the illness and the duration of the absence.[42]

Enforcement

Employees who believe that their rights under this statute have been violated have a choice of filing a private lawsuit or filing a complaint with the Secretary of Labor. Private lawsuits must be filed within two years of the date on which the employee claims the violation occurred or three years if the violation is considered willful. Remedies for violations of the Act include wages, employment benefits, or other compensation denied or lost to the employee by reason of the violation. Additionally, the employee may recover for any monetary loss incurred as a direct result of the violation, such as the cost of providing care, with reimbursement not to exceed 12 weeks of wages for that employee. Additionally, an amount equaling the preceding sums may be also awarded as liquidated damages unless the amount is reduced by the court because the violation was in good faith and the employer had reasonable grounds for believing its conduct was permissible.[43]

Effect on employer operations

Many employers have expressed concern about the law's impact on their operations. In part, these concerns are rooted in the cost of continuing the health benefits of employees on leave. A study conducted by the Small Business Administration in 1990 entitled *Leave Policies in Small Business* estimated that the cost of providing 12 weeks of unpaid maternity and infant care leave would exceed one billion dollars per year. While other estimates have been lower, they have still predicted the imposition of considerable costs on business. For example, the General Accounting Office

Figure 3 FMLA physician certification form (WH-380).

WH-380, FMLA PHYSICIAN CERTIFICATION

Certification of Physician or Practitioner (Family and Medical Leave Act of 1993)	U.S. Department of Labor Employment Standards Administration Wage and Hour Division
1. Employee's Name	2. Patient's Name (if other than employee)

3. Diagnosis

4. Date condition commenced	5. Probable duration of condition

6. Regimen of treatment to be prescribed (indicate number of visits, general nature and duration of treatment, including referral to other provider of health services. Include schedule of visits or treatment, if it is medically necessary for the employee to be off work on an intermittent basis or to work less than the employee's normal schedule of hours per day or days per week.)

   a. By Physician or Practitioner

   b. By another provider of health services, if referred by Physician or Practitioner

If this certification relates to care for the employee's seriously-ill family member, skip items 7, 8 and 9 and proceed to items 13 thru 20 on reverse side. Otherwise, continue below.

Check **Yes** or **No** in the boxes below, as appropriate

7. Is inpatient hospitalization of the employee required? ☐ Yes ☐ No

8. Is employee able to perform work of any kind? (If "**No**", skip item 9) ☐ Yes ☐ No

9. Is employee able to perform the functions of employee's position? (Answer after reviewing statement from employer of essential functions of employee's position, or, if none provided, after discussing with employee) ☐ Yes ☐ No

10. Signature of Physician or Practitioner	11. Date	12. Type of Practice (Field of Specialization, if any)

Form WH-380
June 1993

WH-380, FMLA PHYSICIAN CERTIFICATION

For certification relating to care for the employee's seriously-ill family member, complete items 13 thru 17 below as they apply to the family member and proceed to item 20.

13. Is inpatient hospitalization of the family member (patient) required? ☐ Yes ☐ No

14. Does (or will) the patient require assistance for basic medical, hygiene, nutritional needs, safety or transportation? ☐ Yes ☐ No

15. After review of the employee's signed statement (**See** item 17 below), is the employee's presence necessary or would it be beneficial for the care of the patient? (This may include psychological comfort.) ☐ Yes ☐ No

16. Estimate the period of time care is needed or the employee's presence would be beneficial.

Item 17 is to be completed by the employee needing family leave

17. When Family Leave is needed to care for a seriously-ill family member, the employee shall state the care he or she will provide and an estimate of the time period during which this care will be provided, including a schedule if leave is to be taken intermittently or on a reduced leave schedule.

---

18. Employee Signature	19. Date

20. Signature of Physician or Practitioner	21. Date	22. Type of Practice (Field of Specialization, if any)

*U.S. GPO: 1993-343-134/83210

estimated that the cost of continuing insurance coverage for employees on leave to companies nationally was $674,000,000 annually. Additionally, employers may incur costs in recruiting, selecting, and training replacements.[44]

On the other hand, studies have also noted that the family leave policies may be beneficial to organizations. A survey of 1,000 employers by Hewitt Associates found that a majority of companies following the implementation of family leave policies experienced improved morale and lower turnover. Furthermore, in many situations employers may not incur substantial increases in cost as their employees will not take the leave available to them. In a survey by BNA only 7 percent of men polled indicated that they would take 12 weeks of leave following the birth or adoption of a child. Significantly, employers can also take steps to reduce their cost.[45] Cross-training of employees may be an effective way to minimize the use of replacement or temporary workers. In other situations, the employer may encourage employees to take part-time leave. In this manner, the employee can be paid, perform his or her essential services, and obviate the need to employ a replacement.[46]

In the first half of fiscal year 1994 the Department of Labor received 513 complaints under the FLA, and found violations in 302 cases (60 percent), of which 278 were successfully settled. Back wage payments were made in 30 cases, totalling more than $55,000, and benefits valued approximately $16,000 were restored in 32 cases. Eighty-four of the complainants got their jobs back with pay, 49 returned to work without lost pay and two returned to work with pay and benefits.[47] According to Dean Speer, the director of policy analysis for the Labor Department's Wage and Hour Division, employers are not providing enough training to their first line supervisors to enable them to deal with requests for leave under the law. The majority of inquiries to the agency are from employees whose requests for emergency leave covered by the Act have been denied or who have been fired for requesting leave to recover from a personal illness or to take care of a sick family member.[48] The willingness of the Department of Labor to pursue these cases highlights the importance that employers must attach to familiarizing their managerial personnel with their compliance responsibilities under the Family Leave Act.

Sexual Harassment

Sexual harassment continues to be one of the major problems facing managers and workers. Depending upon the definition of harassment, surveys have estimated that between 25 and 90 percent of all women workers have been victimized. While sexual harassment against both men and women is illegal most incidents apparently involve female employees.[49] Nearly all district court cases involving sexual harassment that first addressed this problem found in favor of the defendants. Courts were initially reluctant to declare sexual harassment illegal for fear of being overwhelmed with a flood of litigation. Additionally, sexual harassment was not perceived as the kind of practice that Congress intended to outlaw under Title VII. Finally, many took the position that sexual harassment is the kind of innocent horseplay that men and women have come to expect as an element of working life.[50]

Since the mid-1970s, appellate courts, EEOC guidelines and Supreme Court decisions have firmly established the principle that sexual harassment at the work site constitutes illegal discrimination under Title VII. Essentially, the case law distinguishes between two types of sexual harassment: *quid pro quo* and hostile environment harassment. In the former, unlawful sexual attention exists where an employee is subject to unwelcome sexual harassment that affects that worker's term and condition of employment. In the typical situation the employee's rejection of a supervisor's sexual demands results in that employee suffering some tangible job loss, such as more burdensome working conditions, loss of promotions, layoff, or dismissal.[51]

At times, harassment may not be linked to employer threats or decisions to retaliate against employees. However, an employer may nonetheless create a hostile environment by subjecting workers to offensive remarks, sexual innuendos of a verbal and nonverbal nature, and unwelcome physical contacts. In *Meritor Savings Bank* v. *Vinson*, the US Supreme Court upheld the EEOC position that harassment creating a hostile and abusive working environment violates Title VII, even when the harassed employee suffers no tangible job loss.[52] However, the Supreme Court did place limits on what kinds of conduct would be covered. Not every isolated incident would necessarily be actionable. For such harassment to be unlawful, it must be sufficiently severe or persuasive to alter the conditions of the victim's employment and create an abusive working environment.[53]

More recently, in *Harris* v. *Forklift Systems*,[54] the Supreme Court identified the following factors that must be considered in determining whether work environment harassment is sufficiently severe or pervasive to be unlawful.

1 Frequency of the harassing conduct.
2 Its severity: whether it is physically threatening or humiliating, or merely an offensive remark.
3 Whether it unreasonably interferes with an employee's work performance.
4 The effect of the harassment on the employee's psychological well-being.

Significantly, the court noted that while all these factors are relevant, no single one is required. In this regard, the court specifically rejected the lower court's opinion that evidence of psychological injury is necessary to prove the existence of an abusive environment.

Sexual harassment to be actionable must be unwelcome. Evidence that employees solicited or incited the conduct may defeat a sexual harassment claim. For example, a court rejected a plaintiff's claim of hostile environment harassment because the propositions or sexual remarks of coworkers were prompted by the employee's own sexually explicit conversations.[55]

Where an employee has previously indicated a willingness to engage in conduct of a sexual nature but then subsequently acts to terminate the relationship, the EEOC has held that the employee has the responsibility to notify the harasser that hostile conduct is no longer welcome.[56] At the same time, submission or acquiescence to sexual conduct will not undermine a sexual harassment claim if an employee's acquiescence was motivated by fear of job loss. Additionally, an employee's off-duty activities may serve as a basis for concluding that the employee welcomed the sexual conduct at work. For example, one court found it relevant that the plaintiff had posed nude for a magazine outside work, noting: "In view of plaintiff's willingness to display her nude body to the public in Easy Rider publications, crude magazines at best, her testimony that she was offended by sexually directed comments and Penthouse or Playboy pictures is not credible."[57]

Instances of sexual favoritism

Difficult problems arise where a supervisor may afford preferential treatment on the basis of friendship or romantic relationships with a worker. Naturally such conduct is damaging to employee morale and injurious to the employer as it prevents the advancement of individuals on the basis of their merit and performance. Yet is such conduct unlawful? The EEOC has indicated that isolated instances of such preferential treatment may be unfair but not unlawful because typically both men and women are disadvantaged for reasons other than sex.[58]

At the same time such favoritism may be found unlawful where the supervisor conveys the message that such sexual liaisons are necessary for advancement. For example, in *Toscano* v. *Nimmo*,[59] the court found a violation of Title VII because the granting of sexual favors was a condition for promotion. Although the individual who was granted preferential treatment was engaged in a consensual affair with her supervisor, the supervisor had made telephone calls to proposition other female employees at home, had phoned workers to describe his supposed sexual encounters with female employees under his supervision, and had engaged in suggestive behaviors at work.

Reasonable person standard

In *Harris* v. *Forklift Systems*,[60] the Supreme Court reaffirmed the principle that for sexual harassment to be unlawful it must create an environment that "a reasonable person" would find abusive. This standard has been utilized to prevent hypersensitive employees from barraging the workplace and the courts with complaints. Yet this standard has also been criticized for being unfairly prejudicial to women. There is concern that when applying this standard courts may adopt societal norms which reflect sexual behavior that is acceptable to men but offensive to women. For example, in *Rabidue* v. *Osceola Refining Corp.*[61] a female employee complained of sexual harassment because of vulgar and crude comments that were repeatedly made to her at the workplace by a coworker and because of pictures of nude women that were displayed. The court concluded that sexual harassment had not occurred because a reasonable person would not have found the sexually oriented displays, posters, and remarks abusive "in the context of a society that condones and publicly features and commercially exploits written and pictorial erotica."[62]

The *Rabidue* decision has evoked considerable criticism because it would in part condone harassment merely because it was commonly accepted in the workplace. Furthermore, because women are disproportionately victims of racial and sexual assault, they are more concerned about displays of sexual behavior at the workplace. As a result, even milder forms of harassment might be viewed by them as threatening because they may be seen as a prelude to sexual assault. Given the concern that a sex-blind reasonable person standard might ignore the experiences of women, some courts have held that sexual harassment is actionable when "a reasonable women" would consider the harassment sufficiently severe or pervasive to create an abusive working environment.[63]

Significantly, the Supreme Court did not comment on the legitimacy of this standard in its *Harris* decision. Yet in its aftermath the EEOC has continued to support its application. The current EEOC guidelines provide that sexual harassment will be found where a reasonable person in the victim's circumstances would have considered the behaviors abusive.[64]

Scope of employer liability

When a supervisor engages in *quid pro quo* harassment, the EEOC and the courts have applied a policy of strict liability. Under it, employers are always held responsible for their supervisor's misconduct on the theory that when a supervisor acts within the scope of his authority (e.g. to demote, dismiss), his conduct can reasonably be imputed to the employer which had delegated such authority to him.[65] In contrast, an employer is not strictly liable for supervisory or coworker harassment that creates a hostile environment. Liability occurs if the victim can prove that higher level management knew or should have known of the harassment. Management is likely to obtain actual knowledge of harassment through first-hand observation of its supervisors, reports and complaints by employees, and the receipt of charges from civil rights agencies. Constructive knowledge may be imputed where the harassment is widespread or where the higher level employer representatives block the efforts of employees to voice their concerns.[66]

In *Vinson*, the Supreme Court indicated that whether an employer has a policy on sexual harassment is "plainly relevant" in assessing employer liability in hostile environment cases.[67] Significantly, EEOC rulings on employer liability have all but mandated employee implementation of such policies. The EEOC has noted that if the employer fails to establish a complaint mechanism against sexual harassment that is widely disseminated and vigorously enforced, then the employer is implicitly communicating to workers that a harassing supervisor's actions will be ignored, tolerated, or even condoned by higher level management. As a result, if an employer fails to adopt a policy against sexual harassment and a mechanism by which employees can obtain redress, the EEOC will find an employer strictly liable for a hostile environment sexual harassment by a supervisor. On the other hand, if an employee does have a mechanism in place an employee's failure to utilize it may immunize the employer from liability.[68]

Since Title VII now permits plaintiffs to recover not just back pay, but also compensatory and punitive damages, recoveries against organizations for unlawful sexual harassment will be costly. Additionally, employers are also subject to tort suits for such harassment, which similarly expose them to damage judgment. As a result, employers must act vigorously to establish mechanisms to address and deter such misconduct. Such policies should include the following measures.

1   A sexual harassment policy should identify for employees what constitutes sexual harassment. It should note that sexual harassment is not limited to requests for sexual favors in return for job benefits. It can also take the form of verbal abuse, leering, gestures, more subtle advances, and pressures inviting sexual activities, such as intentional touching, patting, and other assaults.

2   The policy must be communicated to every employee, worker and supervisor alike, and it should convey the message that the organization will not tolerate sexual harassment or pressures. Workers should be informed that the employer has remedies available and they should be directed to report any allegations to their supervisors or senior level managers.[69]

3   Complaints of sexual harassment should be immediately investigated. An impartial investigator should be selected from the company's personnel or human resource department. All investigations must be strictly confidential. The investigator should have the authority to deal effectively and forcibly with line management. In examining the sexual harassment charge, try and determine what kind of sexual harassment charge you are dealing with, when it occurred, whether or not the victim has complained before, if there have been complaints initiated by other employees against the alleged perpetrator, and whether the alleged conduct was offensive and unwelcome to the victim. Where sexual harassment has occurred, it may result in a sudden deterioration in the employee's performance. On the other hand, organizations have to be careful and sensitive that a sexual harassment charge may be initiated by an employee against a supervisor in retaliation for a poor evaluation. All facts supporting or refuting the complaint should be documented carefully. In this regard, the investigator should maintain documentation in each step of the investigation process, including the names of all interviewed, what they said, and what personal records were reviewed.[70]

4   Take vigorous disciplinary measures. Where sexual harassment has occurred, it is the employer's responsibility to take appropriate disciplinary

measures against the perpetrator. Depending upon the actual conduct that occurred, these may include transferring the offender, putting that individual on probation, suspension, and even dismissal. Many female employees in general are reluctant to file formal complaints. The vigorous enforcement of a policy will instill in workers the necessary confidence to confront harassment. On the other hand, their inclination to do so will be undermined if meritorious complaints are met with management indifference and/or a failure to penalize offenders. Even if the management finds no violation and the employee has only perceived harassment, an effort should be made to improve communication and understanding between the supervisor and the employee. Where necessary, a non-disciplinary transfer to a similar job in another department may be appropriate.

5   Train managers and workers. Sexual harassment frequently occurs because employees are ignorant that their actions will be perceived as offensive by others. The objective of training is to increase the awareness of employees as to the kinds of language, attitudes, and behaviors that are considered not only objectionable but illegal. To the degree that workers and staff will have a better awareness of what is expected of them and the limits placed upon them, the incidence of sexual harassment complaints should be reduced.[71]

Equal Pay Act

The Equal Pay Act (EPA), which was originally enacted as an amendment to the Fair Labor Standards Act in 1963, is the first federal law in the area of equal employment opportunity. Its exclusive focus is upon the elimination of sex-based wage disparities, where men and women perform work requiring "equal skill, effort and responsibility and which [is] performed under similar working conditions."[72]

When originally enacted the statute was administered by the Wage and Hour division of the United States Department of Labor. Effective in 1979, this responsibility was transferred to the Equal Employment Opportunity Commission.[73] As administered previously by Labor and currently by the EEOC, the equal work standard does not require that jobs be identical, only that they be substantially similar in job duties and content.[74] This focus on job content is further amplified in EEOC guidelines defining the statutory terms equal skill, effort, responsibility, and working conditions.

Equal skill

This factor considers one's experience, training, education, and ability. It must be measured in terms of skills used on the job and not in the abstract. For example, a male employee has a master's degree and a woman worker performing the same job task has only a high school education. Yet if both are performing only clerical duties not requiring the use of a college education, a wage disparity based on education would not be appropriate.[75]

Equal effort

This factor addresses the physical and mental exertion needed in performing a job. Where the amount of effort extended is comparable, the mere fact that two jobs call for effort of different kind will not render them unequal. For example, a male checker employed in a supermarket may be required to spend part of his time carrying out heavy packages or replacing stock involving the lifting of heavy items. At the same time, a female checker spends an equivalent amount of time performing fill-in work requiring greater dexterity, such as rearranging displays of spices or other small items. Although both are involved in different tasks, a wage differential cannot be established for the two positions since the amount of effort is similar.[76]

Some employers have rationalized higher pay for male employees on the basis of the additional tasks they and not women employees perform. Wage differentials because of "extra work" have been found unlawful in the following situations: (a) some male employees receive higher pay without doing the extra work;[77] (b) female employees also perform extra duties of equal skill, effort, and responsibility;[78] (c) qualified female workers are not given the opportunity to do the work;[79] (d) the supposed extra duties do not in fact exist;[80] (e) the extra task consumes a minimal amount of time and is of peripheral importance;[81] and (f) third persons who do the work as their primary job are paid less than the male employees in question.[82]

Equal responsibility

This factor is concerned with the degree of accountability required in the performance of the job. For example, employees may merit higher compensation if they assume supervisory duties. In *Estrada* v. *Siros Hardware*,[83] the court dismissed the Equal Pay Act charge of a female department manager because a male manager with whose job she had compared herself was in fact responsible for supervising the activities of three separate departments. Increased responsibility may be also exercised by employees who are granted greater decision making authority over financial matters. A sales clerk who not only sells merchandise but is authorized to approve checks exercises more responsibility than one whose job is restricted to selling.[84]

Similar working conditions

For pay to be equal, jobs must be similar in terms of working conditions. The mere fact that jobs are in two different departments will not necessarily mean that they are performed under dissimilar working conditions. Similarity or disparity in conditions of employment refer to surroundings and hazards. Surroundings relate to the elements regularly encountered by a worker, their intensity, and their frequency. For example, a mechanic regularly employed in sub-freezing weather outdoors confronts a significantly harsher working environment than one working normally in a heated indoors facility. Hazards address the medical and physical hazards regularly encountered, their frequency, and the severity of injury or illness that they cause.[85] Jobs in which workers confront dangerous or hostile working conditions obviously are less attractive and management could pay a wage differential to attract workers to fill them.

Statutory defenses

The statute permits wage differentials based on the following criteria: (a) a seniority system; (b) a merit system; (c) a system which measures earnings by quantity or quality of production; or (d) a differential based on any other factor apart from sex.[86]

Under these exceptions, employers are generally permitted to afford employees longevity increments, production bonuses, incentives, and raises based on performances when applied to both male and female workers.[87] To ensure that a system of seniority, merit, or production is viewed as bona fide, employers should: (a) communicate a system's components to all affected employees; (b) have the plan in writing; and (c) apply uniformly all criteria of evaluation to both male and female employees.[88] Such plans will more likely be upheld when based on objective rather than on subjective measures of job performance.[89]

The last exemption "other than sex" has been used to defend differences in pay on the basis of the following factors.

1 Red circling of wage rates. Where an employee because of ill health is temporarily transferred, the EEOC will permit an employer to pay the transferred employee his or her prior salary even though it may be greater than that being offered a member of the opposite sex who is currently performing the same work on a regular basis.[90]

2 Matching outside offers. In *Winkes* v. *Brown University*,[91] the university had raised the salary of a female associate professor of art history above that of a male colleague. Although the two were employed in essentially equal positions in terms of their research, teaching, and administrative responsibilities, the court found that matching an outside offer to keep a promising employee was permissible. At the same time, an employer would be violating the Act if it paid female employees less because they were in greater supply and would accept lower beginning salaries.[92]

3 Training programs. For a training program to be considered a bona fide factor other than sex, employers have to be careful that a training program incorporates the following features.

- Both men and women have equal access to training opportunities.
- Programs should be produced in writing and communicated to all workers.
- The program has ascertainable starting and termination points.
- Trainees must be supervised and evaluated and their ultimate advancement should be dependent upon their successful completion of the training program.[93]

4   Head of household. Some employers might provide workers with supplementary pay if they are considered "the family head" and responsible for the support of their spouse and children. Such a wage criterion must be applied equally to both men and women. At the same time, if its application results in female employees earning less than male workers, the wage disparity is suspect since the EEOC maintains that head of family status bears no relationship to job requirements or performance on the job.[94]

5   Shift differentials. The Supreme Court in *Corning Glass* v. *Brennan*[95] indicated that while working at night is not an element in determining "working conditions" it does fall within the category "other than sex" because of the extra physiological and emotional stress borne by employees who work on the evening shifts.

6   Prior salary. Some employers will consider an employee's prior salary, either with another organization or internally within the firm, as a factor in determining compensation levels. The courts are divided with regard to the legitimacy of this standard. For example, in *Kouba* v. *Allstate Insurance*[96] the company computed the minimum salary guaranteed new sales agents in part on the basis of an employee's prior salary. As a result, the average salary of female agents was less than that of their male counterparts. The court found that reliance on prior salary, although not related to an employee's duties or job performance, is nonetheless valid where it would promote a legitimate business requirement. Applying this standard, courts have found that prior salaries can be used where they help to enable the employer to (a) compete for qualified workers by encouraging them to take positions without a reduction in salary and (b) attract workers with needed experience and skills.[97]

Other courts have held otherwise. In *Glenn* v. *General Motors*,[98] the company paid clerical employees who had transferred from hourly jobs more than female employees who had been hired off the street because of the company's policy not to reduce the pay of employees who transfer from hourly to salary positions. The court ruled that a factor other than sex is limited to: (a) characteristics unique to the job; (b) factors relating to an individual's experience, training, or ability; or (c) compelling business circumstances. Since an individual's prior salary does not relate to these considerations, its use, which resulted in pay differences between men and women performing essentially the same job duties, violated the Equal Pay Act. Given these conflicting rulings, employers should be aware that they are vulnerable to Equal Pay Act violations if their use of prior salaries when determining compensation levels results in significant differences in pay received by men and women employees performing the same job duties.

Administration and enforcement

Under the EPA, sex-based wage disparities for similar jobs are unlawful within an "establishment." The EEOC and the courts have defined this term to limit the application of the statute to a comparison of jobs occurring within a geographically and operationally distinct facility rather than to an entire business, which may include several locations and operations.[99] As a result, Equal Pay Act violations normally cannot be supported by references to wage data obtained from distinct business enterprises that constitute separate places of business.

Individual suits may be initiated either by an affected employee or by the EEOC.[100] Charges must be brought within two years from the date of the wage violation or, in the case of a willful violation, three years.[101] Curing a violation requires raising the wage levels of those unfairly paid less and not reducing the wages of those previously paid more.[102] Besides the right to a higher rate, relief includes back pay and an additional sum equal to the amount of wages lost as liquidated damages, plus attorneys' fees and court costs.[103] Since 1963 there have been tens of thousands of complaints alleging violations of the Equal Pay Act and investigations have disclosed over $150,000,000 in wage underpayments involving hundreds of thousands of workers.[104] Because of the heavy potential liability of organizations, managers should constantly reappraise their compensation systems to determine that no violations are occurring. As part of this effort, managers should:[105]

- Review all job descriptions to determine if they accurately mirror the actual duties employees performed. Wage disparities may result because female employees may be performing additional duties not reflected in the job descriptions.
- Determine whether there are significant differences in pay received by male and female employees working on the same job. Are these differences related to legal considerations (performance appraisal, seniority, responsibility, skill, or effort)?
- Re-evaluate measures of performance to make them as objective as possible. If their application results in adverse impact then engage in appropriate validation studies. All performance appraisal systems must be uniformly administered.
- Critically review the measures used to determine starting salaries. Avoid utilizing abstract notions of market worth in determining compensation levels as courts have rejected paying women a lower starting salary on the basis that they would settle for less than an equally qualified male candidate would agree to.
- Examine company records to ensure that male and female employees in the same position are afforded the same fringe benefit and overtime opportunities.

Comparable Worth

Title VII in Section 703(H) incorporates what has been designated as the Bennett Amendment. It provides as follows:

> It shall not be an unlawful employment practice under this subchapter for any employer to differentiate upon the basis of sex in determining the amount of compensation paid or to be paid to employees of such employer if such differentiation is authorized by the provisions of (the Equal Pay Act).

Basically this amendment incorporates into Title VII the four major defenses available to firms under the Equal Pay Act, which include: (a) seniority; (b) merit; (c) quality or quantity of work; and (d) any condition other than sex (e.g. experience, training). The Bennett Amendment was, however, the source of substantial debate and conflict among commentators and the appellate courts.[106] One view was that the incorporation of the equal work test into Title VII meant that sex-based wage differences violated Title VII only when employees performed the same or substantially similar work.[107] Under this approach, challenges over pay for work in comparable but different positions were outside the scope of Title VII. Other courts, however, ruled that the Bennett Amendment's effect was only to incorporate the Equal Pay Act defenses in Title VII and not the equal work requirement. In *Gunther* v. *County of Washington* (1979),[108] the Supreme Court upheld the latter view, ruling that the purpose of the Bennett Amendment was only to incorporate into Title VII the four affirmative defenses of the Equal Pay Act. As a result a female charging party could bring an equal pay proceeding under Title VII without first proving that the job she sought to compare to the male job was substantially equal. It is this ruling that permitted the comparable worth controversy to continue. At the same time, the court was careful to disclaim any notion that it was endorsing the controversial concept of comparable worth.

The argument underlying comparable worth is that jobs traditionally held by women (teachers, nurses) are of equal worth or value to an organization as jobs traditionally held by men. Nonetheless, the jobs occupied by women pay less. The resulting differences in pay that are not reflective of the differences in the true worth of jobs are indicators of pay discrimination. Proponents of comparable worth maintained that through bias-free job evaluations pay equality could be achieved. On the other hand, opponents of comparable worth argue that comparable worth notions unrealistically ignore the role of the market place in determining wage levels. Additionally, by imposing a system of wage comparability, employers would be compelled to restructure the United States economy in a way that would cost billions of dollars, and such actions would create wage inflation and threaten the competitiveness of American business.[109]

By the mid-1980s it became apparent that courts will routinely uphold the capacity of employers to rely on market factors in determining wage levels, notwithstanding the disparate affect it may have on wages earned by women in traditionally female occupations. The Ninth Circuit Court of Appeals decision in *AFSCME* v. *State of Washington*[110] is illustrative.

> AFSCME argues from the study that the market reflects an historical pattern of lower wages to employees in positions staffed predominantly by women and it contends that the State of Washington perpetuates that disparity in

violation of Title VII by using market rates in the compensation system. Neither law nor logic deems the free market system a suspect enterprise. Economic reality is that the value of a particular job to an employer is but one factor influencing the rate of compensation for that job. Other considerations may include the availability of workers willing to do the job and the effectiveness of collective bargaining in a particular industry . . . We find nothing in Title VII to indicate Congress intended to abrogate fundamental economic principals such as the law of supply and demand, or to prevent employers from competing in the labor market. While the Washington legislature may have the discretion to enact a comparable worth plan if it chooses to do so, Title VII is not obligated to eliminate an economic equality which it did not create.[111]

In other rulings the appellate courts have held that market considerations relevant to different types of jobs justify pay differences between these jobs. Courts, however, are most reluctant to make essentially subjective assessments of the relative value of duties and responsibilities associated with different jobs.[112]

At the same time efforts at promoting comparable worth have been implemented at the state level. In 1983 Minnesota became the first state to adopt a comparable worth plan and approved appropriations to raise the salaries of underpaid female workers. Iowa and New Mexico have also adopted plans to increase through special budget appropriations the salary rates for employees in lower paid female-dominated jobs. Through the period of the 1970s and 1980s approximately 100 state and local governments in the United States initiated some comparable worth action.[113]

While the comparable worth argument lingers on, it may die a natural death as a result of the changing composition of the American labor force. In the United States many industrial employers confronted with international competitive pressures have permitted only moderate wage increases and at times reductions in classifications traditionally occupied by men. At the same time, in the service industries, such as retail trade, banking, and hospitals, in which women are more heavily concentrated wages have relatively increased, as the demand for service products has grown. Thus a recent Federal Reserve Bank study has indicated that the difference in median salaries between workers of the service sector and the manufacturing and industrial sector shrank from $82 a week in 1979 to $18 a week in 1992.[114] The continuing growth in the service sector and the entry of women in formerly male-only occupations should result over time in a continuing decrease in the gender wage gap.

Conditions of Employment

Grooming policies

Grooming requirements which are even-handedly applied to all employees and which have no disparate impact are naturally lawful. Additionally, it is well settled that an employer may apply different grooming requirements for men and women that take into consideration community standards or tastes. For example, a policy barring male employees from wearing shoulder length hair or pony tails, but not women, but at the same time imposing upon women the requirement that they keep their hair well groomed, will be valid. In sanctioning these policies courts have taken judicial notice of an employer's right to protect and maintain a favorable public image.[115] At the same time, employers should be careful not to impose appearance rules only on members of one sex. For example, in *Carroll* v. *Talman Federal Savings and Loan Association*[116] the court noted that while there is nothing offensive about uniforms *per se*, requiring only female employees to wear them is "disparate treatment" and unlawful. Similarly, a policy of only requiring women to wear sexually suggestive and revealing uniforms has been found to constitute illegal sexual harassment, as the effect is to harass and humiliate female employees.[117]

No-spouse policies

Many organizations will employ some policies restricting the employment or actual hire of relatives. The most common prohibition relates to policies prohibiting one relative from supervising another. Another approach is to ban spouses from working in the same department while in other settings there is a total ban against the employment of spouses within the same facility.[118]

Having close family members or spouses work in the same departments or in a supervisory–subordinate type of relationship can create problems by creating the reality or appearance of improper influence. Such policies have rarely been challenged by employees. The policies that have come under critical review are those which have banned spouses from working together within the same organization. Such policies will be considered unlawful if they are applied in a disparate manner. For example, a no-spouse policy in which wives but not husbands of employees are barred from employment would constitute a direct violation of Title VII. Similarly, a no-spouse policy enforced by the dismissal of a female employee and the retention of the male worker, because he is considered presumptively the head of the household, has been held unlawful.[119]

No-spouse policies have also been challenged on the basis of their disparate effect. These cases will be difficult to prove in the absence of a significant sample size to demonstrate that female employees have suffered a real adverse impact. For example, in *Thomas* v. *Metro Flight Incorporated*,[120] the court noted that a sample of two is too small to make even a 100 percent impact rate significant. Similarly, in *Harper* v. *Transworld Airlines*,[121] evidence that four or five applications of the no-spouse rule resulted in female job losses was held to be an inadequate basis for demonstrating adverse effect. Yet even where a definite disparate discriminatory effect is shown, courts are apparently divided over the legality of a no-spouse policy that is on the surface even-handedly applied. In *Yuhas* v. *Libby-Owens-Ford Corporation*,[122] a substantial discriminatory effect was established when 71 of 74 applicants excluded by the no-spouse hire rule were women. Nonetheless, the court found that the policy was job-related because the employment of spouses together at the same work site might: (a) interfere with a worker's job performance; (b) impede the expeditious resolution of grievances; (c) eliminate the possibility of the already employed marriage partner intervening in the hiring process on behalf of her spouse to the detriment of the employer; and (d) create a situation where spouses might enter into supervisory–subordinate type relationships, thereby creating the appearance of or actual conflict of interest problems.

Other courts are not so willing to accept a no-spouse policy on the basis of presumptions that spouses working together might create problems for the work environment. In *EEOC* v. *Rath Packing Company*,[123] the Eighth Circuit held that a no-spouse policy having an adverse effect can only be justified on the basis of a compelling need for its implementation. Applying this standard, the court felt that concrete evidence and not presumption or speculation was necessary. While the employer had asserted that dual absenteeism was a problem when both spouses had worked, the court indicated that company records revealed that production was not detrimentally affected by the minimal amount of dual spouse absenteeism. Similarly, problems created when both spouses scheduled vacations at the same time could be prevented by subjecting leave requests to management review and approval. Finally, potential abuses when spouses are placed in supervisory–subordinate type relationships could be effectively addressed by not assigning spouses to positions in which they would occupy such relationships.

Pensions and fringe benefits

Women employees have also been discriminated against in terms of lower pension and fringe benefits received. Prior to the Supreme Court's landmark decision in *Manhart* v. *City of Los Angeles*,[124] employers would either provide women retirees smaller pensions or require that they contribute a greater sum towards the purchase of monthly annuity incomes than similarly situated male retirees because of actuarial assumptions that women as a group live longer than men. In *Manhart* the Supreme Court held unlawful such pension policies. While not disputing that women as a class live longer than men, the court noted that Title VII required fairness to individuals and not to class. Since there are some women who will not live as long as men and it is impossible in advance to predict which women fall within this category, to require all women to contribute more towards the purchase of monthly annuity incomes constitutes unlawful discrimination based on sexual classifications.

In 1983 the Supreme Court in *Arizona Governing Committee* v. *Norris*[125] held unlawful an employer's deferred compensation plan, which relied on sex-based mortality tables to calculate monthly retirement benefits. Under these tables a man received larger monthly payments than a woman who deferred the same amount of compensation and retired at the same age, because the tables classify annuities on the basis of sex and women on the average live longer than men. The court noted that while sex was the only factor in the table that was used to classify individuals of the same age, the tables did not incorporate other factors correlating with longevity, such as smoking habits, alcohol consumption, weight, medical history, or family history. Noting that Title VII prohibits the use of sex-segregated actuarial tables to calculate retirement benefits, the court ruled that employers cannot adopt retirement plans that treat every individual woman less favorably than every individual man. These decisions effectively have compelled insurance companies to terminate use of sex-based actuarial tables and to substitute for them unisex actuarial tables when calculating pension premium payments and retiree annuities.

Fetal protection policies

To immunize themselves from potential liability many employers in the 1980s began to institute policies which excluded women of reproductive age from jobs where they might be exposed to chemicals or substances that would pose a health risk to the fetuses they might conceive. The legality of such policies was examined by the Supreme Court in *Auto Workers* v. *Johnson Controls*.[126] At Johnson Controls women who were pregnant or who were capable of bearing children were excluded from jobs involving lead exposure. This policy was challenged by a female employee who had chosen to be sterilized in order to avoid losing her job, by some employees who had suffered a loss in compensation upon being transferred out of jobs where there was exposure to lead, and by one male employee who had been denied a request for a leave of absence for the purpose of lowering his lead level because he had intended to become a father. The district court had granted summary judgment in favor of Johnson Controls and ruled that the policy was justified by business necessity.[127] This decision was affirmed by the seventh circuit court of appeals.[128]

In a unanimous decision, the Supreme Court reversed, finding that fetal protection policy was facially discriminatory; thus the policy created a facial classification based on sex since it denied fertile women a choice given to fertile men "as to whether they wish to risk their reproductive health for a particular job."[129] Given its obvious bias the Supreme Court noted that such a policy was permissible if it met the BFOQ exception. This burden would require the company to demonstrate that a person's sex or pregnancy actually interfered with her ability to safely perform job duties. Since concerns raised by Johnson Controls – protecting the fetus – did not relate to a female worker's ability to perform the job, the court found the exclusion of women from these positions unlawful. As a result of this decision, the exclusion of women from jobs because of concerns or even evidence that a substance will endanger the health of a fetus is no longer lawful.

The Supreme Court's decision has met with a mixed reaction. Labor and women's groups have generally praised the ruling, believing that fetal protection plans have generally been subterfuges by which to keep women out of higher paying jobs. On the other hand, the business community is concerned about the potential liability of employers. Addressing these concerns, Justice Harry Blackman noted that an employer would be immune from tort liability if it fully informed the woman of the risk, had not acted negligently, and complied with OSHA protections which should effectively minimize the risk to the fetus and newborn child. Notwithstanding Justice Blackman's disclaimer, the potential liability of employers is not clear. Justice Byron White indicated that it is not well established that Title VII will preempt state tort liability. Furthermore, although warnings may preclude claims by injured employees, they will not necessarily preclude claims by injured children because of the general rule that parents cannot waive causes of action on behalf of their children and that parents' negligence cannot be imputed to their children.

One expert in the area of occupational safety and health has advised employers to pursue the following steps to reduce their potential liability from employee exposure to hazardous substances.[130]

1 Maintain a safe workplace. The best solution is for employers to minimize the risk by keeping their workplace as free as possible from hazardous substances. Employers should ascertain if there is a more safe way to do business that will not expose their workers, particularly women of childbearing age, to hazardous risks.

2 Comply with applicable safety laws and regulations. Employers should carefully monitor the workplace for compliance with all state and federal laws and regulations concerning workplace safety and chemical exposure levels.

3 Inform employees of the risks. Now that employers can no longer exclude women from jobs that involve exposure to hazardous substances, it is the responsibility of employers to inform all employees of the risks they assume in occupying certain jobs. This factor alone, according to the majority, will provide employers with some protection in lawsuits resulting from the harm to the children of such employees. Full disclosure will provide employees with an opportunity to have access to all information, which will enable them to make a reasoned choice as to whether or not they want the job.

4 Document employee acceptance. It is best to have some kind of written document which explains to employees in detail the risks that they assume in occupying a job and the employee's willingness to accept that position despite the risks.

All these measures may not fully immunize the employer from liability. They will, however, demonstrate the employer's good faith to any jury with responsibility to determine potential damages. Furthermore, by making the job as safe as possible the employer helps to avoid situations where any employee is subjected to hazardous substances and injury to the employee or that employee's offspring.

Bias against Homosexuals and Transsexuals

The courts have held that Title VII's prohibition against sex does not apply to individuals discriminated against on the basis of their sexual preference, such as homosexuality. Furthermore, even assuming that such bias would have a greater adverse effect upon men than women because of the greater incidence of male homosexuals in our society, the courts have been unwilling to extend protection to them under the guise of protecting men generally.[131] Similarly, discrimination against individuals because they have undergone gender conversion surgery has also been held as outside Title VII's coverage.[132]

Two states, Wisconsin and Massachusetts, have enacted statutes prohibiting discrimination on the basis of sexual orientation. Additionally, many cities and counties have enacted some form of anti-discrimination protection to homosexuals. Discrimination against federal government employees because of their homosexual status has been declared a violation of a worker's due process rights under the Fifth Amendment, and is illegal unless the employer can demonstrate a nexus between a person's job performance and the employee's off-duty conduct.[133] As a result, within federal government service personnel policies have been revised so that persons are not normally disqualified solely on the basis of their sexual preference. The unique duties and responsibilities of police officers and teachers have led some state courts to uphold employer actions to dismiss or reassign employees involved in homosexual activities.[134]

Summary

The Equal Pay Act and particularly Title VII have been responsible for major alterations in organizational policies and practices regarding the employment of women. In nearly all circumstances, women must be afforded the same employment, promotional, wage, and fringe benefit opportunities as are afforded male employees working on the same job. Negative stereotypical characterizations of a woman's ability to work because of such conditions as on-the-job hazards, pregnancy, or family circumstances are not an appropriate basis for limiting their employment opportunities. Similarly, the ability of charging parties to recover compensatory and punitive damages in sexual harassment situations dictates that employers act vigorously to establish mechanisms to address and deter such misconduct. Under the Family Leave Act both men and women are entitled to take up to 12 work weeks of unpaid leave during any 12-month period for child care reasons or because of serious medical problems they or their immediate family members may confront.

Over the past 20 years women have entered the labor force in increased numbers. Currently 51 percent of all adult women work outside the home, and by the year 2000 it is projected that women will account for 47 percent of the total labor force.[135] Yet working women still feel that they are not receiving the pay, benefits, or recognition they merit. In a recent survey of 250,000 women conducted by the US Department of Labor's Women's Bureau, two-thirds indicated that improving pay scales is a high priority and half responded that they were not earning what they thought they are worth. Significantly, 14 percent of white women and 26 percent of minority women reported loss of a job or a promotion because of sex or race. It is therefore no wonder that a majority of all Hispanic, black, and white women indicated that ensuring equal opportunities in the workplace is an important change that must be made.[136] Continued enforcement of Title VII, the Equal Pay Act, and the Family Leave Act will help to ensure that women and men will maximize their opportunities and have a distinct and vital economic impact on organizations.

Questions for discussion

1   The local YMCA has a policy requiring employees and particularly youth counselors to be role models. Pursuant to such a policy it prohibits employees from parenting children out of wedlock. Jane Doe is a single female who has worked satisfactorily as a youth counselor for ten years. In the eleventh year of her employment she becomes pregnant out of wedlock and is terminated. Is this dismissal lawful? See *Chambers* v. *Omaha Girls Club*, 45 FEP 698 (8th Circuit, 1987).

2   Aero Airlines is attempting to increase the number of male business passengers. As part of its marketing campaign it imposes a 120 pound weight limitation on female flight cabin attendants. Additionally, it requires them to wear short skirts and low cut blouses. Subsequent to the implementation of this policy, Aero experiences a 15 percent increase in male passenger traffic. Are the company's grooming requirements lawful? See *EEOC* v. *Sage Realty*, 24 FEP 1521 (S.D.N.Y., 1981) and *Gerdom* v. *Continental Airlines*, 30 FEP 235 (9th Circuit, 1982).

3   Plato College consists of an engineering school, a medical school, and nursing schools, which share the same campus. Ninety percent of the engineering and medical school faculty are male, whereas 90 percent of the nursing school staff are female. The average seniority of faculty in each of three schools is approximately 20 years. The average faculty salary in the medical school is $125,000, in engineering $85,000, and in nursing $55,000. Female faculty in the nursing school feel they are underpaid and threaten to file Title VII and Equal Pay Act charges unless their salaries are substantially increased. How would the EEOC respond to such charges? What defenses might the university offer? See, for example, *Wilkins* v. *University of Houston*, 26 FEP 1230 (5th Circuit 1981).

4   Ajax, Incorporated, is a small business of 50 workers providing accounting services. It seeks to employ a CPA. Following its recruitment efforts one male and two female employees apply. The two female candidates have superior credentials. Nonetheless, the president of Ajax decides to

offer employment to the male applicant, who is the son of a close friend. Has the employer violated Title VII? *See DeCintio* v. *Westchester County Medical Center*, 42 FEP 921 (2nd Circuit, 1986). At what point may discrimination based on social relationships result in a breach of Title VII?

5 To avoid absenteeism problems, many employers have promulgated "no fault" attendance policies in which workers may be subjected to increased discipline for a specific number of absences without regard to the reasons for the absence. Such policies may permit workers to clear their attendance records by some specified period of perfect or near perfect attendance. In some situations absences for specific reasons may be excluded from consideration. To what degree would such policies be affected by the Family and Medical Leave Act?

NOTES

1 Charles and Barbara Whalen, *The Longest Debate: a Legislative History of the 1964 Civil Rights Act* (Seven Locks Press, Washington, DC, 1985), pp. 115–17.
2 Kenneth Lawrence and Katherine Klos, eds, *Sex Discrimination in the Workplace* (Aspen Systems Publications, Germantown, MD, 1978), pp. 28–9.
3 US Equal Employment Opportunity Commission, *Status and Trends* (September 1991), p. 14.
4 Ronald Ehrenberg and Robert Smith, *Modern Labor Economics* (Harper Collins, New York, 1994), p. 401.
5 1 FEP 656, 408 F.2d 228 (5th Cir. 1969), at 661.
6 *Diaz* v. *Pan American Airways*, 3 FEP 337, 442 F.2d 385 (5th Cir. 1971), at 339.
7 See, for example, *Dothard* v. *Rawlinson*, 15 FEP 10, 433 US 321 (1977).
8 Guidelines on Discrimination Because of Sex, 29 CFR, section 1604.2(a)(2).
9 *Gunther* v. *Iowa State Men's Reformatory*, 21 FEP 1031, 612 F.2d 1079 (8th Cir. 1980); *EEOC* v. *Mercy Health Center*, 29 FEP 159 (1982).
10 Supra, note 7.
11 3 FEP 40, 400 US 542 (1971).
12 *Inda* v. *United Air Lines*, 16 FEP 251, 565 F.2d 554 (9th Cir. 1977); *Jacobs* v. *Martin Sweets Co.*, 14 FEP 687, 550 F.2d 364 (6th Cir. 1977).
13 Barbera Bergmann, *The Economic Emergence of Women* (Harper Collins, New York, 1986), pp. 18, 22–3, 30–3.
14 13 FEP 1657, 427 US 125 (1976).
15 *Gardner* v. *National Airlines*, 14 FEP 1806, 434 F.Supp. 249 (1977).
16 *California Federal Savings and Loan Association* v. *Guerra* 42 FEP 1073, 479 US 272 (1987).
17 *Newport News Shipbuilding and Dry Dock Co.* v. *EEOC*, 32 FEP 1, 462 US 669 (1983).
18 Section 701(k), Public Law 95-555 (1978).
19 29 Code of Federal Regulations section 825(II)(A) (1993).
20 Department of Labor-ESA, "Fact sheet on Family and Medical Leave Act," July 22, 1993, *BNA Fair Employment Practice Manual*, section 405:251.
21 Ibid.
22 Ibid., at 405:252.
23 29 CFR section 825.114.

24 29 CFR section 925.203(a)(b) and (c).
25 "Fact sheet on Family and Medical Leave Act," supra, note 20, section 405.252.
26 29 CFR section 825.204(a)(b) and (c).
27 29 CFR section 825.207.
28 29 CFR section 825.209(a) and (b).
29 29 CFR section 825.213(a)(1) and (2).
30 29 CFR section 825.214.
31 29 CFR section 825.216(a).
32 29 CFR section 825.216(c).
33 29 CFR section 825.217(a).
34 29 CFR section 825.219(a–d).
35 29 CFR section 825.218(a–c).
36 29 CFR section 825.302(a).
37 29 CFR section 825.304(b).
38 "Fact sheet on Family and Medical Leave," supra, note 20, section 405.253.
39 29 CFR section 825.305(a).
40 29 CFR section 825.307(a) and (c).
41 29 CFR section 825.309(a).
42 29 CFR section 825.310(a).
43 29 CFR section 825.400(a–c).
44 Dawn Gunsch, "The Family Leave Act: a financial burden?" *Personnel Journal* (September 1993), pp. 49–50.
45 BNA, *Family and Medical Leave Act of 1993* (June 4, 1993), No. 106, p. 55.
46 Ibid., pp. 56–7.
47 BNA, *Daily Labor Reporter* (June 2, 1994), p. A-3.
48 BNA, *Daily Labor Reporter* (May 11, 1994), p. A-19.
49 Clifford Koen, "Sexual harassment: criteria for defining hostile environment," *Employee Responsibilities and Rights Journal*, 2 (No. 9, 1989), p. 289.
50 See, for example, *Tomkins* v. *Public Service and Electric*, 13 FEP 1574, 422 F.Supp. 553 (1976), rev. 16 FEP 22, 568 F.2d 1044 (3rd Cir. 1977).
51 *Henson* v. *City of Dundee*, 29 FEP 787, 682 F.2d 897 (11th Cir. 1982).
52 40 FEP 1822, 477 US 57 (1986).
53 Ibid., at 1827.
54 63 FEP 225 (1993).
55 *Gan* v. *Kepko Circuit Systems*, 28 FEP 639 (1982).
56 EEOC Policy Guidance on Sexual Harassment Issues, March 19, 1990, *EEOC Compliance Manual* (Commerce Clearing House, New York, 1990), pgh. 81,441.
57 *Burns* v. *McGregor Electronics*, 60 FEP 695 (1992), at 701.
58 Policy Guide on Employer Liability for Sexual Favoritism under Title VII, Jan. 12, 1990, BNA, No. 694, pgh. 405:6817.
59 32 FEP 1401, 570 F.2d 1197 (1983).
60 63 FEP 225 (1993).
61 42 FEP 631, 805 F.2d 611 (6th Cir. 1986).
62 Ibid., at 639.
63 *Ellison* v. *Brady*, 54 FEP 1346, 924 F.2d 872 (6th Cir. 1991); *Yates* v. *Avco Corp.*, 43 FEP 1595, 819 F.2d 1371 (6th Cir. 1987).
64 EEOC Enforcement Guidance on Harris v. Forklift Systems, March 8, 1994, BNA *Fair Employment Practice Manual*, Section 405.7168.
65 *Sparks* v. *Pilot Freight Carriers, Inc.*, 45 FEP 160, 830 F.2d 1554 (11th Cir. 1987); EEOC Policy Guidance on Sexual Harassment Issues, supra, note 56, pgh 81,441.

66 Ibid., at pgh 81,472-81,474.
67 Supra, note 52, at 1829.
68 Supra, note 56, at pgh 81,476.
69 Frederick L. Sullivan, "Sexual harassment: the Supreme Court ruling," *Personnel* (December 1986), pp. 42–5.
70 Mary E. Kurz, "Investigating sexual harassment complaints," Michigan State University, September 2, 1993.
71 Sullivan, supra, note 69.
72 29 USCA section 206(d).
73 43 Fed. Reg. 19807 (1978).
74 29 CFR section 1620.13(a).
75 29 CFR section 1620.15(a) and (b).
76 29 CFR section 1620.16(a) and (b).
77 *Shultz* v. *American Can Co.*, 9 FEP 524, 424 F.2d 356 (8th Cir. 1970).
78 *Hodgson* v. *Fairmont Supply Co.*, 9 FEP 706, 454 F.2d 490 (4th Cir. 1971).
79 *Shultz* v. *Wheaton Glass Co.*, 9 FEP 502, 421 F.2d 259 (8th Cir. 1972).
80 *Hodgson* v. *Security National Bank*, 9 FEP 761, 460 F.2d 57 (8th Cir. 1972).
81 *Hodgson* v. *Behrens Drug Co.*, 9 FEP 816, 475 F.2d 1041 (5th Cir. 1973).
82 Supra, note 79.
83 39 FEP 597 (1984).
84 29 CFR section 1620.17(a) and (c).
85 29 CFR section 1620.18(a).
86 29 USCA section 206(d).
87 Michael Levin-Epstein, *Primer on Equal Employment Opportunity* (BNA, Washington, DC, 1987), p. 57.
88 Mack A. Player, Elaine Shoben, and Risa Lieberwitz, *Employment Discrimination Law: Cases and Materials* (West Publishing Co., St Paul, MN, 1990), p. 396.
89 Thomas Basnight and Benjamin Wolkinson, "Evaluating managerial performance: is your appraisal system lawful?" *Employee Relations Law Journal*, 3 (No. 2, August 1972), pp. 244–6.
90 29 CFR section 1620.26.
91 36 FEP 120, 747 F.2d 792 (1st Cir. 1984).
92 *Marshall* v. *Georgia Southwestern College*, 23 FEP 451, 489 F.Supp. 1322 (1980).
93 Mack A. Player, *Employment Discrimination Law* (West Publishing Co., St Paul, MN, 1988), p. 172.
94 29 CFR section 1620.21.
95 9 FEP 74, 417 US 188 (1974).
96 30 FEP 57, 691 F.2d 873 (1982).
97 *Groussman* v. *Respiratory Home Care*, 40 FEP 122 (1986).
98 46 FEP 1331, 841 F.2d 1567 (11th Cir. 1988).
99 29 CFR section 1620.9(a).
100 29 USC section 216(b).
101 29 USC section 255(a).
102 29 USC section 296(a)(1).
103 29 USC section 216(c).
104 Donald Elisburg, "Equal pay in the United States: development and implementation of the Equal Pay Act of 1963," *Labor Law Journal* (April 1978), p. 201.
105 See, in general, Frederick S. Hills and Thomas J. Bergmann, "Conducting an equal pay for equal work audit," in *New Perspectives on Compensation*, ed. David Balkin and Luis R. Gomez-Meija (Prentice-Hall, Englewood Cliffs, NJ, 1987), pp. 80–9.

106 Robert Vercruysse, "Comparable worth before and after Gunther," *Michigan Bar Journal* (September 1984), pp. 793–7.

107 *Lemon* v. *City and County of Denver*, 22 FEP 959, 620 F.2d 228 (10th Cir. 1980).

108 25 FEP 1521, 425 US 161 (1981).

109 Bruce Nelson, Edward M. Opton, Jr, and Thomas E. Wilson, "Wage discrimination and Title VII in the 1980s: the case against comparable worth," *Employee Relations Law Journal*, 6 (No. 3, 1980), pp. 380–91.

110 38 FEP 1353, 770 F.2d 1401 (9th Cir. 1985).

111 Ibid., at 1357–8.

112 *UAW* v. *State of Michigan*, 50 FEP 1560, 886 F.2d 766 (6th Cir. 1351); *American Nurses Association* v. *Illinois*, 40 FEP 244, 783 F.2d 716 (7th Cir. 1981); *Plemer* v. *Parsons-Gilbane*, 32 FEP 1351, 713 F.2d 1127 (5th Cir. 1983).

113 Richard I. Henderson, *Compensation Management* (Prentice Hall, Englewood Cliffs, NJ, 1994), p. 116.

114 *The Wall Street Journal* (July 19, 1994), p. A2.

115 *Willingham* v. *Macon Telegraph Publishing Co.*, 9 FEP 189, 507 F.2d 1084 (5th Cir. 1975); *Dodge* v. *Giant Food, Inc.*, 6 FEP 1066 (DC Cir. 1973); *Knott* v. *Missouri Pacific Railroad*, 11 FEP 1231, 527 F.2d 1249 (8th Cir. 1975).

116 20 FEP 764, 604 F.2d 1028 (7th Cir. 1979).

117 *EEOC* v. *Sage Realty Corp.*, 24 FEP 1521 (1981).

118 Bureau of National Affairs, *Nepotism, Office Romance, and Sexual Harassment* (BNA, Washington, DC, 1988), pp. 17–20.

119 *George* v. *Farmers Electrical Co-op*, 32 FEP 1801, 715 F.2d 175 (5th Cir. 1983).

120 43 FEP 703, 814 F.2d 1506 (10th Cir. 1987).

121 11 FEP 1074, 525 F.2d 409 (8th Cir. 1975).

122 16 FEP 891, 562 F.2d 496 (7th Cir. 1977).

123 40 FEP 580, 787 F.2d 318 (8th Cir. 1986).

124 17 FEP 395, 435 US 702 (1978).

125 32 FEP 233, 463 US 1073 (1983).

126 55 FEP 365, 499 US 187 (1991).

127 46 FEP 110, 680 F.Supp. 309 (1988).

128 50 FEP 1627, 886 F.2d 871 (1989).

129 Supra, note 126, at 370.

130 Howard A. Simon, "Mixed signals: the Supreme Court's 1991 Title VII decisions," *Employee Relations Law Journal*, 17 (Autumn 1991), pp. 213–15.

131 *DeSantis* v. *Pacific Telephone Co.*, 19 FEP 1493, 608 F.2d 327 (9th Cir. 1979).

132 *Ulane* v. *Eastern Air Lines*, 35 FEP 1398 (7th Cir. 1984).

133 *Norton* v. *Macy*, 9 FEP 1382, 417 F.2d 1161 (DC Cir. 1969).

134 *Childers* v. *Dallas Police Dept*, 28 FEP 1072, 609 F.2d 732 (5th Cir. 1982); *Gaylord* v. *Tacoma School District No. 10*, 16 FEP 596 (1977).

135 Marc G. Singer, *Human Resource Management* (PWS-Kent, Boston, 1990), p. 517.

136 *New York Times*, October 15, 1994, p. 8; *Detroit Free Press*, October 15, 1994, pp. 16A–17A.

Chapter 5
Other Equal Employment Opportunity Classifications: Age, Religion, and National Origin Discrimination

Age Discrimination

When it was signed into law by President Johnson on December 15, 1967, the major concern of the Age Discrimination Employment Act (ADEA) was the elimination of age discrimination and the hiring of older workers. Governmental studies conducted prior to the Act's passage reported that applicants over 55 years of age were excluded from 50 percent of all private sector job openings while 25 percent were closed to applicants 45 years and older.[1] Underlying restrictive practices were stereotypical perceptions that older workers were unsuitable for employment. These included notions that: (a) younger workers were more productive, motivated, and capable of working under pressure; (b) older workers were more accident prone; (c) older employees have greater difficulty learning new skills and techniques; and (d) younger employees are more creative. The Act combated reliance on these stereotypical perceptions, requiring employers to evaluate workers not on the basis of their chronological age, but on the basis of their functional abilities to perform the duties of a particular job.

The effort to protect older workers has taken on increased significance in the 1980s and 1990s as the American workforce continues to age. By the year 2000 it is projected that 32 percent of the United States population will be aged 55 years or more, while the median age of the labor force will be 38.9 years.[2] The massive layoffs of workers during the 1980s and the growing awareness of older workers of their rights has led to a major expansion in the number of charges filed. In 1968 approximately 1,000 age discrimination charges were filed. By 1985, 25,000 were being processed annually by the United States Equal Employment Opportunity Commission. These charges can be broken down into the following categories: termination (75 percent), refusal to hire (10 percent), failure to promote (7 percent), demotion (6 percent), and compensation and benefits (2 percent).[3] Through the 1990s, it is anticipated that the volume of age discrimination complaints will continue to grow.

Jurisdictional scope and critical provisions

The ADEA is patterned after Title VII and applies nearly the same definitions to the terms employers, labor unions, and employment agencies. All firms with at least 20 employees (15 under Title VII), all labor unions with at least 25 members (20 under Title VII), and all employment agencies are covered.[4] Since 1974, state and local governments have been included in its scope.[5]

When the ADEA was originally enacted in 1967 only workers between the ages of 40 and 65 were protected. In 1978 the upper age limit was extended to 70.[6] Effective January 1, 1987, the maximum age limit was removed altogether.[7] Currently, all workers aged 40 years and older are protected against age discrimination. The statute renders unlawful the following employee practices.

- Refusing to hire or discharging or otherwise discriminating against any individual with respect to compensation, terms, conditions, or privileges of employment because of age.[8]
- Limiting, segregating or classifying employees in any way which would deprive any individual of employment opportunities or otherwise adversely affect his or her status as an employee because of age.[9]
- Reducing the wage rate of any employee in order to comply with the Act.[10]
- Indicating a preference, or limitation, or specification based on age in any notice or advertisement for employment.[11] As a result, employers should eschew notices or advertisements containing such terms or phrases as wanted, "young college student," "recent college graduate," "boy," "girl," or others of a similar nature which suggest that preference will be given to employees of a given age and which may discourage older workers from applying.[12] Similarly, to avoid potential litigation it would be advisable for most employers to avoid asking applicants to state their age except to determine if they meet the legal age requirements in a state (usually 18 or 21).
- Operating a seniority system or employee benefit plan that requires or permits the involuntary retirement of employees.[13]

Proof of discrimination

The Age Discrimination Employment Act also borrows its standards of proof from Title VII. Commonly adopted criteria for establishing a *prima facie* case of age discrimination are that the individual: (a) is aged 40 or older; (b) was not hired, was discharged or was otherwise adversely affected by the employer's decision; (c) was qualified for the position; and (d) was ultimately replaced by a person sufficiently younger to permit an inference of age discrimination.[14]

As in Title VII cases the ultimate burden of proving discrimination remains with the employee. An employer may rebut a *prima facie* case of employment discrimination by clearly explaining and articulating non-discriminatory reasons for its actions. Where an employer provides a non-discriminatory reason (e.g. the person's lack of qualifications, poor job references), the employee will be given the opportunity to demonstrate that the proffered reason was not the true reason and that the employer's justification was a mere pretext for discrimination.

In proving pretext courts will frequently rely on a company's history of employing older workers, the performance record of aggrieved employees, and prejudicial statements made by management against them. For example, in *Duffy* v. *Wheeling Pittsburgh Steel Corporation*,[15] the employer had terminated the four oldest and most highly paid salesmen. In finding the termination unlawful, the court noted that the performance of the dismissed employees was superior to that of younger men retained, and that management officials had been eager to get younger and more aggressive people in the field. Similarly, in *Hodgson* v. *First Federal Savings and Loan Association*, the court relied upon the interviewer's note indicating that the applicant was "too old for teller' and the bank's record of hiring 35 tellers within a ten-month period, all of whom were below the age of 40.[16]

Statutory exceptions and defenses

The ADEA has created several exemptions from the scope of the Act's coverage.

- Preference in employment may be afforded where age is a bona fide occupational qualification reasonably necessary to the normal operations of the business.[17]
- The differentiation is based on a reasonable factor other than age.[18]
- Compliance with the terms of a bona fide seniority system or any bona fide employee benefit plan that is not intended to evade the purposes of the act.[19]
- The discharge or discipline of an individual is for good cause.[20]

BFOQ defense An employer claiming its conduct was based on a bona fide occupational qualification admits age-based treatment but maintains that the differential treatment is necessary to promote legitimate business objectives. As with Title VII's BFOQ provision, the courts will permit the BFOQ defense only in limited circumstances. In *Western Airlines* v. *Criswell*,[21] the Supreme Court identified the two prong test required to validate a BFOQ in age cases. An employer asserting a BFOQ must demonstrate that age is reasonably necessary to the operation of the business. This requirement precludes an organization from establishing an age qualification for purposes that are unrelated to or tangential to the employer's central mission. For example, a desire to create a youthful environment by only hiring employees younger than 40 would normally not be viewed as "reasonably necessary" to the business.[22] Secondly, even where the employer could show that the age qualification is necessary to the normal business operations, the employer must prove that (a) all or substantially all persons excluded by the age requirement would be unable to perform safely and efficiently or (b) age is a legitimate proxy for safety-related qualifications because it is impossible or impracticable to screen older persons on an individual basis.[23]

In most settings employers establishing a BFOQ would be subject to the first standard by which management must screen workers on an individual basis. This evidentiary burden of proof is most difficult to satisfy, since the unpredictability of the aging process will make it nearly impossible for employers to demonstrate that workers above a certain age are unable to perform.[24] At the same time, where safety is at issue and the individual testing of workers is not feasible, then age may be a BFOQ if objective evidence demonstrates that older workers are generally unable to perform.

This more flexible and lighter standard has been accepted in the transportation industry, where jobs have an immediate and direct effect on public safety. In *Usery* v. *Tamiami Trail Tours Incorporated*,[25] the employer had presented medical evidence that the physiological and psychological changes that accompany the aging process and decrease a person's ability to drive safely justify the establishment of age 40 as a cutoff age for hiring. In *Tamiami* the court ruled that the normal requirement to evaluate persons and drivers on an individual basis could be dispensed with and that age could be the basis for a BFOQ where the evidence indicated that medical tests could not adequately determine which individuals over 40 would be affected by the age-related impairments, such as loss of stamina, which negatively affected driving safety.

At the same time, even in such situations the evidence presented must be objective in nature and specifically related to the duties of the particular job for which the BFOQ has been established. For this reason the Supreme Court in *Western Airlines* v. *Criswell* rejected the establishment of age 60 as a retirement date for engineers because it had been adopted as an extension of the company's rule for pilots and failed to consider that the qualifications for flight engineer were less rigorous than those required for a pilot.[26]

Employers concerned over the performance of older employees must also consider that while aging may result in a lessening of one's physical abilities, such disadvantages may be offset or counterbalanced by workers' increased seniority and maturity. Thus, one court noted that older fire fighters are less likely to be injured or killed than younger fire fighters because of their better judgment and experience.[27]

Employers seeking to screen out older employees because of the alleged waning physical and psychological abilities must be careful to impose minimum health and physical requirements not just on older employees but on the entire workforce. In *EEOC* v. *Commonwealth of Pennsylvania*,[28] the Seventh Circuit noted that the ADEA bars selective age-based enforcement of a health and fitness requirement. As a result, it held that the State of Pennsylvania could not justify the mandatory retirement of police officers at age 60 because of their presumed inadequate fitness when the department did not require all state troopers to maintain a minimal level of health and fitness. Similarly, in *Heiar* v. *Crawford County*[29] the Seventh Circuit rejected the mandatory retirement of deputy sheriffs at age 55 because of medical concerns that their higher risk of developing heart disease would preclude their response to emergencies, since the county failed to require deputy sheriffs to take annual or periodic physical examinations at any age to determine their fitness.

Under 1986 amendments to the ADEA,[30] police and fire agencies were permitted to establish age requirements for hiring or retirement as long as such plans were not implemented as a subterfuge to evade the purposes of this Act. The amendment reflected congressional opinion that the municipalities should be given the discretion based on their experience to establish BFOQ policies. This exemption terminated on December 31, 1993. At the same time, many states and municipalities are maintaining their policies in anticipation of congressional action to reinstate this exemption. On November 8, 1993 the House of Representatives gave voice approval to legislation authorizing state and local governments to impose mandatory retirement and maximum hiring ages for their safety public employees.[31]

As part of the 1986 amendments, the EEOC was commissioned to examine the use of physical and mental fitness tests to measure the ability and competency of police and fire personnel. A study commissioned by the EEOC found that age is a poor predictor of "ability," meaning stamina, strength, reasoning and comprehension, and that age-related decline in job-related abilities is slight. It also found that tests are a safe and effective alternative to age in making hiring and retirement decisions. These reported findings have helped to spur senatorial opposition to reinstating the exemption.[32]

Reasonable factors other than age The employer who invokes the BFOQ exception essentially admits that differentiations were made on the basis of age, but seeks to legitimize those differentiations by demonstrating that they were necessary given the nature of the business. On the other hand, the employer who invokes "the reasonable factor" justification asserts that there was no differentiation on the basis of age, because its employment decisions were based on some other legitimate consideration. Under this exception, employers can make employment decisions based upon such factors as physical fitness, education, testing, production, and performance. Similarly, courts have found that lack of training for a particular job,[33] chronic tardiness,[34] or elimination of a position[35] could serve as reasonable factors to justify the dismissal of employees within the protected age group.

At the same time, the EEOC has noted that when an employment practice including a test is claimed as a basis for different treatment of employees or applicants and such a practice has an adverse impact on individuals within the protected age group, reliance on the selection factor will require its validation in accordance with the EEOC's uniform guidelines on employee selection procedures.[36]

Employer layoff decisions   Take a situation where because of poor economic conditions the employer is compelled to reduce its workforce. Recognizing that more senior personnel are earning substantially more than younger employees, the employer decides to lay off executives who are 50 years of age and older in order to achieve significant cost reductions. Can the employer lawfully contend that the dismissal of older workers to achieve substantial cost savings is a reasonable factor other than age?

The EEOC maintains that the layoff of older employees to achieve cost savings is illegal.[37] The EEOC's position has generally been affirmed by the appellate courts. For example, in *Leftwich* v. *Harris-Stowe State College*,[38] the court found that the college as a cost saving measure had adopted a job elimination plan that had targeted tenured faculty for layoff because of their higher salaries as compared with nontenured personnel. Although the university's plan was based on tenure status rather than explicitly on age, because of the close relationship between tenure status and age, the court found that the plain intent and effect of the college's plan was to eliminate older workers who have built up through years of satisfactory service higher salaries than their younger counterparts. As a result, utilizing higher salaries as a basis for layoff undermined the purpose of the Age Discrimination and Employment Act. Similar rulings that salary differences are not age-neutral and cannot qualify as a factor other than age have been found by the Seventh and Second Circuits.[39]

Where employers engage in major cutbacks it is not unusual that some workers over age 40 within the protected age group will be adversely affected. To minimize potential age discrimination suits, employers should take the following precautions. Make layoff decisions on the basis of objective performance criteria. Treat all employees uniformly and do not apply a more rigorous standard to older workers. Inform all employees of the reasons for their termination and provide them with an opportunity to review evaluations of their job performance. Document the performances of individuals retained and laid off and be able to identify the specific job related deficiencies that led to a worker's dismissal. Attempt to avoid the economic impact upon those terminated by establishing a placement program.[40]

Bona fide seniority system   The Act also permits differentiations pursuant to a bona fide seniority system. Under EEOC guidelines, a valid seniority system must include the following components: (a) job benefits and employment opportunities must be allocated on the basis of an employee's length of service; (b) the plan must be communicated and applied uniformly to all affected regardless of age.[41]

Mandatory retirement

As originally enacted, section 4f(2) of the ADEA provided as follows:

> It shall not be unlawful for an employer . . . to observe the terms of a bona fide seniority system or any bona fide employee benefit plan such as a retirement, pension, or insurance plan, which is not a subterfuge to evade the purposes of this Act, except that no such employee benefit plan shall excuse the failure to hire any individual.

Relying on this language, the Supreme Court in *McMann* v. *United Airlines*[42] ruled that an employer could require the retirement at age 60 of workers who were participating in a retirement plan that had been adopted prior to the Act's passage. Since United Airlines's plan had been established well before the ADEA's enactment, the court ruled that it could not be viewed as a subterfuge to evade its purposes.

In 1978 Congress responded by amending section 4f(2) to ban the mandatory retirement of workers:

> It shall not be unlawful for any employer . . . to observe the terms of a bona fide seniority system or any bona fide employee benefit plan such as a retirement, pension, or insurance plan, which is not a subterfuge to evade the purposes of this [Act], except that no such employee benefit plan shall excuse the failure to hire any individual, and no such seniority system or employee benefit plan shall require or permit the involuntary retirement of any individual specified . . . because of the age of such individual.[43]

Congress concurrently amended the ADEA to extend protection of the statute to persons through age 70,[44] and in 1986 the upper limit was removed entirely.[45] The sentiment underlying this major change was expressed by Senator John Heinz of Pennsylvania.

> The importance of removing the age 70 cap is its message to present and future older workers; you are to be employed on the basis of your ability, not on the basis of your birthdate. . . .
>
> Age discrimination is unfair and we should rid our society of it without further delay . . .
>
> The ADEA does not require employers to keep unfit or unproductive employees. All that the ADEA requires is that the employer make individualized assessments where it is possible and practical to do so. I believe that such determinations are possible and that it is reasonable to require them rather than imposing age limits based solely on age.[46]

The 1978 amendments do permit the retirement at age 65 of bona fide "executive and high policy makers" who, prior to their retirement, are in such positions for a minimum of two years. Additionally, these employees must be entitled to an immediate non-forfeitable retirement benefit of at least $44,000.[47]

The statute does not define the terms "bona fide executive" or "high policy maker." At the same time, based on the conference committee report that drafted the language, the EEOC has indicated that this exception will be applied narrowly to only a few top level employees who exercise substantial authority over a significant number of employees and a large volume of business.

> Typically the head of a significant and substantial local or regional operation of a corporation, such as a major production facility or retail establishment, but not the head of a minor branch, warehouse or retail store, would be covered by the term "bona fide executive." Individuals at higher levels in the corporate organizational structure who possess comparable or greater levels of responsibility and authority as measured by established and recognized criteria would also be covered.
>
> The heads of major departments or divisions of corporations are usually located at corporate or regional headquarters. With respect to employees whose duties are associated with corporate headquarters operations, such as finance, marketing, legal, production and manufacturing (or in a corporation organized on a production basis, the management of product lines), the definition would cover employees who head those divisions.
>
> In a large organization the immediate subordinates of the heads of these divisions sometimes also exercise executive authority, within the meaning of this exemption. The conferees intend the definition to cover such employees if they possess responsibility which is comparable to or greater than that possessed by the head of a significant and substantial local operation who meets the definition.
>
> The phrase "high policymaking position" is limited to certain top level employees who are not "bona fide executives" within the exemption. These [include] individuals who have little or no line authority but whose position and responsibility are such that they play a significant role in the development of corporate policy and effectively recommend the implementation thereof.
>
> For example, the chief economist or the chief research scientist of a corporation typically has little line authority. His duties would be primarily intellectual as opposed to executive or managerial. His responsibility would be to evaluate significant economic or scientific trends and issues, to develop and recommend policy direction to top executive officers of the corporation, and he would have a significant impact on the ultimate decision on such policies by virtue of his expertise and direct access to the decisionmakers. Such an employee would meet the definition of a "high policymaking" employee.[48]

Few cases are litigated because of the clear requirements of the statute, the willingness of executives to retire by the age of 65, and the disinclination of some managers to acknowledge that they have not served in executive or high policy making positions.[49]

Employee benefit plans

Section 4(f)(2) allows employers to administer bona fide employee pension and insurance plans. To be bona fide the EEOC requires the plan to be in writing and to provide the benefits in accordance with its plan.[50] Additionally, the EEOC implemented rules that permitted benefit levels for older workers to be reduced only when necessary to achieve equivalency of costs for older and younger workers. Under this approach a benefit plan was bona fide if the actual payment or cost on behalf of an older worker was equal to that incurred on behalf of a younger one.[51] Thus, for example, higher group term life insurance costs for older workers would justify a correspondingly lower amount of group life insurance coverage for older workers. Consequently, if a $100 monthly contribution purchased $50,000 coverage for an employee at age 35 and only $25,000 for employees at age 60, the difference in coverage was lawful.

The EEOC's approach, however, was invalidated by the Supreme Court in *Public Employment Retirement System of Ohio* v. *Betts*.[52] Betts had been hired and employed as a speech pathologist by the County of Hamilton. Because of a deteriorating medical condition she chose to retire. The State of Ohio had previously established a disability retirement plan whereby benefits were made available to employees who suffered a permanent disability and who had at least five years of total service credit and were under the age of 60 at retirement. Because she was over 60 and otherwise entitled to retiree benefits, she was denied disability retirement benefits despite her medical condition. Because of this denial she lost $158 a month in pension benefits, the difference between her age and service retirement benefits and the disability retirement benefits.

Following the denial Betts sued and won judgments at the district and appellate levels. These courts found that Ohio's public employment retirement plan was facially discriminatory for denying workers over 60 the opportunity to receive disability retirement benefits. Moreover, relying on EEOC guidelines, the courts held that a reduction in benefits to workers under age 60 was not lawful as the State of Ohio had provided no empirical evidence that the reduction in benefits was necessitated by cost considerations.

On review the Supreme Court rejected the EEOC contention that the statute prohibited age-related distribution of pension benefits that were not justified on the basis of cost considerations. Instead, the court decided that any employee benefit plan that did not adversely affect an older worker's employment status, wages, salaries, or other non-benefit aspects of employment would be considered legitimate. Additionally, the court noted that for a charging party to win an age discrimination suit it was required to demonstrate that the employer in reducing the level of pension benefits had an actual intent to discriminate in the non-fringe benefit aspects of the employment relationship.

Older Workers Benefit and Protection Act

Betts sparked widespread protests by civil rights advocacy groups, including the American Association of Retired Persons (AARP), and a number of bills were introduced in congress to overturn it. On October 16, 1990 President Bush signed into law the Older Workers Benefit and Protection Act (OWBPA).[53]

The OWBPA overturned *Betts* and reinstated EEOC policy on benefits plans through the following provisions. (a) The term "compensation" was expanded to include all employee benefits (section 102). As a result, discrimination against older employees in receipt of any employee benefits (health, pension, insurance) is unlawful regardless of the non-fringe aspects of the employment relationship. (b) The Act codified the EEOC principle of "equal benefit or equal cost," whereby employers must provide older workers with the benefits provided younger employees unless the employer can demonstrate that the cost of providing an equal benefit is greater for an older worker than a younger one.[54] In the latter circumstance the employer would be required to prove that the cost incurred for providing benefits to younger and older employees would be the same. (c) Benefit plans are covered regardless of their date of implementation.[55] (d) Employers will have the burden of proving that their benefits are bona fide.[56]

Early retirement plans The Act also permits voluntary early retirement incentive plans that are "consistent with the statute." According to the legislative history early retirement incentives that provide a flat dollar amount, service based benefits (i.e. $1,000 multiplied by number of years of service), or a percentage of salary which reward service and which encourage the employment of older workers based upon their ability would remain lawful. At the same time, early retirement that is not truly voluntary or plans that deny or reduce benefits to older workers while continuing to make them available to younger employees on the basis of stereotypical assumptions that older workers would be retiring anyway will conflict with the Age Discrimination and Employment Act.[57]

An employer may require the attainment of a minimum age as a condition of eligibility for normal or early retirement benefits.[58] Additionally, the Act permits employers when structuring early retirement plans to provide payments of Social Security supplements for plan participants that begin before and terminate at the age when the participants would otherwise be eligible to receive reduced or unreduced old age insurance benefits under the Social Security Act.[59] These supplements or bridge payments were explained in the Senate Report:

> Typically, a social security bridge payment is a fixed monthly payment intended to substitute for social security benefits that will become available to the plan participant either at age 62 (eligibility for reduced Social Security benefits) or age 65 (eligibility for unreduced Social Security benefits).
>
> The Committee concludes that the payment of such supplemental pension

benefits . . . is lawful . . . so long as the supplement does not exceed the amount of the Social Security benefits.

The fact that younger retired workers may receive the benefits for a greater number of years and may therefore receive greater total benefits does not make these plans unlawful. *See Dorsch* v. *L.B. Foster Company*, 782 F.2d 1421 (7th Cir. 1986). If a plan provides these benefits, the benefits may not terminate at an age earlier than the first age of eligibility for reduced old-age insurance benefits.[60]

One of the more difficult issues confronting the courts prior to passage of the OWBPA was whether an employer could lawfully reduce or deny severance benefits to laid off employees who are otherwise eligible for retirement benefits. Under the new Act employers have been given flexibility to engage in narrowly drawn forms of benefit packaging that prior to *Betts* may have been unlawful under EEOC regulations. Specifically, the Act provides that in the event of a plant closing or layoff, an employer may reduce a worker's severance payments by the value of retiree health benefits received by a worker eligible for a pension.[61] If, however, an employee's pension benefits are actuarily reduced, then the amount of the reduction in health benefits allowable to severance payments must be proportionately reduced.[62] "Thus, for example, if an individual receiving retiree health benefits received a pension that is actuarily reduced by 18 percent, the value of that individual's retiree health benefits (as calculated under this section) must be reduced by 18 percent before any deduction is taken."[63]

In some situations workers may receive additional pension benefits solely because of a plant closing or layoffs. These additional benefits may be deducted from severance payments where the individual is able to receive a pension at an unreduced level.[64] For example, assume that at the time of the plant closing an employee was entitled to 80 percent of his normal pension, and because of the shutdown received an amount equal to 100 percent of his retirement pension. In this instance, the additional 20 percent value of the pension as well as the value of the retiree health benefits could be offset against severance benefits.[65] Finally, in calculating employee severance pay, an employer may include supplementary unemployment compensation benefits of up to 52 weeks that may be available until an individual becomes eligible for an immediate and unreduced pension.[66]

The Act also permits coordination of pension and long-term disability (LTD) benefits. Employer contributions may be deducted from LTD benefits received by employees where: (a) the individual voluntarily elects to receive such disability benefits, and (b) the individual who is eligible to receive such disability benefits has reached either age 62 or the normal retirement age, whichever is later.[67] However, where the LTD benefits exceeded the pension benefits, the employer would be obliged to pay the excess until the employee reached 65 or five years had elapsed from the date benefit payments were issued.[68]

Waivers under the Age Discrimination Employment Act

In April of 1989 a General Accounting Office study disclosed that approximately 80 percent of Fortune 500 companies had sponsored exit incentive programs at least once between 1979 and 1988. Approximately 28 percent of these companies required that workers sign a waiver releasing all rights that they may have to sue their former employer as a precondition of receiving enhanced benefits. Additionally, investigation by a Senate Subcommittee on Labor revealed that older workers are at times manipulated or coerced into waiving their statutory rights.[69] Responding to these concerns, Congress incorporated within the OWBPA a section on waiver of rights or claims. For an employee waiver to be valid, the employer must now satisfy the following requirements.[70]

- The waiver must be written in a manner that can be understood by an average individual. If the agreement is not understandable it is unenforceable.
- The waiver refers to rights or claims arising under the statute; it does not address prospective claims that arise after the date of the waiver has been executed.
- In return for the waiver, the employee must receive consideration, something of value in addition to what he or she is already entitled to. For example, if an employee is entitled to severance pay upon his separation, then the severance pay plan would not constitute consideration for the waiver. The consideration must therefore consist of monies or other benefits to which the employee had no pre-existing right.
- The individual must be advised in writing to consult with an attorney prior to executing the agreement.
- The individual who signs a waiver must be given a period of at least 21 days within which to consider the agreement.
- The employee must be granted at least seven days to revoke the waiver agreement and the waiver remains unenforceable until the revocation period has expired.

Additionally, if a waiver is requested of a group or class of workers who participate in an employment termination program, then each individual within that group must be given at least 45 days within which to consider the agreement. Furthermore, the employer must advise each employee regarding the identity of all other participants, their ages and job titles, the eligibility factors and any time limits applicable to it. Furthermore, the employer must inform participants of the individuals in the same job classification, organization, or unit who are not eligible for selection.[71] Through these enhanced informational and review requirements, it is expected that older workers will be able to make more informed judgments as to whether a particular termination or retirement is reasonable and legitimate under the ADEA.

Administration and enforcement

Charges are processed by the EEOC.[72] As with Title VII, both the charging party and the EEOC may institute suits in federal courts after a minimum time period has elapsed to give the EEOC the opportunity to conciliate. The individual complainant is subject to two time limitations. To file with the EEOC charges must be brought within 180 days of the alleged unlawful act (300 days if the complainant initially filed with a state agency).[73] Additionally, suits must be initiated within two years from the date of the claim, and three years in the case of a willful violation.[74] Judicial remedies include back pay reinstatement and liquidated (double) damages in the case of willful violations. The Supreme Court has said that a violation is "willful" if the employer "either knew or showed reckless disregard for the matter of whether its conduct was prohibited."[75]

The new damage provisions under the 1991 Civil Rights Act do not apply to suits filed under the ADEA. Legislation, however, has been introduced that would extend to ADEA complainants the same damage remedies available under Title VII. Nonetheless, the current availability of jury trials under the ADEA and the prospect of liquidated damages for willful violations expose employers to the risk of serious financial liability if found guilty of age discrimination.

Religious Discrimination Issues

Religion defined and scope of protected activity

Title VII prohibits discrimination based on a worker's religion. The proscription against religious discrimination addresses primarily the problem of disparate treatment. For example, discrimination for or against individuals because they are Protestant, Roman Catholic, Muslim, or Jewish would be disparate treatment in violation of Title VII.[76] By religion the Act includes not only beliefs but "all aspects of religious observance and practice."[77]

In its guidelines the EEOC has broadly defined religion to include "moral or ethical beliefs as to what is right or wrong which are sincerely held with the strength of traditional religious views."[78] As a result, Title VII would protect atheists who are acting out of deeply rooted moral convictions. In *Young* v. *Southwestern Savings and Loan Association*,[79] the Fifth Circuit upheld this view when it found unlawful an employer's effort to require an employee who professed atheism to attend prayer sessions that were conducted on company time. Furthermore, the EEOC maintains that one need not have to respond to the commands of the particular religious organization to have one's actions viewed as religious in nature.[80] This view was endorsed by the Supreme Court in *Frazee* v. *Illinois Department of Employment Security*[81] when it unanimously held that an individual did not lose his right to unemployment compensation because his rejection of an offer to work on Sunday was grounded in his personal religious view that working on this day is immoral.

At the same time activities primarily influenced by political or social considerations are not protected. The courts have denied relief to an employee who was dismissed for membership in the Ku Klux Klan, maintaining that the racist and antisemitic ideology of the Klan is inconsistent with the meaning of religion under Title VII and constitutes in essence political views not protected by Title VII.[82] Similarly, the courts have held that personal preferences are not to be confused with deeply held religious convictions. In *Brown* v. *Pena* the court dismissed the religious discrimination charge of an employee fired for eating cat food on the job. Although the employee maintained that his unique food tastes were influenced by a personal religious creed, the court was unwilling to characterize such a bizarre preference as a bona fide religious belief.[83] Courts have also refused to overturn employer dismissals of employees for having extramarital affairs or practicing polygamy, rejecting claims that such practices are entitled to protection as religious beliefs.[84]

A critical aspect of a religious belief is that it be sincere. While the sincerity of an employee's religious belief is rarely challenged, evidence of employee inconsistency in following the tenets of a religion may result in a judicial determination that the individual beliefs are grounded more in convenience rather than conviction and hence not entitled to statutory protection.[85] At the same time courts accept the reality that an individual's religious beliefs may change over time. As a result, the adoption of more stringent religious beliefs subsequent to one's original date of employment, as may arise where an employee converts to a new faith, is typically accepted as a sincere religious activity warranting protection.[86]

Duty of accommodation

The major issue in religious discrimination cases involves employee requests for time off because their religious beliefs preclude them from working at designated times. This problem generally concerns Orthodox Jews, Seventh Day Adventists, and members of the Worldwide Church of God who refrain from working between Friday sunset and Saturday sundown, and members of the Dutch Reform Church and smaller Christian sects whose beliefs preclude them from working on Sundays. Under Title VII an employer is required to accommodate the employee's religious beliefs as long as in doing so the employer's operation would not sustain any "undue hardship."[87] Possible mechanisms for accommodation include employer efforts to secure voluntary substitutes who could perform the needed work. Alternatively, an employer may provide employees with flexible scheduling so that the individual requesting the accommodation could perform the needed work either before or after the time he or she needs to be off because of the observance of his or her religious practices. Where such accommodations are not feasible, the employer can consider whether it is possible to change the employee's job assignment or effect lateral transfer to a position in which there is no conflict between the employee's religious beliefs and the employer's work requirements.[88]

The most significant case addressing the scope and nature of an employer's duty to accommodate is the Supreme Court's decision in *Trans World Airlines* v. *Hardison* (1976).[89] This case provides the standard against which we can evaluate and assess the employee's right to be accommodated against the employer's right to manage its business operations efficiently. Hardison was a member of the Worldwide Church of God whose religious doctrine precludes work on Saturdays. In a previous position at TWA, Hardison had enough seniority to transfer to a facility wherein work on Saturday would not be required. However, to assume a day position he bid for a different job and found himself in a department where his lack of seniority under the contract required his working on Saturday. Hardison notified his supervisors that his religious beliefs prevented him working on Saturday and as a result the employer requested that the union find a substitute who might exchange shifts with Hardison. The union, however, informed management that no employee was willing to engage in any such exchange. It also refused to force an employee with greater seniority to work the less desirable shift, claiming that to do so would violate the contract's seniority system. Hardison then asked for a four-day work week. The company rejected this request, maintaining that Hardison's job was essential and that on weekends he was the only available person on his shift to perform it. To leave the position empty would have impaired functions which were crucial to airline operations. On the other hand, to fill Hardison's position with a supervisor or an employee from another area would simply have undermanned another operation. Finally, to employ someone not regularly assigned to work Saturdays would have unfairly required TWA to pay premium wages. When an accommodation was not reached Hardison refused to report for work on Saturdays. He was then discharged on grounds of insubordination for refusing to work during his designated shift.

The court's decision narrowed the scope of an employer's duty to accommodate. The court noted that the duty to accommodate does not (a) take precedence over or supersede the seniority provision of a collective bargaining agreement, or (b) justify the denial of shift and job preference rights of other workers. For this reason any effort by TWA or the union to extinguish seniority rights of employees in order to accommodate would be not only undesirable but improper. Additionally, the court noted that undue hardship exists and the duty to accommodate is liquidated when the employer's efforts at accommodation require it to bear more than a *de minimis* cost. Finding that replacing Hardison with supervisory personnel would result in a loss of efficiency, while bringing in other bargaining unit personnel to perform his work would have required the payment of premium wages, the court reasoned that accommodating Hardison would involve more than a *de minimis* cost. Consequently, it was not required of TWA.

In post *Hardison* cases a common omission of employers which has resulted in adverse judgments has been their failure to consider any effort at accommodation.[90] Before an employer can take disciplinary action against an employee for refusing a job assignment because it conflicts with his religious beliefs, the employer must attempt to find a suitable alternative. Even when a reasonable accommodation is not likely, that does not remove the employer's obligation to seek one. Furthermore, the courts have noted that it would be illegal for employers to refuse to accommodate on the basis of hypothetical or anticipated negative consequences. In *Brown* v. *General Motors*,[91] management discharged Brown because of his refusal to work Friday evenings after he had joined the Worldwide Church of God. The Appellate Court noted that the cost of replacing Brown was negligible as the plant had maintained relief crews available at no extra cost to fill in for employees otherwise absent from work. Additionally, the court rejected the company's defense that to accommodate Brown would result in numerous other individuals seeking accommodation as the refusal to accommodate must be based upon objective data and not upon speculative considerations.

Where an employer has tried to accommodate and such efforts impose more than minimal economic costs or impose a serious burden on co-workers, the duty to accommodate may be lifted. For example, in *Brener* v. *Diagnostic Center*,[92] a hospital's staff of five pharmacists worked rotating shifts on the weekend. A Jewish pharmacist's effort not to work on Saturdays was accommodated through shift changes arranged by the employer, the hospital, and the employee himself. Thereafter, the hospital began receiving complaints from coworkers regarding the preferential treatment of Brener when he sought additional days off on Jewish holidays. The court found that given these complaints and the consequential lowering of morale among the hospital's pharmaceutical staff, the hospital was no longer required to arrange shift changes for Brener. When Brener could not obtain cooperation from other employees, the hospital was permitted to accept his resignation.

The capacity of employers to accommodate will naturally depend on many factors, including the availability of substitutes and the nature of employer operations. In general, companies which operate on a seven days a week, 24 hours a day basis impose the least favorable conditions for accommodation, as the essential nature of operations makes it difficult to allow work to be delayed or made up at a subsequent time. Thus in settings such as hospitals, transportation operations, and police and fire agencies the opportunity to accommodate may be limited.

While the focus in most cases is on employer efforts to accommodate, the statute also imposes a corresponding obligation on the part of the worker to cooperate with management. Such an obligation requires the employee to give adequate notice to the employer of his or her need for accommodation.[93] Through such notice the organization is in a better position to search for available substitutes or to rearrange production schedules. Similarly, employees may have to postpone leave requests; for example, an employee may delay attendance at Bible retreats to times when the employer is not operating on a full production schedule.[94] Finally, the employee must accept any reasonable accommodation and cannot insist on the accommodation that he or she finds most favorable. For example, non-paid leave for a teacher who takes time off to observe religious holidays is a reasonable accommodation, although not necessarily the preferred accommodation sought by the teacher.[95]

Although it is uncommon, an employer may be confronted with situations where an employee because of religious reasons objects to duties assigned him or her. Take, for example, a postal employee whose religious beliefs require that he or she does not handle military draft registrations or an IRS agent who refuses to process the tax exemption applications of groups favoring abortions. Where such duties form a very small part of an employee's overall responsibilities, courts have imposed an obligation on organizations to accommodate by reassigning the work to other employees.[96]

Many organizations may establish policies that require employees to maintain dress and grooming codes. These may conflict with the beliefs of employees adhering to certain religious faiths. For example, Sikhs and some Orthodox Jewish sects require their followers to grow beards. In other situations female employees because of religiously based considerations of modesty may object to wearing pants or short skirts. The obligation of an employer to accommodate in these circumstances will be controlled by the *Hardison* decision. Where employers can demonstrate more than a *de minimis* cost, as might occur if non-compliance with the dress code would create a safety hazard, the employer's grooming regulations will be upheld. For example, in *Batia* v. *Chevron, Incorporated* the court upheld a company policy requiring all employees potentially exposed to toxic gases to shave any facial hair that might interfere with the wearing of a respirator. The company was permitted to apply this requirement to Batia, whose unwillingness to shave was due to his religious beliefs as a member of the Sikh faith.[97]

Similarly, another court upheld the right of an employer to require restaurant managers to shave because facial hair on restaurant employees might diminish the clean-cut image of the eating establishment and might be in violation of sanitation regulations.[98] On the other hand, in *EEOC* v. *Electronic Data Systems*[99] the court found illegal the dismissal of a computer programmer because of his refusal to shave, because the organization failed to provide any evidence that accommodating the person's religious beliefs would impose any hardship on the organization.

Unions and accommodations

The definition of religion in section 701J of the statute states that it is "the employer's obligation" to accommodate the religious practices or observance of employees. However, unions also have been required to make reasonable accommodations under the same standards that are imposed on employers. The major area of conflict arises in situations where employees because of their religious beliefs refuse to pay initiation fees or membership dues. Unions have opposed waivers of initiation fees or membership dues for fear that in doing so they would be creating free riders, employees receiving the benefits of unionization but not sharing in the cost. Unions have also been concerned that the waiver of initiation fees and membership dues would impose financial hardship on them if a substantial number of employees would seek such a waiver. Under EEOC guidelines[100] and court rulings,[101] unions, as a means of accommodation, must permit employees to pay a sum equivalent to union dues and initiation fees to a charity. This type of accommodation addresses the free rider concern by removing the economic incentive other employees might otherwise have to claim a religious exemption. On the other hand, if a religious employee whose dues are waived uses the grievance arbitration procedure, the union would be permitted to charge the employee the reasonable cost of using its procedures.[102]

Statutory defenses: religious institutions and BFOQs

The Act permits religious institutions to discriminate on the basis of religion with regard to the employment of individuals to perform work that helps to carry out the activities of the institution.[103] This exemption is extremely broad and would actually permit the institution to hire persons of a particular faith to fill any job vacancy. For example, a Catholic university would be permitted to hire only Catholics for the position of janitors and secretaries. At the same time, this exemption is limited to religion alone and does not allow for discrimination on the basis of race, sex, or national origin.

The Act also allows discrimination on the basis of religion where the latter is a bona fide occupational qualification reasonably necessary to the normal operation of the business.[104] Most such situations arise in the context of religious institutions: the employment of ministers or rabbis in churches and synagogues or teachers in church-run religious schools. Obviously the schools themselves would be permitted to discriminate in favor of hiring those who practice the church's religion by virtue of the exemption afforded religious institutions. However, in unique circumstances secular organizations might contend that religion operates as a BFOQ. In *Kern* v. *Dynalectron Corporation*,[105] the company had a contract to fly helicopters over crowds of Muslims making their pilgrimage along Muhammad's path to Mecca. The purpose of these flights was twofold, to protect against any violent outbreaks and to help fight fires. The pilots who were stationed at Jeddah would be required to fly into the holy area of Mecca. Saudi Arabian law, based upon the tenets of the Islamic religion, prohibited under the penalty of death the entry of non-Muslims into Mecca. As a result of this legal policy, Dynalectron required all pilots stationed at Jeddah to become Muslim. Kern, a pilot, had converted to the Muslim religion and was assigned to Jeddah. However, upon his assignment he renounced his conversion and was subsequently discharged. In rejecting the claim of discrimination, the court noted that religion was a valid qualification necessary to ensure a pilot's safety.

Finally, the prohibition against religious discrimination not only applies to employer policies or rules that restrict an employee's religious beliefs or practices but also addresses problems of religious harassment on the job.

As with race and sex discrimination, employers have a responsibility to maintain their work environment free of oppressive considerations. Employers are required to ensure that workers do not subject employees to religious slurs or jokes that would create an intimidating or hostile work environment.[106]

National Origin Discrimination

One of the most dominant characteristics of the US population is the increased presence of persons with ancestral ties to countries from Asia and Central and South America. Currently Asian Americans represent 3 percent of the population (up from 1.4 percent in 1970) while Hispanic Americans constitute nearly 9 percent.[107] Within the next 25 years persons of Hispanic origin may surpass blacks as the single largest minority group in the United States.[108]

There are major differences among and between Hispanic and Asian American communities in terms of their degree of acculturation, English language fluency, and educational and employment experiences, and these factors undoubtedly influence these groups' assimilation into the US economy.[109] Yet there is increased concern that the position of ethnic minorities may be impaired by the discriminatory policies that they confront in the labor market. A recent Urban Institute report on the hiring practices of employers in Chicago and San Diego identified the differential treatment of Hispanic and Anglo job seekers.[110] Similarly, the US General Accounting Office concluded that people with a foreign appearance or accent experience job discrimination across a wide variety of industries in all cities of the nation.[111] The US Commission on Civil Rights has noted that artificial barriers prevent Asian Americans from rising to management positions for which they are qualified.[112] Reflecting these problems is the substantial number of charges that are filed by ethnic minorities with the Equal Employment Opportunity Commission. In fiscal year 1988 over 10,000 charges of national origin discrimination were filed.[113]

Title VII coverage

Title VII prohibits discrimination on the basis of an individual's national origin. This term has been interpreted broadly by the EEOC to prohibit discrimination based on:

- an individual or his or her ancestor's place of origin;
- physical, cultural or linguistic characteristics of the national origin group;
- marriage to or association with a member of a national origin group;
- membership in or association with organizations promoting the interest of a national origin group;
- attendance or participation in schools, churches, temples, or organizations generally used by persons of a national origin group;

- an individual's name or spouse's name that is associated with a national origin group.[114]

Generally the same principles of equal employment opportunity law that apply to problems of race discrimination are equally relevant to national origin issues. For example, a policy not to hire employees with an arrest record may disqualify more Hispanics than Anglo-Americans in the Los Angeles area and would normally not be considered a business necessity. Similarly, word of mouth recruiting might be considered discriminatory if the company's work force was disproportionately Anglo.

At the same time the EEOC has identified certain policies that may well operate to exclude on the basis of national origin. One of these is height and weight requirements. The EEOC has compiled data that the average height of white males is five feet eight inches, while that of Hispanics is only five feet four and a half inches. As a result, the application of a height requirement may exclude disproportionately greater numbers of Hispanics. Unless validated, this requirement would be found unlawful.[115] The leading case supporting the EEOC's approach is *Davis* v. *County of Los Angeles*.[116] Here the County of Los Angeles had established a five foot seven inch height requirement for the position of fire fighter. This requirement operated to exclude 45 percent of eligible Mexican American applicants. Finding no evidence that a height requirement was in fact job-related, the court ruled that the requirement discriminated against Mexican American applicants on the basis of their national origin.

Certain language requirements may also affect national origin groups. Employers may require individuals to speak in accent-free English. Such a requirement will typically be found discriminatory where a person's accent does not interfere with his or her ability to be understood by coworkers or supervisors.[117] For example, the EEOC found unlawful the IRS's removal of a tax auditor from a training program because she spoke English with a Korean accent, since the auditor had no oral or written communication problems despite her accent. Additionally, the EEOC noted that the IRS's concern over its image and customer preferences not only was speculative but independently could not serve as a basis for discriminating against an otherwise qualified person.[118]

At the same time, courts have upheld English fluency requirements where they are viewed as job-related. For example, one court upheld the requirement of a major urban hospital that employees in nearly all job classifications speak English because English was found to be the common language of the majority of the patients and staff alike, and deficiencies in English would likely create problems.[119] Similarly, hotels have been permitted to establish an English fluency requirement for front office positions where employees must communicate with English speaking guests.[120]

Taking into consideration the millions of Americans who are not native born, the EEOC has issued guidelines severely restricting an employer's right to promulgate rules that would require that only English be spoken at the work site. Viewing one's language as an essential national origin characteristic, the EEOC maintains that restricting one's right to speak one's native language is presumptively unlawful unless justified by considerations of business necessity.[121] For example, the EEOC would uphold the right of an employer to require salespeople to speak only English when dealing with English speaking customers. Similarly, an English-only rule may be upheld during working time for safety reasons. In 1983, the EEOC upheld the imposition of an English-only rule during work time for refinery employees who worked in processing areas where there was a potential of fires and explosion. Such a rule was viewed as necessary to promote effective communication among employees during emergency situations.[122]

Courts themselves are divided over the legality of English-only rules. In *Garcia* v. *Gloor*,[123] the Fifth Circuit held that requiring bilingual employees to speak only English on the job did not violate Title VII. When dealing with bilingual employees the court noted that the language utilized by an employee is a question of individual preference and that equal employment opportunity laws were only meant to prohibit discrimination based upon immutable characteristics, such as race, color, or national origin. As these individuals have the option and the ability to speak either English or Spanish, requiring that they speak only English on the job was not discriminatory. On the other hand, the Ninth Circuit has upheld EEOC guidelines that English-only rules are discriminatory unless justified by considerations of business necessity. In *Gutierrez* v. *Municipal Court*,[124] a municipal court had forbidden its Spanish speaking translators to speak Spanish except while on break or at lunch or during the work time when they were actually translating. Finding no evidence that the English-only rule was necessary to promote racial harmony or that permitting Spanish to be spoken between employees would otherwise be disruptive, the court found the policy discriminatory.

The apparent conflict between these courts is limited to circumstances where English-only rules are applied to bilingual workers. Consequently, where employees do not have equal fluency in English and in their native language, employers should eschew English-only rules unless they can be justified on the basis of compelling business considerations. Thus, the imposition of an English-only rule upon employees most comfortable speaking a native language might be viewed as producing an atmosphere of ethnic harassment. Finally, while some courts may permit narrowly tailored job-related rules requiring English to be spoken during work time there is no apparent justification to extend such restrictions during an employee's free time, lunch, or work breaks.

National origin as a BFOQ

Title VII permits an employer to afford preferences to members of particular national origin groups where the latter is a bona fide occupational qualification.[125] Yet the EEOC has indicated that any such exemptions would be "strictly construed."[126] A possible BFOQ situation might arise where a

French or Italian restaurant would employ waiters or chefs of French or Italian origin.[127]

After the Second World War the United States and some foreign countries signed commerce and navigation treaties whereby foreign corporations operating in the United States would have the right to select experts, executive personnel, agents, attorneys, and other specialists of their choice. The courts have held that treaties may afford foreign corporations operating in the United States the right to give job preferences to their citizens. For example, in *MacNamara* v. *Korean Airlines*,[128] on the basis of such a treaty Korean Airlines was permitted to replace an American citizen in an executive position with a Korean.

At the same time the immunity granted foreign corporations from the proscriptions of Title VII are limited. Foreign corporations do not have the right to discriminate on the basis of race, age, sex, religion, or national origin when they select among American citizens for positions. Furthermore, even when selecting their own foreign nationals, they must do so because of citizenship concerns and not because they seek to avoid the employment of Americans because of considerations of race, religion, sex, or age. As a result, American citizens who feel that they have been discriminated against by foreign-based corporations operating in the United States may file disparate treatment claims alleging that but for the race, sex, age, or religion they would have been hired or retained. In short, the right to give preference to foreign nationals cannot be used to effect intentional discrimination against American workers on the basis of race, age, sex, or religion.

Employment of aliens: public sector constitutional protections

The Fourteenth Amendment to the Constitution provides as follows: "Nor shall any state deprive any person of life, liberty or property without due process of law, nor deny any person within its jurisdiction to equal protection of the laws." This constitutional provision, which is known as the equal protection clause, has been relied upon to prohibit states from imposing policies that exclude aliens from public employment. In *Sugarman* v. *Dougall*,[129] the Supreme Court held that a provision of the New York Civil Service law that prohibited the employment of all resident aliens in competitive Civil Service jobs violated the equal protection clause of the Fourteenth Amendment. This decision was influenced by the court's belief that since lawful residents pay taxes and are subject to the draft and all other legal requirements, they ought not to be deprived of the right to earn a livelihood.

At the same time the court suggested that a refusal to employ aliens may be permitted if related to legitimate state interests. For example, a state could employ only American citizens for positions involving the formulation and execution of broad public policy functions. Additionally, the Court has upheld policies reserving for citizens positions filling critical governmental functions. For example, the Supreme Court has upheld state laws denying aliens the right to serve as police officers,[130] public school teachers,[131] and probation officers.[132]

Policy concerning the right of aliens to employment in the federal sector has undergone radical change, shifting from one of protection to one of exclusion. In *Hampton* v. *Wong*,[133] the Supreme Court invalidated a Civil Service Commission policy barring the employment of aliens in the competitive Civil Service, finding such a policy in breach of the equal protection clause of the Fifth Amendment. However, the Court also noted that either Congress or the President could verbally impose a citizenship requirement to encourage aliens to become naturalized or to provide the President with a expendable token for treaty negotiating purposes.

This option was immediately seized upon by President Ford. By executive order dated September 2, 1976, barely two months after the Supreme Court decision, the President amended the Civil Service rule to provide for the exclusion of aliens from the Civil Service except in limited circumstances where necessary for the efficiency of the service.[134] This new executive order effectively terminates the ability of most aliens lawfully residing in the United States to obtain employment in the federal sector.

The constitutional protection enjoyed by resident aliens under the Fifth and Fourteenth Amendments applies only to governmental employment. As firms in the private sector are not subject to these constitutional constraints, the question soon arose as to whether or not resident aliens could obtain relief from discrimination by resorting to other legal forums. Initially, the Equal Employment Opportunity Commission maintained that discrimination against aliens constituted unlawful discrimination on the basis of national origin under Title VII.[135] This position, however, was rejected by the Supreme Court in *Espinoza* v. *Farah Manufacturing Company*,[136] which ruled that the term national origin refers to the country where one is born or from which one's ancestors have come and not to one's citizenship. At the same time the court warned that discrimination on the basis of citizenship would be illegal if it had the purpose or effect of discrimination on the basis of national origin or race. For example, employers would be guilty of a Title VII violation where they would employ citizens of European countries but refused to employ aliens with a Mexican or Spanish speaking background or from Black African nations.

Immigration Reform Control Act of 1986

While federal law has primarily been focused upon promoting the employment rights of minorities, a major shift occurred in 1986 with the congressional enactment of the Immigration Reform Control Act (IRCA). By 1986 it was estimated that there resided in the United States over 12 million undocumented aliens. These were workers from other countries who lacked the right to either reside or be employed in the United States. The presence of these individuals was viewed as constituting an enormous strain on the social welfare and educational resources of the country. Additionally, some observers felt that the employment of illegal aliens would reduce the employment opportunities of US citizens.[137] In response to these concerns the IRCA was enacted.

Record keeping and verification requirements

The Act prohibits an employer from hiring, recruiting for a fee, or referring for a fee workers who are not eligible for employment in the United States.[138] To enforce this prohibition, the Act imposes on employers a systematic record keeping and verification procedure that must be followed in the hiring of all workers.[139] This includes the following requirements.

- An employer must examine documents that at the time of hiring demonstrate the individual is eligible to work in the United States. Among the documents that may be used to establish eligibility are US passport, birth certificate, residency, alien card, social security card, and resident alien card.
- After examining the documents the employer must indicate on an INS form I-9 (see figure 4) the documents it has examined. The employer must certify on the basis of his or her examination that the employee is entitled to work because he or she is a US citizen, a legal permanent resident, or a non-immigrant alien with temporary employment rights.
- The INS form must also be signed by the individual, who also certifies under penalty of perjury that he or she has presented genuine documents that prove eligibility for employment.
- The employer must retain the I-9 form for a period of three years after the date of hire or one year after the date the individual's employment has terminated. This form must be made available for inspection to employees of the Immigration Naturalization Service or the Department of Labor.
- If the employer determines that the individual is no longer eligible to work in the United States this employee must be immediately terminated.[140]

Documents that applicants can use to establish work eligibility are:

1. US passport.
2. Certificate of US Citizenship (issued by INS).
3. Certificate of Naturalization (issued by INS).
4. A foreign passport that includes an authorization to work.
5. Resident Alien INS form I-551.
6. Temporary Resident Card, INS form I-688.
7. Employment Authorization Card, INS form I-688.
8. Social Security Card.
9. Re-entry Permit, INS form I-327.
10. Refugee Travel Document, INS form I-571.

Figure 4 Employment eligibility verification form (I-9).

☐1☐ EMPLOYEE INFORMATION AND VERIFICATION: (To be completed and signed by employee.)

Name: (Print or Type) Last	First	Middle	Birth Name
Address: Street Name and Number	City	State	ZIP Code
Date of Birth (Month/Day/Year)		Social Security Number	

I attest, under penalty of perjury, that I am (check a box):

☐ 1. A citizen or national of the United States.
☐ 2. An alien lawfully admitted for permanent residence (Alien Number A_____).
☐ 3. An alien authorized by the Immigration and Naturalization Service to work in the United States
(Alien Number A _____ , or Admission Number _____ , expiration of employment
authorization, if any _____).

I attest, under penalty of perjury, the documents that I have presented as evidence of identity and employment eligibility are genuine and relate to me. I am aware that federal law provides for imprisonment and/or fine for any false statements or use of false documents in connection with this certificate.

Signature	Date (Month/Day/Year)

PREPARER, TRANSLATOR CERTIFICATION (To be completed if prepared by person other than the employee). I attest, under penalty of perjury, that the above was prepared by me at the request of the named individual and is based on all information of which I have any knowledge.

Signature	Name (Print or Type)		
Address (Street Name and Number)	City	State	Zip Code

☐2☐ EMPLOYER REVIEW AND VERIFICATION: (To be completed and signed by employer.)

Instructions:
Examine one document from List A and check the appropriate box. *OR* examine one document from List B *and* one from List C and check the appropriate boxes. Provide the *Document Identification Number* and *Expiration Date* for the document checked.

List A Documents that Establish Identity and Employment Eligibility	List B Documents that Establish Identity	and	List C Documents that Establish Employment Eligibility
☐ 1. United States Passport ☐ 2. Certificate of United States Citizenship ☐ 3. Certificate of Naturalization ☐ 4. Unexpired foreign passport with attached Employment Authorization ☐ 5. Alien Registration Card with photograph	☐ 1. A State-issued driver's license or a State-issued I.D. card with a photograph, or information, including name, sex, date of birth, height, weight, and color of eyes. (Specify State)_____) ☐ 2. U.S. Military Card ☐ 3. Other (Specify document and issuing authority) _____		☐ 1. Original Social Security Number Card (other than a card stating it is not valid for employment) ☐ 2. A birth certificate issued by State, county, or municipal authority bearing a seal or other certification ☐ 3. Unexpired INS Employment Authorization (Specify form) #_____
Document Identification #_____	*Document Identification* #_____		*Document Identification* #_____
Expiration Date (if any) _____	*Expiration Date (if any)* _____		*Expiration Date (if any)* _____

CERTIFICATION: I attest, under penalty of perjury, that I have examined the documents presented by the above individual, that they appear to be genuine and to relate to the individual named, and that the individual, to the best of my knowledge, is eligible to work in the United States.

Signature	Name (Print or Type)	Title
Employer Name	Address	Date

Form I-9 (05/07/87)
OMB No. 1115–0136

U.S. Department of Justice
Immigration and Naturalization Service

11 Certification of Birth issued by the State Department.

12 Certification of Birth Abroad issued by the State Department.

13 An original or certified copy of a birth certificate issued by a state, county, or municipal authority.

14 An Employment Authorization Document issued by INS.

15 Native American tribal document.

16 US Citizen Identification Card, INS form I-197.

17 Identification Card for Use of Resident Citizens in the US, INS form I-179.

There is one exception to the verification requirements imposed upon an employer. A state employment agency may conduct the employment verification process and issue a certification on form I-9 as part of this referral process. Where a certified form I-9 from a state employment agency is submitted to the employer, that employer is not required to repeat the verification process. The employer, however, is required to retain that form for the time period identified in the Act.[141]

The importance attached to employer record keeping and verification requirements is underscored by the statutory imposition of fines on employers guilty of non-compliance. Penalties ranging from $100 to $1,000 will be assessed for every employee hired where the employer has failed to engage in appropriate inspection and verification of documents.[142] Additionally, where an employer knowingly employs an unauthorized alien, fines ranging from $250 to $2,000 will be assessed for a first offense, up to $5,000 for a second offense and up to $10,000 for a third offense.[143] An employer who engages in a pattern or practice of violation may be assessed for further fines and can be imprisoned for up to six months.[144]

Proscriptions against national origin discrimination

When considering immigration reform legislation, Congress was seriously concerned that the IRCA's requirements and sanctions might be used by some employers as a basis or pretext for discriminating on the basis of national origin or citizenship against persons who are lawfully entitled to work in the United States. It was also felt that some employers may simply decide not to hire "foreign" appearing individuals to avoid sanctions.[145] Addressing these concerns, Congress incorporated within the IRCA anti-discrimination provisions. Under the IRCA it is unlawful to discriminate in the hiring, recruitment, or referral for a fee or to discharge any individual because of an individual's national origin. Recognizing that Title VII contains parallel provisions against national origin discrimination, these provisions only apply to employers otherwise exempt from Title VII's coverage because of the small number of employees they employ. Under the IRCA employers with between four and 14 employees are covered. Additionally, the statute prohibits all employers from discriminating on the basis of citizenship either against US citizens or against aliens who are entitled to work in the United States.[146]

Statutory exemptions and defenses

The scope of prohibited conduct is significantly more limited under the IRCA than under Title VII. The IRCA does not prohibit discrimination in terms and conditions of employment. As a result employer decisions on promotions, compensation, layoffs, and other working conditions are immune from challenge. Additionally, the IRCA establishes a BFOQ on the basis of citizenship when the employer hires citizens in order to comply with any law, regulation, or executive order or federal, state, or local governmental contracts.[147] Futhermore, employers are permitted to give preference to US citizens over aliens when the two applicants are judged equally qualified.[148] The latter exemption would normally come into play only where the employer had actually compared the credentials of the citizen and alien and had determined that the citizen has qualifications equal to those of the non-citizen.[149] Finally, under interpretive guidelines of the United States Department of Justice a violation of the anti-discrimination provisions must be based on a record of disparate treatment and cannot be premised on evidence of disparate impact. As a result, policies which are neutral on their face but which have the effect of excluding from consideration a disproportionately greater number of aliens as opposed to citizens would not be legal.[150] Instead, complainants seeking relief would have the more difficult task of proving intentional discrimination.

Violation of the anti-discrimination provisions of the IRCA may result in the following penalties.

- Cease and desist from the discriminatory practice.
- Requirement that the employer comply with the verification and record keeping requirements, and the hiring of the discriminatee with or without back pay.
- Posting of notices.
- Requirement to acquaint all personnel involved in hiring with IRCA requirements.
- Removal of a tainted performance reviews or discipline.[151]

Additionally, under the Immigration Act of 1990 penalties for violating the anti-discrimination provisions have been increased and now equal those assessed when employers hire unauthorized aliens. For a first offense an employer may be fined between $250 and $2,000, for a second offense from $2,000 to $5,000 and for a third offense from $3,000 to $10,000. Additionally, if an employer requires more documents than the law requires, but refuses documents that on their face appear genuine, the employer may be subject to a civil fine between $100 and $1,000.[152]

Employment of temporary agriculture workers

Historically farm owners throughout the country, particularly in the southwest and western regions, have relied on alien labor, especially from Mexico, to harvest their crops. The IRCA permits this continued reliance by affording employers the right to import temporary agricultural workers. However, for these workers to obtain the necessary visas, the Secretary of Labor must certify (a) that there is an insufficient number of US citizens able, willing, and qualified to perform the necessary services, and (b) that the employment of the alien labor force will not adversely affect the wages and working conditions of similarly employed US citizens.[153] Additionally, permission to employ temporary agricultural workers will be denied if the employer seeking their presence is affected by a strike or lock out. The employer must also ensure that such temporary agricultural workers will be covered by state workers' compensation law or alternatively that the employer itself will provide benefits at least equal to those provided under state workers' compensation systems. The Secretary of Labor may also deny certification where the employer has failed to engage in positive recruitment efforts to find qualified United States workers who, if recruited, would be willing to make themselves available for work at the time and place needed.[154] In employing agricultural laborers, employers are required to furnish them adequate housing that satisfies federal standards for temporary labor camps[155] and to afford them the same transportation assistance that is afforded US citizens employed on a seasonal basis.[156]

Enforcement of the IRCA

A multiplicity of governmental agencies are involved in enforcing various aspects of the IRCA. An inspection of an employer's compliance with verification and record keeping requirements will be conducted by two federal agencies, the Department of Labor and the Immigration Naturalization Service (INS) of the United States Department of Justice. Department of Labor wage and hour inspectors currently conduct some 80,000 checks of employer records a year and these inspectors will be utilized to examine compliance with the IRCA.[157] Additionally, the INS has approximately 1,300 agents assigned to investigations and their time as well may be devoted to an examination of IRCA violations. Their inspections of employer facilities might involve educational visitations, the issuance of warning letters, or the execution of notices of intent to fine. Although the Department of Labor inspectors do not possess the authority to issue notices or fines, they will report the result of their inspections to the INS, which will follow up on any inconsistencies or irregularities that are reported. The penalties for violating IRCA verification requirements and for knowingly hiring unauthorized workers can be quite severe. A fine of $144,800 was imposed against a San Jose and Oakland security firm. This fine involved 226 paperwork violations, specific violations for not having I-9s for employees and for not having the employee/employer sections of forms filled out properly.[158]

An employer can seek to challenge the findings of an investigation by seeking a hearing presided over by an administrative law judge of the INS. The employer may appeal the award of the hearing officer by filing a petition in a court of appeals for the appropriate circuit. If an employer fails to appeal the award and fails to comply with the final order of an administrative law judge, the attorney general is authorized to file suit to seek compliance with the order in any appropriate district court.[159]

Charges that the anti-discrimination provisions of the IRCA have been violated are investigated by the Office of Special Counsel, an agency established within the United States Department of Justice. As under Title VII, individual complainants must file charges within 180 days from the date of the alleged act of discrimination. An employer who wishes to challenge the determination of the special counsel may obtain a hearing presided over by an administrative law judge specially designated by the attorney general to hear such cases. The administrative law judge can issue cease and desist orders and assess fines. Decisions of the administrative law judge are subject to review by the United States Courts of Appeal.[160]

In addition, there will be other governmental agencies involved in administering the IRCA. The Department of Labor and the United States Department of Agriculture will determine whether shortages of agriculture workers justify the admission of immigrant farm workers. The Department of Health and Human Services reimburses states for their costs in supplying educational, medical, and public assistance to newly legalized aliens. The Social Security Administration is involved in issuing cards to new legal aliens while states are required to verify the immigration status of all non-citizens applying for federally funded assistance programs.[161]

Impact of the IRCA

In 1990, the General Accounting Office (GAO) did a major review which sought to identify the impact of the statute. The GAO reported that the statute appears to be reducing illegal immigration and employment. It noted that more than half of employers surveyed who believed that they could evaluate the law's effectiveness indicated that employer sanctions had reduced unauthorized alien employment in their industry. Additionally, INS interviews of unauthorized aliens apprehended at work suggested that the law had made it more difficult for some to find jobs.[162] Supporting the GAO finding was a July 1989 study of the Urban Institute which found that the IRCA had reduced illegal immigration across the US southern border.[163]

Many employers remain opposed to the law. The two most commonly cited reasons for opposition are (a) the paperwork burden and (b) problems with employee documentation. About 78 percent of employer respondents indicated that they want a simpler form of verification. This involves creating a simpler system that relies on fewer documents. Currently the wide variety of documents can lead to confusion and may promote the use of counterfeit or fraudulently obtained documents. This problem may be resolved by the mid-1990s when the INS plans to standardize work eligibility documents and eventually reduce from ten to two the number of cards it issues.[164]

Perhaps the most serious problem is the substantial amount of national origin discrimination practiced by employers seeking to avoid fines imposed under the IRCA for employing unauthorized aliens. An estimated 227,000 employers reported that because of the IRCA they do not hire job applicants whose foreign appearance or accent lead them to suspect that they might be unauthorized aliens. Additionally, contrary to IRCA regulations, an estimated 346,000 employers said that they applied the IRCA's verification system only to persons who had a "foreign" appearance or accent. Some employers engage in both unlawful practices. Furthermore, an additional 430,000 employers who responded to a GAO survey (9 percent) said that because of the law they began hiring only persons born in the United States or not hiring individuals with temporary work eligibility documents.[165]

The GAO has concluded that confusion and uncertainty in determining employee eligibility and the prevalence of counterfeit and fraudulent documents are the major factors fostering employer discrimination. It has suggested that these problems could be effectively addressed by increased educational efforts, reducing the number of work eligibility documents, making these documents harder to counterfeit, and applying them to all members of the workforce.

On the other hand, the US Commission on Civil Rights has issued a statement calling for the repeal of IRCA employer sanction provisions.[166] Those who feel that the anti-discrimination and sanction provisions of the IRCA should be eliminated maintain that efforts to control illegal immigration could be achieved through other means. These would include increased border enforcement and the impositions of more substantial penalties on those who engage in the smuggling and harboring of aliens for profit. Finally, increased labor law enforcement, such as that involving minimum wage and hour legislation, could be used to remove the economic incentive employers would have to hire illegal aliens.[167]

In September of 1991 several bills were introduced in the Congress to repeal the sanctions, but to date no action has been taken on them. The IRCA therefore remains basically intact. Most recently a federal advisory commission chaired by former Congresswoman Barbara Jordan proposed that the government establish a computerized registry of the names and social security numbers of all citizens and aliens authorized to work in the United States, so that employers could check the immigration status of job applicants. The proposed registry would include data provided by the immigration service and the social security administration. Employers would have to check the registry before hiring people. The commission said it would not require people to carry identification cards. This proposal, too, has generated controversy. Many groups, such as the American Civil Liberties Union, Hispanic organizations, Chinese American groups, Jewish groups, and immigration lawyers, have expressed concern over the proposed registry, saying its use could increase job discrimination against members of racial and ethnic minorities. On the other hand, some senators from both parties expressed support for the commission's recommendations at a hearing of the Judiciary Committee, and view it as a long overdue step to discourage illegal discrimination.[168]

Summary

In *Workforce 2000*,[169] the Hudson Institute projected for American business a dramatically different labor market than the one to which it has been accustomed. Over the next decade employers can expect the following changes: (a) the number of new workers in the workforce will fall; (b) the average age of workers will rise; (c) more women will be on the job; (d) one-third of all workers will be minorities; and (e) there will be more immigrants than at any time since the First World War. These developments are due to a complex mix of social and economic factors. The average age of workers will rise as those born in the 1940s (the baby boomers) will remain on the job in full force. Furthermore, advances in medicine will make the ages of 65 and 70 younger than they were previously in practical terms, thereby providing employees an incentive to work beyond normal retirement age. Continued immigration and higher birth rates will likely make the Hispanic population in the United States the largest minority group within the next 25 years. And as it is the destination of choice for those seeking economic opportunity or political refuge, close to half a million new immigrants are expected to enter the United States lawfully by the end of the century.[170]

While these changes are occurring, managers will be under increased pressure to satisfy their workforce needs. Demographic data suggest that the rate of increase in the entry of new workers into the workforce will fall with the decline in both fertility and marriage rates. Additionally, most of the new jobs will be in the service and information sector. They will require higher skills. A company's competitive edge then clearly will depend in part on its capacity to attract and keep good workers. In meeting this challenge, companies will have to accept a more diverse workforce. This will require companies to evaluate employees not on the basis of their chronological age, but on the basis of their functional capacity to perform. As a result, employers should eliminate age-related criteria to the employment of workers and must also adopt seniority, benefits, and retirement plans that are consistent with the Age Discrimination and Employment Act. Similarly, organizations must, where feasible, accommodate the religious needs of their employees. Consistent with requirements under Title VII and the IRCA, employers must be willing to employ and promote individuals from diverse cultural and ethnic backgrounds. In summary, vigorous compliance with the federal equal employment opportunity mandate will serve the best interests of the organization.

Questions for discussion

1   In *TWA* v. *Hardison* the Supreme Court found that the employer had satisfied its obligation to accommodate in part because management had permitted the union steward to find a substitute worker who might be willing to assume Hardison's shift. Should the responsibility to find

such substitute workers fall on management, the union steward, or the employee? Should the company have been required to accommodate Hardison by permitting him to reimburse it for the additional overtime cost it had to expend in employing a substitute?

2 Peter Welfare is employed as a machinist in an auto parts facility. He is called in to work overtime Thursday evening. He informs management that he cannot because he must attend a fund-raising meeting at his local church. Must the company accommodate him? See *Dorr* v. *First Kentucky NAT Corporation*, 41 FEP 421 (6th Circuit, 1986) and *Wessling* v. *Kroger*, 30 FEP 1222 (1982).

3 In filling the position of plant manger, an employer is unwilling to consider any worker younger than 35. Is the company's action lawful under the ADEA? The employer also has a policy of not admitting into its apprenticeship training program employees above the age of 50. This policy is motivated by its concern that if workers aged 50 years old or more retire, the company will not recoup its training costs. Is the company's apprenticeship training admission policy lawful?

4 Measuring adverse impact is difficult in age discrimination cases because of the problems involved in identifying the affected class. Assume a company has 140 workers, 80 whom are 39 or younger, 40 who are 40 to 50 years old and another 20 who are over 60 years old. It must lay off 35 employees. In doing so, it selects for layoff 20 workers who are younger than 40, five who are between 40 and 50 and ten who are over 60. Does this pattern of layoff suggest that older workers have been disproportionately and illegally affected under the ADEA? See *Lowe* v. *Commack Union School District*, 50 FEP 1400 (2nd Circuit, 1989).

5 Sanyo, Inc., a Japanese firm based in Tokyo, has recently purchased Avascar Communication, a manufacturer of communications equipment with 500 production workers. Upon the acquisition, Sanyo dismisses the president of Avascar and replaces him with a Japanese national. To expedite the integration into Avascar of Japanese manufacturing practices, Sanyo dismisses 250 production workers and replaces them with Japanese workers. Additionally, it requires that all US production workers pursue instruction in the Japanese language, and that Japanese be spoken, if possible, throughout the entire plant. Are Sanyo's practices lawful? See *Fortino* v. *Quasar Co.*, 950 F.2d 389 (7th Cir. 1991).

NOTES

1 Daniel P. O'Meara, *Protecting the Growing Number of Older Workers: the Age Discrimination in Employment Act* (Wharton School, Philadelphia, 1989), p. 13.
2 Ibid., pp. 20–1.
3 Ibid., p. 30.
4 Sections 11(b), (c), and (e).
5 Section 11(b), Public Law No. 93-259 (1974).
6 Section 3(a), Public Law 95-256 (1978).
7 Section 2(c)(1), Public Law 99-592 (1986).

8 Section 4(a)(1).
9 Section 4(a)(2).
10 Section 4(a)(3).
11 Section 4(e).
12 EEOC Interpretive Rules on Age Discrimination, 29 CFR Section 1625.4 (1981).
13 Section 4(f)(2).
14 *Bruno* v. *W. B. Saunders Co.*, 48 FEP 1613 (1988), aff. 50 FEP 898, 882 F.2d 760 (1989).
15 35 FEP 246, 738 F.2d 1393 (3rd Cir. 1984).
16 4 FEP 269, 455 F.2d 818 (5th Cir. 1972).
17 Section 4(f)(1).
18 Ibid.
19 Section 4(f)(2).
20 Section 4(f)(3).
21 37 FEP 1829, 472 US 400 (1985).
22 Zachary Fasman and Michael Album, *Employment Law Compliance Handbook* (Executive Enterprises Publications Corp., New York, 1988), p. 438.
23 *Western Air Lines* v. *Criswell*, supra, note 21, at p. 1835.
24 EEOC Regulations under the Age Discrimination in Employment Act, 29 CFR Section 1620.6(b).
25 12 FEP 1233, 531 F.2d 224 (5th Cir. 1976).
26 Supra, note 21, at p. 1837.
27 *Aaron* v. *Davis*, 12 FEP 1506, 414 F.Supp. 2153 (1976).
28 44 FEP 1470, 829 F.2d 392 (3rd Cir. 1987).
29 35 FEP 1458, 746 F.2d 1190 (7th Cir. 1984).
30 Section 3, Public Law 99-592 (1986).
31 Bureau of National Affairs, *Daily Labor Report* (January 10, 1994), p. A13.
32 Bureau of National Affairs, *Government Employment Relations Report* (April 25, 1994), p. 550.
33 *Hinote* v. *Dworshak Dam Constructors*, 26 FEP 1094 (1973).
34 *Brennan* v. *Reynolds and Co.*, 7 FEP 369, 367 F.Supp. 440 (1973).
35 *Moses* v. *Falstaff Brewing Co.*, 14 FEP 813, 550 F.2d 1113 (8th Cir. 1977).
36 EEOC Regulations under the Age Discrimination in Employment Act, 29 CFR section 1625.7(d).
37 Ibid., 29 CFR section 1626.7(f).
38 31 FEP 376, 702 F.2d 686 (8th Cir. 1983).
39 *Metz* v. *Transit Mix*, 44 FEP 1339, 828 F.2d 1202 (7th Cir. 1987) and *Geller* v. *Markham*, 24 FEP 920, 635 F.2d, 1027 (2nd Cir. 1980).
40 N. Thompson Powers, "Reductions in force under the Age Discrimination in Employment Act," *The Labor Lawyer*, 1 (Spring 1986), pp. 197–228.
41 EEOC Guidelines, supra, note 36, section 1625.8(a) and (c).
42 16 FEP 146, 434 US 192 (1977).
43 Section 2(a), Public Law No. 95-256 (1978).
44 Supra, note 6.
45 Supra, note 7.
46 132 Cong. Rec. S 16851-52 (Oct. 16, 1986), as reported in O'Meara, supra, note 1, p. 240.
47 Section 631c(1), Public Law No. 95-256 (1978).
48 EEOC Guidelines, supra, note 36, section 1625.1(d)(2) and 1625.1(e).
49 O'Meara, supra, note 1, p. 354.
50 29 CFR section 1625.10(b) (1987).

51 29 CFR section 1625.10(a)(1).

52 50 FEP 104, 492 US 158 (1989). For an excellent review of this decision and its aftermath, see John Runyan, "Hedging Betts: the Older Worker's Benefit Protection Act," *Michigan Bar Journal* (February 1993), pp. 168–74.

53 Public Law 101-433 (1990).

54 Section 103(b).

55 Section 103.

56 Ibid.

57 *Older Workers Benefit Protection Act*, Senate Report, 101st Cong. 2d Session, Report 101-263, April 6, 1990, pp. 27–8; Runyan, supra, note 52, p. 171.

58 Section 103.

59 Section 103 L(1)(c).

60 Senate Report, supra, note 57, p. 21.

61 Section 103 (2)(A)(1).

62 Section 103 (2)(A)(B).

63 Senate Report, supra, note 57, p. 24.

64 Section 103 2(A)(ii).

65 Senate Report, supra, note 57, p. 24.

66 Section 103 2(A)(C).

67 Ibid., at p. 25.

68 Section 103(1)(3)(a) and (b); Runyan, supra, note 52, at pp. 172–3.

69 Robert J. Alberts and Eileen P. Kelly, "Waivers under the ADEA: An analysis of the Age Discrimination in Employment Waiver Protection Act of 1989," *Labor Law Journal* (December 1989), p. 739.

70 Section 201(f)(1), OWBPA. See also Bennett Alsher, "Validity of waivers in discrimination cases," *Labor Law Journal* (February 1991), pp. 89–91.

71 Section 201(f)(1), OWBPA.

72 Originally, the Department of Labor enforced the ADEA. This authority was transferred to the EEOC in 1978 by President Carter, Reorganization Plan No. 1, 3 CFR section 321 (1978).

73 Section 7(d), 29 USC section 626(d) (1986).

74 29 USC section 255(a) (1982). Under the ADEA, a complainant is also required to wait 60 days after filing his or her EEOC charge before commencing suit.

75 *Trans World Airlines* v. *Thurston*, 469 US 111, 36 FEP 977 (1985), at 984.

76 See, for example, *Smith* v. *University of North Carolina*, 18 FEP 913 (1978).

77 Section 701(j), Title VII.

78 Guidelines on Discrimination Because of Religion, 29 CFR section 1605.1 (1980).

79 10 FEP 522, 509 F.2d 140 (1975).

80 EEOC Guidelines, supra, note 78.

81 *Frazee* v. *Illinois Department of Labor*, 49 FEP 469, 489 US 829 (1989).

82 *Bellamy* v. *Mason's Stores*, 9 FEP 1, 508 F.2d 504 (4th Cir. 1974).

83 *Brown* v. *Pena*, 19 FEP 887, 589 F.2d 1113 (5th Cir. 1979).

84 *Potter* v. *Murray City*, 37 FEP 1652, 760 F.2d 1065 (10th Cir. 1985); and *McCrory* v. *Rapides Regional Medical Center*, 40 FEP 750 (1986).

85 *Hansard* v. *Johnson-Manville Products Corporation*, 5 FEP 707 (1973).

86 *TWA* v. *Hardison*, 14 FEP 1697, 432 US 63 (1977).

87 Section 701(j), Title VII.

88 EEOC Guidelines, supra, note 78, 29 CFR section 1605.2(d).

89 Supra, note 86.

90 Douglas Massengill and Donald Peterson, "Job requirements and religious practices: conflict and accommodation," *Labor Law Journal* (July 1988), pp. 402–10.

91 20 FEP 94, 601 F.2d 956 (8th Cir. 1979).

92 28 FEP 907, 671 F.2d 141 (5th Cir. 1982).

93 *Chrysler Corp.* v. *Mann*, 15 FEP 788, 561 F.2d 1282 (1977).

94 *J. Schoenemann, Inc.*, 69 LA 325 (1977)

95 *Ansonia Board of Education* v. *Philbrook*, 42 FEP 366, 479 US 60 (1986).

96 *Haring* v. *Blumenthal*, 19 FEP 744, 471 F.Supp. 1172 (1979); *American Postal Workers Union* v. *Postmaster General*, 35 FEP 1484 (1984).

97 34 FEP 1816, 734 F.2d 1382 (9th Cir. 1984).

98 *EEOC* v. *Sambo's of Georgia*, 27 FEP 1210, 530 F.Supp. 86 (1981).

99 31 FEP 588 (1988).

100 Supra, note 78, 29 CFR, section 1605.2(d)(iii)(2).

101 *Yott* v. *North American Rockwell Corp.*, 20 FEP 870, 602 F.2d 904 (9th Cir. 1979) and *International Association of Machinists Lodge 751* v. *Boeing Corp.*, 45 FEP 791, 833 F.2d 165 (9th Cir. 1987).

102 National Labor Relations Act, section 10, 29 USCA, section 169 (1980).

103 Section 702, Title VII of the Civil Rights Act of 1964.

104 Ibid., section 703e(1).

105 36 FEP 1716, 746 F.2d 86 (5th Cir. 1984).

106 *Weiss* v. *US*, 36 FEP 1, 596 F.Supp. 1050 (1984).

107 US Commission on Civil Rights, *Civil Rights Issues Facing Asian Americans in the 1990s* (February 1992), p. 15.

108 Gregory DeFreitas, *Inequality at Work: Hispanics in the US Labor Force* (Oxford University Press, New York, 1991), pp. 65–6.

109 Ibid., pp. 66–73.

110 Urban Institute, *Employer Hiring Practices: Differential Treatment of Hispanic and Anglo Job Seekers* (Urban Institute Press, Washington, DC, 1990).

111 General Accounting Office, *Employer Sanctions and the Question of Discrimination* (GAO, Washington, DC, March 1990), p. 37.

112 US Commission on Civil Rights, supra, note 107, p. 130.

113 US Equal Employment Opportunity Commission, Reports for Fiscal Years 1986, 1987, 1988 (GPO, Washington, DC, 1990), p. 20.

114 EEOC Guidelines on Discrimination Because of National Origin, 29 CFR 1606.1 (1980).

115 EEOC Decision, Number 74-25, 10 FEP 260 (1973), at p. 262.

116 13 FEP 1217, 566 F.2d 1334 (9th Cir. 1976).

117 *Berke* v. *Ohio Dept of Public Welfare*, 30 FEP 387 (1978), aff. 30 FEP 395 (6th Cir. 1980).

118 Joy Cherian, "National origin discrimination affecting civilian employees overseas," *Labor Law Journal* (July 1990), pp. 387–8.

119 *Garcia* v. *Rush Presbyterian Medical Center*, 26 FEP 1556, 660 F.2d 1217 (7th Cir. 1981).

120 *Mejia* v. *New York Sheraton Hotel*, 18 FEP 602, 459 F.Supp. 375 (1978).

121 EEOC Guidelines, supra note 114, section 1606.7(a) and (b).

122 EEOC Decisions, Number 83-7, 31 FEP 1861 (1983).

123 22 FEP 1403, 618 F.2d 264 (5th Cir. 1980).

124 51 FEP 435, 838 F.2d 1031 (9th Cir. 1988).

125 Section 703e(1), Title VII 1964 Civil Rights Act.

126 EEOC Guidelines, supra note 114, section 1606.4.

127 Arthur and Lex Larson, *Employment Discrimination, Vol. 3* (Matthew Bender Publishers, New York, 1989), section 95-90.

128 48 FEP 980, 863 F.2d 1135 (3rd Cir. 1988).

129 5 FEP 1152, 413 US 634 (1973).

130 *Foley* v. *Connelie*, 17 FEP 1, 435 US 291 (1978).

131 *Ambach* v. *Norwich*, 19 FEP 467, 441 US 68 (1979).

132 *Cabell* v. *Chavez-Salido*, 27 FEP 1129, 454 US 432 (1982).

133 12 FEP 1377, 426 US 88 (1976).

134 Charles Agege, "Employment discrimination against aliens: the constitutional implications," *Labor Law Journal* (February 1985), pp. 93–4.

135 EEOC Guidelines, supra, note 114, 29 CFR section 1606.1(d), 1972.

136 6 FEP 933, 414 US 86 (1973).

137 Bureau of National Affairs, Immigration Reform (1987), pp. 1, 8–9.

138 IRCA, section 274(A)(a)(1)(A).

139 IRCA, section 274A(b).

140 Austin Fragomen, Jr and Steven Bell, *1992 Immigration Employment Compliance Handbook* (Clark, Boardman, Callaghan, New York, 1992), section 1-3.

141 8 CFR section 274(a)(3)(1), 1987.

142 IRCA section 274A(e)(5).

143 IRCA section 274A(e)(4)(i)–(iii).

144 IRCA section 274A(f)(1).

145 David Cathcart and J. Kevin Lilly, "The Immigration Reform and Control Act of 1986 – key compliance issues," *Employee Relations Law Journal*, 13 (Autumn 1987), pp. 224–5.

146 IRCA section 274B(1) and (2).

147 IRCA section 274B(2)(C).

148 IRCA section 274B(4).

149 Fragomen and Bell, supra, note 140, section 5-16.

150 29 CFR section 44.200(a) (1989).

151 Fragomen and Bell, supra, note 140, section 5-31.

152 Ibid., sections 5-31 and 5-32.

153 IRCA section 216(a)(A) and (B).

154 IRCA section 216(b)(B)(3)(4).

155 IRCA section 216(c)(4).

156 IRCA section 210(f)(1).

157 Bureau of National Affairs, supra, note 137, p. 65.

158 Fragomen and Bell, supra, note 140, sections 3-2, 3-3.

159 IRCA section 274A(e)(1)–(8).

160 IRCA section 274B(c)–(g).

161 Bureau of National Affairs, supra, note 137, pp. 63–5.

162 General Accounting Office, *Immigration Reform: Employer Sanctions and the Question of Discrimination* (GAO, Washington, DC, 1990), pp. 5, 103–4.

163 US Immigration Reform and Control Act and Undocumented Migration to the US (Urban Institute, Washington, DC, 1989).

164 General Accounting Office, supra, note 111, p. 67.

165 Ibid., p. 6.

166 US Commission on Civil Rights, news release, March 29, 1990.

167 Cecilia Munoz, *Unfinished Business: the Immigration Reform and Control Act of 1986* (National Council of La Raza, Washington, DC, 1990), p. 54.

168 *New York Times*, August 4, 1994, pp. 1, 7.

169 William B. Johnstone, *Workforce 2000* (Hudson Institute, Indianapolis, June 1987), pp. 75–103.

170 Ibid.

Chapter 6
Employment of the Handicapped

Background

Prior to 1920, Congress's concern over the handicapped was limited to Army veterans who had served in the First World War. In 1920, however, in the Smith–Fess Act Congress began to address the needs of all handicapped citizens. This statute provided training, counseling and placement services for physically handicapped persons regardless of their prior Army service. In 1943 Congress extended such services to the mentally ill and the mentally retarded. Amendments to the Social Security Act in 1954 and in the 1960s increased federal financial support, enlarged the target population, and expanded the scope of available services for the handicapped.[1]

By the early 1970s there was increased recognition and concern that discrimination contributed to serious unemployment problems among the handicapped and significant disparities between their incomes and those of the non-handicapped. In 1972, one year prior to the enactment of the Rehabilitation Act, Congress recognized that of the 22 million physically handicapped persons in the United States, only approximately 800,000 were employed.[2] In the mid-1970s the median family income of non-disabled individuals was nearly double that of the severely disabled population.[3] Promoting these outcomes were stereotypical judgments that a worker's disability rendered him or her unfit for employment. The disabled would also face rejection when their handicap promoted feelings of discomfort and unease in non-handicapped people.

The Rehabilitation Act of 1973 was the federal government's first comprehensive effort to challenge and remedy discriminatory barriers against the handicapped. Approximately 20 years later Congress would enact an even more far-reaching statute, the Americans with Disabilities Act (ADA). Yet the latter's passage has not reduced the significance of the Rehabilitation Act. The former statute remains the exclusive source of rights for federal employees. Furthermore, not only does it serve as the conceptual framework for the Americans with Disabilities Act, but the precedents adopted under the Rehabilitation Act will undoubtedly serve to guide both administrative agencies and courts in defining the scope and nature of worker rights and management's responsibilities under the ADA. Consequently, it is appropriate that we first examine the requirements established under the Rehabilitation Act.

Rehabilitation Act of 1973

The Rehabilitation Act of 1973, as amended in 1978, was part of a comprehensive effort to integrate handicapped citizens into American society. The Act was composed of different chapters or titles. Title I set up programs whereby handicapped people would receive diagnostic services, medical care, counseling, and training. These services would be provided by local agencies or private organizations under contract with states. Title II established the National Institute for Handicapped Research, while Title III provided funding for construction and training programs and for such services as interpreters for the deaf and readers for the blind. Title IV established the National Council on the Handicapped to assess services and programs for the handicapped. Title VI established a pilot employment program and project designed to give handicapped persons training and employment to prepare them for outside employment, while Title VII funded comprehensive programs for independent living.[4]

It is Title V of the Act which established the national policy of protecting the employment rights of handicapped people. Title V is divided into several critical parts, which impose separate responsibilities and obligations on recipients of federal funds (section 504), governmental contractors (section 503), and the federal government (section 501). Section 504 provides as follows:

> No otherwise qualified handicapped individual in the United States, shall solely by reason of his handicap be excluded from the participation in, be denied the benefits of, or be subjected to discrimination under any program or activity receiving federal financial assistance or under any program or activity conducted by any executive agency or by the United States Postal Service.

The prohibition against discrimination by the recipient of federal funds applies to all areas to which funding is used, including the education, housing, transportation, health, and human services. It also includes a prohibition on the part of the federal recipient not to discriminate in employment.[5]

Section 503 imposes on federal contractors an obligation to engage in affirmative action and is enforced by the Office of Federal Contract Compliance. It provides:

Any contract in excess of $2,500 entered into by any federal department or agency for the procurement of personal property and non-personal services including construction for the United States shall contain a provision requiring that in employing persons to carry out such contract the party contracting with the United States shall take affirmative action to employ and advance the employment of qualified handicapped individuals.

Additionally, companies with 50 or more workers and with contracts valued at $50,000 or more a year are required to develop written affirmative action plans and to act affirmatively to eliminate discriminatory practices against the handicapped. While not obliged to submit the plans for governmental scrutiny, companies must make them available for inspection to all employees at their request. In contrast to the written affirmative action plans for minorities and women, the plan for the handicapped need not incorporate goals and timetables.[6]

Section 501 of the Rehabilitation Act manifests the congressional commitment to make the federal government a model employer of the handicapped. It requires each department agency:

To engage in an affirmative action program plan for the hiring, placement and advancement of handicapped individuals.... Such plan shall include a description of the extent to which and methods whereby the special needs of the handicapped employees are being met.

The United States Equal Employment Opportunity Commission administers section 501 through regulations and the prosecution of discrimination complaints.

Defining Who Is Handicapped

The Rehabilitation Act of 1973 provides an initial framework for defining the term "handicapped" individual. The Act provides that a "handicapped individual" means any person who (a) has a physical or mental impairment which substantially limits one or more of the person's major life activities, (b) has a record of such impairment, or (c) is regarded as having such an impairment.[7]

The Office of Federal Contract Compliance Programs (OFCCP) and the United States Department of Justice have issued detailed guidelines operationalizing this definition. Those of the OFCCP are:

"Life activities" may be considered to include communication, ambulation, self care, socialization, education, vocational training, employment, transportation, adopting to housing, etc. For the purpose of Section 503 of the Act, primary attention is given to those life activities that affect employability.

The phrase "substantially limits" means the degree that the impairment affects employability. A handicapped individual who is likely to experience difficulty in securing, retaining or advancing in employment would be considered substantially limited.

"Has a record of such an impairment" means that an individual may be completely recovered from a previous physical or mental impairment. It is included because the attitude of employers, supervisors and co-workers toward that previous impairment may result in an individual experiencing difficulty in securing, retaining, or advancing in employment. The mentally restored and those, for example, who have had heart attacks or cancer often experience such difficulty. Also, this part of the definition would include individuals who may have been erroneously classified and may experience discrimination based on this misclassification. This group may also include persons such as those who have been misclassified as mentally retarded or mentally restored.

"Is regarded as having such an impairment" refers to those individuals who are perceived as having a handicap, whether an impairment exists or not, but who, because of the attitudes or for any other reason, are regarded as handicapped by employers or supervisors who have an effect on the individual securing, retaining or advancing in employment.[8]

The Department of Justice regulations more specifically describe protected disabilities. These include:

"Physical or mental impairment" means (1) Any physiological disorder or condition, cosmetic disfigurement or anatomical loss affecting one or more of the following body systems: Neurological; musculoskeletal; special sense organs, respiratory, including speech organs; cardiovascular; reproductive; digestive; genitourinary; hemic and lymphatic; skin and endocrine or (2) any mental or psychological disorder such as mental retardation, organic brain syndrome, emotional or mental illness and specific learning disabilities. The term "physical or mental impairment" includes, but is not limited to, such diseases and conditions as orthopedic, visual, speech, hearing impairments, cerebral palsy, epilepsy, muscular dystrophy, multiple sclerosis, cancer, heart disease, diabetes, mental retardation, emotional illness and drug addiction and alcoholism.[9]

In enforcing the statute, courts have identified a wide variety of conditions as falling within the definition of handicap. These include amputation, cerebral palsy, blindness, asthma, dyslexia, bilateral carpal tunnel syndrome, alcoholism, diabetes, deafness, paranoia, hemophilia, manic depression, hypertension, congenital back anomalies, and tuberculosis.[10]

In School Board of *Nassau County* v. *Arline*,[11] the Supreme Court affirmed the principle that individuals with contagious diseases are considered handicapped. In so doing the court rejected the contention that communicability of the disease is not an element that qualifies as a handicap.

We do not agree with petitioners that in defining a handicap under section 504 the contagious effects of a disease can be meaningfully distinguished from the disease's physical effects on a claimant in such a case as this. Arline's contagiousness and her physical impairment each resulted from the same underlying condition, tuberculosis. It would be unfair to allow an employer to seize upon the distinction between the effects of a disease on others and the effects of a disease on a patient and use that distinction to justify discriminatory treatment.[12]

Merely concluding that an individual has a handicap does not afford that person the right to a position. The statute prohibits discrimination against "otherwise qualified individuals." In *Southeastern College* v. *Davis*,[13] a unanimous Supreme Court rejected the Fourth Circuit's construction of section 504 which interpreted "otherwise qualified" as requiring federally funded programs to consider a handicapped person's qualifications without regard to the handicap. Instead the Supreme Court indicated that "an otherwise qualified person is one who is able to meet all of a program's requirements in spite of his handicap."[14] In this case Davis, a severely hearing impaired person, sought to be trained as a registered nurse. Finding that Davis was not otherwise qualified, because the training program could not reasonably be modified to accommodate her handicap, the Court upheld the college's refusal to admit her into its nursing program.

In determining whether an individual is otherwise qualified, the Supreme Court in Arline has also indicated that employers may address the legitimate concerns of avoiding or exposing others to significant health and safety risks. In the context of employing a person handicapped with a contagious disease, the Supreme Court suggested that employers should consider: (a) the nature of the risk (how the disease is transmitted); (b) the duration of the risk (how long the carrier is infectious); (c) the severity of the risk (what is the potential harm to the third parties); and (d) the probability that the disease will be transmitted and cause varying degrees of harm. In making such judgments employers should rely on the reasonable medical judgments of public health officials.[15]

Not all disabilities qualify as a handicap. Physical conditions that are temporary in nature may not. For example, in *Evans* v. *City of Dallas*,[16] an employee whose knee injury required surgery was not considered an individual with a handicap even though the injury may have impaired his life activities during his recuperation, since the injury was considered transitory in nature and would not subsequently limit the individual's activities. Additionally, even physical conditions that are longer lasting may not be covered. Thus, the courts have held that physical disabilities such as acrophobia[17] (fear of heights) and strabismus[18] (cross-eyedness), which have the effect of only disqualifying a person from a particular job in a facility, do not constitute being limited in a major life activity and hence do not qualify as a handicap.

Under guidelines of the United States Department of Labor[19] and the Health and Human Services[20] alcoholics and drug addicts may be handicapped within the meaning of the Rehabilitation Act. Underlying this determination is the recognition that both conditions are generally considered diseases which can substantially impair major life activities. Again, however, the recognition of alcoholism and drug addiction as handicaps does not guarantee any employee a position. In 1978 the Rehabilitation Act was amended to provide:

> For purposes of Sections 503 and 504 as such sections relate to employment, [the] term ["handicapped individual"] does not include any individual who is an alcoholic or drug abuser whose current use of alcohol or drugs prevents such individual from performing the duties of the job in question or whose employment, by reason of such current alcohol or drug use, would constitute a direct threat to the property or safety of others.[21]

Many cases interpreting sections 503 and 504 concern recovering alcoholics, that is alcoholics who are not currently using alcohol. Former alcohol and drug users and abusers who are currently performing adequately and who do not pose a safety threat have been held to be protected from discrimination by the statute.[22] In evaluating the performance of alcoholics and drug addicts, the employer may consider such factors as past personnel records, absenteeism, dangerous behavior, violation of rules, and unsatisfactory work performance. The employer is free to apply the rules and regulations of the work site to an alcoholic or drug addict provided such rules are applied in a non-discriminatory fashion.[23]

HIV/AIDS

In 1986 the United States Department of Justice issued a memorandum addressing the question of whether an individual carrying HIV was covered under the Rehabilitation Act. The Justice Department concluded that simply to be a carrier of the disease, that is to be capable of spreading the disease without suffering any physical ailment or other symptoms associated with the disease, did not render one handicapped. Under this view, the contagious aspects of the disease, the real or perceived ability to transmit the disease to others, did not qualify as a handicap notwithstanding the realization that employers may act on such fears in not employing those carrying HIV.[24] This position was rejected by the Supreme Court in *Arline*, which held that in defining a handicapped individual one cannot meaningfully distinguish between the disease's physical effects on the individual and the effects the disease may have on others.[25]

Chalk v. *US District Court*[26] is one of the few cases to specifically address the employment rights of workers carrying HIV. There the Ninth Circuit examined an accumulated body of medical evidence which demonstrated that in a normal work setting there is no basis for concluding that a worker with AIDS could transmit his disease to his coworkers or to others with whom he may come into contact. On the basis of this medical evidence, the court issued an injunction requiring the school district to restore to classroom duties a teacher who had been removed because of the fear that he would transmit HIV to his pupils. In *Doe* v. *Garrett*,[27] the Eleventh Circuit reaffirmed the protection that persons with HIV or AIDS have under the Rehabilitation Act.

Duty of Accommodation

In *Southeast Community College* v. *Davis*,[28] the Supreme Court held that an otherwise qualified handicapped individual is one who is able to meet a program's requirements in spite of her handicap. Yet the determination of whether a reasonable individual is qualified must consider the nature of accommodation that reasonably can be made to the person's handicap.

Under section 501 of the Rehabilitation Act that applies to federal contractors, a qualified handicapped individual had been defined by the US Department of Labor as a "person who is capable of performing the job with reasonable accommodation."[29] The US Department of Justice[30] and the US Equal Employment Opportunity Commission,[31] in implementing guidelines applicable to the recipients of federal funds and federal governmental employers, have applied the same accommodation construct to the definition of qualified handicapped person.

All three agencies responsible for administering the Rehabilitation Act have required employers to engage in reasonable accommodation unless it can be shown that "accommodation would cause undue hardship."[32] Since the United States Supreme Court decision in *Davis*, courts pursuant to section 504 have required accommodation in a variety of situations, including the use of readers for blind employees,[33] establishing for a dyslexic worker a different means for determining employee eligibility for entrance to an apprenticeship training program,[34] and offering a handicapped worker alternative and more suitable employment.[35] Under Justice Department guidelines facilities will also have to be rendered readily accessible and usable for handicapped workers.[36] As examples of potential accommodation, the United States Department of Labor has cited use of special equipment, changes in the physical layout of the job, and elimination of certain duties.[37] Similarly, the Equal Employment Opportunity Commission has noted that reasonable accommodation may include but shall not be limited to: (a) making facilities readily accessible and usable; (b) job restructuring, such as part-time or modified work schedules, acquisition or modification of equipment or devices, modification of examinations, the provision of readers and interpreters, and other similar action.[38]

Significantly, it is the employer and not the employee that has the primary responsibility to determine how to accommodate the employee in terms of machinery modification, schedule adjustments, or redistribution of job responsibilities. The logic for imposing this responsibility on the employer and not the employee has been articulated in *Prewitt* v. *US Postal Service*.[39]

> The employer has greater knowledge of the essentials of the job than does the handicapped applicant. The employer can look to its own experience or if that is not helpful to that of other employers who have provided jobs to individuals with handicaps similar to those of the applicant in question. Furthermore, the employer may be able to obtain advice concerning possible accommodations from private and government sources.[40]

Employers are required to accommodate unless they sustain undue hardship. In determining the scope of an employer's accommodation responsibility, the Labor Department has indicated that federal contractors should consider (a) business necessity and (b) financial costs.[41] Within the federal government the EEOC has identified the following factors to be considered in determining whether or not an accommodation is reasonable: (a) the overall size of the agency's program with respect to the number of employees, number and type of facilities, and size of budget; (b) the type of agency operation including the composition and structure of the agency's workforce; and (c) the nature and cost of the accommodation.[42]

At the same time reasonable accommodation does not require the elimination of essential job functions if they are not to be performed by the handicapped worker. For example, in *Coleman* v. *Darden*,[43] the court upheld the EEOC's refusal to place a blind attorney in the position of research analyst as much of his duties would have to be performed by a reader. Similarly, a paraplegic was denied a position as a police officer as his condition would have precluded him from effectively participating in forceful arrests.[44]

Employers must nonetheless be careful not to screen out handicapped individuals because of their inability to perform non-essential or tangential aspects of their position. In *Davis* v. *Frank*,[45] a deaf employee was denied the position of time and attendance clerk because of his inability to satisfy the job requirement of answering phones. The court, however, found that this task was such a small part of the job that it could have been easily allocated to other clerks. As a result, the denial of the time and attendance clerk position to the deaf employee was considered discriminatory.

Where an employee is unable even with reasonable accommodation to perform his or her job, the general consensus of the courts under the Rehabilitation Act is that the employer is not obligated to reassign that employee to a different position.[46] In general, the duty to accommodate only contemplates accommodation of a qualified handicapped employee's present position. Similarly, at least one court has held that the obligation to accommodate does not require an employer to consider handicapped applicants for jobs for which they have not applied if the employer does not do so for all other applicants who are not handicapped and the applicant's failure or inability to apply for other positions was not a function of his or her handicap.[47]

Under the Rehabilitation Act there appears to be a collective bargaining agreement exception to the requirement of reasonable accommodation. Courts have held that an employer cannot be required to accommodate a handicapped employee by restructuring a job in a manner which would usurp legitimate rights of employees under a contract. For example, if light duty assignments are reserved for more senior employees regardless of their handicap, an employer is not required to assign a handicapped employee with an inadequate amount of seniority to such a position.[48] Additionally, nothing in the Rehabilitation Act precludes management from dismissing handicapped workers for cause. In this regard poor performance, excessive absenteeism, illegal drug use, and loss of security clearance have been upheld as a legitimate basis for either the demotion or dismissal of handicapped workers.[49]

A difficult question that may confront employers is whether to employ a handicapped worker who carries a risk of future injury. Here the courts have suggested that employers are required to accumulate all relevant data regarding the applicant's work history and medical records, and independently assess the probability and severity of any potential injury.[50] Such an approach naturally requires a case-by-case determination. Only when the information suggests that the individual poses a reasonable probability of substantial harm to himself or herself or to others would the employer be justified in bypassing the handicapped worker.

One case where an employer was permitted to exclude an otherwise qualified handicapped worker because of future risk of injury was *Davis* v. *Meese*.[51] This concerned the blanket policy of the FBI to preclude all insulin-dependent individuals who have diabetes from employment as special agents. The danger of employing such an individual arose from the possibility that he or she could have a sudden and incapacitating hypoglycemic incident. The medical evidence also indicated that there existed no reliable method of predicting when such insulin-dependent diabetics would have such an attack. Given the extremely sensitive and sometimes dangerous nature of FBI activity and the potential harmful consequences that would arise if a special agent in the field was subject to a hypoglycemic attack, the court upheld the employer's blanket exclusion of insulin-dependent diabetics.

Enforcement

The US Department of Labor through its Office of Federal Contract Compliance Programs enforces a federal contractor's obligations under section 503. Meritorious complaints may lead the OFCCP to recommend a contract's termination, an employer's debarment, or affirmative relief to make whole discriminatees.[52] Under sections 504 and 505, individual complainants may sue for relief in federal courts. Section 505(a)(1) of the Rehabilitation Act specifically gives the federal courts the authority to issue an "equitable or affirmative action remedy" which considers "the reasonableness of the cost of any necessary work place accommodation . . . or other appropriate relief in order to achieve an equitable and appropriate remedy."

The Americans with Disabilities Act

The Rehabilitation Act of 1973 did not cover private sector firms or state or local government entities that are not recipients of federal aid or contracts. As a result, tens of millions of workers were not eligible for relief if they encountered discrimination because of an actual or perceived handicap. This glaring omission was rectified by passage of the Americans with Disabilities Act (ADA). Signed into law by President Bush on July 26, 1990 and taking into effect exactly two years thereafter, the statute provides comprehensive protection to the disabled.

Congressional recognition of the serious problems of discrimination in American society against the disabled and the need for comprehensive legislation is identified in section 2 of the ADA.

(a) Findings — The Congress finds that —

(1) Some 43,000,000 Americans have one or more physical or mental disabilities, and this number is increasing as the population as a whole is growing older;

(2) historically, society has tended to isolate and segregate individuals with disabilities, and, despite some improvements, such forms of discrimination against individuals with disabilities continue to be a serious and pervasive social problem;

(3) discrimination against individuals with disabilities persists in such critical areas as employment, education, transportation, communication, recreation, institutionalization, health services, voting, and access to public services;

(4) unlike individuals who have experienced discrimination on the basis of race, color, sex, national origin, religion, or age, individuals who have experienced discrimination on the basis of disability have often had no legal recourse to redress such discrimination;

(5) individuals with disabilities continually encounter various forms of discrimination, including outright intentional exclusion, the discriminatory effects of architectural, transportation, and communication barriers, overprotective rules and policies, failure to make modifications to existing facilities and practices, exclusionary qualification standards and criteria, segregation, and relegation to lesser services, programs, activities, benefits, jobs, or other opportunities;

(6) census data, national polls, and other studies have documented that people with disabilities, as a group, occupy an inferior status in our society, and are severely disadvantaged socially, vocationally, economically, and educationally;

(7) individuals with disabilities are a discrete and insular minority who have been faced with restrictions and limitations, subjected to a history of purposeful unequal treatment, and relegated to a position of political powerlessness in our society, based on characteristics that are beyond the control of such individuals and resulting from stereotypic assumptions not truly indicative of the individual ability of such individuals to participate in, and contribute to, society;

(8) the Nation's proper goals regarding individuals with disabilities are to assure equality of opportunity, full participation, independent living, and economic self-sufficiency for such individuals; and

(9) the continuing existence of unfair and unnecessary discrimination and prejudice denies people with disabilities the opportunity to compete on an equal basis and to pursue those opportunities for which our free society is justifiably famous, and costs the United States billions of dollars in unnecessary expenses resulting from dependency and nonproductivity.

The basic framework of the ADA is modeled on two statutes, the Civil Rights Act of 1964 and the Rehabilitation Act of 1973. The jurisdictional yardsticks (15 or more employees), the nature of employment practices prohibited, and the remedies for violations are nearly identical to those contained in Title VII. At the same time the pivotal concepts relating to the meaning of the term disabled or handicapped and concepts of undue hardship are derived directly from the Rehabilitation Act and regulations issued by administrative agencies in implementing it. As with Title VII, the EEOC has been vested with the authority to administer and enforce the ADA.

Employment provisions of the ADA[53]

Employers cannot discriminate against people with disabilities in regard to any employment practices or terms, conditions, and privileges of employment. This prohibition covers all aspects of the employment process, including:

- application;
- testing;
- hiring;
- assignments;
- evaluation;
- disciplinary actions;
- training;
- promotion;
- medical examinations;
- layoff/recall;
- termination;
- compensation;
- leave;
- benefits.

Actions which constitute discrimination

The ADA specifies the types of actions that may constitute discrimination. These include:

1 Limiting, segregating, or classifying a job applicant or employee in a way that adversely affects employment opportunities for the applicant or employee because of his or her disability.
2 Participating in a contractual or other arrangement or relationship that subjects an employer's qualified applicant or employee with a disability to discrimination.
3 Denying employment opportunities to a qualified individual because he or she has a relationship or association with a person with a disability.
4 Refusing to make reasonable accommodation to the known physical or mental limitations of a qualified applicant or employee with a disability, unless the accommodation would pose an undue hardship on the business.
5 Using standards, employment tests, or other selection criteria that screen out or tend to screen out individuals with a disability unless they are job-related and necessary for the business.
6 Failing to use employment tests in the most effective manner to measure actual abilities. Tests must accurately reflect the skills, aptitude, or other factors being measured, and not the impaired sensory, manual, or speaking skills of an employee or applicant with a disability (unless those are the skills the test is designed to measure).

7 Denying an employment opportunity to a qualified individual because he or she has a relationship or association with an individual with a disability.

8 Discriminating against an individual because he or she has opposed an employment practice of the employer or filed a complaint, testified, assisted, or participated in an investigation, proceeding, or hearing to enforce provisions of the Act.[54]

Definition of disability

The Act defines a person with a disability as one who (a) has a physical or mental impairment that substantially limits one or more of the major life activities of such an individual; (b) has a record of such impairment; or (c) is regarded as having such impairment.[55] This definition mirrors that used by Congress to define handicap under the Rehabilitation Act of 1973. In utilizing the same definitional approach, Congress reaffirmed its support for agency regulations and judicial decisions which have expansively defined the types of individuals classified as handicapped or disabled.

An impairment is a physiological or mental disorder. Consequently, the EEOC has noted that physical characteristics such as eye or hair color, left-handedness, or height and weight which are within a normal range and are not the result of a physiological disorder are not disabilities. In addition, personality traits such as poor judgment or a quick temper where these are not symptoms of a mental or psychological disorder will also not qualify. Similarly, environmental, cultural, or economic disadvantages such as poverty, lack of education, or a prison record are not viewed as impairments. While advanced age is not an impairment, various medical conditions commonly associated with age, such as hearing loss, osteoporosis, or arthritis would qualify as a disability.[56]

Certain mental impairments and sexual disorders are excluded from coverage. These include psychoactive substance use disorders resulting from current illegal use of drugs, compulsive gambling, kleptomania, pyromania, transvestism, transsexualism, pedophilia, exhibitionism, voyeurism, gender, identity disorders not resulting from a physical impairment, and other sexual behavior problems.[57] The statute also indicates that homosexuality and bisexuality are not viewed as impairments and as such are not considered disabilities.[58] Consequently, an individual's sexual orientation is not protected under the ADA; however, if a gay man or lesbian has a disability that is otherwise covered by the statute, such an individual would be protected from discrimination on the basis of that covered disability.

The ADA also provides protection to a new class of individuals not previously covered by the Rehabilitation Act. It is now illegal to discriminate against an individual who does not have a disability because of the relationship that this person maintains with a person who has a disability.[59] Thus, it would be illegal for an organization to fire an employee because that person's spouse or friend has a particular disability.

Who Are the Disabled?

Major life activities

To be a disability covered by the ADA, an impairment must "substantially" limit one or more of the major life activities. These are basic activities that an average person in the general population can perform with little or no difficulty. These include caring for one's self, walking, seeing, talking, learning, performing manual tasks, and working.[60]

The EEOC considers three factors in evaluating whether an impairment is substantially limiting: (a) the nature and severity of the impairment; (b) its duration; and (c) its permanent or long-term impact or expected impact.[61] These are judgments that routinely will have to be made on a case-by-case basis. Additionally, whether the limitation on working is "substantial" will depend on such factors as:

- the geographical area in which the person may expect to find employment;
- the number of types of jobs using similar skills and training for which the individual is disqualified within the geographical area because of the disability.[62]

Thus, an individual is not considered "substantially limited" because of an inability to perform a particular or specialized job. Rather, the term refers to an individual restricted from performing a class or broad range of jobs. For example, a computer programmer may develop a vision impairment preventing her from working in a range of jobs requiring use of the computer, including computer operator, programmer, and systems analyst. Because the impairment precludes the employee from working in a class of jobs requiring computer use, she would be viewed as substantially limited in working. On the other hand, a person whose allergic reactions prevent her from working in a particular office and who is able to work in other offices would not be viewed as significantly restricted in working.

Record of substantially limiting conditions

The Act protects people who have a history of disability, even if not currently limited by it. As a result, persons with a history of cancer, heart disease, or other illnesses that are cured, controlled, or in remission are protected from discrimination.[63]

Is regarded as having an impairment

Also considered disabled are people without any limiting impairment, but who are wrongly treated as having a disability. An example would be an individual with high blood pressure. If the employer removes the employee because of unsubstantiated fears that the employee would suffer a heart attack, the employer has regarded this individual as impaired and has unfairly discriminated against him.[64]

Medical Examination and Inquiries

The Act generally precludes employers from conducting pre-employment medical inquiries and examinations.[65] As a result, employers are prohibited from requiring applicants to undergo a physical examination which could identify the nature and scope of an employee's disability. The prohibition against medical examination includes psychological testing. Similarly, neither a recruiter nor a physician could ask a job applicant about the presence of any disability or its severity. This prohibition extends to all application forms and inquiries made in reference checks. Underlying this prohibition is the effort to eliminate employer utilization of pre-employment screening to identify and reject disabled applicants.[66] Questions to be avoided include:[67]

- Have you ever had or been treated for the following conditions or diseases?
- Please list any conditions or diseases for which you have been treated in the past three years.
- Have you ever been hospitalized? If so, for what condition?
- Have you ever been treated by a psychiatrist or psychologist? If so, for what condition?
- Have you ever been treated for any mental condition?
- Is there any health-related reason you may not be able to perform the job for which you are applying?
- Have you had a major illness in the past five years?
- How many days were you absent from work because of illness last year?
- Do you have any physical defects which preclude you from performing certain kinds of work? If yes, describe them and the specific work limitations.
- Do you have any disabilities or impairments which may affect your performance in the position for which you are applying?
- Are you taking any prescribed drugs?
- Have you ever been treated for drug addiction or alcoholism?
- Have you ever filed for worker's compensation insurance?

At the same time an employer may ask questions that address the applicant's ability to perform job-related functions. These questions, however, should not be phrased in terms of disability. For example, an employer may ask an individual with one leg who applies for the position of home washing machine repairman to demonstrate or explain how, with or without accommodation, he would be able to transport himself and his tools down basement stairs. However, the employer may not inquire into the nature or severity of his disability.[68]

One exception to the bar against pre-employment screening of job applicants concerns the testing of job applicants for illegal drug use. Employers are permitted to subject even job applicants to a drug screen because, under the statute, a test to determine the illegal use of drugs is not considered a medical examination.[69] If, however, the drug screen produces a false positive and the job applicant is erroneously perceived as having been on drugs, the employer would be liable for any act of discrimination.

On the other hand, the employer may subject workers to physical examinations once an offer of employment has been made. However, such examinations are subject to the following qualifications: (a) all employees are subjected to such examinations regardless of disability; (b) all information obtained will be kept strictly confidential and maintained in separate medical files.[70] The employer may condition the offer of employment on the result of the examination. However, the job applicant may only be screened out on the basis of factors that are job-related and consistent with business necessity. In this regard, the employer must also demonstrate that there is no reasonable accommodation that would enable the individual with the disability to perform the essential functions of the job.[71]

Employers are also permitted to require employees to undergo medical examinations when necessary to determine their ability to perform essential job functions. For example, employees returning from extended medical leaves may undergo fitness for duty examinations. Similarly, employers are permitted to compel workers to undergo periodic physical examinations that are required by federal, state, or local law. For example, OSHA standards require that employees exposed to certain toxins and hazardous substances be medically monitored at specific intervals.[72]

A growing number of employers today are offering voluntary wellness programs in the workplace. These programs often include medical screening for high blood pressure, weight control, and detection of diseases such as cancer. As long as the programs are voluntary and the medical records are maintained in a confidential manner and not used for the purpose of limiting health insurance eligibility, these activities are acceptable.[73]

Employment Standards

The ADA defines a qualified disabled individual as one who with or without accommodation is able to perform "essential" functions of the job.[74] While not defining the term "essential" the ADA indicates that both the employer's judgment and job descriptions prepared before advertising or interviewing applicants will be considered in determining whether job functions are essential.[75]

The EEOC has developed some criteria which help to identify whether a function is essential. The job function would more likely be viewed as essential if: (a) the position was created specifically to perform it; (b) there are few employees available to perform the function; and (c) the function involves a highly specialized task for which individuals with specific skills and expertise have been sought to perform it. Other factors to be considered in determining essentiality of job function are the amount of time spent performing it and the work experience of past employees holding the position.[76]

Significantly, the ADA does not require an employer to lower job qualifications or to employ individuals lacking the requisite qualifications. It does, however, require an employer to spend more time evaluating job candidates. Thus, individuals can no longer be screened out because of stereotypical perceptions that a disabled individual cannot perform. To protect themselves against liability, employers are best advised to place additional resources in both identifying the prerequisites of satisfactory job performance and in evaluating job candidates.[77]

Reasonable Accommodation

The ADA imposes an affirmative obligation on employers to accommodate handicapped or disabled persons. This objective is achieved by rendering employers liable if they refuse to accommodate. Thus, the ADA defines discrimination to include:

> not making reasonable accommodations to the known physical or mental limitations of an otherwise qualified individual with a disability who is an applicant or an employee, unless such covered entity can demonstrate that the accommodation would impose an undue hardship on the operation of the business of such covered entity.[78]

The ADA requires accommodation in three aspects of employment:[79]

- To ensure equal opportunity in the application process: for example, a person who uses a wheelchair may need accommodation if an employment office or interview site is not accessible. A person with cerebral palsy may need assistance filling out an application form.
- To enable a qualified individual with a disability to perform the essential functions of the job: modification or adjustments in the job in the way it is customarily performed may be feasible.
- To enable an employee with a disability to enjoy equal benefits and privileges of employment: employees with disabilities must have equal access to lunchrooms, lounges, restrooms, meeting rooms, and other employer provided or sponsored services, such as health programs, transportation, and social events.

Basic principles of reasonable accommodation

The EEOC has identified the parameters within which accommodation requirement operates. These include the following components.[80]

Effectiveness The accommodation offers a person with a disability the opportunity to perform or to enjoy benefits equal to those of a non-disabled person who is similarly situated. The accommodation does not have to ensure equal results or provide exactly the same benefits or privileges. For example, assume a wheelchair-bound individual working in a two-story building with no elevator has no access to a second floor cafeteria. If installing an elevator would be unduly costly, the employer would not be required to install a separate cafeteria on the first floor for the handicapped employee. It would be sufficient for the employer to provide food (vending machines) and space for that employee and other workers to eat on the first floor.

Limited focus   Accommodation seeks to reduce barriers to employment. It need not apply to accommodation that a disabled person may request for some other reason. For example, if a blind computer operator working at an employer's Michigan facility requested reassignment to a Florida facility because of a preference for a warmer climate, this would not be a required accommodation under the ADA.

Employer options   Accommodation needs to be effective, yet it need not be the one preferred by the employee. Where there are two alternative means of accommodation available, the employer may select the one that is most appropriate from a cost and convenience perspective as long as the one selected effectively eliminates the barrier for the disabled employee. For example, an employer would not have to hire a full-time reader for a blind employee if a coworker is available on a part-time basis, which will enable the blind employee to perform his or her job duties effectively.

Personal needs of workers   Accommodation is not required to address the personal needs of an employee. Equipment or devices that assist a person in daily activities on and off the job are considered personal items that an employer is not required to provide.

When is an employer required to make a reasonable accommodation?

An employer is required to accommodate only the known limitations of an individual's disability. Generally it is the applicant or employee's responsibility to inform management that accommodation is necessary. Thus, an employer cannot be expected to provide an accommodation when it is unaware of an individual's need. At the same time the employer must inform job applicants of the availability of accommodation opportunities. This requirement is typically satisfied by posting notices containing the provisions of the ADA, including the reasonable accommodation obligation, in conspicuous places on its premises. Such notices should also be posted in employment offices and other places where applicants and workers can see them. The EEOC provides such posters. Information about reasonable accommodation may be included in job application forms and personnel manuals, and may be communicated orally as well.[81]

An applicant or an employee does not have to specifically request a reasonable accommodation but can inform management that some adjustments or changes are necessary for a more effective performance of the job because of the limitations caused by a disability. If a job applicant or employee has "a hidden disability," one that is not so obvious, it is the responsibility of the employee to make known his or her need for an accommodation. If an applicant has a known disability, such as the loss of a limb, that appears to limit or otherwise interfere with his or her ability to perform, the employer may ask the applicant to describe or demonstrate how he or she would perform the function with or without reasonable accommodation. Additionally, if a person requests an accommodation and the need for it is not obvious or is suspect, the employer may require documentation to support the employee's request.[82]

Examples of reasonable accommodations

The statute[83] and EEOC regulations[84] provide many illustrations of accommodations an employee may be required to offer. These include the following.

Job restructuring and reassignment of duties Job restructuring means modifying a job so that a person with a disability can perform the essential functions of the position. It also means removing barriers to performance by eliminating non-essential functions. It may include redelegating assignments, exchanging assignments with other employees, and redesigning procedures for accomplishing certain job tasks. However, an employee is not required to reallocate essential job functions.

Modified work schedules The EEOC has noted that people with disabilities may need modified work schedules because their conditions may require special medical treatment (cancer patients who require chemotherapy) or they may need special rest periods. Alternatively, people with visual impairments may find it difficult to drive at night. Shifting arrival and departure hours may lessen commuting problems.

Flexible leave policies Individuals with impairments may require leave for medical treatment. While an employer is not required to provide additional paid leave, it should consider allowing use of accrued leave, leave without pay, or advance leave.

Reassignment to vacant positions This type of accommodation should be considered if an employee cannot be accommodated in his or her current job. An employer is not required to consider a different position for a job applicant who was unable to perform the essential functions of the position for which that person applied. An employer should attempt to reassign an employee to a position which is equivalent to the one previously held in terms of pay and other job benefits. Individuals cannot be reassigned only to certain undesirable positions or only to certain offices or facilities from which future promotion might be restricted. If no position is currently available the employer should consider the disabled employee for vacancies that will become available within a reasonable amount of time. The EEOC indicates that a reasonable amount of time should be determined on a case-by-case basis with due regard to such factors as the frequency with which such jobs become available, general policies regarding job reassignments, and any specific policies regarding sick or injured employees. An employer may also reassign an individual to a lower graded position if there is no accommodation that would enable the employee to remain in his or her current job and there are no other positions vacant at his or her level. In such a situation the employer does not have to maintain the employee's salary at the higher level unless it has a policy of red circling salaries and wages of other employees reassigned to lower level positions. An employer is also not required to create a new job or to bump another employee from a job in order to provide reassignment as a reasonable accommodation, nor is an employer required to promote an individual with a disability to make such accommodation.

Acquisition or modification of equipment and devices There are many devices and instruments that make it possible for people to overcome existing barriers to performing functions. These may range from a simple element, such as an elastic band that can enable a person with cerebral palsy to hold a pencil and write, to high tech electronic equipment that can be operated with eye or head movements by people who cannot use their hands. An employer should seek advice from applicants and employees with disabilities as to the availability of effective and low cost equipment, as they may have a great deal of experience in its use. Where a job requires special adaptations of equipment, the employer can utilize various informational sources on technical assistance. They include Job Accommodation Network, a free consulting service on accommodations, as well as vocational rehabilitation specialists and occupational therapists who may come to the site, conduct a job analysis, and recommend appropriate equipment or job modifications. An employer, however, is only required to provide equipment that is needed to facilitate the performance of a job. There is no obligation to provide equipment that an individual uses regularly in daily life, such as glasses, a hearing aid, or a wheelchair.

Examples of equipment and devices that may be used by the impaired include:

- *Blind and visually impaired persons.* Braille, large type, or recorded materials allow blind and visually impaired employees to read the same printed materials as sighted persons. Braille typewriters enable a person who is blind or visually impaired to take notes and write reports. Occasionally, providing sighted reading assistance may be a reasonable accommodation. Other options may include speech synthesizers, braille computer printers, or scanners that print or store text and magnify it on a screen.

- *Persons with hearing impairments.* Accommodations for such persons may include telephone handset amplifiers, telecommunication devices for deaf persons (TDDs), lights that flash to indicate break, lunch, and quitting times.
- *Persons with limited physical dexterity.* Employers may need to modify or purchase special equipment, such as gooseneck telephone headsets, hands-free telephones, voice-activated dictation machines, one-handed typewriters, mechanical page turners, and raised or lowered furniture.

Adjusting and modifying examinations, training materials, and policies
Accommodation may be required to ensure that tests and examinations measure the actual ability of an individual to perform job functions rather than reflecting the limitations caused by his disability. To people who have sensory, speaking, or manual impairments, tests must be given in a format that does not require the use of an impaired skill unless it is a job-related skill the test is designed to measure. For example, an individual with dyslexia who has difficulty reading should if possible be given an oral rather than a written test unless reading is an essential function of the job. Alternatively, an individual with a visual disability may be given the materials in large type or braille. Employers must also provide accessible training sites.

Providing readers and interpreters This may involve one of the more expensive mechanisms of accommodation. It would not be required if its implementation would impose an undue hardship. Yet even when such a service is provided it need not necessarily be afforded on a full-time basis. For example, few jobs require an individual to spend all day reading. A reader, therefore, may be a part-time employee or a full-time person who performs other duties for the employer. Whether or not qualified interpreters and readers are required would depend upon an examination of the resources available to the particular organization.

Altering existing facilities Facilities must be "readily accessible and usable."[85] This may include redesigning an employee's workstation to accommodate a wheelchair, installing ramps by stairways, widening doorways, rearranging files or shelves, adaptive levers or machinery, raised door numbers for the blind, and alternative warning devices for the deaf and blind.

The ADA's problem solving approach

Frequently an appropriate accommodation is obvious and can be made without difficulty and at little or no cost. Individuals with a disability may be able to suggest a simple change or adjustment based on their work experience. Yet in some cases the appropriate accommodation may not be readily identifiable. The person requesting accommodation may be unfamiliar with the equipment being used and not knowledgeable enough about the exact nature of the work site to suggest an accommodation. Alternatively, the employer may not know enough about the individual's functional limitations in relationship to specific jobs. EEOC regulations suggest that employers and workers engage in an interactive problem solving approach to find an effective accommodation.[86] This process should incorporate the following steps.

- Determine the particular purpose and essential functions of the job.
- Consult with the worker to ascertain the precise job-related limitations created by the individual's disability.
- Identify means by which the employer may accommodate the individual's disabilities to permit the employee to perform the essential functions of the position.
- The reasonableness of each potential means of accommodation should be assessed in terms of its effectiveness in permitting the employee to perform. They should also be examined in terms of their timeliness of applications and costs of implementation. If more than one accommodation would be effective, the employer is free to choose the one that is less expensive or easier to provide.

The undue hardship limitation

An employer is not required to accommodate if it would impose undue hardship on the operation of the business. However, if a particular accommodation would impose an undue hardship, the employer must consider whether there are alternative accommodations that would not impose such costs. Under the ADA an undue hardship is an action that requires "significant difficulty or expense."[87] The concept of undue hardship includes any action that:

- is unduly costly;
- is extensive;
- is substantial;
- is disruptive;
- would fundamentally alter the nature or operation of the business.[88]

The statute[89] and EEOC regulations[90] identify factors to be considered in determining whether or not accommodation would impose an undue hardship. These include:

- the nature and net cost of the accommodation;
- the overall financial resources of the facility or facilities involved;
- the number of people employed at the facility;
- the effect of expenses and resources or any other impact that the accommodation would have on the operation of the facility;
- the overall financial resources of the employer;
- the overall size of the business of the employer in terms of number of employees and the number, type, and location of its facilities;
- the composition, structure, and function of the workforce;

- the geographic, administrative, and fiscal relationship between the facility involved and the overall employer.

It is evident that employers must determine undue hardship on a case-by-case basis. At the same time, it will be difficult for large employers to demonstrate that any one accommodation imposes an "undue hardship," unless the accommodation is extreme. Furthermore, the legislative history indicates congressional rejection of the test of *de minimis* costs that the Supreme Court applied in religious discrimination cases to define "undue hardship."[91] Specific federal tax credits and tax deductions are also available to employers for making accommodations required by the ADA. If an employer receives tax credits, only the net cost to the employer will be considered in determining undue hardship.[92]

The EEOC has also indicated that an employer may not be able to claim undue hardship because the cost of accommodation is high in relationship to an employee's wage or salary. In this regard, when enacting the ADA, Congress specifically rejected an amendment that would have permitted firms to eschew accommodation if the costs exceeded 10 percent of an employee's salary. Such an approach would have adversely affected low pay workers who need to be accommodated. Instead the focus in determining undue hardship is the overall resources available to the firm.[93]

Undue hardship is also not measured by employee fears or prejudices about an employee's impairment. At the same time, if accommodation is unduly disruptive to other employees or the employer's operations, then accommodation need not occur. For example, if an employee requested that a thermostat in the workplace be raised to a certain level to accommodate his or her disability, no accommodation would be required if the raised level would make it uncomfortably hot for other employees or customers. Finally, reflective of the congressional mandates to encourage accommodation is the requirement that if a firm finds the financial costs of accommodation excessive, then the applicant or employee should be offered the option of sharing in the costs and thereby eliminating the undue hardship that an employer may otherwise incur.[94]

Financial and technical assistance for accommodation

There are several sources of financial assistance to help employers make accommodations and comply with the ADA requirements.

Tax credit for small business   In 1990 Congress established a special tax credit to help smaller employers making accommodations. An eligible small business is defined as one with gross receipts of a million dollars or less for a taxable year or 30 or fewer full-time employees. Such businesses may take a tax credit of up to $5,000 per year for accommodations. The credit is available for one-half the cost of "eligible access expenditure" that is more than $250 but less than $10,250.[95]

Eligible access expenditures for which tax credits may be taken include the following.

- Removal of architectural, communication, physical, or transportation barriers.
- Providing qualified interpreters or other methods to make communication accessible.
- Providing qualified readers, taped texts, or other methods to make information accessible.
- Acquiring or modifying equipment for people with disabilities.
- Tax deduction for architectural and transportation barrier removal. Any business may take a full tax deduction of up to $15,000 per year for expenses of removing specified architectural or transportation barriers. Expenses covered include the cost of removing barriers created by steps, narrow doors, inaccessible parking spaces, toilet facilities, and transportation vehicles. Both the tax credit and the tax deduction are available to eligible small businesses.[96]

Targeted job tax credit   Tax credits are also available under the targeted jobs tax credit program (TJTCP) for employers who hire individuals with disabilities referred by state or local vocational rehabilitation agencies. This program includes the hiring of special disadvantaged groups, including people with disabilities. Under the TJTCP a tax credit may be taken for 40 percent of the first $6,000 of an employee's first year salary.[97]

Other funding sources   State or local vocational rehabilitation agencies and state commissions for the blind may provide financial assistance for equipment and accommodations for their clients. Additionally, the US Department of Veteran Affairs provides financial assistance to disabled veterans for equipment needed to help them perform.[98]

Drug and Alcohol Abuse

The ADA specifically permits employers to ensure that the workplace is free from illegal use of drugs and the use of alcohol and to comply with the federal laws and regulations regarding alcohol and drug use.[99] Yet the ADA provides limited protection from discrimination for recovering and rehabilitated drug addicts and for alcoholics.[100] Reflecting this balance, the EEOC has identified the following employer rights and responsibilities:[101]

- An employer may prohibit the illegal use of drugs or the use of alcohol at the workplace.
- It is not a violation of the ADA for an employer to give tests for the illegal use of drugs.
- Such testing is not considered a medical test under the ADA.
- An individual who currently uses illegal drugs is not covered by the statute when the employer acts on the basis of such use.

- An employer may discharge or deny employment to persons who currently engage in the illegal use of drugs. The illegal use of drugs includes the use, possession, or distribution of drugs which are unlawful under the Controlled Substances Act. It includes the use of illegal drugs and the illegal use of prescription drugs that are controlled substances. However, the illegal use of drugs does not include drugs taken under supervision of a licensed health care professional, including experimental drugs for people with AIDS, epilepsy, or mental illness.
- An employer may not discriminate against a drug addict who is not currently using drugs and who has been rehabilitated because of a history of drug addiction. Persons addicted to drugs but who are no longer using them and are receiving treatment for an addiction are also protected by the ADA from discrimination. To ensure that drug use is not recurring an employer may request evidence that an individual is participating in a drug rehabilitation program. Such programs may include inpatient, outpatient, or employee assistance programs.
- A person who is an alcoholic is an individual with a disability under the ADA, and may be entitled to consideration or accommodation if the individual is qualified to perform the essential functions of a job. However, an employer may discipline, discharge, or deny employment to an alcoholic whose use of alcohol adversely affects job performance. Unsatisfactory behavior, such as absenteeism, tardiness, poor job performance, or accidents caused by alcohol or illegal drug use, need not be accepted or accommodated.

Many employers have established employee assistance programs for employees who have been addicted to drugs or alcohol. The ADA does not require an employer to provide such an opportunity for rehabilitation in place of discipline or discharge. At the same time, the ADA may require an employer to accommodate a drug addict who is rehabilitated, is not currently using drugs or alcohol, and remains qualified to perform. For example, a modified work schedule to permit the individual to attend an ongoing self help program might be a reasonable accommodation for such an employee. In certain cases an employer may be able to fire or to refuse to hire an individual with a previous history of illegal drug use even if the person no longer uses drugs. For example, a law enforcement agency might be able to show that excluding an individual with a history of illegal drug use from the position of police officer is necessary because such prior illegal conduct would undermine the credibility of that officer as a witness for the prosecution in a criminal proceeding.[102]

Pre-employment inquiries about drug and alcohol use and drug testing

An employer may make certain pre-employment pre-offer inquiries regarding the use of alcohol or illegal drugs. An employer may ask a job applicant whether he drinks and whether he or she is currently using drugs illegally.

However, an employer may not ask whether an applicant is a drug addict or an alcoholic, nor inquire whether the person has ever been in a drug or alcohol rehabilitation program. After a conditional offer of employment has been made, an employer may ask any questions concerning past or present drug or alcohol use. However, the employer may not use such information to exclude an individual with a disability unless it can be shown that the reasons for exclusion are job-related and consistent with business necessity.[103]

Drug tests are not considered medical examinations and an applicant can be required to take a drug test before a conditional offer of employment has been made. An employee can also be required to take a drug test whether or not such a test is job-related and necessary for the business. On the other hand, a test to determine an individual's blood alcohol level would be a medical examination and could only be required by an employer in conformity with the ADA.[104]

Health Benefits

The ADA covers discrimination with regards to "terms, conditions, and privileges of employment."[105] Discrimination, therefore, is illegal with respect to provision for health benefits. As a result, it would be unlawful for an employer to deny disabled employees access to health insurance or other benefits plans, such as life insurance and pension plans, because of their disability. At the same time, where an employer provides health insurance through an insurance carrier, it may provide coverage in accordance with accepted principles of risk assessment and/or risk classification even if this causes limitations in coverage for individuals with disabilities. EEOC guidelines specifically note that an employer may continue to offer health insurance plans that limit coverage for certain procedures and/or limit particular treatments to a specified number per year, even if these restrictions affect individuals with disabilities, as long as the restrictions are uniformly applied to all insured individuals. For example, an employer may offer a health insurance plan that limits coverage of blood transfusions to five a year even though a hemophiliac may require more than five per year.[106] On the other hand, the EEOC has noted that an employer will be considered in violation of the ADA if it singles out a particular disability (e.g. deafness, AIDS, schizophrenia) for exclusion from a health insurance plan. Similarly, an insurance plan that would place a cap of $100,000 of benefits for all illnesses, but limit the cap at $5,000 for AIDS, would be considered unlawful as well.[107]

Labor Unions and the ADA

Labor unions are covered by the ADA and are subject to the same obligation as employers. There remain, however, many unanswered questions concerning the potential conflict between the scope of an employer's duty to accommodate and a union's rights under the National Labor Relations Act (NLRA). The ADA envisions employers interacting with employees to effect workplace accommodations. Yet if accommodation results in a major change in a worker's pay, duties, or seniority, the employer could be charged with a unilateral change in conditions of employment in violation of section 8(A)(5) of the NLRA. Also, employer accommodations may be viewed as negating an employee's contractual rights. For example, assume an employer wishes to offer a light duty assignment to an employee with a disability. If jobs are normally allocated on the basis of a person's seniority and the employee with the disability does not possess adequate seniority, placement of this individual in that job may arguably breach the seniority rights of other workers in the facility. On the other hand, an employer who fails to effect such accommodations may be liable under the ADA.

Efforts by the EEOC and NLRB to develop a memorandum of understanding which would indicate how such problems would be resolved have proven unsuccessful. In the face of this vacuum the NLRB's general counsel issued a preliminary memorandum concerning the ADA in August of 1992.[108] With respect to the duty to bargain over reasonable accommodation, the general counsel suggested that a unilateral change that did not effect a substantial or significant change in working conditions would not violate an employer's obligation to bargain in good faith. For example, providing a ramp for an employee in a wheelchair or putting a desk on a block would be examples of changes in working conditions that are sufficiently insignificant that they would not trigger an employer's duty to bargain. On the other hand, a change that would result in modifications in job classifications or in established employment practice might.[109] It would appear that the more prudent approach for employers would be to involve the union in their deliberations with employees over workplace accommodations.

EEOC regulations do not address the relationship between an employer's rights under the NLRA and the ADA. The EEOC has, however, indicated that the terms of the contract may be relevant in determining whether a particular accommodation would cause an employer undue hardship.[110] For example, if a contract reserves certain jobs for employees with a given amount of seniority, this may be considered as a factor in determining whether it would be undue hardship to reassign an individual with a disability who does not have the seniority to be eligible for that position. When similar conflicts arose under the Federal Rehabilitation Act of 1973 between the contract and the employer's duty to accommodate, courts gave deference to collective bargaining agreements.[111] Ultimately, court action will be necessary to settle these issues under the ADA.

Enforcement and remedies

Procedures available to enforce the ADA are identical to those available under Title VII.[112] Thus a charging party and the EEOC may initiate suits against offending employers. The remedies also parallel Title VII relief and include:

- hiring or reinstatement;
- promotion;
- increase in wages and benefits;
- back pay;
- reporting requirement;
- review and modification of employment practices;
- injunctions.

In addition, depending on an employer's size, damage awards ranging from $50,000 to $300,000 may be imposed. Additionally, 43 states have enacted their own legislation to prohibit discrimination against the handicapped, and state forums may be used to obtain added damages.[113]

Compliance with the ADA is essential to avoid the risk of EEOC charges and adverse legal judgments. At the same time, employers should be aware that the employment of the disabled satisfies important business needs. Disabled persons represent a large and frequently untapped pool of qualified workers. The case of Kreunile Corporation in Wichita, Kansas, is instructive. In the 1980s, the company experienced a turnover rate of 33 percent, at a cost of $1,000 per worker. In part as a result of hiring and accommodating the disabled, turnover was reduced to 10 percent. Today 15 percent of the company's workforce consists of "disabled" employees functioning well in their positions.[114]

To facilitate the employment of the disabled, legal experts have recommended the following measures:[115]

- Issue a policy statement affirming an employer's intent to recruit as employees disabled applicants.
- Avoid general conclusions about categories of disabilities.
- Review job application forms and interview procedures.
- Permit greater flexibility regarding part-time work, shift assignments, and leave policies.
- Review selection procedures to ensure that they do not unnecessarily screen out a disproportionately greater number of disabled employees.
- Review and revise job descriptions to ensure that they identify essential functions of the position.
- Examine the physical structure and layout of the facility to make those modifications that will ensure that disabled employees and applicants have easy access to them.
- Communicate and train supervisors with regard to their responsibilities to accommodate.
- Solicit suggestions from disabled job applicants and employees about reasonable accommodation.
- Be flexible and open-minded in your search for them.

Summary

The passage and enforcement of the Rehabilitation Act and the Americans with Disabilities Act have significantly expanded the employment rights of the handicapped worker. No longer can an organization reject workers because of perceived actual impairments or because of a prior record of a disability. Instead, such workers must be judged on the basis of their ability to perform essential job functions. When making such assessments, employers must be willing to effect reasonable workplace accommodations. While organizations are now effectively barred from engaging in pre-employment medical inquiries and accommodations, such restrictions and other protections afforded handicapped workers do not preclude an employer's effort to ensure that its workplace is free from the illegal use of drugs and alcohol.

Questions for discussion

1 Jane Doe is a trained computer programmer. She seeks employment with a software company. She has no disqualifying physical or mental problems. She is, however, extremely overweight, being five foot six inches tall and 245 pounds. The company's medical doctor advises the company to reject her because of obesity. Has the company violated the Rehabilitation Act or the ADA? See "EEOC: definition of term disability", March 14, 1995, Section 902.2(c)(5), *BNA Fair Employment Practices Manual*, pp. 405: 7259–60.

2 Distinguish between the meaning afforded the term "undue hardship" under Title VII, which limits an employer's obligation to accommodate a worker's religious beliefs or practices, and its meaning under the Rehabilitation Act of 1973 and the ADA. What accounts for the differences and, given the respective interests of workers and managers, are such differences with respect to the accommodation obligation reasonable?

3 The company in 1995 initiates a policy that all employees whose duties involve potential exposure to toxic gases must wear respirators. All machinists are included in the category of affected workers. Machinists' duties include field work, involving potential exposure to toxic gases, and shop work, where there is no direct exposure to hazardous fumes. The company also decides to rely on its machinist labor pool for emergency fire fighting, toxic gas containment, and rescue in cases of accident. John Doe has been working satisfactorily as a shop machinist for several years. He informs the company that a respiratory condition precludes him from wearing a respirator. He requests that the company restructure his position so that he is not assigned fire or rescue duties requiring use of a respirator. The company refuses and removes him from his position. Has the company violated Doe's rights?

4 The employer's health insurance plan provides full reimbursement to employees for costs incurred in the treatment of physical conditions. At the same time, it provides only partial reimbursement for the treatment of mental problems. Are such distinctions in coverage reasonable or lawful? See EEOC Interim Guidelines on Application of ADA to Health Insurance, June 8, 1993, *BNA Fair Employment Practices Manual*, p. 405: 7117.

5 In 1993 John Doe drove a school bus for Plymouth School District. In 1994 his left leg was amputated and since that time he has undergone rehabilitative training to relearn driving skills. After he learned to drive again, Doe reapplied for his former position. The board of education refused to hire him, citing a local ordinance which provides that "no person shall drive a school bus who does not possess both of these natural body parts: feet, legs, hands, arms, eyes and ears." Additionally, it notes that for Doe to drive the bus effectively it would have to install a hand clutch. Would the employer be required to accommodate? Can an employer rely on a local or state regulation to refuse employment to the handicapped? See *Coleman* v. *Casey County Board of Education*, 26 FEP 357 (1980).

NOTES

1 David Malikin and Herbert Rusalem, eds, *Vocational Rehabilitation of the Disabled: an Overview* (New York University Press, New York, 1969), pp. 39–60, 113.
2 Statement of Senator Williams, 118 *Congressional Record*, 3320–1 (1972).
3 US Commission on Civil Rights, *Accommodating the Spectrum of Individual Abilities* (USCCR, Washington, DC, 1983), pp. 27–32.
4 Ibid., pp. 47–8.
5 Ibid., pp. 50–1.
6 41 CFR section 60-741. (5).
7 29 USC section 706(B).
8 Affirmative Action Obligations of Contractors and Subcontractors for Handicapped Workers, 41 CFR section 60-741, appendix A.
9 Justice Department Regulations on the Handicapped, 28 CFR section 41.31 (b)(1).
10 Arthur Larson and Lex Larson, *Employment Discrimination, Vol. 3* (Mathew Binder, New York, 1989), Section 106.14(a).
11 43 FEP 81, 480 US 273 (1987).
12 Ibid., at 84.
13 442 US 397 (1979).
14 Ibid., at 406.
15 Supra, note 11, at 87.
16 52 FEP 418, 861 F.2d 846 (5th Cir. 1988).
17 *Forrisi* v. *Bowen*, 41 FEP 190, 794 F.2d 931 (4th Cir. 1986).
18 *Jasany* v. *US Postal Service*, 37 FEP 210, 755 F.2d 1244 (6th Cir. 1988).
19 29 CFR section 32.3(a), (b)(iii) (1990).
20 45 CFR part 84, appendix A, pgh 3 (1993).
21 29 USC section 706(7)(B).
22 Robert B. Fitzpatrick, "Alcoholism as a handicap under federal and state employment discrimination laws," *The Labor Lawyer*, 7 (1991), pp. 401–46.
23 "Non-discrimination on the basis of handicap in program and activities receiving federal financial assistance," 45 CFR part 84, appendix A, pgh 3.
24 Joseph B. Broadus, "Arline: the application of the Rehabilitation Act of 1973 to communicable diseases," *Labor Law Journal* (May 1988), pp. 277–8.
25 *School Board of Nassau County* v. *Arline*, supra, note 11.

26 46 FEP 279, 840 F.2d 701 (9th Cir. 1988).

27 53 FEP 335, 903 F.2d 1455 (11th Cir. 1990).

28 442 US 397 (1979).

29 41 CFR section 741.2.

30 28 CFR section 41.32.

31 29 CFR section 1613.702(f).

32 41 CFR section 60.741.5(d) (Dept of Labor); 28 CFR section 41.53 (US Dept of Justice); 29 CFR Section 1613.704 (EEOC).

33 *Nelson* v. *Thornburgh*, 34 FEP 835, 732 F.2d 146 (3rd Cir. 1984).

34 *Stutts* v. *Freeman*, 30 FEP 1121, 694 F.2d 666 (11th Cir. 1983).

35 *Harrison* v. *Marsh*, 46 FEP 971 (1988).

36 28 CFR section 41.57.

37 41 CFR section 10.741, appendix B.

38 29 CFR section 1613.704.

39 27 FEP 1043, 662 F.2d 292 (5th Cir. 1981).

40 Ibid., at 1054.

41 41 CFR 741.6(D).

42 29 CFR section 1613.704.

43 19 FEP 137, 595 F.2d 533 (10th Cir. 1979).

44 *Simon* v. *St Louis County*, 26 FEP 1003, 656 F.2d 316 (8th Cir. 1981).

45 50 FEP 1188, 711 F.Supp. 447 (1989).

46 *Carter* v. *Tisch*, 44 FEP 385, 822 F.2d 465 (4th Cir. 1987); and *Jasany* v. *US Postal Service*, supra, note 18.

47 *Dexler* v. *Carlin*, 40 FEP 633 (1986).

48 *Jasany* v. *US Postal Service*, supra, note 18; and *Daubert* v. *US Postal Service*, 34 FEP 1260, 733 F.2d 1367 (10th Cir. 1984).

49 Larson and Larson, supra, note 10, section 106.33(b).

50 *Mantolete* v. *Postal Service*, 38 FEP 1081, 767 F.2d 1416 (9th Cir. 1985).

51 48 FEP 1894, 865 F.2d 592 (3rd Cir. 1989).

52 41 CFR section 60-741.23(g)(3) and Executive Order 11246, section 209.

53 Sections 101(7), 102, and 107.

54 Section 102, ADA.

55 Section 3(2), ADA.

56 Equal Employment Opportunity Commission, *Americans with Disabilities Act – Equal Employment Regulations*, 29 CFR 1630, appendix to section 1630.2(h).

57 Section 511(b), ADA.

58 Section 511(a), ADA.

59 Section 102(b)(4), ADA.

60 Equal Employment Regulations, supra, note 56, appendix to section 1630.2(i).

61 Ibid., appendix to section 1630.2(j).

62 Ibid.

63 Ibid., appendix to section 1630.2(k).

64 Ibid., appendix to section 1630.2(l).

65 Section 102(c)(2)(A), ADA.

66 Lawrence P. Postol and David K. Kadue, "An employer's guide to the Americans with Disabilities Act," *Labor Law Journal* (April 1991), pp. 325–6.

67 Equal Employment Opportunity Commission, "A technical assistance in the employment provisions of the ADA: explanation of key legal requirements," Bureau of National Affairs, January 28, 1992, *Daily Labor Report*, No. 18, p. 24.

68 Appendix to section 1630.14(a), supra, note 56.

69 Section 104(d), ADA.

70 Section 102(c)(3)(A–B).
71 Appendix to section 1630.14(b), supra, note 56.
72 Appendix to section 1630.14(c), supra, note 56.
73 Appendix to section 1630.14(d), supra, note 56.
74 Section 101(8), ADA.
75 Ibid.
76 Appendix to section 1630.2(h), supra, note 56.
77 Philip Gordon, "The job application process after the Americans with Disabilities Act," *Employee Relations Law Journal*, 18 (No. 2, Autumn 1992).
78 Section 102(b)(5)(A), ADA.
79 Technical assistance in the employment provisions of the ADA, section 3.3, supra, note 67, p. 10.
80 Ibid., section 3.4, p. 10.
81 Ibid., section 3.6, p. 11.
82 Ibid.
83 Section 101(9)(a–b).
84 Section 3.10, supra, note 67, pp. 13–17.
85 Section 101(9)(A).
86 Section 3.8, supra, note 67, p. 12.
87 Section 101(10)(a), ADA.
88 Section 3.9, supra, note 67, p. 12.
89 Section 101(10)(B)(i–iv), ADA.
90 Section 3.9, supra, note 67, p. 12.
91 Postol and Kadue, supra, note 66, pp. 338–9.
92 Section 34, supra, note 67, p. 12.
93 Ibid., section 3.9.5, p. 13.
94 Ibid.
95 Section 3.11(a), supra, note 67, p. 17.
96 Ibid., p. 18.
97 Ibid., section 3.11(a)(3).
98 Ibid., section 3.11(a)(4).
99 Sections 104(a) and 104(c).
100 Section 104(b), ADA.
101 Section 8.2, supra, note 67, p. 34.
102 Section 8.7, supra, note 67, p. 35.
103 Ibid., section 8.8.
104 Ibid., section 8.9, p. 36.
105 Section 102(a), ADA.
106 Section 7.9, supra, note 67, p. 33.
107 EEOC Guidelines on ADA and Health Insurance, June 8, 1993, Bureau of National Affairs, *Fair Employment Practices Manual* (1993), p. 405: 7115.
108 Bureau of National Affairs, *Daily Labor Report*, No. 158 (August 14, 1992), p. E-1.
109 James H. Coil III and Charles M. Rice, "The tip of the iceberg: early trends in ADA enforcements," *Employee Relations Law Journal*, 19 (No. 4, Spring 1994), pp. 491–2.
110 Section 3.9(5), supra, note 67, p. 12.
111 *Jasany* v. *US Postal Service*, supra, note 18; and *Daubert* v. *US Postal Service*, supra, note 48.
112 Section 10, supra, note 67, pp. 38–40.
113 Jeffrey Allen, *Complying with ADA* (John Wiley, New York, 1993), p. 74.

114 Ibid., pp. 2–3.
115 Elliot Shaller, "Reasonable accommodation under the ADA – what does it mean?" *Employee Relations Law Journal*, 16 (No. 4, Spring 1991), pp. 441–8; Philip Gordon, "Job application process under the ADA," *Employee Relations Law Journal*, 18 (No. 2, Autumn 1992), pp. 206–10.

7
Courts and Affirmative Action

Affirmative Action Plans

State governments, local governments, and, most importantly, the federal government have required that in order to do business with them, a contractor (or subcontractor) must be committed to the government's goal of equal employment opportunity and must demonstrate that commitment by developing an affirmative action plan. The specifications for such plans differ between state governments, local governments, and the federal government. The most significant requirements, of course, are those arising for *federal* contractors.

Federal contractors have had equal employment opportunity related requirements placed upon them since 1941, when President Franklin D. Roosevelt issued Executive Order 11141 requiring that defense contractors cease discriminatory practices in hiring. In 1961 President John F. Kennedy issued Executive Order 10925, requiring that federal contractors take whatever action necessary to "insure that applicants are treated during employment without regard to their race, color, or national origin." The most significant of these Executive Orders, and the one currently in place, is Executive Order 11246, signed by President Johnson on September 24, 1965. Executive Order 11246 as amended[1] prohibits federal contractors from discriminating against any employer on the basis of race, color, religion, sex, or national origin. It further requires that contractors take "affirmative action." The types of affirmative action stipulated in the order "shall include, but not be limited to the following: employment, upgrading, demotion, or transfer; recruitment, or recruitment advertising; layoff or termination; rates of pay or other forms of compensation; and selection for training, including apprenticeship." The Executive Order also provides that in the event of non-compliance with its provisions, federal contracts can be canceled, terminated, or suspended, and the contractor can be declared ineligible for further government contracts. Regulations implementing Executive Order 11246 were issued in 1968. Order Number Four of those regulations describes in great detail the steps that contractors must take to develop a written affirmative action plan. These regulations were significantly amended by Revised Order Four, which continues to guide federal employers in the development of affirmative action plans that cover discrimination because of sex, race, and ethnicity.

In addition to Executive Order 11246, two federal statutes require that most federal contractors take affirmative action in employment and develop written affirmative action plans. The Rehabilitation Act of 1973, Section 503,[2] requires that federal contractors take affirmative action for handicapped individuals.[3] Also, disabled veterans and veterans of the Vietnam War era are protected against employment discrimination by government contractors under the Vietnam-era Veterans Readjustment Act of 1974.

Two premises can be used to explain the rationale for requiring that government contractors be committed to equal employment opportunity and affirmative action. First, in using presidential executive orders, the executive branch of government is expected to procure goods and services in a manner advantageous to the government in terms of economy and efficiency. The government's position is that discrimination in employment is uneconomical; hence, contractors must not discriminate (i.e. must be committed to equal employment opportunity) and must be able to convince the government that they are not discriminating (i.e. must develop a written affirmative action plan).

The affirmative action efforts of federal contractors are regulated by the US Department of Labor's Office of Federal Contract Compliance Programs. The guidelines in Revised Order Four (41 CFR 60-2) cover federal contractors that have contracts of at least $10,000. Additionally, they require that non-construction contractors with 50 or more employees and contracts of $50,000 or more develop a written affirmative action plan for each of their establishments.[4] The regulations under Revised Order Four define an affirmative action plan as:

> A set of specific and results-oriented procedures to which a contractor commits himself to apply every good faith effort . . . to achieve prompt and full utilization of minorities and women at all levels and in all segments of the workforce where deficiencies exist.

The written affirmative action plan

The requirements for a written affirmative action plan can differ depending upon which governmental body has required that it be developed. Additionally, the affirmative action plan required of federal contractors for individuals with disabilities and for Vietnam-era and disabled veterans does not require the kind of statistical analysis that is required under Executive Order 11246. But while the specific ingredients differ in contractual affirmative action efforts depending upon the governmental agency involved, some key concepts run through them all. First, while equal employment opportunity is the goal, without a specific, action-oriented plan one does not really have a goal; one has, perhaps, a lofty intention. Second, such plans are premised on the idea that if an employer does not discriminate, its workforce should reflect the demographics of the labor market from which it recruits employees. While there may be many reasons besides illegal discrimination to explain why an employer's workforce does not reflect the demographics of the labor market, the basic idea remains – if an employer's workforce does not look like the relevant labor market then it should be prepared to explain the disparity and it should be developing a plan to make the workforce more representative of that labor market. Third, a critical issue, therefore, is determining what the relevant labor market is. The basic question upon which availability data gathering hinges is, *"From where could someone reasonably come for this job?"* For example, if one were examining the job classification "clerical employee," candidates are rarely promoted or transferred from within and usually do not move from other locales; the relevant statistics, therefore, are those for the local metropolitan area. For the job classification "first line supervisors," emloyees may not move from outside the local area, but the organization may promote from within; therefore, the employer must concentrate on local labor market data and internal promotion possibilities. However, for the job classification "nuclear engineer," most employers recruit on a national basis; hence, employment statistics for the country as a whole must be utilized since the relevant labor market is national.

Basic elements of an affirmative action plan as required of federal contractors

Regulations from the Office of Federal Contract Compliance Programs specify many sections and mandatory ingredients for an affirmative action plan. However, the plan must contain six basic elements:

1   Development or reaffirmation of the company's equal employment opportunity policy (41 CFR 60-2.20).
2   Establishment of responsibilities for implementation of the affirmative action program (41 CFR 60-2.22).
3   Procedures for internal and external dissemination of the policies (41 CFR 60-2.21).
4   Identification of problem areas by organizational units and job groups (41 CFR 60-2.23), including a workforce analysis of all jobs (41 CFR 60-2.11).
5   Establishment of goals and objectives by organizational units and job classifications (41 CFR 60-2.12), and the development and execution of

action-oriented programs designed to eliminate problems and further designed to attain goals and objectives (41 CFR 60-2.24).
6   Designation and implementation of internal audits and reporting systems to monitor effectiveness of the program (41 CFR 60-2.25).

Development or reaffirmation of the company's policy   An affirmative action plan must include a statement of the organization's policy with respect to affirmative action. The policy of the facility chief executive officer (CEO) must be clearly stated. In addition, OFCCP regulations require that the facility CEO sign the affirmative action plan, indicating the company's commitment to it.

Responsibility for implementation of the AAP   The OFCCP stipulates that primary responsibility and accountability for directing and implementing the affirmative action plan rest with the chief executive officer. He or she normally designates a responsible individual, who must be identified by name and job title in the facility's affirmation action plan. The plan must indicate the support given to the equal employment opportunity or affirmative action officer. More importantly, an effective plan recognizes that ultimate success lies with line managers, not with human resources specialists. Hence, the commitment from top management is critical, but as importantly, individual managers and unit heads must be held responsible for helping the organization achieve its affirmative action goals. In fact those organizations truly committed to a successful program view affirmative action in a way quite similar to that in which other organizational goals and objectives are viewed. Such goals are made a part of the performance plans of managers, their progress is monitored and evaluated, and rewards are allocated based upon the extent to which goals are accomplished. In other words, affirmative action criteria should become a part of the performance plan and appraisal of managers and should contribute to performance-based rewards that such individuals receive.

Dissemination of policy   OFCCP regulations require that contractors disseminate, both internally and externally, their equal employment opportunity policy. The written plan should summarize these dissemination efforts, which often include:

- including an equal opportunity statement on company publications;
- having appropriate statements in the organization's human resources policy statements, advertisements, recruitment announcements, etc.;
- Sending reminders from the CEO to all employees of the equal employment opportunity policy of the employer;
- Covering equal employment opportunity and affirmative action in orientation and training programs.

Externally, the company is to notify its major stakeholders (suppliers, customers, recruitment sources, etc.) of its commitment to equal employment opportunity and affirmative action. This can include:

- sending notices of the policy to recruitment agencies;
- notifying community organizations;
- including minority and female employees in company advertisements;
- including an equal employment opportunity and affirmative action statement on all company publications and letterhead.

Active dissemination of the contractor's affirmative action program, internally and externally, serves to buttress an employer's claim that it made a good faith effort to achieve its affirmative action goals.

The identification of problem areas OFCCP regulations require not only a narrative explanation of the contractor's problem areas, but also a careful statistical analysis which is critical in identifying those problem areas. The statistical section includes four components:

1 Workforce analysis or array.
2 Job grouping.
3 Availability analysis.
4 Utilization analysis.

In the *workforce analysis*, the employer is required to "take a snapshot of its organization." In the snapshot, the organization, on a unit-by-unit or department-by-department basis, reports the number of employees in every job title, both in total and also by sex and race/ethnicity. For example, the human resources department might have a vice president for human resources, a director of labor relations, a director of human resource services, two labor relations specialists, four human resources representatives, one payroll administrator, three payroll technicians, and six clerical employees. The workforce analysis would list each of these job titles, and detail for each, the number of incumbents in total, the number of men, women, blacks, Hispanics, Native Americans or Alaskan Natives, and Asian and Pacific Islanders. This presentation of information allows the OFCCP (and of course the employer) to identify positions in which women and minorities are concentrated as well as those in which they hold few positions.

Job grouping is a process in which the contractor groups together jobs that are similar in terms of skill, salary, promotional opportunities, and availability, regardless of the unit or department in which the jobs happen to be located. For example, an organization may have data entry specialists in a number of departments and there may be two or three levels within that broad job classification. But additionally, the employer may have other secretarial and clerical positions that are, in a broad sense, quite similar to the data entry specialists in terms of skills, wages, and promotional opportunities. An employer would then pull together all such job titles into a single job group that might be named "office and clerical." A good starting point for constructing job groups is to work from the categories on an employer's EEO-1 form (Standard Form 100 from the Joint Reporting Commission). Those categories (e.g. officials and managers, professionals, technicians, sales, office and clerical, craft workers, operatives, laborers, and service workers) usually provide a good first cut, but may not be specific enough for some employers. For example, in a hospital the broad category of professionals might include a job group for nurses, but there might also be job groups for other professionals, such as accountants, pharmacists, or human resources specialists. Developing job groups is an art, not a science. In constructing the job group, the contractor generally seeks to construct the job groups that are large enough in size that, when one sets a goal, one does not end up with a fraction of a person. (For example, if the job group only has five people and if the goal is 10 percent, then mathematically the goal becomes one-half person.)

Once job groups are constructed, the employer must determine *availability*. Availability answers the question, "In a world free of discrimination, how would my workforce look?" In other words, what should be the employer's goals with respect to the employment of women and minorities in each job group? In this section the employer must gather relevant statistics and apply judgment in determining the weight given to those statistics in order to determine what the representation of women and minorities should look like given the labor market (those with relevant skills within a reasonable recruitment area).

OFCCP regulations require that availability data be developed separately for women and total minorities in each job group using eight factors, i.e. "eight factor analysis." The factors are:

1a The minority population of the labor area surrounding the facility, or
1b The availability of women seeking employment in the labor or recruitment area of the facility.
2   The size of the minority and female unemployment force in the labor area surrounding the facility.
3   The percentage of the minority and female workforce as compared with the total workforce in the immediate labor area.
4   The general availability of minorities and women having requisite skills in the immediate labor area.
5   The availability of minorities and women having requisite skills in an area in which the contractor can reasonably recruit.
6   The availability of promotable and transferable minority and female employees within the facility.
7   The existence of training institutions capable of training persons in the requisite skills (i.e. the availability of minorities and women in those institutions that will be entering the labor force).
8   The degree of training which the contractor is reasonably able to undertake as a means of making the job group available to minorities and women (i.e. the availability of minorities and women who could be trained for the job group).[5]

Generally, an employer must *consider* all eight factors in determining availability for each job. Thus, an employer must first gather data, i.e. raw statistics, about each of the factors. The first three factors remain constant for each job group, as they relate to general population and employment statistics concerning the area around the facility. The last five factors are skill- or job-specific and will therefore differ for each job group. Of the eight factors, factors 6 and 8 relate to internal availability, i.e. within the employer's workforce, while the remaining six factors measure external availability.

Availability factor computation next requires that each of the eight factors be "weighted" according to its importance to the job group. In some job groups, some factors are likely to be unimportant and will be weighted zero. For example, if the employer is a hospital and if the job group is nurses, factors 1 (a and b), 2, and 3 are too general and not likely to be particularly critical in determining availability. Similarly, nurse candidates are not likely to be promoted or transferred from other jobs, so factor 6 will not prove helpful in determining availability. And assuming the hospital does not have its own nursing school, factor 8 will not be useful. These factors, 1, 2, 3, 6, and 8, might receive a value weight of 0 percent. By contrast, factors 4, 5, and 7 are likely to be critical in determining availability. The hospital is concerned about persons in the local area and reasonable recruiting areas that have the skills, training, and certification required for nursing jobs, and also about those in the education pipeline, i.e. training institutions graduating nurses from which the hospital could attract candidates.

The final step of availability analysis is to calculate a weighted average for each job group. This requires multiplying the raw statistic for each of the eight factors by that factor's value weight, then adding to calculate final availability.

Utilization analysis requires that an employer compare the racial and ethnic composition of its present workforce on a job group to job group basis with availability statistics on that same job group to job group basis. Where the employer's workforce has a smaller percentage of women or minorities than the availability analysis indicates it should, the employer must declare that it is "underutilized." Where an employer is underutilized it is required to establish a goal and to develop action plans for the accomplishment of those goals.

Having statistically analyzed its employment situation, the employer now is able to more carefully identify problem areas. The narrative description of these apparent problem areas must be identified by organizational unit and job groups. This analysis is designed to evaluate all human resources practices and policies and to identify those which are creating or could potentially create an adverse impact on minorities and women.

Establishment of goals and the development of action-oriented programs
Having analyzed the organization and identified its problem areas the employer is now in position to develop and execute action-oriented programs to achieve its goals. This is where the contractor commits itself to undertake every good faith effort. And the contractor must in the next year's affirmative action plan comment on its success with respect to these efforts.

Internal auditing and reporting systems The final major component of the affirmative action plan is the description of the organization's internal auditing and reporting system used to monitor the facility's progress toward achievement of its goals and objectives. At a minimum, an employer should monitor on a quarterly basis. Among the information to be monitored is records of new hires (applicant flow), transfers, training program attendees, promotions, layoffs, and terminations.

The affirmative action plan for individuals with disabilities, and for Vietnam-era and disabled veterans

The Office of Federal Contracts Compliance Programs requires that federal contractors with 50 employees and $50,000 in government contracts have a written affirmative action plan for individuals with disabilities, disabled veterans, and veterans of the Vietnam War. This plan is narrative only. Employers are not required to perform a statistical analysis of their workforce or establish numerical goals. Among the major factors important in such plans is that the employer provide proper consideration of the qualifications of such individuals to ensure that there are not any inhibitors to the recruitment, hiring, or advancement of individuals with disabilities or Vietnam-era veterans. Additionally, the OFCCP monitors closely the physical and mental job qualifications set by the contractor to ensure that they are job-related and have no adverse impact. The accessibility of the organization's physical environment to employees and prospective employees is also a major OFCCP concern. Finally, the OFCCP pays special attention to a contractor's outreach efforts, internally and externally, with regard to its affirmative action commitment for individuals with disabilities and Vietnam-era veterans. Dissemination efforts that the contractor utilizes must be detailed and should include educational efforts for employees, and local and national recruiting sources which specialize in the placement of individuals with disabilities.

Judicially Imposed Affirmative Action

Where unlawful employment practices have been found, the federal courts are authorized under section 706G of Title VII to "order such affirmative action as may be appropriate." Pursuant to this authority the federal courts have required employers and unions to comply with race conscious hiring, promotion, and union admission requirements to remedy "longstanding or egregious" discrimination. For example, in *Local 28 Sheet Metal Workers* v. *EEOC*[6] the Supreme Court dealt with a local union that had excluded blacks from membership and from its apprenticeship training program over several decades. Recognizing its continuous and deep rooted pattern of discrimination, the court required the local to establish a 29 percent minority membership goal by August of 1987. This remedy was based on the percentage of minorities in the labor pool within the local union's jurisdiction. This case is most significant because the court specifically upheld the principle that race-conscious affirmative action relief may be extended not only to actual victims of discrimination but to minorities in general to promote minority employment and deter future misconduct.

Similarly, the Supreme Court has found that race-conscious affirmative action hiring requirements are compatible with the equal protection clause of the Fourteenth Amendment. In *the US* v. *Paradise*,[7] the application of non-validated and biased testing and interview procedures operated to exclude Afro-Americans from upper level positions in the Alabama State Police force. Of six majors, 25 captains, 35 lieutenants, and 65 sergeants, none were minority. Of 66 corporals, four were black. To remedy the department's utilization of discriminatory promotion practices, the court upheld a 50 percent minority promotional quota.

Yet a promotional quota is not a remedy that can be rigidly applied. In approving its implementation, the court indicated that the 50 percent promotional quota was contingent upon the existence of vacancies and the availability of qualified minority employees. Furthermore, the court revealed that the quota need only endure until the department came up with a promotion procedure that did not have a discriminatory impact on blacks, something that the department had failed to do over a 12-year period. Given these considerations, the court found that the 50 percent minority promotion requirement did not impose an unacceptable burden on white troopers in violation of their rights under the Fourteenth Amendment.

Furthermore, the authority of the federal courts to impose race-conscious requirements on employers to remedy past discrimination is not unlimited. In *Fire Fighters Local Union 1784* v. *Stotts*[8] the Supreme Court addressed the authority of the federal courts to modify seniority systems in order to protect newly hired minorities from layoff. In this case the district court had entered into a consent decree with the City of Memphis establishing interim annual goals for minority hiring and promotions. Subsequently, the city announced layoffs because of budgetary deficits and indicated its intent to lay off on the basis of "last hired, first fired." Recognizing that the application of the seniority system would result in the layoff of a disproportionate number of minorities, and would interfere with the city's affirmative action obligations under the consent decree, the district and appellate courts had ordered modifications of the seniority system to protect minority workers from layoff. This approach, however, was explicitly rejected by the Supreme Court, which ruled that federal courts under Title VII cannot overturn bona fide seniority systems and mandate the layoff of more senior white employees to make room for blacks with less seniority.

Legality of Employer Established Affirmative Action Programs

The Supreme Court's decision in *United Steel Workers* v. *Weber*[9] has established the framework for determining the legal parameters for voluntarily established affirmative action programs. This case arose from the operation of an affirmative action program at a Kaiser Aluminum plant in Gramercy, Louisiana. Until the mid-1970s Kaiser hired as craft workers only persons who had prior craft experience. Because blacks had long been excluded from craft unions in the Gramercy area, few were able to present the necessary credentials. As a consequence, prior to 1974, fewer than 2 percent of the skilled craft workers at the Gramercy plant were black, although the workforce in the area was approximately 39 percent minority.

Pursuant to a national agreement, Kaiser altered its craft hiring practices at the Gramercy plant. Rather than hiring already trained outsiders, Kaiser established a training program to train its production workers to fill craft openings. Selection of craft trainees was made on the basis of seniority, with the critical proviso, however, that at least 50 percent of the new trainees were to be black until the percentage of skilled craftsmen in the Gramercy plant approximated the percentage of blacks in the local labor force. In implementing this plan in its first year of operation, Kaiser and the union selected 13 craft trainees, seven of whom were black and six white. The most junior black selected into the program had less seniority than several white production workers whose bids for admission were rejected. One of the white production workers bypassed was Brian Weber, who filed a Title VII claim charging that the affirmative action program which gave preferences to minorities in filling the craft training program discriminated against white employees in violation of Title VII.

The Court of Appeals for the Fifth Circuit had found that all employment preferences based on race, including those that are a component of a bona fide affirmative action plan, violated Title VII's prohibition against racial discrimination in employment. The Supreme Court, however, reversed. Its determination was strongly predicated upon its reading of the legislative history to Title VII. While recognizing that Title VII makes it unlawful to discriminate on the basis of race in hiring and in the selection of apprentices for training programs, the court's review of the legislative history led it to conclude that Congress did not intend in Title VII to prohibit the private sector from taking effective voluntary steps to eradicate racial imbalances in a company's workforce. Additionally, the court noted that such voluntary preferences did not violate section 703J of Title VII, which provided that the act cannot be interpreted "to require employers with racially imbalanced work forces" to grant preferential treatment to racial minorities in order to integrate. The court interpreted section 703J's prohibition as limited to governmental efforts to "require" employers to grant preferential treatment because of a *de facto* racial imbalance in an employer's workforce. At the same time, Title VII does not prohibit employers and unions from voluntarily engaging in such affirmative action efforts to correct a racially segregated workforce.

The *Weber* decision is significant because it identifies the line of demarcation between permissible and impermissible affirmative action plans. A voluntarily established affirmative action plan will be legal if: (a) it is designed to open employment opportunities for minorities in occupations which have been traditionally closed to them; (b) it does not unnecessarily trammel the interests of white employees (thus, an affirmative action plan which would require the discharge of white workers and their replacement with new black hires would be illegal); (c) it does not create an absolute bar to the advancement of white employees (in this regard, the court noted that half of those trained at the Kaiser facility would be white); and (d) it is a temporary measure and is not intended to maintain racial balance. At Kaiser the plan was scheduled to terminate when the percentage of black skilled craft workers in the Gramercy plant approximated the percentage of minorities in the local labor force.

This decision has served as a safety valve to employers caught between competing legal pressures. On the one hand, employers with strong imbalances in their workforce are eager to implement affirmative action programs to reduce the likelihood of suits initiated by minorities alleging employment discrimination in hiring and promotion. On the other hand, prior to *Weber*, employers engaging in such affirmative action programs would be vulnerable to suits filed by disaffected white employees. The *Weber* decision allows employers to escape this legal tightrope by affording them the opportunity to implement affirmative action programs to rectify imbalances in their workforce without fear of liability to whites as long as the guidelines set forth in the *Weber* decision are satisfied.

While the parameters for lawful affirmative action programs were identified in *Weber*, which is a Title VII case, they have also been applied by the courts in reverse discrimination cases litigated under the Fourteenth Amendment. In 1972 the Jackson Board of Education and the Jackson Education Association amended their collective bargaining agreement to protect minority groups against layoff. A result was the layoff of tenured non-minority teachers while minority teachers on probationary status were retained. The Court of Appeals had held that the board's interest in providing minority role models for its minority students as an attempt to alleviate the effects of societal discrimination was sufficiently important to justify the racial classification embodied in the layoff provision.[10] The Supreme Court, however, reversed, citing its earlier decisions in *Fire Fighters* v. *Stotts* and *Weber*. The court noted that efforts to promote and protect minority employment cannot unfairly burden innocent third parties. Because of the adverse financial and psychological effects that a layoff has upon incumbent employees, the court found that the layoff of non-minority teachers with greater seniority in order to retain minority teachers with less seniority breached the equal protection clause of the Fourteenth Amendment.[11]

The previous cases have dealt with preferences afforded minorities. In *Johnson* v. *Transportation Agency, Santa Clara County*,[12] the Supreme Court for the first time dealt with a voluntary affirmative action plan that gave employment preferences to women. In December of 1978 Santa Clara County had adopted an affirmative action program for promotions to positions within a traditionally segregated job classification in which women had been significantly underrepresented. Under the program the employer would consider the sex of the qualified applicant as one factor in the selection process. When a female employee was selected for a skilled craft position over a male employee who had scored somewhat higher, the male employee filed a Title VII claim charging sex discrimination.

In upholding the affirmative action plan, the court applied the *Weber* criteria. The plan was limited in scope and designed to remedy a serious underrepresentation of women in traditionally segregated job categories. In particular, women were most egregiously underrepresented in the skilled craft job category, since none of the 238 positions was occupied by a woman. Additionally, the plan did not unnecessarily injure the interests of male employees as it did not require their discharge or their replacement with female employees. The bypassed male employee had no absolute entitlement to the disputed position as he, the female applicant, and other employees were both qualified and eligible. Furthermore, the bypassed male employee retained employment with the agency at the same salary and seniority, and remained eligible for other promotions. The plan also did not operate as a bar to the advancement of other male workers. No quotas were imposed for the promotion of female employees. While the affirmative action plan had as a benchmark goal the employment of women in major job classifications that mirrored their representation in parallel jobs within the area labor market, the goal took into account such factors as turnover, layoffs, transfers, new openings, retirement, and the availability of qualified minority workers in the labor force. Additionally, sex was but one factor among many that were considered in making a selection decision. Finally, as with *Weber*, the plan was intended only to attain a balanced workforce, not to maintain it.

From these cases we can identify the following principles which characterize legitimate affirmative action efforts.

- Preferences must be narrowly tailored to address the specific problem of minority underutilization. For example, an affirmative action plan may be warranted to promote the employment of minorities who are underrepresented. However, minority underrepresentation would not justify preferences for Hispanics if their presence in the workforce was equal to or greater than their composition within the surrounding labor market in the relevant job classification.
- Preferences must be temporary and the plan must terminate once a racial, ethnic, or sexual imbalance in the company's workforce has been remedied.
- Whereas courts have imposed hiring quotas in cases of egregious discrimination and have permitted them at times even when voluntarily established (*Weber*), absolute bars to the advancement of non-minorities or plans resulting in their layoff or displacement will be prohibited.
- Plans are also more likely to succeed when preferences are just one and not the determining factor in the selection process.
- Those making the hiring or promotion decision should have the discretion to select candidates from a given list and to reject those lacking requisite qualifications.

Preferences for Indians

Section 703I of Title VII provides an exception to Title VII's general non-discrimination principles allowing employers under certain circumstances to exercise an employment preference in favor of American Indians. That section provides as follows:

> Nothing contained in this title shall apply to any business or enterprise on or near an Indian reservation with respect to any publicly announced employment practice of such business or enterprise under which preferential treatment is given to any individual because he is an Indian living on or near a reservation.

According to the EEOC an employer seeking to avail itself of the Indian preference exception must meet three conditions: (a) the employer must be located on or near an Indian reservation; (b) the employer's preference for Indians must be publicly announced; and (c) the individual to whom preferential treatment is accorded must be an Indian living on or near a reservation. At the same time, various critical terms within the exception of 703I require clarification. The term "Indian reservation" and "near a reservation" are not defined. The EEOC, however, has indicated that it will define the term "Indian reservation" in accordance with the Indian Financing Act of 1974, which defines reservations to include Indian reservations, public domain Indian allotments, and former Indian reservations in Oklahoma, as well as village corporations under the provisions of the Alaskan Native Claims Settlement Act. Additionally, should a dispute arise as to whether a particular tract of land falls within this definition, the EEOC will present the question to the Bureau of Indian Affairs and will make a determination after considering the conclusions reached by that agency. The EEOC will also accept the definition "near an Indian reservation" that is provided by the Office of Federal Contract Compliance Programs in its regulations. The OFCCP had previously defined the term "near" to include "all that area where a person seeking employment could reasonably be expected to commute to and from in the course of a workday."[13]

According to the EEOC, employment practices for which preferential treatment may be accorded to Indians include hiring, promotion, transfer, and reinstatement, as well as layoffs and reduction in force. The commission has not yet reached a determination whether employment preferences may be afforded American Indians with regard to other terms and conditions of employment, such as compensation, benefits, work assignments, or training.[14]

Affirmative Action and the 1991 Civil Rights Act

It is likely that the 1991 Civil Rights Act will have no effect on the law of affirmative action. Thus, section 116 of the 1991 Act provides: "Nothing in the amendments made by this Title shall be construed to affect court ordered remedies, affirmative action or conciliation agreements that are in accordance with the laws." Section 107 of the Act does make it illegal to make any employment decision in which "race, color, religion, sex or national origin was a motivating factor for any employment practice even though other factors also motivated the practice." This provision overturned the Supreme Court's decision in Price Waterhouse.[15] Under this section an employment practice or decision is rendered unlawful where a motivating factor for its implementation is also the employee's protected minority status. Some concern, however, was expressed that this new section might outlaw affirmative action programs which are in part designed specifically to afford preferences to employees on the basis of race, sex, or national origin. At the same time it is apparent from the legislative history that Congress did not intend in section 107 to affect lawfully established affirmative action plans. Thus, the Edwards memorandum provides:

> It is our clear understanding and intent that this section [107] is not intended to provide an additional method to challenge affirmative action. As section 116 of the legislation makes plain, nothing in this legislation is to be construed to affect court ordered remedies, affirmative action, or conciliation agreements that are otherwise in accordance with the law. This understanding has been clear from the time this legislation was first proposed in 1990, and any suggestion to the contrary is flatly wrong.[16]

Given this legislative history, it is doubtful that parties will be able to challenge affirmative action programs on the basis of section 107. Most recently the Ninth Circuit rejected a contention that section 107 negates a previously ordered affirmative action program.[17]

Impact of Affirmative Action Programs

While the position of minorities and women in the labor market has radically improved since 1965, it is difficult to determine the degree to which such changes are the result of affirmative action. Thus, it is difficult to separate the effects of affirmative action from other social and economic forces improving minority opportunities. For example, improvements in the quality and amount of education attained by minorities have been cited as playing an important role in raising incomes of blacks relative to whites since 1965.[18]

At the same time, there is some evidence that governmentally directed affirmative action programs also contributed significantly to minority employment through the 1970s. The OFCCP reported a substantially higher percentage of minorities and women employed by federal contractors than by non-contractors.[19] Similarly, Leonard found that affirmative action goals do have a measurable and significant correlation with improvements in the employment of minorities and females at reviewed establishments.[20]

Yet for affirmative action programs to be effective key variables must be in place. The federal government must be willing to devote the necessary resources to ensure contractor compliance. In this regard, Leonard has indicated that between 1980 and 1984 male and female minority employment grew more slowly among federal contractors than non-contractors. He notes that during this period staffing and budgets for governmental compliance were reduced.[21] Similarly, within the firm progress will be contingent on the commitment of management personnel at all levels to recruit and employ minorities.

Beyond measuring the effectiveness of affirmative action on minority employment, employers must also be sensitive to its impact on those directly affected. Data suggest that most workers, regardless of race or sex, dislike quotas, presumably because such an approach disregards a worker's qualifications.[22] While quotas are not typically an ingredient of affirmative action and will rarely be implemented unless effected as a result of a court order, many workers may associate affirmative action with them. Generating favorable employer/employee support and cooperation for affirmative action is dependent upon an organization's capacity and willingness to communicate and effect affirmative action programs in which a worker's qualifications remain an indispensable element to the selection of workers and the evaluation of their continued performance. Where workers fully recognize that only qualified workers will be selected and promoted, there will be less likelihood of either racial polarization or minority self-stigmatization, which may arise when workers believe that selection decisions are made not on the basis of a worker's effort, but because of a worker's race or sex.

Questions for discussion

1   Two employees, one black and one white, are caught stealing scrap metal. The white employee is discharged for theft. Sensitive to criticisms that it has made inadequate efforts to employ minorities, the employer decides to only suspend the minority employee for 30 days. Is the employer's conduct lawful? What factors may justify the imposition of disparate penalties upon two employees who have committed the same offense? See *McDonald* v. *Santa Fe Trail Transportation Company*, 427 US 273 (1976).

2   The debate in the United States over affirmative action has continued to intensify. California in 1996 at either the legislative level or in a state-wide referendum will vote to affirm or repeal affirmative action programs. At the federal level, a bill has been introduced in the senate (S. 477) to bar the federal government from requiring or granting preferences in employment on the basis of race, sex, or national origin. See 141 *Congressional Record – US Senate*, no. 40, March 3, 1995, p. 3473. What factors influence continued support or opposition to affirmative action programs?

3   XYZ Company is a tobacco manufacturing facility which employs 100 females and 500 males. It is located in a community where women constitute 40 percent of the labor force. The two major job classifications at XYZ Corporation are industrial chemists and non-skilled production

workers. Women constitute 15 percent of the company's labor force in these two classifications. On January 1, 1995 the plant manager introduces an affirmative action program whereby 35 percent of the job openings are reserved for female workers. All job applicants have to also pass a satisfactory interview. On January 5, 1995 the company advertises ten job openings. There were 20 male and ten female applicants. To promote affirmative action, the plant manager restricted interviews to ten male and ten female applicants. Of the 20 interviewed the plant manager hired eight women and two men. Has the company committed any violations of Title VII?

4 John Doe is a white male psychiatric social worker with ten years' working experience for the City of Dubuque, Idaho (population 50,000, less than 1 percent minority). Desiring to move east, he applies for a social worker position with the City of Highland Park, Michigan (population 25,000, 99 percent minority). The position involves counseling disadvantaged minority youth. During his interview he is informed that he will not be hired because his race and/or background preclude him from being an effective role model for Highland Park's troubled youth. Is Highland Park's employment policy lawful? See *Rucker* v. *Higher Educational Aids Board*, 27 FEP 1553 (7th Circuit, 1982); *Chaline* v. *KCOH, Incorporated*, 30 FEP 834 (5th Circuit, 1982); *EEOC* v. *Kamehameha Schools*, 61 FEP 621 (9th Circuit, 1993).

5 Jane Miller and John Doe are two recent LIR graduates who are applying for the position of human resource specialist at XYZ, Incorporated. They are interviewed by the president, who decides to hire both. Doe is offered a salary of $35,000 per year and Miller is offered a salary of $40,000. Both accept the job offers. Upon discovering the higher salary being paid Miller, Doe approaches the president and asks for equal compensation on the grounds that both are performing the same work. Anderson responds that the higher salary paid Miller is due to the affirmative action effort to employ women professionals and is designed to rectify the previous pattern of female workers' under-utilization. Is the company's salary policy lawful? See *Hein* v. *Oregon College of Education*, 33 FEP, 1538 (9th Circuit, 1983); *Ring Radio*, 24 FEP 776, 1980; *Dawes* v. *University of Nebraska*, 11 FEP 283 (8th Circuit, 1975); and *Ende* v. *Northern Illinois University*, 37 FEP 575 (7th Circuit, 1985).

NOTES

1 President Johnson issued Executive Order 11375 October 13, 1967, extending the coverage of Executive Order 11246 to "expressly embrace discrimination on account of sex."

2 Rehabilitation Act of 1973, section 503, 41 CFR 60-741.

3 The Rehabilitation Act uses the term handicap; the Americans with Disabilities Act of 1990 uses the term disabled. The definitions in the two statutes are virtually identical; only the semantics with regards to "disabled" versus "handicap" have changed.

4 The regulations for section 503 of the Rehabilitation Act and section 402 of the Vietnam-era Veterans Act have similar thresholds for coverage. Fifty employees and a federal contractor or subcontractor of at least $50,000 leads to a requirement for a written affirmative action plan. However, contractors with federal contracts of at least $2,500 are required to take affirmative action with respect to individuals with disabilities under the Rehabilitation Act.

5 41 CFR section 60-2.11(b)(1) and (2).

6 41 FEP 7, 478 US 421 (1986).

7 43 FEP 1, 480 US 147 (1987).

8 34 FEP 1707, 467 US 561 (1984).

9 20 FEP 1, 443 US 193 (1979).

10 36 FEP 153, 746 F.2d 1152 (1984).

11 *Wygant* v. *Board of Education*, 40 FEP 1321, 476 US 267 (1986).

12 43 FEP 411, 480 US 616 (1987).

13 EEOC: Policy Statement on Indian Preference Under Title VII, May 16, 1988, *BNA Fair Employment Practice Manual*, section 405, 6647–51.

14 Ibid., at section 405, 6652–3.

15 49 FEP 954, 490 US 228 (1989).

16 137 Congressional Record 9529, November 7, 1991.

17 *Officers for Justice* v. *Civil Service Commission of the City and County of San Francisco*, 62 FEP 869 (9th Cir. 1992).

18 John J. Donohue, III and James Heckmen, "Continuous versus episodic changes: the impact of civil rights policy on the economic status of blacks," *Journal of Economic Literature*, 29 (December 1991), pp. 1603–44.

19 Cited in D. A. Taylor, "Affirmative action and presidential executive orders," in *Affirmative Action in Perspective*, ed. F. A. Blanchard and F. J. Crosby (Springer-Verlag, New York, 1989), pp. 21–9.

20 Jonathan S. Leonard, "The impact of affirmative action regulation and equal employment law on black employment," *Journal of Economic Perspectives*, 4 (No. 4, Fall 1990), p. 56.

21 Ibid.

22 Susan D. Clayton and Faye J. Crosby, *Justice, Gender and Affirmative Action* (University of Michigan Press, East Lansing, 1992), p. 104.

Part II
Health and Safety

Chapter 8
Occupational Safety and Health

With the enactment of the Occupational Safety and Health Act (OSHA) in 1970, the US Congress fundamentally altered the role of the federal government in protecting the safety and health of working people. Prior to the passage of the OSHA individual states rather than the federal government, except in certain industries, provided limited protection to workers through workers' compensation statutes, factory inspection laws and widows' pension laws. In response to criticism leveled against the effectiveness of this patchwork approach, Congress attempted to create a comprehensive legal framework that would assure safe and healthful working conditions for every working man and woman and would preserve our human resources.[1] In this chapter we will examine the administrative structure and enforcement procedures designed by Congress to address workplace safety and health issues. This chapter will also discuss court decisions that have affected implementation of the OSHA.

Background

The most important factor that led to the enactment of the OSHA was the increase in the rate of industrial accidents. Between 1961 and 1970, the accident rate had increased by 29 percent.[2] When the OSHA was adopted, the National Safety Council estimated that 14,000 workers died each year as a result of industrial accidents and another 2.2 million experienced disabling injuries. The US Department of Health, Education and Welfare (now Health and Human Services) calculated an additional 100,000 deaths per year could be attributed to occupational disease.[3] When a coalmining explosion in Farmington, West Virginia, left 78 miners dead, the Coal Mine Safety and Health Act was enacted and two years later the OSHA was signed by President Richard Nixon.

The primary purpose of the OSHA is to ensure uniformity in the application of safety and health regulations. As adopted, the OSHA applies to any employer engaged in a business affecting commerce, including agriculture. Places of employment covered by other federal statutes are exempt only to the extent that other federal agencies have exerted authority over safety and health in the workplace. For example, the Federal Railroad Administration (FRA) is responsible for protecting the safety and health of rail workers, but the OSHA still covers rail employees who respond to chemical spills because the FRA has not exercised jurisdiction for this subject area.

Under section 19(a) of the OSHA, each federal agency is responsible for establishing and maintaining a comprehensive occupational safety and health program. However, the Occupational Safety and Health Administration (also known as OSHA), which is responsible for enforcing the OSHA has limited authority to ensure total compliance. While federal employees do receive some protection, more than seven million public employees in 27 states are not covered by the OSHA.[4] This includes public employees in states which have not adopted state-administered safety and health legislation.

The Congress created three agencies to administer and enforce the provisions of the OSHA. The Occupational Safety and Health Administration, located within the US Department of Labor, is charged with setting standards, conducting inspections, issuing citations, and assessing penalties. In addition, OSHA is authorized to: establish record keeping requirements for employers; create advisory committees to assist in standards development; conduct research relating to occupational safety and health; provide training, directly or by grants, ensure an adequate supply of personnel to carry out the purposes of the OSHA; and provide information to employers and employees. OSHA is located in ten regional offices, each of which is managed by a regional administrator. Each OSHA region is also divided into areas, managed by area directors. For example, the region 5 office of the Occupational Safety and Health Administration is located in Chicago and covers the states of Michigan, Ohio, Indiana, Illinois, Wisconsin, and Minnesota. The state of Ohio is further divided into areas with offices located in Toledo, Cincinnati, Columbus, and Cleveland. Each area office is responsible for conducting workplace inspections, issuing citations, and providing assistance to employers and employees in the area.

The second agency created by the OSHA is the Occupational Safety and Health Review Commission (OSHRC). The commission was established as an independent board charged with reviewing decisions made by OSHA. Three commission members, appointed by the President, rule on challenges submitted by employers relating to enforcement actions. If an employer formally objects to an action taken by OSHA, the commission appoints a hearing examiner to hear the case. The commission can review the hearing examiner's decision, and the employer can seek a review of the commission's decision in federal court.

The third agency created by the OSHA is the National Institute for Occupational Safety and Health (NIOSH). The principal duties of NIOSH include conducting research and recommending regulatory action to OSHA. In addition, NIOSH assists employers and employees in evaluating health hazards in the workplace, publishes lists of known toxic substances, and promotes training of safety and health professionals.

Occupational Safety and Health Standards

Standards setting process

One of OSHA's primary responsibilities is the promulgation of safety and health standards. Section 6 of the OSHA explains the process that must be followed for standards promulgation. When OSHA was created in 1970, the Secretary of Labor was given the authority to adopt pre-existing national consensus standards immediately in order to expedite the standards setting process. These included standards previously adopted by organizations such as the National Fire Protection Association and the American National Standards Institute. These standards were recognized as representing a national consensus because of the diverse representation of these groups and the substantial agreement that was reached before the standards were adopted.

When OSHA adopts new standards or revises these national consensus standards, the process is considerably more complex. According to section 6(b) of the OSHA the Secretary of Labor may promulgate a standard based on information provided by any interested person, an organization representing employers or employees, the Secretary of Health and Human Services, NIOSH, or any state or political subdivision. The Secretary of Labor then has the authority to appoint an advisory committee, which is charged with developing a recommended standard. After OSHA has reviewed and evaluated the recommendations of the advisory committee, the proposed standard is published in the Federal Register. OSHA must then provide interested parties an opportunity to submit comments on the proposed standard. If any parties object to portions of the standard, OSHA will conduct public hearings to allow for comments from impacted individuals or organizations. After comments have been received and hearings conducted, a final standard is published in the Federal Register. Within 60 days after a standard has been promulgated, any affected person may challenge the validity of the standard with the United States Court of Appeals for the circuit where the person resides or has a principal place of business.[5]

If the Secretary of Labor determines that employees are exposed to a grave danger from exposure to a new hazard, the Secretary may issue a temporary emergency standard.[6] The emergency standard is effective immediately upon being published in the Federal Register. The emergency standard may remain in effect for six months, at which time the Secretary of Labor must promulgate a permanent standard, or the emergency standard will expire.

Case study: standards setting process   In December 1972, the Oil, Chemical and Atomic Workers International Union (OCAW) and the Health Research Group submitted a petition to OSHA requesting that a temporary emergency standard be promulgated to protect employees from exposure to ten cancer-causing chemicals. In April 1973 OSHA had still not acted, so the OCAW filed a complaint in US District Court, District of Columbia, seeking an order directing OSHA to issue the emergency standard.

OSHA finally issued an emergency standard protecting employees from exposure to 14 cancer-causing chemicals in May 1973. In October of that year, as a result of a suit brought by the Chemical Manufacturers' Association, the US Court of Appeals, Third Circuit, struck down standards for two of the chemicals, ruling that OSHA failed to give sufficient reasons for including these two substances in the rule making.

In July 1973, OSHA proposed permanent standards for the 14 carcinogens. In November the OCAW again filed suit requesting OSHA to adopt the permanent standard. The OCAW sought this action because of OSHA's failure to meet the six-month time limit for adopting a permanent standard after the issuance of the emergency standard. In January 1974 OSHA finally published its standards for the 14 carcinogens in the Federal Register. The OCAW sought judicial review of the final standard, arguing that it did not adequately address medical surveillance and air monitoring. The OCAW also protested OSHA's failure to set a zero exposure level for these chemicals. Two industry groups also sought review of the standards. In May 1975 the Third Circuit Court of Appeals upheld the standards for all the cancer-causing chemicals except one, which was vacated on procedural grounds.[7]

Types of safety and health standards

OSHA may promulgate several types of safety and health standards. A specification standard will require employers to use a specific piece of equipment or to design the facility in a specific fashion. For example, railings to protect employees from falls may need to be of an exact height (42 inches) or made of a particular material (3 inch steel tubing). Performance standards, on the other hand, permit a variety of methods for protecting employees. For example, OSHA could require that a guardrail withstand a force of 200 pounds per square inch. In this instance, the employer is responsible for determining the actual method by which this will be accomplished.[8]

Standards are also distinguished according to their application. Vertical standards apply to a particular industry, operation, practice, or process. For example, OSHA has promulgated standards that are specific to sawmill operations. Horizontal standards will apply when a vertical standard is not in effect. The Hazard Communication standard, which requires the labeling of containers of hazardous materials and employee training, applies to a variety of industries, operations, and processes. When a hazard in a particular industry is covered by vertical and horizontal standards, the vertical standard takes precedence, even if the horizontal standard is more stringent.

If an employer believes that employee safety and health can be protected by means other than those required by a permanent or emergency standard, the employer can seek a variance from OSHA. The request for a variance must be in writing and must include a description of the proposed work process or method, a statement regarding the equal level of protection that will be created, and evidence that employees were informed of the application and their right to petition. An employer might seek a variance if an alternative method for protecting employee safety and health was available and was easier or more cost-effective to achieve than that required by the OSHA standard. Employees could petition OSHA for a denial of the variance if they believed the employer's alternative method was not equally protective of employee safety and health.

General duty clause

If a hazardous situation occurs for which OSHA has not promulgated a standard, the employer must still comply with section 5(a), the general duty clause. Under this section, the employer must "furnish to each of his employees employment and a place of employment which are free from recognized hazards that are causing or likely to cause death or serious physical harm to his employees."[9]

In most cases, an employer will be in violation of the general duty clause only if no standard applies to the hazard involved. In addition, all elements described in section 5(a) must be present. OSHA can establish the existence of a "recognized hazard" based on general practice in the industry, based on the employer's own recognition of the hazard, or in special situations based on common sense, meaning that any reasonable person would have recognized the hazard. The elements that will determine whether a hazard is recognized include: statements by industry safety and health experts; manufacturers' warnings on equipment; studies conducted by the industry, the government, or insurance carriers; written or oral statements made by the employer; company memorandums, safety rules, or operating manuals; employee complaints or grievances to supervisory personnel; or corrective actions taken by employers that are not completed or maintained.

If an actual death or serious injury results from exposure to a recognized hazard, the employer would be in violation of the general duty clause. However, the employer could also be in violation if no death or serious injury occurred. This situation would arise if OSHA determined that in the event of an accident caused by the hazard, the likely result would be death or serious physical harm. Finally, in order for OSHA to find a violation of the general duty clause, a feasible and useful method to correct the hazard must be available. An employer will not be liable for a violation of the general duty clause if the hazard was created by unauthorized or disobedient actions by employees that could have been prevented by reasonable employee supervision.[10]

The general duty clause is not normally used to impose stricter requirements than those mandated by a standard. However, if an employer knows that a particular standard is inadequate to protect employees against a specific hazard, OSHA may find a violation of the general duty clause if protective action is not taken.

Case study: general duty clause In April 1987, the US Court of Appeals for the District of Columbia ruled that an employer could be in violation of the general duty clause regardless of compliance with an existing standard. The case involved General Dynamics employees who used freon as a solvent to clean up oil spills in the manufacture of M-1 Abrams tanks. Freon is heavier than air and in high concentrations may cause cardiac arrhythmia and even arrest. In cleaning up hydraulic oil spills, employees would dump gallons of the solvent into the tank hull, where it would evaporate or exit through a drain on the floor. When employees performed this procedure, General Dynamics required the tank hulls to be ventilated.

From August 1982 through September 1983 three employees became ill when using the freon. One employee experienced dizziness and weakness; another lost consciousness; and a third was discovered inside a tank shaking and foaming from the mouth. In November 1983 an employee at another General Dynamics plant died from exposure to freon. As a result of a complaint from the international union, United Automobile, Aerospace and Agricultural Implement Workers of America (UAW), OSHA conducted an investigation of the first three incidents and cited General Dynamics for violations of the general duty clause and of OSHA's specific standard on employee exposure to freon. General Dynamics contested the citation, and the administrative law judge ruled that the violation of the general duty clause was inappropriate and must be vacated because the alleged hazard is addressed by a specific standard.[11] The judge also ruled that OSHA failed to prove a violation of the specific standard on freon.

The Court of Appeals reversed and found that section 5(a)(1) "clearly and unambiguously imposes on an employer a general duty to provide for the safety of his employees that is distinct and separate from the employer's duty, under section 5(a)(2), to comply with administrative safety standards promulgated under section 6 of the Act."[12] The court continued, "In sum, if an employer knows that a specific standard will not protect his workers against a particular hazard, his duty under section 5(a)(1) will not be discharged no matter how faithfully he observes that standard."[13] At the same time, the court stipulated that an employer could rely on compliance with a specific standard in the absence of any knowledge regarding the standard's ineffectiveness. In addition, this case involved the use of freon in a confined space. This created a hazard that is not addressed by the standard, which limits the amount of freon exposure in the general work environment. In some cases, then, the employer must comply with the general duty clause even if a specific standard may address the same subject.

Feasibility

When promulgating standards dealing with toxic materials or harmful physical agents, section 6 of the Act requires OSHA to "set the standard which most adequately assures, to the extent feasible, on the basis of the best available evidence, that no employee will suffer material impairment of health or functional capacity even if such employee has regular exposure to the hazard dealt with by such standard for the period of his working life."[14]

In determining whether a proposed standard is feasible, OSHA considers two separate issues – technical and economic feasibility. Technical feasibility pertains to the existence of materials and methods that could be utilized to comply with the new standard. Economic feasibility is determined by assessing the financial ability of impacted employers to comply with citations that might be received using the new standard. The US Supreme Court addressed OSHA's responsibilities regarding this feasibility test in *American Textile Manufacturers Institute* v. *Donovan in* 1981.

Case study: feasibility In 1978 the Secretary of Labor promulgated a standard limiting exposure to cotton dust in the workplace. The American Textile Manufacturers filed suit, arguing that OSHA failed to demonstrate a reasonable relationship between the costs and benefits associated with the standard.

OSHA developed the cotton dust standard with the assistance of a NIOSH recommendation and as a result of three public hearings lasting over 14 days, 263 written comments, and 109 notices of intent to appear at the hearings.[15] On the basis of the evidence presented, the Secretary of Labor determined that cotton dust exposure represented a significant health risk to employees.

In enacting this standard, OSHA interpreted the Act to require the most protective health requirements, limited only by technical and economic feasibility. Although OSHA did not determine whether the costs of implementing the standard were justified by the benefits, the agency did analyze whether it was economically feasible for the cotton industry to bear this cost. OSHA decided that "although some marginal employers may shut down rather than comply, the industry as a whole will not be threatened by the capital requirements of the regulation."[16]

The Supreme Court affirmed the decision of the Appeals Court in this case and ruled that "Congress itself defined the basic relationship between costs and benefits, by placing the 'benefit' of worker health above all other considerations save those making attainment of this 'benefit' unachievable."[17] In short, cost–benefit analysis is not required by the Act because feasibility is required. In deciding this case the Supreme Court recognized that Congress did not intend to achieve absolute safety and health with the passage of the OSHA. Safety and health must be achieved within the realm of technical and economic feasibility.

Case study: health standards   In a more recent case, the US Court of Appeals for the Eleventh Circuit has defined more precisely OSHA's responsibilities in setting health standards. In 1988 OSHA proposed to issue new or revised permissible exposure limits (PEL) for over 400 substances. The PELs, originally promulgated in 1971, were designed to limit employee exposure to chemicals or toxic substances that can cause harm by being breathed into the lungs or absorbed through the skin. Because the original PELs had undergone little or no revision, OSHA hoped in its 1988 rule making to lower existing PELs and create PELs for new substances. The AFL-CIO and several companies filed challenges to the final standard in numerous US Courts of Appeals.

The Eleventh Circuit found nothing in the OSHA to prevent OSHA from addressing multiple substances in a single rule making. Nor did the Court disagree with OSHA's assessment that health effects caused by exposure to these substances are material impairments. However, OSHA's determination of significant risk and feasibility failed to pass judicial scrutiny.

In the first instance, the court ruled that OSHA has a responsibility to "quantify or explain, at least to some reasonable degree, the risk posed by each toxic substance regulated."[18] Since OSHA failed to make this determination, the court could not evaluate the seriousness of the risk posed by any one substance. Second, the court rejected OSHA's feasibility analysis regarding this generic rule making. In order to support a finding of technological feasibility, OSHA must demonstrate that strategies or devices are available which could be utilized to lower the permissible exposure limit for substances being regulated. This must be demonstrated for specific exposure standards in specific industries, and OSHA failed to make this showing.[19]

On the subject of economic feasibility, OSHA also proved unequal to the task. Although OSHA attempted to demonstrate economic feasibility by industrial sector, the court rejected this approach, asserting that substantial evidence of economic feasibility must be demonstrated for affected industries separately, not by aggregate. Furthermore, OSHA never justified the use of its industrial sector approach. The court reasoned that studying the economic impact for an entire industrial sector could disguise financial hardships experienced by a specific industry within that sector.

In its conclusion, the court criticized OSHA for exceeding its statutory authority to set health standards. At the same time the court recognized OSHA's good intentions and its inability to adopt standards that protect workers' health in a timely fashion. Rather than using a generic approach that does not comply with the statute, the court recommended that OSHA seek authorization from Congress by amending the OSHA itself.[20]

Enforcement Procedures

Section 8 of the Act provides OSHA with the authority necessary to ensure compliance with the various safety and health standards. By this authority,

OSHA may enter without delay and at reasonable times any workplace in order to inspect and investigate conditions pertaining to the safety and health of employees.

Types of inspections

OSHA conducts two major types of inspections – programmed and unprogrammed. Programmed inspections include those which have been scheduled in advance for the purpose of accomplishing certain objectives, such as reducing injuries in high risk industries. Because of limited staffing, OSHA must direct its priorities, and conducting programmed inspections in high hazard sectors of employment, such as construction or logging, is one way to accomplish that objective. Unprogrammed inspections are those scheduled as a result of hazardous conditions identified at specific worksites. These include situations reported as imminent dangers, reported fatalities, employee complaints, and referrals from other agencies.

Imminent dangers include those situations in which an employee or employees face(s) death or serious physical harm. They represent OSHA's highest inspection priority. However, in order for a condition to be considered an imminent danger, the threat must be immediate. In these cases, OSHA makes every attempt to inspect the imminent danger in an expeditious fashion. If OSHA cannot conduct an immediate inspection, the employer is notified and an attempt is made to have the employees removed from the dangerous situation. A more in-depth discussion of imminent danger will be presented later in this chapter.

OSHA's second highest inspection priority includes those cases in which a fatality has occurred or in which five or more employees have been hospitalized. This is followed by investigations of complaints and referrals and then by programmed inspections. OSHA also conducts follow-up investigations, which are intended to determine whether previous violations have been corrected.

Under section 8(f) of the OSHA, employees or employee representatives who believe standards violations are occurring or imminent danger exists may request OSHA to conduct an inspection. The request must be in writing, and it must specify the reasons why the request is being made. The request also must be signed by the employees or representative of employees. A copy of this complaint will be provided by OSHA to the employer; however, if the employees so specify, their names will be removed from the complaint in order to maintain their anonymity. This requirement is designed to protect employees from employer retaliation.

Preparation for the inspection

Before conducting an inspection, the Compliance Safety and Health Officer (CSHO) must prepare for the assignment by reviewing data on the place of employment scheduled for inspection. The CSHO must be knowledgeable of the potential hazards that may exist, violations that have been discovered in the past, and equipment, such as air monitoring devices, that may be necessary for conducting the inspection. The inspection is normally conducted during regular business hours except when special circumstances dictate otherwise. For example, the hazard may only occur on an evening shift. Before the inspection, the CSHO attempts to locate the owner or person in charge and presents his or her credentials. The CSHO will also ask to examine injury and illness statistics the employer is required to keep. Prior to entry, the employer is permitted to demand an inspection warrant. This particular employer right was established in *Marshall* v. *Barlow's, Inc.*, decided by the US Supreme Court in 1978.

Case study: search warrants   In 1975 an OSHA compliance officer entered Barlow's, Inc., an electrical and plumbing installation business in Pocatello, Idaho. Mr Barlow asked if a complaint had been lodged against his company, and the CSHO indicated that the firm had been chosen using OSHA's programmed inspection selection process. Barlow asked if the CSHO had a search warrant, and when he discovered no search warrant had been secured, Barlow refused to allow the inspector to enter the employee area of the business.

Three months later the Secretary of Labor petitioned the US District Court to issue an order compelling Barlow to permit the inspector to enter. Barlow refused and instead sought his own injunctive relief against the warrantless search.

The Secretary of Labor argued that some industries have such a history of government oversight that no reasonable expectation of privacy exists. In addition the Secretary urged that "warrantless inspections are essential to the proper enforcement of OSHA because they afford the opportunity to inspect without prior notice and hence to preserve the advantages of surprise."[21]

The Court disagreed with this rationale and instead ruled that OSHA could easily obtain the necessary warrant by providing evidence of an existing violation or by explaining the process by which certain employers are designated for inspection based on the types of hazards that may be expected. The court continued by stressing the importance of the warrant in advising the employer of the "scope and objects of the search, beyond which limits the inspector is not expected to proceed."[22] In general the court upheld the necessity of obtaining a warrant in order to establish the search as reasonable.

Since this decision was handed down, OSHA has sought and obtained search warrants to enter places of employment. In fact, OSHA's Field Operations Manual directs CSHOs to seek a warrant prior to the inspection if the CSHO has reason to believe the employer will demand one.

The inspection tour

The compliance officer or any other person is prohibited from giving an employer advance notice regarding the conduct of an inspection. This prohibition is designed to ensure the element of surprise and to prevent the employer from altering or disguising hazardous conditions. However, advance notice may be given in the following circumstances: (a) in cases of apparent imminent danger so the employer can correct the situation as soon as possible; (b) when the inspection can be most effectively conducted after business hours; (c) to ensure the presence of employer or employee representatives; and (d) when the area director determines that it would enhance the effectiveness of an inspection, for example when a complex fatality has occurred.

Before conducting the inspection tour or walkaround of the workplace, the CSHO must give the employer and employees an opportunity to select a representative to participate in the inspection. Anyone designated to represent the employer is acceptable, but determining the employee representative may present more of a challenge.

If the employees are represented by a certified or recognized bargaining agent, the CSHO will ask the employer to contact the designated employee representative promptly and that individual will be given an opportunity to participate fully in the inspection.[23] If employees are not represented by a bargaining agent, the compliance officer may designate an employee member of a safety and health committee who has been designated by other employees or an individual selected by employees as the walkaround representative for that facility. Most importantly, the employee representative must be selected by employees and not the employer. If no authorized representative is present, the CSHO must consult with a reasonable number of employees during the inspection tour.[24] If an employer refuses to accept or interferes with the employee's right to participate in the inspection and the resistance by the employer is continuous, the CSHO will construe the employer's actions as constituting a refusal to permit an inspection.[25] If more than one employer is present at a site, such as a construction job, more than one employer and employee representative may be present for different phases of the inspection. The compliance officer is responsible for determining who will participate in the inspection and may deny the right to accompany to anyone whose conduct interferes with a full and orderly inspection.

Before the actual inspection takes place, the CSHO conducts an opening conference for those who will be participating. At this point the CSHO outlines the scope of the inspection that is about to take place. OSHA has advised its compliance officers to keep this meeting as brief as possible, so it should not exceed one hour. Wherever practical, the opening conference will be joint, unless either party chooses to have a separate conference.

After the opening conference, the CSHO conducts a walkaround inspection of the workplace. The main purpose of the walkaround is to identify potential hazards. In order to be effective, the CSHO must be familiar with workplace processes, must evaluate the employer's safety and health program, must identify conditions that were previously considered to be in violation, and must record all facts that are pertinent to the investigation. The OSHA Field Operations Manual advises compliance officers that a free and open exchange of information with employees is also an essential ingredient of an effective inspection.[26]

During the walkaround, the CSHO may take photographs and may videotape if necessary. However, under section 15 of the OSHA the inspector must ensure the confidentiality of any trade secret information. As stated previously, the inspector may consult with employees privately at any time during the investigation. If an employee requests the presence of an employee representative during the interview, the CSHO is required to make every reasonable effort to honor such a request. During these interviews or at any time during the inspection, employees or their representatives may notify the inspector in writing of any violations of the OSHA which may exist in the workplace.[27] The CSHO is then obligated to investigate these specific complaints.

At the conclusion of the walkaround, the CSHO conducts a closing conference with representatives from the employer and employees. As with the opening conference, the closing conference is joint whenever practical, but either party may request a separate conference. The CSHO describes apparent violations, advises both sides of their right to participate in any subsequent conferences or meetings, and outlines the strengths and weaknesses of the employer's safety and health program. Because environmental sampling results may need further analysis, the CSHO can discuss these at a later date by phone or in person.

If a violation is discovered, a citation will be issued to the employer. The citation lists the violation, a date for abating the hazard, and penalties that have been assessed. The citation must be posted at or near where the violation occurred so that employees will be informed of the hazard. The citation must remain posted for three working days or until the violation is corrected, whichever is longer.

The CSHO must inform the employer of the right to contest the citation. If the employer chooses to contest, he or she must notify the area director in writing within 15 working days after receipt of the citation and penalty. If the employer does not contest the citation, the citation becomes a final order, and hazardous conditions must be abated and penalties paid. If the employer does contest a citation, he or she must also inform the employee representative of this fact. The employee representative may then choose to participate fully in future actions related to the citation, such as meetings with OSHA. This is referred to as electing party status. The employer may contest the item cited, the penalty assessed, or the abatement date. Any uncontested items must be corrected. The employees may contest the abatement date only, but in this case the original date remains in effect.

OSHA will attempt to resolve any disputes informally with the employer and employees; however, a properly filed contest will ultimately be forwarded to the Occupational Safety and Health Review Commission. If an employee organization has requested party status, OSHA may not conduct hearings or reach a settlement agreement with the employer unless the authorized employee representative has been given an opportunity to participate. In a case involving American Airlines, Inc., the Review Commission reversed an agreement reached between a hearing judge and the employer because the settlement was not served on the union prior to acceptance by the hearing judge.[28]

If the employer does not contest a citation, he or she must notify the OSHA area director when conditions have been corrected. The failure to report this information may trigger a follow-up inspection. The date for correcting the hazard, referred to as the abatement date, will be the shortest period of time required for the employer to effectuate necessary changes in a reasonable manner.

The abatement date determined by OSHA will be a specific date rather than a number of days. The date itself will be determined based on information collected during the inspection. The abatement period will normally be less than 30 calendar days, particularly for safety hazards that are easy to correct. If the employer is granted more than 30 days, justification must be provided in writing in the case file. An abatement of more than one year will not be granted without the prior approval of OSHA's regional administrator. If the employer contests the abatement date, the abatement period does not begin until final resolution of the contest.

OSHA will inspect workplaces regardless of a strike or other labor dispute, between a union and employer or between two unions competing for bargaining rights. OSHA will investigate the seriousness and reliability of a complaint in such a situation in an effort to ensure the complaint reflects a good faith belief that a hazard exists. OSHA may not conduct an inspection if the complaint is simply being used to harass an employer. Finally, the OSHA prohibits forcible conduct against a compliance officer and forbids threats of any action that limit the CSHO's freedom of action or choice.

Violations

One of several types of violations may be listed on the citation. An other-than-serious violation is one where the accident or illness that would most likely result from a hazardous condition would probably not cause death or serious physical harm but would have a direct or immediate relationship to the safety and health of employees. On the other hand, a serious violation will be issued if there is a substantial probability that death or serious physical harm could result from an exposure to a condition that violates the OSHA. Injuries that would provoke a serious violation include amputations, concussions, fractures, burns, or lacerations. If an employee experienced illnesses such as cancer, lung disease, poisoning, or hearing loss, OSHA would also cite the employer for a serious violation.

A willful violation occurs when the employer intentionally violates the OSHA or demonstrates indifference to the requirements of the Act. For example, when officials of the employer were aware of an OSHA requirement but made little or no effort to notify lower level supervision or employees, OSHA found a willful violation.[29] If the willful violation results in the death of an employee, the employer is subject to a criminal penalty that may include imprisonment of not more than six months, a fine of $10,000, or both. Criminal penalties are restricted to situations where the employer violated an OSHA standard and does not encompass violations of the general duty clause. OSHA may also seek criminal penalties for individuals who give advance notice of an OSHA inspection or who knowingly make false statements or supply false documents to OSHA.

OSHA may cite an employer for a repeated violation if the employer was cited previously for a substantially similar condition and the citation has become a final order. A repeated violation must be issued within three years of the final order of a previous citation or final abatement date, whichever is later. A failure to abate citation will be issued by OSHA when the item previously cited has never been fixed.

As previously mentioned, OSHA's area directors have the authority to reach settlements with employers regarding citations that have been issued. These informal conferences are intended to expedite the correction of hazardous situations and to provide a forum for resolving disputes among OSHA, employers and employees. The informal conference may occur before the employer contests a citation and before the case goes to the Occupational Safety and Health Review Commission. If the authorized employee representative has elected party status, OSHA must include him or her in any informal settlement. This will ensure that all sides of any controversy are fairly represented.

The employer may advance several defenses in responding to an OSHA citation. The employer may present the following arguments: (a) the violation could not be avoided because of unpreventable employee misconduct; (b) compliance with the OSHA requirement was functionally impossible or would prevent performance of required work, and no alternative means of protection are available; and (c) compliance with the standard in question would create a greater hazard than non-compliance. When arguing that employee misconduct was responsible for the violation, the employer must be prepared to document the existence of work rules that were communicated to employees and that the rules were enforced. If an error has occurred in issuing the citation, the area director may amend or withdraw the citation. If a citation is amended, the amendment must be attached to the original citation and posted in the workplace. If the citation is withdrawn, a copy of the letter withdrawing the citation must be provided to the authorized employee representative.

Penalties

OSHA's penalty structure is intended to create an incentive for correcting violations voluntarily, not only for employers found in violation of the Act, but for others who may be guilty but have not yet been inspected. The penalties are not intended to inflict punishment or to serve as a source of revenue, but the amounts must be sufficient to serve as a deterrent.[30]

The maximum fine for a serious or other-than-serious violation is $7,000. For a willful or repeat violation, the maximum fine OSHA may impose is $70,000. For repeat violations, the penalty may be multiplied by a factor ranging from two to ten based on the size of the employer and the history of previous citations. In a 1986 case OSHA implemented a new policy regarding the use of penalties. For especially flagrant violations, the policy permits OSHA to assess penalties for each violation, rather than grouping them together.[31] Although OSHA does not utilize this policy often, it has been used as a deterrent because fines can be increased dramatically.

If a willful violation results in the death of an employee, the fine is not more than $10,000 for the first offense and not more than $20,000 for a second offense. A minimum fine of $5,000 must be assessed for a willful violation. If OSHA has cited an employer for failing to abate a hazard, the fine may be as high as $7,000 for each calendar day the hazard is not corrected.

The actual amount of the penalty will be based on the gravity of the violation and various reduction factors. OSHA determines the gravity of the violation by examining the severity of the injury or illness that could or did result and the probability that an injury or illness could occur. OSHA will reduce penalties based on the size of the business, good faith efforts by the employer, and the history of past violations. In general the ability to pay is not considered unless the employer presents convincing evidence of financial difficulties.

OSHA may reduce penalties by up to: 60 percent for business with one to 25 employees; 40 percent for employers with 26 to 100 employees; and 20 percent for establishments that have 101 to 250 employees. OSHA will not reduce penalties based on size for employers with over 250 employees. Good faith efforts by the employer, as documented by a written safety and health program that is effectively implemented, may result in reductions of 25 percent from OSHA. This written program should provide evidence of the following: management commitment to safety and health; employee involvement in decision making; worksite analysis that is utilized to identify hazards; hazard prevention and control; and safety and health training. OSHA will reduce a penalty by up to 15 percent if the employer has a documentable and effective safety and health program but OSHA has identified incidental deficiencies. Finally, a 10 percent reduction is available to employers who have not been cited by OSHA for any serious, willful, or repeat violations in the past three years.[32] For willful or repeat violations, OSHA will only apply the reduction factor based on size of the firm.

Record Keeping

Section 8(c) of the OSHA empowers the Secretary of Health and Human Services and the Secretary of Labor to promulgate regulations requiring employers to maintain records relating to workplace injuries and illnesses. The two most significant regulations can be found at 29 Code of Federal Regulations Part 1904 (Recording and Reporting Occupational Injuries and Illnesses) and 29 CFR Section 1910.20 (Access to Employee Exposure and Medical Records).

Recording and reporting occupational injuries and illnesses

Employers are required to keep records pertaining to injuries and illnesses in order to ensure proper enforcement, to develop information regarding the causes and prevention of injuries and illnesses, and to maintain a program of collection, compilation, and analysis of safety and health statistics.[33]

Employers covered by the regulation are required to maintain a log and summary of all recordable injuries and illnesses. Recordable injuries and illnesses include the following: (a) fatalities, regardless of the time between the injury and death, or the length of the illness; (b) lost workday cases, other than fatalities; and (c) non-fatal cases without lost workdays which result in transfer to another job or termination of employment, or which require medical treatment other than first aid, or which involve loss of consciousness or restriction of work or motion. Occupational illnesses reported to the employer but which are not classified as fatalities or lost workday cases are also included.[34] For further clarification, the OSHA defines lost workday as any day in which the employee cannot perform all or any part of his or her normal assignment during all or any part of the workday or shift.

The employer must enter each recordable injury or illness on the log and summary no later than six working days after receiving information that an injury or illness has occurred. OSHA provides a form for recording this information, which is referred to as OSHA No. 200. The annual summary of each recordable injury and illness must be completed and posted by February 1 of each year and must cover incidents for the previous calendar year. The summary must remain posted in a conspicuous location until March 1. Failure to maintain the log or post the summary may result in an OSHA citation. In addition to the log and summary, each employer must maintain a supplementary record for each recordable case. This record provides detailed information regarding the specific incident. OSHA refers to the supplemental record as Form OSHA No. 101.

In the event of an employee fatality or an accident that results in the hospitalization of five or more employees, the employer must report the accident orally or in writing to the nearest OSHA area office. In the report the employer must indicate the circumstances of the accident, the number of fatalities, and the extent of any injuries. The area director may require the employer to provide additional information as is deemed necessary.

The employer must provide access to the log, summary and supplemental record to any representative from OSHA, from Health and Human Services, or a representative from a state which administers its own safety and health legislation. The employer must also make the log and summary available upon request to employees, former employees, and their representatives. The employer is not required to provide copies of the records free of charge, but the records must be made available for examination and copying in a reasonable manner and at reasonable times. The employer would be in violation of the regulation if access to the records were restricted to times or places that would discourage employee access. The regulation makes clear that employees and their representatives may bargain collectively for access to employer information that exceeds the requirements of the regulation.[35]

Several categories of employers are exempt from these record keeping requirements. An employer who has had no more than ten employees at any time during the previous calendar year need not comply. However, the small employer must still report fatalities or multiple hospitalization accidents and must maintain the log and summary if requested to do so by the Bureau of Labor Statistics (BLS). The BLS may make such a request as part of a statistical survey. In addition to small employers, employers in the following Standard Industrial Classification Codes are exempt from record keeping requirements: SICs 55–69 (retail trade); SICs 60–67 (finance, insurance, real estate); and SICs 71–74, 77–78, and 81–89 (business services). As with small employers, this group must report fatalities and multiple hospitalizations and must maintain a log and summary if requested to do so by the BLS.

Any employer covered by the regulation may petition the Regional Commissioner of the Bureau of Labor Statistics to maintain these records in a different manner than that required by OSHA. In making this request, the employer must indicate why relief is necessary, and a description of the proposed record keeping procedures must be provided.

Case study: falsification of injury reports In 1987 OSHA issued a series of willful violations against employers for falsifying injury and illness records. The most prominent case involved a Chrysler facility in Belvidere, Illinois; however, citations were also levied against Ford Motor Company, Caterpillar, American Motors, Volkswagen, USX, Shell Oil, and Union Carbide.

The most frequent violations cited by OSHA included: instances where workers' compensation claims were paid and not recorded on the OSHA log; cases where employees were assigned light-duty positions which were later classified as injuries without lost workdays; and injuries in which employees received medical treatment, as defined by the OSHA, that were classified as first aid by the employer.[36]

Chrysler Corporation agreed to several measures in an effort to abate violations of the record keeping requirements. As part of its settlement with OSHA, Chrysler agreed to the following: (a) each patient visiting the plant medical facility to report injuries or illnesses will be asked if the condition is caused or aggravated by work and responses will be recorded; (b) workers' compensation claims that are filed will be entered on the OSHA log pending final determination; (c) medical staff and safety personnel will investigate any claims for sickness and accident insurance in which occupational causation is claimed; (d) medical restrictions or job transfers resulting from alleged work-related injuries or illnesses will be entered on the log pending final determination; (e) if a case is removed from the log, the reasons will be documented and a record of the investigation maintained; and (f) all personnel responsible for investigating injury and illness reports or maintaining records will receive training in Bureau of Labor Statistics guidelines. This agreement with Chrysler became a model used by OSHA for abating similar record keeping violations.[37]

Access to employee exposure and medical records

Under 29 CFR 1910.20, the OSHA requires employers to provide their employees, employee representatives, health professionals, and OSHA with access to exposure and medical records the employer has on file. As stated in the regulation, access is intended to "yield both direct and indirect improvements in the detection, treatment, and prevention of occupational disease."[38] The regulation applies to employers in general industry, maritime, and construction who make, maintain, contract for, or have access to employee exposure or medical records. The regulation does not require employers to create employee exposure and medical records in the absence of other regulations. However, any records that are kept on file, legally or voluntarily, must be made available to employees and others.

An employee exposure record includes: (a) environmental monitoring or measuring, such as results from air sampling conducted to detect the presence of toxic materials; (b) biological monitoring results, such as tests conducted to determine the level of chemicals in an employee's urine or blood; (c) material safety data sheets, which provide hazard information on products used in the workplace; and (d) any other record, such as chemical inventories, that reveals the identity of a toxic substance or harmful physical agent.

An employee medical record includes: (a) medical and employment questionnaires and histories; (b) the results of medical examinations; (c) medical opinions, diagnoses, progress notes, and recommendations; (d) descriptions of treatments and prescriptions; and (e) employee medical complaints. Medical records do not include physical specimens, health insurance claims maintained separately, or records concerning voluntary employee assistance programs, such as those related to drug and alcohol abuse.

The employer must make exposure and medical records, as well as analyses of these records, available to current and former employees, employees who are being transferred to work involving exposure to toxic substances, and designated employee representatives. The employer must provide access no later than 15 days after the request for access is made. The employer can provide access in one of the following ways: (a) provide a copy of the record without cost; (b) make the necessary copying facilities available and allow photocopying of the records without charge; or (c) loan the record to the requesting party for a reasonable time to enable copies to be made. In the case of an original X-ray, the employer may restrict access to onsite examination or temporary loan of the X-ray. After an employee or others have received one copy of a record without cost, the employer may charge a reasonable administrative fee for providing additional copies. If new information is added to the record, a copy of this new material must be provided without charge. For OSHA representatives, the employer must provide immediate access to exposure and medical records.

For employee representatives, the rules of access regarding exposure records are identical to those for employees, except that requests for uncontested access must specify the records to be disclosed and the occupational health need for gaining access. For medical records, the employee representative may gain access to information only after receiving specific written consent from the employee. In the appendix to the regulation, the OSHA provides a sample form which can be used to establish this consent. As with the regulation pertaining to record keeping of occupational injuries and illnesses, employees and bargaining agents may gain access to additional information through collective bargaining. For example, some employers have agreed to provide copies of employee death certificates, which have been used by labor organizations to research the causes of workplace diseases.[39]

When providing access to exposure and medical records, the employer may delete any trade secret data that disclose manufacturing processes or the percentage of a chemical substance in a mixture. The employer must notify the employee or employee representative if such information has been withheld. The employer may also withhold the specific chemical identity of a substance provided that: (a) the information withheld is a legitimate trade secret; (b) all other information on the properties and effects of the substance is provided; (c) the employer notifies the requesting party that the specific chemical identity is being withheld; and (d) the specific identify is provided to health professionals. The employer must immediately disclose the specific chemical identity to a treating physician or nurse if the health professional determines that a medical emergency exists and the specific identify is necessary for emergency or first-aid treatment. In non-emergencies, health professionals may gain access to trade secret identities provided the request is in writing and as long as the health professional adheres to other stipulations in the regulation.[40]

Under the regulation, the employer is responsible for informing employees of the existence, location, and availability of such records, the person responsible for maintaining the records, and the employee's rights of access. This information must be provided initially and annually thereafter.

The employer must maintain exposure records for 30 years and medical records for the duration of employment plus 30 years. Preservation of records is critical because occupational diseases may not be manifested until many years after the employee has retired or transferred to another job. If the employer ceases to do business, the records must be transferred to the successor employer. If no successor employer exists, the employer must transfer the records to the NIOSH or notify the director of the NIOSH in writing of the impending disposal of the records at least three months in advance.

Discrimination

Section 11(c) of the OSHA prohibits employers from discharging or discriminating against any employee who exercises his or her rights under the act. Section 11(c)(1) states: "No person shall discharge or in any manner discriminate against any employee because such employee has filed any complaint or instituted or caused to be instituted any proceeding under or related to this Act or has testified or is about to testify in any such proceeding or because of the exercise by such employee on behalf of himself or others of any right afforded by this Act."[41]

In an effort to interpret section 11(c), OSHA adopted a regulation in 1973. In the regulation OSHA emphasizes the importance of protection against discrimination by asserting that "effective implementation of the Act and achievement of its goals depend in large part upon the active but orderly participation of employees, individually and through their representatives, at every level of safety and health activity."[42] Clearly, without protection from discrimination, employees would be reluctant to raise concerns about workplace safety and health or to request OSHA to enforce its standards and regulations.

Persons prohibited from discriminating and protected classes

According to the OSHA, those prohibited from discriminating against employees include any individuals or groups. In addition to the employer of the employee, this broad category includes other employers, labor organizations, employment agencies, or anyone who is capable of taking discriminatory action. Those protected by section 11(c) include all employees, as defined by the OSHA. This may include job applicants, if they are currently employed elsewhere, and others who are employees at the time they are engaging in protected activities. Employees of states or their political subdivisions would not be covered by section 11(c), but may be protected by anti-discriminatory legislation enacted at the state level (see discussion of state OSHA plans).

Protected activities

Several employee activities fall under the coverage of section 11(c). An employee who suffers discharge or discrimination for filing "any complaint" is protected. This includes complaints to OSHA, as well as complaints filed with other federal or state agencies that regulate occupational safety and health. In order to be protected, the employee's complaint must be related to conditions in the workplace, not simply those touching upon general public safety and health. Protected activity also includes filing a complaint with the employer, if it is made in good faith.[43]

Other protected activities include requesting an OSHA inspection of the workplace, contesting an abatement date included in an OSHA citation, initiating the creation of a new OSHA standard, applying for modification or revocation of a variance granted to the employer by OSHA, challenging an OSHA standard, or appealing an order of the Occupational Safety and Health Review Commission. Employees who refuse to comply with OSHA

standards or valid safety rules implemented by the employer are not protected from discipline. This exception, however, does not pertain to situations in which an employee refuses to perform a dangerous assignment.

Refusing dangerous work

OSHA recognizes in its explanatory regulation that the Act does not afford
employees the right to walk off the job because of unsafe conditions. However, OSHA does list a special circumstance in which an employee may
refuse to perform a dangerous job. The regulation states at 29 CFR section
1977.12(2):

> However, occasions might arise when an employee is confronted with a choice
> between not performing assigned tasks or subjecting himself to serious injury
> or death arising from a hazardous condition at the workplace. If the employee,
> with no reasonable alternative, refuses in good faith to expose himself to the
> dangerous condition, he would be protected against subsequent discrimina-
> tion. The condition causing the employee's apprehension of death or injury
> must be of such a nature that a reasonable person, under the circumstances
> then confronting the employee, would conclude that there is a real danger of
> death or serious injury and that there is insufficient time, due to the urgency
> of the situation, to eliminate the danger through resort to regular statutory
> enforcement channels. In addition, in such circumstances, the employee, where
> possible, must also have sought from his employer, and been unable to obtain,
> a correction of the dangerous condition.

Case study: the right to refuse   The validity of OSHA's regulation granting
employees the right to refuse certain dangerous work assignments was tested
in *Whirlpool Corporation* v. *Marshall*, decided by the US Supreme Court in
1980. In this case employees at a Whirlpool plant in Marion, Ohio, had
refused to perform maintenance work on a screen below a conveyor. The
screen was suspended above the plant floor and was designed to catch
parts that fell off the conveyor system. It was necessary for employees
working on the conveyor to stand on the screen.

Prior to the refusal in question, several employees had fallen through the
screen when it collapsed underneath them. In addition a maintenance worker
fell to his death when a section of the screen gave way while he was
retrieving parts. Employees at the plant had complained about the unsafe
conditions related to the screen before and after these incidents occurred.
In response, the employer began replacing older sections of the screen.
However, when two employees refused to perform maintenance work while
standing on an older section of the screen, the employer ordered them to
leave work, they were docked six hours' pay, and both were given written
reprimands.

When the employees complained to OSHA, the agency brought action in
federal district court, alleging that the employer had violated section 11(c)
of the Act by issuing the written reprimands and refusing to pay the
employees for the six hours of lost pay. Whirlpool argued that OSHA

exceeded its authority in promulgating the regulation because the Act itself did not grant employees the right to refuse. Despite this argument, the Supreme Court ruled that OSHA's regulation "clearly conforms to the fundamental objective of the Act – to prevent occupational deaths and serious injuries."[44] The Court reasoned that the preventive nature of the legislation compelled a finding in support of an employee who, with no other alternative, withdraws from a workplace environment that he or she reasonably believes is highly dangerous.[45]

In refusal cases the burden is on the employee to demonstrate the presence of the conditions outlined in the regulation. In order for the refusal to be protected, the employee must demonstrate the following: (a) the employee had a reasonable apprehension under the circumstances that the working conditions presented a danger of death or serious injury; (b) there was insufficient time to utilize normal enforcement procedures under the Act; and (c) the employee made an attempt to correct the hazard by discussing it with the employer.[46] The employee need not show that an actual injury occurred before refusing the assignment.

Filing discrimination complaints

In the event of employer discrimination, the employee must file a complaint with the OSHA area director within 30 days after such a violation occurs. OSHA may extend this time limit under extenuating circumstances, such as a case where the employer misleads the employee about the grounds for dismissal, and the employee does not discover the actual cause until 30 days has elapsed. OSHA may also toll the 30-day limit if the employee has, in good faith, resorted to the grievance arbitration process under an existing collective bargaining agreement before complaining to the OSHA.

Alternative remedies

As mentioned above, an employee who faces discrimination for safety and health activity may file a grievance under an existing collective bargaining agreement. This is particularly true in refusal to work cases. Although a general principle of arbitration requires employees to carry out an order by management, even if the order violates the contract, an exception exists where obedience would expose the employee to an unusual or abnormally dangerous safety or health hazard.[47] In these cases the majority of arbitrators attempt to determine whether a reasonable person would have feared for his or her safety or health given similar facts and circumstances.[48] As with the OSHA regulation, the employee carries the burden for demonstrating that a "reasonable person" would have taken the same course of action. This burden may shift to supervision once the employee has raised a question regarding safety. In this situation, the supervisor would be responsible for explaining the dangers of the job and the measures the employee can take to prevent injury or illness.

Employees who experience discrimination for safety and health activities may also file complaints with the National Labor Relations Board. Section 7 of the National Labor Relations Act permits employees to engage in "concerted activities" for mutual aid or protection, and section 8(a)(1) prohibits employers from interfering with those rights. The Supreme Court has ruled in favor of employees who seek protection for safety and health activity under this provision.[49] However, an employee must be acting on behalf of or in concert with other employees in order to gain protection under section 7. Whereas section 11(c) complaints with OSHA must be filed within 30 days, employees have six months to file discrimination complaints with the NLRB.

Section 502 of the Labor Management Relations Act also provides limited protection for employees who refuse to perform dangerous work. Section 502 reads, "The quitting of labor by an employee or employees in good faith because of abnormally dangerous working conditions for work at the place of employment of such employee or employees [shall not] be deemed a strike under this chapter."[50] In these cases the employee must prove that the work was "abnormally dangerous." Furthermore, the dangerous conditions must be demonstrated by competent evidence. Unlike arbitration cases, the subjective state of mind of the employee is not governing in section 502 cases.[51]

Finally, because of a national policy favoring the voluntary resolution of collective bargaining disputes, OSHA will defer to arbitration or other agency proceedings. However, deferral is done on a case-by-case basis, and OSHA must be convinced that these alternative proceedings are fair and the decisions do not contradict the purpose and policy of OSHA.[52]

State OSHA Programs

Section 2(b)(11) of the OSHA encourages states to enact their own occupational safety and health legislation. Furthermore, section 18 gives the individual states the authority to assume responsibility for the development and enforcement of occupational safety and health standards. Where no federal OSHA standard exists, any state may assert jurisdiction over an occupational safety and health issue. However, in order for a state to regulate subject areas that are already covered by the OSHA, the state must submit a plan to OSHA for the development and enforcement of such standards. Currently, 23 states have requested and received permission to administer and enforce their own safety and health legislation. As evidence of its support for these state plans, OSHA has paid up to 90 percent for their development and continues to pay 50 percent of ongoing costs related to their administration.[53]

Approval of state plans

Section 18(c) of the Act requires the Secretary of Labor to approve a state plan based on several criteria. In order to secure approval from OSHA, the state must: (a) designate a state agency responsible for administering its plan; (b) provide for the development and enforcement of standards which are at least as effective as OSHA standards in protecting employee safety and health; (c) provide for a right of entry and inspection of all workplaces covered by the legislation; (d) include a prohibition on advance notice of inspections; (e) assure it will have the legal authority and qualified personnel necessary for standards enforcement; (f) assure it will devote adequate funds to the administration and enforcement of safety and health standards; (g) provide safety and health coverage for all employees of the state and its political subdivisions; and (h) make reports to the Secretary of Labor as may be periodically required.

Monitoring of state plans

Besides granting initial approval, the Secretary of Labor is also responsible for continuously evaluating the manner in which each state is carrying out its plan. If the state fails to comply with any provision of its plan or fails to meet the above criteria, the Secretary of Labor must notify the state that approval of the plan has been withdrawn or that concurrent federal jurisdiction will be exercised. The state may obtain a review of this decision by the US Court of Appeals.

Case study: termination of Operational Status Agreement In 1991 a fire occurred in a North Carolina poultry processing plant, killing 25 workers and injuring another 49. Witnesses reported that doors in the plant were locked when the fire broke out, trapping employees who could have escaped. As a result of the fire, the US Secretary of Labor directed OSHA to conduct a complete re-evaluation of North Carolina's state plan and other state plans as well.[54] The AFL-CIO had petitioned OSHA to withdraw approval of North Carolina's plan, claiming the state was unable to fulfill its statutory obligations. The fact that North Carolina safety and health inspectors had never been in the plant added fuel to the controversy.[55]

In October of 1991, OSHA announced the termination of the Operational Status Agreement with the state of North Carolina. Instead of eliminating the state program, OSHA announced that it would maintain concurrent jurisdiction "necessary to assure occupational safety and health protection to employees of the State of North Carolina."[56] In making this decision OSHA relied on North Carolina's acknowledged need for additional resources and personnel. Rather than assuming complete jurisdiction in North Carolina, OSHA declared its intention to exercise enforcement authority with regard to section 11(c) cases, and all issues of occupational safety and health in private sector maritime employment and on military bases.[57]

OSHA also announced its intention to retain general enforcement authority for the following: (a) cases where employers refused entry to state inspectors; (b) safety or health standards promulgated by OSHA but not yet promulgated by North Carolina; (c) joint inspections for newly promulgated standards; and (d) provision of inspection personnel because of a reduction in staffing at the state level. After initial approval but prior to final approval of a state plan, concurrent federal and state jurisdiction is permissible under section 18(e) of OSHA.

As part of OSHA's continuing responsibility to evaluate state plans, the agency may also provide recommendations for state improvement. In its 1990 evaluation of the Michigan state plan, OSHA urged the state to address several shortcomings. These included the state's reluctance to issue serious violations, unexplained reductions in fines for serious and willful violations, failure to conduct follow-up inspections after an employer had been cited, interviewing too few workers during workplace inspections, and taking more than six months to adopt new OSHA standards.[58] OSHA's overview function is implemented not only by quarterly and annual reports of state program activity, but also by visits to state agencies, and investigations of complaints lodged against the state plan.

Any person or organization may complain to OSHA about the administration and operation of a state plan. The complaint, which may be delivered orally or in writing, is handled by the regional administrator for the OSHA region in which the state is located. The complaint, which is referred to as a Complaint about State Program Administration (CASPA), is intended to provide employees, employers, and the public an opportunity to address specific concerns. CASPAs also provide OSHA with an additional source of information on the effectiveness of state enforcement, and they provide the basis for corrective action by the state when a complaint is valid.[59]

Preemption

OSHA expressly preempts state law pertaining to occupational safety and health issues already covered by OSHA standards, unless the state has a plan approved by the Secretary of Labor.[60] The issue of preemption was paramount in a case brought by the New Jersey State Chamber of Commerce against the State of New Jersey's Right-to-know Act.

Case study: preemption In 1984 OSHA promulgated its standard on hazard communication. The standard required employers in the manufacturing sector to provide information to their employees on the hazards of chemicals and substances used in the workplace. The standard required the labeling of hazardous workplace chemicals, employee access to material safety data sheets, employee information and training, and the development by the employer of a written hazard communication program.

In 1984 the New Jersey legislature created its own Right-to-know Act, which was intended to make information about toxic chemicals available to all New Jersey residents who might be exposed to such chemicals, in the workplace or elsewhere, and to public safety officers who might need such information to prevent or respond to emergencies.[61] At the time, New Jersey did not have an OSHA-approved state plan.

The issue before the US Court of Appeals, Third Circuit, was whether the OSHA and OSHA's hazard communication standard preempted the New

Jersey law. In rendering its decision, the Court reasoned, "state laws are expressly preempted only to the extent that a federal standard regulating the same issue is already in effect."[62] Since the OSHA hazard communication standard applied to the manufacturing sector only, the court ruled that the New Jersey law was preempted for employers classified as manufacturers (Standard Industrial Classification codes 20–39) but not for employers in other sectors of the economy. The court also gave New Jersey permission to implement its law as it applied to the identification and reporting of environmental hazards, since these were not addressed in OSHA's standard. The courts buttressed this decision by arguing that employers could comply with both the federal and the state law in this case and that the state law did not conflict with OSHA's purpose of promoting safe and healthful working conditions.[63] Eventually, OSHA expanded coverage of the hazard communication standard to include non-manufacturers, so the New Jersey law as applied to this sector was also preempted.

Related Issues

Criminal liability

In the past several years state and local prosecutors have increased their investigations of workplace fatalities and injuries. Charges of murder, manslaughter, or criminal negligence have been filed where prosecutors find evidence of serious workplace safety hazards, company knowledge of the hazards, the feasibility of corrective action combined with the absence of any corrective action being taken, and an employee death or serious injury.[64] Although the OSHA contains limited provisions for criminal liability, these provisions have rarely been invoked. Between 1977 and 1983, OSHA referred only 15 cases to the Department of Justice for criminal prosecution.[65] This perceived inactivity at the federal level has contributed to the increase in state and local prosecutions. Although some employers have argued that provisions for criminal liability in the OSHA preempt state and local action, the Supreme Courts of Michigan and Illinois and the New York Court of Appeals have ruled that the OSHA does not preempt state criminal law, arguing that preemption would be the equivalent of granting criminal immunity to reckless employers.[66] Because of the growing interest in these types of cases by state and local prosecutors, OSHA has undergone a review of its enforcement policies. As a result, employers can expect closer scrutiny, particularly in cases involving death or serious injuries to employees.

On-site consultation

Section 21(c)(2) requires the Secretary of Labor to consult with and advise employers and employees. This service cannot be provided onsite because of a ruling by the US Solicitor for the Department of Labor prohibiting onsite consultations unless citations are issued. This ruling obviously discouraged employers from seeking OSHA's advice. As a result of this ruling, OSHA promulgated a regulation providing for grants of 50 percent federal funding for onsite consultation programs for states without approved state plans.[67] Those states with approved plans already offer such services. By funding onsite consultation programs, OSHA hopes to increase the incidence of employers' voluntary compliance.

OSHA reform

In 1991 US Senators Edward Kennedy and Howard Metzenbaum introduced the Comprehensive Occupational Safety and Health Reform Act. Similar legislation was also introduced in the US House of Representatives. The legislation is intended to address weaknesses in the OSHA as identified by the General Accounting Office, the Office of Technology Assessment, and the Administrative Conference.[68] As stated by Senator Kennedy, "the bill includes provisions to streamline and expedite the standard setting process, to require better targeting of limited resources to high-risk workplaces, to speed up and improve the hazard abatement process, to strengthen criminal penalties for the most egregious violations of the Act, and to expand coverage of the Act to federal, state and local government employees."[69]

The most controversial sections of this reform legislation include those which will: (a) create mandatory safety and health committees and employee representatives for employers of not fewer than 11 employees; (b) require employers to correct serious hazards by the abatement date on the citation, even if the employer appeals the abatement date; (c) allow unions and employees to contest all aspects of a citation, not just the abatement date; (d) permit OSHA inspectors to place a tag or notice on dangerous equipment that has been identified as an imminent danger; and (e) increase penalties for criminal violations of the act to $250,000 for individuals and $500,000 for organizations.[70]

Despite concerns expressed by employer organizations, sponsors of the legislation maintain that increasing worker involvement is the key to improving workplace safety in an era of limited government resources.[71] Although the progress on this legislation in the US Congress has been slow, the toll of workplace injuries, illnesses, and fatalities will continue to create pressure for meaningful reform.

Summary

In 1970 the US Congress enacted the Occupational Safety and Health Act in an attempt to assure safe and healthful working conditions for working men and women. The Occupational Safety and Health Administration within the US Department of Labor is charged with promulgating and enforcing health and safety standards that are designed to accomplish the Congressional mandate. Individual states may also adopt and enforce workplace safety and health requirements, as long as state administration and enforcement provide equivalent protection for employees.

Employees are afforded several rights under the Occupational Safety and Health Act, including the right to request an inspection of the workplace, to petition OSHA to create a new standard, to receive information from employers on workplace hazards, and under certain circumstances to refuse dangerous work assignments. Employers may also exercise certain rights, including the right to appeal an OSHA citation, to seek a variance from an OSHA standard, to challenge the legality of an OSHA standard, and to request a warrant before an OSHA inspection is conducted.

OSHA has generated a great deal of controversy because decisions made by the agency have a direct impact on workers' physical well-being and employers' financial well-being. Limited federal resources combined with increasing threats from a host of newly recognized hazards, such as second-hand smoke, workplace violence, and poor job design, will create additional debate about the agency's role in accomplishing its responsibility.

Questions for discussion

1 How could the standards setting process be streamlined to limit delays in enacting important safeguards while also protecting the interests of employers?
2 Does OSHA's system of inspections and citations provide an adequate mechanism for eliminating workplace hazards? How could this system be improved?
3 What are the advantages and disadvantages of permitting states to enforce safety and health legislation that is parallel to federal enforcement?
4 Does the OSHA provide adequate protection for employees who refuse dangerous work assignments?
5 Should OSHA adopt tougher criminal penalties for employers in situations involving serious injuries and fatalities of employees?

NOTES

1 Occupational Safety and Health Act of 1970, section 2(b).
2 Nicholas Ashford, *Crisis in the Workplace: Occupational Disease and Injury* (The MIT Press, Cambridge, MA, 1976), p. 46.
3 Ibid.
4 "Death on the job: the toll of neglect," AFL-CIO Department of Occupational Safety and Health, April 1992, p. 7.
5 The Occupational Safety and Health Act of 1970, Section 6(f).
6 Ibid., section 6(c)(1).
7 Ashford, supra, note 2, p. 158.
8 Ibid., p. 179.
9 The Occupational Safety and Health Act of 1970, section 5(a)(1).
10 Ashford, supra, note 2, p. 161.
11 *UAW* v. *General Dynamics Land Systems Division*, the Bureau of National Affairs, 13 *Occupational Safety and Health Cases* 1203, 1987.

12 Ibid., at 1205.
13 Ibid., at 1207.
14 The Occupational Safety and Health Act of 1970, section 6(b)(5).
15 *American Textile Manufacturers Institute* v. *Donovan*, 9 *Occupational Safety and Health Cases* 1917 (1981).
16 Ibid., at 1928.
17 Ibid., at 1920.
18 *AFL-CIO* v. *OSHA*, BNA, *Daily Labor Report* (July 10, 1992), p. D-6.
19 Ibid., p. D-9.
20 Ibid., p. D-12.
21 *Marshall* v. *Barlow's, Inc.*, 436 US 317.
22 Ibid., at 323.
23 29 CFR section 1903.6(b).
24 OSHA Field Operations Manual, as printed by the Bureau of National Affairs, Occupational Safety and Health Report, Reference Manual, p. 77:2304.
25 Ibid., 77:2308.
26 Ibid., 77:2320.
27 The Occupational Safety and Health Act of 1970, section 8(f)(2).
28 Ashford, supra, note 2, p. 165.
29 OSHA Field Operations Manual, supra, note 24, p. 77:2509.
30 Ibid., p. 77:2701.
31 Michael B. Bixby, "Was it an accident or murder? New thrusts in corporate criminal liability for workplace deaths," *Labor Law Journal* (July 1990), p. 421.
32 Supra, note 24, p. 77:2701–4.
33 29 CFR part 1904.
34 Ibid.
35 Ibid.
36 *UAW Health & Safety Newsletter* (No. 1, 1987), p. 1.
37 Ibid., pp. 2, 6.
38 29 CFR section 1910.20.
39 *The Case of the Workplace Killers*, International Union, UAW, November 1980, p. 15.
40 29 CFR section 1910.20(f)(4).
41 The Occupational Safety and Health Act of 1970, section 11(c)(1).
42 29 CFR section 1977.1(c).
43 29 CFR section 1977.9(c).
44 *Whirlpool Corporation* v. *Marshall*, 8 OSHC 1004 (1980).
45 Ibid., at 1005.
46 Larry Drapkin, "The right to refuse hazardous work after Whirlpool," *Industrial Relations Law Journal*, 4 (No. 1, 1980), p. 34.
47 Elkouri and Elkouri, *How Arbitration Works*, 4th edn (Bureau of National Affairs, Washington, DC, 1985), p. 713.
48 Ibid., p. 715.
49 Drapkin, supra, note 46, p. 46.
50 Ibid., p. 51.
51 Ashford, supra, note 2, p. 190.
52 29 CFR section 1977.18(c).
53 Ashford, supra, note 2, p. 210.
54 *Occupational Safety & Health Reporter*, Bureau of National Affairs (October 30, 1991), p. 616.

55 *Occupational Safety & Health Reporter*, Bureau of National Affairs (September 4, 1991), p. 387.
56 Department of Labor, Occupational Safety and Health Administration, 29 CFR section 1952 (October 24, 1991).
57 Ibid.
58 *Detroit News and Free Press* (August 25, 1990), pp. 1, 4.
59 OSHA Field Operations Manual, supra, note 24, p. 77:5151.
60 The Occupational Safety and Health Act of 1970, section 18(b).
61 *NJ State Chamber of Commerce* v. *Hughey*, 774 F.2d 587 (1985), p. 591.
62 Ibid., p. 593.
63 Ibid., p. 594.
64 Bixby, supra, note 31, p. 417.
65 *Occupational Safety and Health Law* (Business Laws, Inc., Chesterland, OH, 1994), p. 1.033.
66 Ibid., p. 1.034.
67 Ashford, supra, note 2, p. 166.
68 *Congressional Record-Senate* (August 1, 1991), S 11833.
69 Ibid., S 11833.
70 Statement of the US Chamber of Commerce, before the House Committee on Education and Labor, April 8, 1992.
71 *Congressional Record-Senate*, supra, note 68, p. S 11833.

Chapter 9
Workers' Compensation

Introduction

Workers' compensation is the system by which we compensate individuals who become disabled as a result of their employment. Although, as discussed below, there are a couple of federal programs that apply to certain classes of employees, workers' compensation is primarily a state program. It is administered by state agencies and there is great variation among the laws of the 50 states. The variation is greatest with regard to the evaluation of permanent partial impairment and procedures.

This chapter will provide an overview of the system and suggest some of the various alternatives that are used by individual states. It will not, however, attempt to provide specific information about the workers' compensation law in any one state. Appendix 1 provides a listing of state workers' compensation agencies. These would be the best starting point for obtaining information about the specific laws of an individual state.

Origins

Workers' compensation was the first form of social legislation enacted in the United States. It came to the country from Germany via the United Kingdom. Wisconsin's law, enacted in 1911, is the oldest in the country. By 1920, about 40 states had enacted workers' compensation laws, although it was not until 1940 that all states had workers' compensation laws in operation.

Prior to the enactment of workers' compensation laws, a worker injured on the job could not sue his or her employer unless the worker could prove that the employer's *negligence* was responsible for the disability. In addition, the employer had available three defenses. An employer would not be held liable if it could show any of the following: (a) that the employee's negligence contributed to the injury; (b) that a fellow employee was responsible for the injury; or (c) that the worker knew a danger existed and assumed the risk.

As a result of this, it was rare for workers to win claims arising out of their employment-related injuries. It is generally said that society enacted workers' compensation laws to remedy this situation and guarantee some benefits to injured workers. A few people suggest, however, that in fact workers were occasionally beginning to win law suits and employers enacted workers' compensation laws for their own protection.[1]

Workers' compensation laws are a compromise. A worker whose injury occurs as a part of his or her employment is guaranteed benefits regardless of the cause. They were the first "no-fault" systems. In return for the guarantee of some benefits, the amount of benefits is severely limited. Under workers' compensation laws, a worker is entitled to receive certain wage-replacement benefits, health care benefits, and, more recently, vocational rehabilitation benefits, but nothing more.

The Exclusive Remedy and Civil Lawsuits

Workers' compensation is the *exclusive remedy* for workers injured on the job. While workers are guaranteed prescribed benefits regardless of fault, they are not allowed to file through a civil action against their employer.

Intentional torts are an exception to the exclusive remedy provision. If Ms A is a sole proprietor and Ms A hits an employee over the head with a two by four, Ms A cannot claim the exclusive remedy protection of the Workers' Compensation Act. During the 1980s, the courts in some states expanded the intentional tort exception. Generally, they did it by including circumstances which the employer "should have known" would result in injury. In most states, the legislature responded promptly to the judicial expansion of this principle, passing more restrictive statutory language. Today, intentional torts are a very carefully circumscribed exception in most states. Other exceptions include contracts between employers and their employees and other statutory provisions, such as civil rights laws.

Workers' compensation is the exclusive remedy a worker has against his or her employer. It does not, however, prohibit a worker from suing some other person, a third party. If Mr B is a truck driver, and is injured in a collision with an automobile, he may file a civil action against the driver of the automobile if that person was responsible for the injury. The driver of the automobile is a "third party." If Mr B has received workers' compensation benefits from his employer, he must repay the employer out of the proceeds of the third party claim. In most such cases, there will be an attorney's fee to be paid, and Mr B and the employer will generally share the attorney's fee in proportion to their recovery. In most states, fellow employees of the injured worker enjoy the protection of the exclusive remedy provision and cannot be sued for negligence.

Coverage

Workers' compensation is primarily a state program. Employees of the federal government are covered by the Federal Employees' Compensation Act and employees working on or around navigable waters are covered by the Longshore and Harbor Workers' Act. These are the only two federal workers' compensation laws. Employees injured on merchant ships are covered by the Merchant Marine Act (Jones Act) and employees working on interstate railroads are covered by the Federal Employers' Liability Act. The latter two, however, are not strictly speaking workers' compensation laws since they, at least in theory, require that the worker prove negligence on the part of the employer and allow damage awards by juries.

Workers' compensation is mandatory in all states except New Jersey, Texas, and South Carolina. By this it is meant that employers must either purchase workers' compensation insurance or obtain permission from the state agency to be self-insured.

Some 14 states have some form of *size test*. These tests might require, for example, that an employer have one or more full-time employees or three employees at one time in order to be subject to the Workers' Compensation Act. In many states, public employees were not originally covered. But all states now cover public employees to the same extent as other workers.

Workers' compensation covers *employees*. Some individuals who perform services for others are *independent contractors* rather than employees. Thus, if Ms C runs a law firm and hires Mr D, a plumber, to install some fixtures, Mr D is probably not an employee of the law firm and thus the law firm is not required to pay workers' compensation benefits if he is injured. If, on the other hand, the law firm called in its secretaries and told them that it was going to make them independent contractors, the law would still consider them employees. This would apply even if the individuals signed an agreement that they would now be considered independent contractors. It is possible, however, for the law firm to hire a secretary on a short-term basis from a temporary agency and for that person to be an employee of the agency rather than the law firm.

There are often disputes as to whether an individual is an employee or an independent contractor. Workers leased on a long-term basis are often problematic in this regard. Some employers attempt to escape their responsibility under workers' compensation laws by creating firms whose only purpose is to lease workers back to the original company. Generally, this is seen by the law as a subterfuge.

Most states provide exceptions to their workers' compensation laws for agricultural employees and for domestic help.

"Arising out of and in the Course of"

It is generally said that to be compensable an injury must "arise out of and in the course of" the employment. While this formulation seems rather straightforward, it gives rise to many controversies.

Originally, most workers' compensation laws covered only *accidents*. Over the years, the definition of an accident has been greatly expanded. Originally, it applied only to unexpected events, but most states have expanded it to cover situations in which the result is unexpected, even though the event was not. Thus, if a worker suffers a back injury as a result of a routine lifting task, it is said that this was an accident since the injury was unexpected even though the lifting was a routine task. Some states have completely eliminated the accident requirement.

Generally, going to and coming from work is not covered. However, if the worker is on the employer's premises an injury is usually covered if it is within a reasonable time before or after work. Thus, injuries on company parking lots are usually covered.

Employees, such as sales people or truck drivers, who travel as part of their employment are generally covered during all of their travels. They would also usually be covered during lunch hours or overnight stays if travel was part of their employment. If, however, they *deviate* too far they may remove themselves from the course of their employment. The deviation is usually analyzed geographically, but sometimes the activities can be so different from those expected of an employee that the nature of the activities results in a deviation. Thus, if Mr E travels from Chicago to New York on business he would ordinarily be covered during the entire trip. If, however, he deviated from his route and went to Washington to visit a friend, he would not be covered while he was in Washington. If he returned from Washington to New York, and then traveled back to Chicago, his coverage would resume once he returned to his employment-related route.

If Mr F traveled to New York on business and engaged in the activities that one would normally expect of a traveling business person, he would probably be covered during the entire trip. If, however, he began drinking and carousing and ended up in a part of town where one would not ordinarily expect to find a traveling business person, he too may have deviated from the course of his employment.

An employer must expect that workers will engage in a certain amount of "horseplay" as part of their work. If activities which are not directly related to the worker's employment are generally expected and tolerated by the employer, the results of those activities will usually be compensable. In recent years, a number of states have passed laws which provide that injuries which are caused by the abuse of alcohol or the use of illegal drugs are not compensable.

A trip can have a *dual purpose*. Thus, if Mr F works in a hardware store and makes a delivery to a customer on his way home from work, the trip will usually be considered to be in the course of the employment, even though there was a personal as well as business purpose to the trip.

The Causal Relationship

Disputes often arise as to whether or not a specific disability was *caused* by the employment. It is the basic principle of English and American law that a person "takes his victim as he finds him." Thus, even though an event might not have caused a disability in the ordinary person, it is generally considered compensable if in fact it caused the disability in a given individual, even though this only occurred because this individual had a pre-existing weakness. It is said that a condition need not be caused by the employment. A condition is compensable if the work contributed to or aggravated the condition. Thus, if Ms G lifts something heavy in her employment and ruptures a disk, it is generally not a defense that she had a pre-existing weakness in her back and that the lift would not have caused a ruptured disk in a healthy individual.

Interpretations of this principle have caused concern among employers and a few states, such as Oregon, have moved recently to limit it. For example, some states have recently added a requirement that a condition is only compensable if a work-related injury was "the major contributing cause."

Mental disabilities are particularly troublesome in this regard. In fact, some states do not provide any coverage for a mental disability caused by mental stress. (This is distinguished from a mental disability which results from physical stress, and from a physical disability, such as a heart attack, which results from mental stress.) Other states limit compensability for mental disability claims by requiring a higher standard of proof.

Heart conditions also cause problems in this area. Generally, if a worker is subject to conditions which are unusually stressful for that worker and a myocardial infarction (heart attack) follows immediately upon the stress, the resulting disability will be compensable. Heart disease under other circumstances is problematic and coverage varies greatly from state to state.

To a certain extent, the difficulties in shaping concise rules for causality result from factual difficulties and a lack of clear answers from the medical and scientific community. We do not really know, for example, the extent to which repeated stress causes the gradual onset of heart disease. As long as we are uncertain of the factual answers, it is very difficult to design a legal system to deal with these situations. In a number of states, if a worker has a pre-existing disability which results in a measurable impairment rating and there is a subsequent injury that increases the impairment rating, the employer is only required to pay benefits attributable to the increased impairment.

Occupational Disease

As mentioned earlier, workers' compensation laws originally covered only accidents and thus did not provide protection for occupational diseases.

Gradually, however, statutes have been amended and courts have interpreted laws to provide almost full coverage for occupational diseases. Some states, however, still treat them differently in terms of the notice and claim requirements and the burden of proof, and a few states provide slightly different levels of benefits.

Disability

Disability benefits can be divided into four categories: temporary total, temporary partial, permanent total, and permanent partial. Cases involving temporary disability are by far the most common, but also the least costly. Cases involving permanent total disability are by far the most costly, but they are rather rare. Although they are not the most common or the most costly, permanent partial disability claims are frequent enough and costly enough to account for the largest share of workers' compensation dollars. They are also the cases most likely to be disputed and the cases in which there are great differences among the states in how they are treated.

Temporary total benefits are paid to a worker during a period immediately following an injury for which he or she is unable to return to any work. The majority of injured workers who receive temporary total benefits recover and return to work without making any further claim.

The level of temporary total benefits is usually based on the worker's pre-injury earnings or *average weekly wage*. Most often, this is based on the 13 weeks of work prior to the injury. Typically, the benefit rate is two-thirds of the worker's gross pre-injury average weekly wage. Some states, however, base the benefit on the worker's *spendable earnings* or after-tax average weekly wage. States that use this approach most commonly pay 80 percent of the spendable earnings.

All states provide a maximum limit on the weekly benefits. Most commonly, this is set at a level equal to the average wage for all wage earners in the state for the previous year. This level is referred to as *100 percent of the state average weekly wage*. Some states, however, have a higher or lower maximum rate.

Many states have a minimum rate so that a worker receives some minimum amount regardless of how low his or her pre-injury wages were. Some states that do have a minimum amount provide that it does not apply to part-time employees or provide that the worker shall receive the minimum amount or the pre-injury earnings he or she received, whichever is lower. Appendix 2 summarizes benefits for temporary total disability.

Many states provide that if the worker returns to work at a lower paying job, while he or she is still recovering from an injury the worker will receive *temporary partial benefits*. These benefits are based on the difference between the current earnings and the average weekly wage and are paid at the same rate as for temporary total disability.

In all states there is a *waiting period* before temporary benefits begin. The exact periods vary, but typically no benefits would be payable until a worker was off for one week. Benefits would begin at that time. If the worker remains off work for more than two weeks, then, the employer is responsible for benefits back to the first day of disability.

The majority of all injured workers receive temporary benefits, recover and return to work with no further wage loss, and receive no further benefits. If this does not occur, temporary total benefits terminate when the worker reaches *maximum medical improvement* or *medical stability*. In other words, these benefits terminate when the worker's medical condition has improved to the greatest extent to be expected. Most states also provide a limit to the number of weeks for which a worker can receive temporary total benefits, even if he or she has not reached maximum medical improvement.

If, after reaching maximum medical improvement, it appears that the worker will never be able to return to gainful employment, the worker is awarded *permanent total* disability benefits. These are often paid at the same rate as temporary total benefits. In many states they may continue for life, but in others they continue for only a limited number of weeks. States vary in how they define permanent total disability. In a few states, it is limited to individuals who have a loss (or lose the use of) two arms, two legs, two eyes, or a combination of two such members. In other states, it is given a broader definition. Disputes often arise as to whether or not a worker fits into this category.

If a worker reaches maximum medical improvement and is not permanently and totally disabled, but it appears that he or she will have some permanent residuals of the injury, the worker is considered to have a *permanent partial* disability. This is the most troublesome area in workers' compensation. There are often disputes concerning the extent of permanent partial disability in a given worker and there are great differences among the states in how they measure permanent partial disability. Typically, the extent of the permanent partial disability is expressed as a percentage. A worker with a severe back injury, for example, might be said to have a 20 percent disability, while a worker with some limitation of motion in the hand might have a 5 percent disability.

The evaluation of the disability generally starts with a measure of the physical *impairment*. States provide various guidelines to physicians in measuring this impairment. The *Guides to the Evaluation of Impairment* published by the American Medical Association are those used most frequently.[2] A few states attempt to use this measure of physical impairment as the only measure of the extent of disability. Most states, however, modify this estimate by considering vocational factors, such as the worker's age, education, and work experience.

Some states also include the worker's position in the labor market. They consider, for example, economic conditions and whether he or she could reasonably be expected to return to work. It is said that they are estimating the individual's *wage earning capacity* rather than his or her impairment.

The final impairment rating is translated into a dollar payment in various ways. A great many states assign a certain number of weeks as the value for a *whole person*. Thus, if a whole person is worth 500 weeks an individual with a 20 percent disability would receive benefits at a specified rate for 100 weeks (20 percent × 500). The rate is most frequently, but not always, the same as the rate for temporary total benefits. A few states assign a dollar value to a whole person and pay a benefit equal to the appropriate percentage of that dollar value. Others provide that each percentage point of disability entitles the worker to benefits for a certain number of weeks. Thus, one percentage point of disability might entitle the worker to three weeks of benefits and a worker with a 5 percent disability would receive benefits at the prescribed rate for 15 weeks. A few states have reached the conclusion that these formulas tend to overcompensate minor disabilities and undercompensate more severe ones. Accordingly, they have adopted schemes that allow more weeks for percentages over a certain level.

A number of states pay benefits based on the worker's *wage loss* rather than on a permanent partial disability rating. This approach is similar to the one used for temporary benefits. If an individual earns no wages, he or she receives benefits equal to a percentage of the pre-injury earnings (usually two-thirds of gross wages or 80 percent of after-tax wages). If a worker returns to work at a lower paying job, he or she receives the specified percentage of the difference between the pre-injury wages and the current earnings. If the worker returns to work at wages equal to or greater than the pre-injury earnings, no benefits are paid.

Most states that use the wage loss approach have some mechanism to deal with the situation in which the worker could obtain earnings but has chosen not to do so. In some states, an employer can produce evidence of the individual's *wage earning capacity* by showing that other individuals with the same disability and similar education and training are able to earn an estimated level of wages. In other states, the worker is required to establish that he or she has performed a job search and has been unable to find work.

Many states have some combination of wage loss and impairment rating systems. Some provide, for example, that a worker receives only impairment benefits if the disability is under a certain level, say 15 percent, but can receive wage loss benefits either instead of or in addition to impairment benefits if the disability exceeds that percentage. Other states provide benefits based on an impairment rating for injuries to the extremities, but provide wage loss benefits for injuries to the trunk or internal organs.

Most states also have some *schedule* of benefits. In virtually all states, the total loss of a limb or eye is compensated by a fixed amount which is listed in the schedule. In most states, this also applies to a loss of use or partial loss of use of an extremity. Some states, such as California, have a schedule which attempts to cover every conceivable disability. In fact, a comprehensive schedule such as this amounts to a system very similar to an impairment rating system as described above.

Death

If a work-related injury results in an employee's death, the employer is responsible to pay benefits to the survivor. Generally, these benefits are paid to a surviving spouse until the spouse dies or remarries. Some states, however, place an arbitrary limit, such as 500 weeks, on the length of time these benefits are available. The surviving children of a worker who dies as a result of his or her employment generally receive benefits until age 18. Most states also provide some burial allowance: this ranges from $1,400 in Montana to $6,000 in Idaho.

Special Funds

Typically, the loss of one arm might result in an impairment rating of say 25 percent, while the loss of both arms would be considered a permanent and total disability and equivalent to an impairment rating of 100 percent. If a worker comes to an employer already having lost one limb, it seems unfair to burden the employer with the cost of a permanent total disability should the worker lose another single limb in the course of his or her employment. Accordingly, most states created *second* or *subsequent injury funds*. Under these arrangements, if Ms H came to a company already having lost one arm and lost a second arm in the course of her employment there, the company would be required only to pay her for the loss of the second arm. The second injury fund would pay her the rest of the benefits to which she would be entitled (or, in many circumstances, the employer would pay those benefits but would be reimbursed by the second injury fund).

Over the years, states have greatly expanded second injury funds. In some states, they provide relief to an employer in any circumstance in which the worker has a pre-existing disability which is aggravated by a subsequent injury. In other states, they provide relief only if the employer knew of the pre-existing injury or if the employee was certified as having a pre-existing disability.

States also use special funds for a variety of other purposes. In some states, an employer is required to pay benefits to a worker while an appeal is pending. Sometimes, second injury funds are used to reimburse the employer should it eventually win the appeal. Other states use special funds to provide relief to employers in selected industries, typically mining or foundries and sometimes fisheries. Under these arrangements, a part of the workers' compensation liability for employers in these industries is borne by the fund rather than by individual employers.

Special funds are generally financed by some form of tax or assessment on all insurers and self-insured employers. This is usually based on the amount of premium collected (or an estimate of what the premium would have been for a self-insured employer) or the total amount of benefits paid out in the previous year. Some funds also receive a prescribed payment in a death case in which there are no survivors.

Health Care Benefits

Workers injured in the course of their employment are entitled to virtually unlimited health care coverage. Except in Florida, there are no co-pays or deductibles and nearly all forms of treatment are covered. Recently, a few states have begun to put some limit on chiropractic care.

There are differences among the states concerning selection of the treating physician. In a few states the worker has complete freedom of choice, and in a few others the employer has complete control over the choice of physician. In other states, the employer has control for the first 30 days and the worker thereafter. In some states the worker chooses the first physician but the employer controls subsequent changes, and in other states the reverse is true.

Recently, there has been a trend to amend workers' compensation laws to allow employers to contract with managed care organizations. These amendments provide that if the employer has entered into such an arrangement, it may require the worker to obtain treatment through the managed care group.

In theory, wage replacement benefits can be terminated or reduced if a worker refuses reasonable medical treatment. In practice, however, this rarely happens. The employer must prove that the proposed treatment is very likely to improve the worker's condition and that there is little or no danger.

For the past several years, there has been a growing concern with the cost of workers' compensation health care. States have responded to this in various ways, including schedules or lists of the maximum fees that providers can charge, allowing or requiring a utilization review, and permitting the use of managed care organizations.

Vocational Rehabilitation

There are some individuals who are injured on the job and who have no hope of returning to their prior work. Some of these people can be greatly helped through vocational rehabilitation. A trained counselor interviews the individual and gathers information about his or her physical condition, education and training, prior work experience, and abilities. The counselor then helps the person to find permanent alternative employment, sometimes with the help of further education and sometimes through direct placement. In appropriate cases, this is by far the best solution for the worker and also saves money for the employer.

During the 1970s and early 1980s, this alternative appeared so attractive that the legislatures in some states mandated the provision of vocational rehabilitation services in a large variety of cases. As a result, a great deal of money was spent on vocational rehabilitation, but the efforts were successful in only a limited number of cases. Accordingly, in the late 1980s and early 1990s, a number of states withdrew from their statutes provisions that mandated vocational rehabilitation.

Today, all states allow vocational rehabilitation and some will require an employer to pay for it in appropriate cases if requested to do so by the worker.

Procedures

In all states, an employer is required to report to the state agency any disability that lasts long enough to entitle the worker to wage-replacement benefits. In the majority of cases, benefits are paid voluntarily and reported to the state agency, the worker recovers and benefits are stopped.

In some states, the employer begins to pay benefits if it feels this is appropriate and may later terminate benefits if it feels that is appropriate. In other states, however, the employer is given a certain period of time during which it must determine whether it wishes to accept or contest the case. If it accepts the case, it must then continue paying benefits until it has permission from the state agency to stop. In states that use an impairment rating or rating of loss of wage-earning capacity as compensation for permanent partial disability, the state must usually approve the rating determination.

Disputes arise over various issues, including whether or not a disability is covered by the workers' compensation law, whether maximum medical improvement has been reached, whether the worker suffers from a total and permanent disability, and the extent of permanent partial disability. The specifics of the dispute resolution procedures vary greatly from state to state; they do, however, follow the same general pattern.

The process usually begins when one of the parties files a request for hearing with the state agency. This may be an employer that wishes to terminate benefits or a worker whose benefits have already been terminated and who wishes to have them reinstated. A dispute may also arise from the necessity of having the state agency establish a permanent partial disability rating. Frequently, there is some form of mediation, alternative dispute resolution, or informal hearing as the first step in the process. If the parties reach an agreement at this level the case is resolved without any formal hearing.

If no resolution is reached at the informal stage, a formal hearing is held by an individual, who may be called a hearing referee, administrative law judge, magistrate, or arbitrator. The worker usually testifies at these hearings. Often representatives of the employer testify. Frequently, the most important issues involve medical testimony. This testimony is usually received in the form of either written reports from physicians or depositions taken of physicians. In a deposition, the attorneys for both parties go to the doctor's office and take his or her testimony there, as if they were in court. A transcript is then typed up, and given to the judge to read.

Generally, if a party is dissatisfied with the finding at the trial level, it has a right to appeal that decision to a commission. In many states the commission has only limited authority to review factual determinations of the hearing officer, and in most states the parties may not introduce new evidence before the commission. Legal issues are treated differently. The parties can always argue to the commission that the trial judge misapplied the law. Most states also allow an appeal from the commission to the civil courts of the state; this, however, is usually limited to legal rather than factual issues.

The workers' compensation laws in most states provide for the payment of benefits over a series of weeks in nearly all circumstances. In practice, however, it very often happens that workers receive these benefits in a single lump-sum payment. In some cases, this is a fairly straightforward calculation. If it is finally determined that Ms H should receive $400 per week for 100 weeks, it is often considered appropriate to simply give her a single payment of $40,000. (Actually she would not receive $40,000, as the payment would be discounted based on the assumption that whoever holds the money can earn interest on it.)

In other cases, however, these lump-sum payments are more problematic. They often represent compromise settlements. Mr I might be claiming, for example, that he is entitled to $400 a week for 600 weeks, while his employer is claiming that he is entitled to benefits for only 200 weeks. They may reach a compromise in the form of a payment which is equivalent to 400 weeks. In other cases, the worker may claim that he or she is entitled to life-long benefits while the employer is denying that the injury arose out of the employment and, accordingly, claiming that it should not pay any benefits at all. Here again, compromises are often reached.

These compromises go by various names in the different states. They are sometimes called a "compromise and release," a "C&R," a "wash-out," or a "redemption." Some people contend that these represent abuses of the system, that workers who are truly deserving should get the full benefits provided by the statute, and that workers who are not deserving should get nothing. Practically speaking, however, the systems in many states depend heavily on such settlements in order to function efficiently.

Security for Compensation

As discussed above, workers' compensation is mandatory in all but two states. Generally, this means that an employer must either purchase insurance or obtain approval to be self-insured. This is referred to as "providing security for compensation." There are a variety of ways in which an employer may do this. The options permitted in each state are summarized in appendix 3.

1 Self-insurance. All states except South Dakota and Wyoming allow self-insurance. Most large employers choose this alternative. This is, of course, different from just not buying insurance. It means that the employer has obtained approval from the state agency, usually the workers' compensation agency, to be self-insured.

2 Retrospectively rated insurance. Some large employers purchase an insurance policy that is *retrospectively rated*. This means that the premium is adjusted to pass on to the employer the cost of the losses that occur plus a fee for servicing the claims. It might be said that it is a "cost-plus"

arrangement. Under a "retro" policy, the employer assumes much of the risk of the losses but little of the responsibility for handling claims. Adjustments to the premium are made periodically after the close of the policy year. They are usually based on "incurred" losses; that is, the amounts actually paid out plus the reserves. It is also possible, however, to have a retro policy in which the premiums are based strictly on the paid losses. The employer does not assume all the risk, because these policies generally include a minimum and maximum premium. In other words, the insurance company is going to charge something for issuing the policy even if there are no losses. Most of these policies also provide that after losses reach a certain level, the insurance company will accept all responsibility. Because of this arrangement these are sometimes called "high-low" or "stop-loss" policies.

3   Insurance with a large deductible. Large deductible workers' compensation insurance policies have become popular recently. Under such a policy, the employer is responsible for the losses up to an agreed upon amount. The deductible may be on a per accident basis or an annual aggregate basis. For example, the parties might agree that the employer would pay the first $150,000 in each case, or that the employer would pay the first $2 million for all cases arising out of a given policy year. In most deductible policies, the deductible amounts are not paid directly by the employer to the workers or providers. Rather, the claims are managed and paid by the insurer just as in any other policy. The costs attributable to the deductible are then charged back to the employer. The "deductible" is, in some sense, really just a way of calculating the premium.

4   Insurance with a small deductible. An increasing number of states (about 20 at last count) allow some form of small deductible. The deductible amounts are usually between $100 and $10,000 per accident. As with large deductibles, claims are generally handled by the insurer and all payments are made by it, but the costs of the deductible amounts are charged back to the employer. Depending on the state, the losses that are included in the deductible amounts may or may not be included when calculating the employer's experience modification.

5   Experience-rated insurance. The vast majority of employers have experience-rated policies. If the annual premiums are above about $4,000, the policy will most likely be experience-rated. At its simplest, experience rating means that the premium is adjusted up or down based on the loss experience of the employer. The adjustment, however, is much less direct than for retrospective policies or policies with deductibles. When an experience modification formula is used, it considers losses for the three previous years. The "losses" are not the amounts paid out to workers and providers, but "incurred" losses, the amounts paid out plus a reserve for future losses. The formula is rather complicated. It puts more weight on frequency than severity and, for statistical reasons, the losses of a small employer are given less weight than the losses of a large employer. The formula results in an "experience modification factor." The manual premium rate is multiplied by this factor. Thus, if an employee has an experience modification factor

or "mod" of 1.20, its premium will be adjusted upward by 20 percent. Likewise a "mod" of 0.80 will result in a reduction of 20 percent. The calculation is always made by comparing the employers with others who have employees in the same job classifications. It thus compares each employer with others doing the same type of work.

6   Non-experience-rated insurance. This is basically the "all others" category. Employers that are too small to be experience-rated, those with premiums under about $4,000 per year, purchase insurance policies for which the premiums are not adjusted based on the losses.

7   Accident funds. In six states workers' compensation insurance is available only from state-run funds and in some 18 others (the number has increased sharply in the past few years) there is a state fund that is an alternative to private insurance. The policies offered by these funds are similar to those offered by private insurers.

8   Group self-insurance. Thirty states allow group self-insurance funds. Most of the policies written by these groups are similar to experience-rated policies written by private insurance companies. Originally, and still in many states such as Michigan, funds were limited to employers in a single industry. Today, several states allow "heterogeneous" funds. In Florida, for example, a significant portion of all workers' compensation insurance is written by four large funds that are sponsored by statewide trade associations and are not limited to a single industry.

9   Assigned-risk pool. If an employer has a bad record or the nature of its risk is very unusual, companies may not wish to sell it insurance voluntarily. In 13 states the state accident fund is required to sell insurance to "all comers." It is the "insurer of last resort." In the remaining states such an employer can purchase insurance through an "assigned-risk pool" or "residual market." Generally the policies available from the pool are of the same nature as those available in the voluntary market as described above. There may, however, be a "surcharge" on employers in the pool.

Firm Level Solutions

Because this book deals primarily with employment law this chapter has emphasized the law of workers' compensation. There are, however, important aspects of this issue that must be dealt with at the firm level rather than through courts or legislatures.

Commentators are very much inclined to make comparisons between the workers' compensation systems in various states, assuming that state laws account for most of the differences experienced by employers. A study in Michigan, however, found that the differences among employers within Michigan were bigger than the differences between Michigan and other states.[3]

The study surveyed 5,000 employers in 29 different industries and compared the experiences of employers in the same industry. At that time, the difference between Michigan and Indiana was twofold (the costs in Michigan were twice those in Indiana). The difference between Indiana and Maine (at that time the lowest and highest cost states) was sixfold. The study found, however, that the difference between the "good" and "bad" employers within Michigan was ten to one. Within every industry the worst employers had ten times as many claims as the best. The study followed up with a survey of the 15 percent of the employers with the fewest claims and the 15 percent with the most claims. It found that the differences could be attributable to three factors: (a) safety and prevention; (b) disability management; and (c) corporate culture.

Those companies that had active safety programs, in which there was a commitment from management to prevent injuries in every way possible, tended to be in the group with the fewest injuries. The companies that were involved in disability management also tended to be in the group with the fewest injuries. These were companies that had wellness programs, that had return-to-work programs, and that were generally proactive in dealing with the health of their workers. Finally, the researchers ask questions dealing with what they called "the corporate culture." The companies in which decision making was shared with first level employees and in which information flowed from the bottom up as well as the top down, companies which had what the researchers called an "open corporate culture," tended to be in the group with the fewest claims.

The lesson from this is that there is much employers can do in the workplace to influence their workers' compensation experience. They need not rely entirely on lawyers and legislators. The good news about this lesson is that these are strategies which help both employers and workers at the same time, as opposed to most legislative strategies, which can only save money for employers by reducing benefits to workers.

Appendix 1: Workers' compensation agencies

Alabama
Workers' Compensation Division
Department of Industrial Relations
Industrial Relations Building
Montgomery, AL 36130
Tel. (205) 242–2868
Fax (205) 240–3267

Alaska
Workers' Compensation Division
Department of Labor
PO Box 25512
Juneau, AK 99802–5512
Tel. (907) 465–2790
Fax (907) 465–2797

Arizona
Industrial Commission
800 West Washington

PO Box 19070
Phoenix, AZ 85005–9070
Tel. (602) 542–4411

Arkansas
Workers' Compensation Commission
Justice Building
625 Marshall Street
Little Rock, AR 72201
Tel. (501) 682–3930
Fax (501) 682–2777

California
Department of Industrial Relations
Division of Workers' Compensation
455 Golden Gate Avenue
Room 5182, 5th Floor
San Francisco, CA 94102
Tel. (415) 703–5161
Fax (415) 703–3971

Workers' Compensation Appeal Board
455 Golden Gate Avenue
Room 2178
San Francisco, CA 94102
Tel. (415) 703–4942

Colorado
Division of Workers' Compensation
Department of Labor & Employment
Chancery Building
1120 Lincoln Street, 14th Floor
Denver, CO 80203
Tel. (303) 764–4325
Fax (303) 894–2973

Industrial Claims Appeals Board
1120 Lincoln Street, 14th Floor
Denver, CO
Tel. (303) 894–2378

Connecticut
Workers' Compensation Commission
1890 Dixwell Avenue
Hamden, CT 06514
Tel. (203) 789–7783
Fax (203) 789–7375

Delaware
Industrial Accident Board
State Office Building, 6th Floor
820 North French Street
Wilmington, DE 19801
Tel. (302) 577–2884
Fax (302) 577–3750

District of Columbia
Department of Employment Services
Office of Workers' Compensation
PO Box 56098
Washington, DC 20011
Tel. (202) 576–6265

Florida
Division of Workers' Compensation
Department of Labor & Employment Security
Forrest Building, Suite 301
2728 Centerview Drive
Tallahassee, FL 32399–0680
Tel. (904) 488–2514
Fax (904) 922–6779

Georgia
Board of Workers' Compensation
South Tower, Suite 1000
One CNN Center
Atlanta, GA 30303–2788
Tel. (404) 656–3875
Fax (404) 656–7768

Hawaii
Disability Compensation Division
Department of Labor & Industrial Relations
830 Punchbowl Street, Room 209
Honolulu, HA 96813
Tel. (808) 586–9151

Labor & Industrial Relations Appeal Board
888 Miliani Street, Room 400
Honolulu, HA 98613
Tel. (808) 586–8600

Idaho
Industrial Commission
317 Main Street
Boise, ID 83720
Tel. (208) 334–6000
Fax (208) 334–2321

Illinois
Industrial Commission
100 West Randolph Street
Suite 8–200
Chicago, IL 60601
Tel. (312) 814–6500

Indiana
Workers' Compensation Board
Room W196 Government Center South
402 West Washington Street
Indianapolis, IN 46204

Tel. (317) 232–3808
Fax (317) 233–5493

Iowa
Division of Industrial Services
Department of Employment Services
1000 East Grand Avenue
Des Moines, IA 50319
Tel. (515) 281–5934
Fax (515) 281–6501

Kansas
Division of Workers' Compensation
Department of Human Resources
600 Merchant Bank Tower
800 SW Jackson
Topeka, KS 66612–1227
Tel. (913) 296–3441
Fax (913) 296–0839

Kentucky
Workers' Compensation Board
Perimeter Park West, Building C
1270 Louisville Road
Frankfort, KY 40601
Tel. (502) 564–5550

Louisiana
Department of Employment & Training
Office of Workers' Compensation
1001 North 23rd Street
PO Box 94040
Baton Rouge, LA 70804–9040
Tel. (504) 3420–7555
Fax (504) 342–6555

Maine
Workers' Compensation Commission
State House Station 27
Augusta, ME 04333–0027
Tel. (207) 287–3751
Fax (207) 287–7198

Maryland
Workers' Compensation Commission
6 North Liberty Street
Baltimore, MD 21201–3785
Tel. (410) 333–4700
Fax (410) 333–8122

Massachusetts
Department of Industrial Accidents
600 Washington Street
Boston, MA 02111

Tel. (617) 727–4900
Fax (617) 727–6477

Michigan
Bureau of Workers' Disability Compensation
Department of Labor
PO Box 30016
201 North Washington Square
Second Floor
Lansing, MI 48909
Tel. (517) 373–3490

Workers' Compensation Board of Magistrates
PO Box 30016
201 North Washington Square
Second Floor
Lansing, MI 48909
Tel. (517) 335–0643

Workers' Compensation Appellate Commission
PO Box 30015
201 North Washington Square
Second Floor
Lansing, MI 48909
Tel. (517) 335–5828

Minnesota
Workers' Compensation Division
Department of Labor & Industry
443 Lafayette Road North
St Paul, MN 55101
Tel. (612) 296–6107
Fax (612) 296–9634

Workers' Compensation Court of Appeals
775 Landmark Towers
345 St Peter Street
St Paul, MN 55102
Tel. (612) 296–6526

Mississippi
Workers' Compensation Commission
1428 Lakeland Drive
PO Box 5300
Jackson, MS 39216
Tel. (601) 987–4200

Missouri
Department of Labor & Industrial Relations
Division of Workers' Compensation
PO Box 599
3315 West Truman Boulevard
Jefferson City, MO 65102
Tel. (314) 751–4231

Labor & Industrial Relations Commission
PO Box 599
3315 West Truman Boulevard
Jefferson City, MO 65102
Tel. (314) 751–2461

Montana
State Compensation Mutual Insurance Fund
5 South Last Chance Gulch
Helena, MT 59604–8011
Tel. (406) 444–6500

Workers' Compensation Court
47 North Last Chance Gulch
PO box 537
Helena, MT 59624
Tel. (406) 444–6520

Employee Relations Division
Department of Labor & Industry
PO Box 1728
Helena, MT 59624
Tel. (406) 444–3022

Nebraska
Workers' Compensation Court
State House, 13th Floor
PO Box 98908
Lincoln, NE 68509–8908
Tel. (402) 471–2568
Fax (402) 471–2700

Nevada
State Industrial Insurance System
515 East Musser Street
Carson City, NV 68509–8908
Tel. (702) 687–5220
Fax (702) 687–3946

Department of Industrial Relations
1390 South Curry Street
Carson City, NV 89710
Tel. (702) 687–3032

New Hampshire
Department of Labor
95 Pleasant Street
Concord, NH 03301
Tel. (603) 271–3176

New Jersey
Division of Workers' Compensation
Department of Labor
Call Number 381
Trenton, NJ 08625
Tel. (609) 292–2516

New Mexico
Workers' Compensation Administration
PO Box 27198
Albuquerque, NM 87125–7198
Tel. (505) 841–6000
Fax (505) 841–6009

New York
Workers' Compensation Board
180 Livingston Street
Brooklyn, NY 11248
Tel. (718) 802–6600
Fax (718) 834–3705

North Carolina
Industrial Commission
Dobbs Building
430 North Salisbury Street
Raleigh, NC 27611
Tel. (919) 733–4820

North Dakota
Workers' Compensation Bureau
500 East Front Avenue
Bismark, ND 58504–5685
Tel. (701) 224–3800
Fax (701) 224–3820

Ohio
Bureau of Workers' Compensation
30 West Spring Street
Columbus, OH 43215
Tel. (614) 466–1000

Industrial Commission of Ohio
30 West Spring Street
William Green Building
Columbus, OH 43215
Tel. (614) 466–6136

Oklahoma
Workers' Compensation Court
1915 North Stiles
Oklahoma City, OK 73105
Tel. (405) 557–7600
Fax (405) 557–7683

Oregon
Department of Insurance & Finance
21 Labor & Industries Building
Salem, OR 97310
Tel. (503) 378–3304

Workers' Compensation Division
Labor & Industries Building

Salem, OR 97310
Tel. (503) 378–3304

Workers' Compensation Board
480 Church Street South East
Salem, OR 97310
Tel. (503) 378–4283

Pennsylvania

Bureau of Workers' Compensation
Department of Labor & Industry
1171 South Cameron Street, Room 103
Harrisburg, PA 17104–2502
Tel. (717) 783–5421

Workmen's Compensation Appeal Board
1171 South Cameron Street, Room 305
Harrisburg, PA 17104–2511
Tel. (717) 783–7838

Rhode Island

Workers' Compensation Court
One Dorrance Plaza
Providence, RI 02903
Tel. (401) 277–3097
Fax (401) 421–3123

Department of Labor, Workers' Compensation Division
610 Manton Avenue
Providence, RI 02907
Tel. (401) 272–0700
Fax (401) 277–2127

South Carolina

Workers' Compensation Commission
PO Box 1715
1612 Marion Street
Columbia, SC 29202–1715
Tel. (803) 737–5700
Fax (803) 737–5768

South Dakota

Department of Labor
Division of Labor & Management
Kneip Building, 3rd Floor
700 Governors Drive
Pierre, SD 57501–2277
Tel. (605) 773–3681
Fax (605) 773–4211

Tennessee

Workers' Compensation Division
Department of Labor
501 Union Building
Second Floor
Nashville, TN 37243–0661
Tel. (615) 741–2395

Texas
Workers' Compensation Commission
4000 IH 35 South
Austin, TX 78704–7491
Tel. (512) 448–7900

Utah
Industrial Commission of Utah
160 East 300 South 3rd Floor
PO Box 146600
Salt Lake City, UT 84114–6600
Tel. (801) 530–6880
Fax (801) 530–6804

Vermont
Department of Labor & Industry
National Life Building
Drawer 20
Montpelier, VT 05620
Tel. (802) 828–2286
Fax (802) 828–2195

Workers' Compensation Division
State Office Building
120 State Street
Montpelier, VT 05602
Tel. (802) 828–2286
Fax (802) 828–2195

Virginia
Industrial Commission
1000 DMV Drive
PO Box 1794
Richmond, VA 23220
Tel. (804) 367–8633

Washington
Department of Labor & Industries
Labor & Industries Building
PO Box 44000
Olympia, WA 98504–4000
Tel. (206) 956–5800

Board of Industrial Insurance Appeals
2430 Chandler Court SW
PO Box 42401
Olympia, WA 98504–2401
Tel. (206) 753–6823
Fax (206) 586–5611

West Virginia
Bureau of Employment Programs
Workers' Compensation Fund
PO Box 3824

Charleston, WV 25338–3824
Tel. (304) 558–0475

Workers' Compensation Appeal Board
601 Morris Street, Room 419
Charleston, WV 25301–1416
Tel. (304) 558–3375

Wisconsin
Workers' Compensation Division
Department of Industry, Labor & Human Relations
PO Box 7901
Madison, WI 53707
Tel. (608) 266–1340

Labor & Industry Review Commission
PO Box 8126
Madison, WI 53708
Tel. (608) 266–9850

Wyoming
Workers' Compensation Division
122 West 25th Street, 2nd Floor
East Wing, Herschler Building
Cheyenne, WY 82002
Tel. (307) 777–7441
Fax (307) 777–5946

United States Department of Labor
Department of Labor
Employment Standards Administration
Washington, DC 20210
Tel. (202) 219–6692

Office of Workers' Compensation Programs
Tel. (202) 219–6692

Division of Planning & Standards
Tel. (202) 219–6692

Division of Coal Mine Workers' Compensation
Tel. (202) 219–6692

Division of Federal Employees' Compensation
Tel. (202) 219–7552

Division of Longshore and Harbor Workers' Compensation
Tel. (202) 219–8572

Branch of Workers' Compensation Studies
Tel. (202) 219–9560

Appendix 2: Benefits for temporary total disability provided by workers' compensation statutes in the USA

| Jurisdiction | Percentage of worker's wage | Payments per week | | Percentage of state's average weekly wage (SAWW) | Maximum period | Notes |
		Minimum	Maximum			
Alabama	66²/₃	$115: 27.5% of SAWW or worker's average wage if less	$419.00	100	Duration of disability	
Alaska	80% of worker's spendable earnings	$110, or $154 if employee shows proof of wages, or worker's spendable weekly wage if less	$700.00	N/A	Duration of disability until date of medical stability	WC benefits subject to offsets under Social Security
Arizona	66²/₃	Payable, but not statutorily prescribed	$323.10	N/A	Duration of disability	Additional $25 monthly added to benefits of dependents residing in the USA
Arkansas	66²/₃	$20	$267.00	70	450 weeks	
California	66²/₃	$126	$336.00	66²/₃	Duration of disability	
Colorado	66²/₃		$432.25	91	Duration of disability	WC benefits subject to Social Security benefit offsets and to reduction by benefits under an employer pension or disability plan

Jurisdiction	Percentage of worker's wage	Payments per week		Percentage of state's average weekly wage (SAWW)	Maximum period	Notes
		Minimum	Maximum			
Connecticut	75% of worker's spendable earnings	$127.60: 20% of SAWW, or an amount not to exceed 80% of worker's average wage if less	$638.00	100	Duration of disability	WC benefits subject to Social Security benefit offset
Delaware	66²/₃	$113.10: 22²/₉% of SAWW, or actual wage if less	$339.29	66²/₃	Duration of disability	
District of Columbia	66²/₃ or 80% of spendable earnings, whichever is less	$169.79: 25% of SAWW	$679.17	100	Duration of disability	
Florida	66²/₃	$20 or actual wage if less	$444.00	100	104 weeks	WC benefits subject to Social Security and UI benefit offsets
Georgia	66²/₃	$25 or average wage if less	$250.00	N/A	400 weeks	Maximum weekly benefit in catastrophic cases shall be paid until such time as employee undergoes a change in condition for the better

State		Minimum	Maximum		Duration	Notes
Hawaii	$66\frac{2}{3}$	$120: 25% of SAWW, or worker's average wage if less, but not lower than $38	$481.00	100	Duration of disability	
Idaho	67	$175.50: 45% of SAWW	$351.00	90	52 weeks, thereafter 67% of SAWW for duration of disability	
Illinois	$66\frac{2}{3}$	$100 to $124.30, or worker's average wage if less, according to number of dependents	$712.92	$133\frac{1}{3}$	Duration of disability	
Indiana	$66\frac{2}{3}$	$50 or worker's average wage if less	$394.00	N/A	500 weeks	Total maximum amount payable is $197,000 Effective July 1, 1994 increased to $214,000
Iowa	80% of worker's spendable earnings	$139: 35% of SAWW, or actual wage if less	$797.00	200	Duration of disability	
Kansas	$66\frac{2}{3}$	$25	$313.00	75	Duration of disability	Total amount payable is $100,000. WC benefits subject to UI and Social Security benefit offsets
Kentucky	$66\frac{2}{3}$	$83.19: 20% of SAWW	$415.94	100	Duration of disability	
Louisiana	$66\frac{2}{3}$	$85: 20% of SAWW, or actual wage if less	$319.00	75	Duration of disability	WC benefits subject to UI benefit offsets

	Payments per week					
Jurisdiction	Percentage of worker's wage	Minimum	Maximum	Percentage of state's average weekly wage (SAWW)	Maximum period	Notes
Maine	80% of worker's after-tax earnings		$441.00	90	Duration of disability	WC benefits subject to UI benefit offsets
Maryland	66²/₃	$50 or actual wage if less	$510.00	100	Duration of disability	
Massachusetts	60	$113.19: 20% of SAWW, or worker's average wage if less	$565.94	100	156 weeks	Additional $6 will be added per dependent if weekly benefits are below $150. Total maximum payable not to exceed 250 times the SAWW at time of injury
Michigan	80% of worker's spendable earnings		$475.00	90	Duration of disability	WC benefits subject to reduction by UI and Social Security benefits, and by those under an employer disability, retirement, or pension plan
Minnesota	66²/₃	$96.80: 20% of SAWW, or actual wage if less	$508.20	105	Duration of disability until 90 days after maximum medical improvement or end of retraining	

State						
Mississippi	66⅔	$25	$243.75	66⅔	450 weeks	Total maximum amount payable is $109,687
Missouri	66⅔	$40	$470.06	105	400 weeks	WC benefits subject to Social Security benefit offsets
Montana	66⅔	Payable, but not statutorily prescribed	$362.00	100	Duration of disability	
Nebraska	66⅔	$49 or actual wage if less	$265.00	N/A	Duration of disability	Maximum weekly benefit increased to $310, eff. June 1, 1994, and to $350, eff. Jan. 1, 1995. Starting Jan. 1, 1996, maximum weekly benefit will be 100% of the SAWW
Nevada	66⅔		$432.39	100	Duration of disability	
New Hampshire	66⅔	$189.20: 40% of SAWW, not to exceed employee's after-tax earnings	$709.50	150	Duration of disability	
New Jersey	70	$123: 20% of SAWW	$460.00	75	400 weeks	
New Mexico	66⅔	$36 or actual wage if less	$333.02	85	700 weeks; 100 weeks (primary and secondary mental impairment)	Total maximum equals the sum of 700 multiplied by the maximum weekly benefit payable at time of injury
New York	66⅔	$40 or actual wage if less	$400.00	N/A	Duration of disability	
North Carolina	66⅔	$30	$466.00	110	Duration of disability	

Jurisdiction	Payments per week				Maximum period	Notes
	Percentage of worker's wage	Minimum	Maximum	Percentage of state's average weekly wage (SAWW)		
North Dakota	66²/₃	$215: 60% of SAWW, or employee's actual wage if less	$358.00	100	Duration of disability	Additional $10 per week for each dependent child, not to exceed worker's net wage. Benefits are reduced by 50% of Social Security disability benefits
Ohio	72% for first 12 weeks; thereafter 66²/₃	$160.00: 33¹/₃% of SAWW or actual wage if less	$482.00	100	Duration of disability	WC benefits subject to Social Security benefit offsets and, if concurrent and/or duplicate, with those under employer non-occupational benefit plan
Oklahoma	70	$30 or actual wage if less	$307.00	75	300 weeks	
Oregon	66²/₃	$50 or 90% of actual wage if less	$478.95	100	Duration of disability	
Pennsylvania	66²/₃	$273.80 or 90% of AWW if less	$493.00	100	Duration of disability	
Puerto Rico	66²/₃	$25	$65.00	N/A	312 weeks	
Rhode Island	75% of worker's spendable earnings		$463.00	100	Duration of disability	Additional $9 for each dependent; including a non-working spouse, aggregate not to exceed 80% of worker's AWW

State	Percentage	Minimum	Maximum		Duration	Notes
South Carolina	66²/₃	$75 or average wage if less	$410.26	100	500 weeks	
South Dakota	66²/₃	$169: 50% of SAWW, or worker's average wage if less	$338.00	100	Duration of disability	
Tennessee	66²/₃	$64.80	$355.97	N/A	400 weeks	Total amount payable is $142,388
Texas	70% of worker's earnings over $8.50 per hour; 75% for all others	$70: 15% of SAWW	$464.00	100	104 weeks, or upon reaching maximum medical improvement, whichever is sooner	
Utah	66²/₃	$45	$413.00	100	312 weeks	Additional $5 for dependent spouse and each dependent child up to 4 under age 18, but not to exceed 100% of SAWW
Vermont	66²/₃	$215: 50% of SAWW, or worker's average wage if less	$644.00	150	Duration of disability	Additional $10 will be paid for each dependent under 21 years of age
Virgin Islands	66²/₃	$60, or actual wage if less	$287.00	66²/₃	Duration of disability	
Virginia	66²/₃	$112.75: 25% of SAWW, or employee's actual wage if less	$451.00	100	500 weeks	

		Payments per week				
Jurisdiction	Percentage of worker's wage	Minimum	Maximum	Percentage of state's average weekly wage (SAWW)	Maximum period	Notes
Washington	60–75	$44.05 to $83.81 according to marital status and number of dependents	$517.16	105% of state's monthly wage	Duration of disability	WC benefits subject to Social Security benefit offsets
West Virginia	70	$140.11: 33⅓% of SAWW	$420.33	100	208 weeks	
Wisconsin	66⅔	$30 or actual wage if less	$466.00	100	Duration of disability	WC benefits subject to Social Security benefit offsets
Wyoming	66⅔ of actual monthly earnings		$413.00	100% of monthly wage	Duration of disability	
United States[a]						
FECA	66⅔	$193.01 or actual wage if less	$1,248.88	See notes	Duration of disability	Maximum weekly benefit is based on the pay of a specific grade level in the Federal Civil Service
LHWCA	66⅔	$184.58: 50% of NAWW, or worker's actual wage if less	$738.30	200% of NAWW	Duration of disability	National average weekly wage is $369.15

[a] Federal Employees' Compensation Act; Longshore and Harbor Workers' Compensation Act.

Source: State Workers' Compensation Laws, US Department of Labor, Office of Workers' Compensation Programs, January 1994, table 6.

Appendix 3: **Insurance requirements for private employment**

Jurisdiction	State fund	Employer may insure through		
		Private insurance	Individual self-insurance	Group self-insurance
Alabama		X	X	X
Alaska		X	X	
Arizona	X	X	X	
Arkansas		X	X	X
California	X	X	X	
Colorado	X	X	X	X
Connecticut		X	X	X
Delaware		X	X	
District of Columbia		X	X	
Florida		X	X	X
Georgia		X	X	X
Hawaii	X	X	X	X
Idaho	X	X	X	
Illinois		X	X	X
Indiana		X	X	
Iowa		X	X	X
Kansas		X	X	X
Kentucky		X	X	X
Louisiana	X	X	X	X
Maine	X	X	X	X
Maryland	X	X	X	X
Massachusetts		X	X	
Michigan	X	X	X	X
Minnesota	X	X	X	X
Mississippi		X	X	X
Missouri		X	X	X
Montana	X	X	X	X
Nebraska		X	X	
Nevada	X		X	
New Hampshire		X	X	X
New Jersey		X	X	
New Mexico		X	X	X
New York	X	X	X	X
North Carolina		X	X	X
North Dakota	X			
Ohio	X		X	
Oklahoma	X	X	X	X
Oregon	X	X	X	X
Pennsylvania	X	X	X	
Rhode Island		X	X	X
South Carolina		X	X	X
South Dakota		X	X	X

Jurisdiction	State fund	Employer may insure through		
		Private insurance	Individual self-insurance	Group self-insurance
Tennessee	X	X	X	X
Texas	X	X	X	
Utah	X	X	X	
Vermont		X	X	
Virginia		X	X	X
Washington	X		X	X
West Virginia	X		X	
Wisconsin		X	X	
Wyoming	X			
Federal Employees' Compensation Act	X		X	
Longshore and Harbor Workers' Compensation Act		X	X	

Maine. Two prerequisites to the operation of the fund are: (a) that on July 1, 1994, if the premium volume in the voluntary market is less than 20 percent of the total statewide premium volume, or if by December 31, 1995, it is less than 25 percent, the operations of the fund may be initiated; and (b) that there be an appropriation of no more than $20 million to start the fund which is to be repaid over a ten-year period.

New Jersey permits ten or more employers licensed by the state as hospitals to group self-insure.

Texas provides for mandatory workers' compensation coverage under Title 25 of state statutes regarding rules and regulations for "carriers" (article 911-A, section II, Motor Bus Transportation and Regulations by the Railroad Commission). Self-insurance coverage is approved for private employers, effective January 1, 1993.

Wyoming. The law is compulsory for all employers engaged in extra-hazardous occupations and elective for all other occupations.

Source: State Workers' Compensation Laws, US Department of Labor, Office of Workers' Compensation Programs, January 1994, table 1.

Questions for discussion

1 Prepare a report to a legislative committee discussing what work and which injuries should be covered in a model workers' compensation act.
2 Describe a system which would, in your view, embody the fairest method for determining how much compensation a worker would receive for on-the-job injuries.
3 How should an employer decide on the best method for providing security for compensation?
4 The last section of this chapter deals with "firm level solutions." Based upon outside readings or personal experience list several specific techniques an employer can use to control workers' compensation costs.

NOTES

1 Emily A. Speiler, "Perpetuating risk? Workers' compensation and the persistence of occupational injuries," Houston Law Review, 31 (No. 1, Symposium, 1994), pp. 162–8.
2 *Guides to the Evaluation of Impairment*, 4th edn (American Medical Association, Chicago, 1993).
3 R. V. Habeck, H. A. Hunt, M. J. Leahy, and E. M. Welch, "Differences in workers' compensation experience among Michigan employers" (Bureau of Workers' Disability Compensation, Lansing, MI, 1988); and R. V. Habeck, M. J. Leahy, H. A. Hunt, F. Chan, and E. M. Welch, "Employer factors related to workers' compensation claims and disability management," *Rehabilitation Counseling Bulletin* (March 1991), pp. 210–42.

Part III
New Developments

Chapter 10
The Law of Unjust Discharge

Introduction

If the 1960s and the 1970s were notable for the development of the law of employment discrimination, perhaps the major employment law development of the 1980s was the evolution of the law on unjust discharge for employees not covered by a collective agreement – the so-called "employment-at-will doctrine." Traditionally in the United States, the common law rule prevailed, an employee not covered by a collective agreement could be dismissed at any time for any reason. That changed during the 1980s, as almost all states carved out exceptions to this doctrine. An interesting aspect of the development of this law is that it is judge-made on a state-by-state basis, rather than legislatively enacted, either at the federal or the state level.

This chapter explores the evolution of the law on employment-at-will. The first section provides a brief history of the doctrine and a summary of the legal foundations of this area of law. The next section of the chapter is divided into three subsections, each examining, through cases and text, one of the three major exceptions to the employment-at-will doctrine: the contractual exception, the public policy exception, and the good faith and fair dealing exception. The last section of the chapter provides a summary of the doctrine as it has evolved.

Historical Overview

The long-held presumption of employers and employees in the United States is that the employment relationship is generally terminable at will by either party, i.e. the employer may dismiss the employee at any time and the employee may quit at any time. Yet, throughout the history of the USA, it has not always been that way. Jacoby points out that, from the mid-sixteenth to the mid-eighteenth centuries, master–servant law in England and the colonies assumed that contracts of employment which did not specify duration were for one year.[1] There was a reason for this. In a period of labor scarcity, the one-year rule was designed to limit the movement of labor. In addition, it was believed that this rule minimized poor relief by maintaining earnings.

By the early nineteenth century, United States society began to view mercantilistic control and regulations as an anachronistic impediment to the economy. Prosperity and personal liberty were thought to depend on removing all barriers to commercial activity, including wage-fixing and dismissal constraints. Thus, after 1800, the notion that employment implied some imposition of moral obligations was viewed as inconsistent with the principle of contract – the parties should be free to design their own relationship. Courts became unwilling to supply obligations unless these had been intended. Thus, by the mid-nineteenth century, the legal doctrine had moved toward freedom of choice and contract and the market, and away from compulsion of the law. The focus of law shifted from prescriptive regulation of the employment relationship to enforcing only that to which the parties had agreed.

Thus, because the American Revolution coincided with the rise of *laissez-faire* philosophies, there has never truly been an acceptance of the annual hiring presumption in the United States. Prior to 1877, there was little employment-related litigation in the United States. Jacoby attributes this to the unwillingness of the United States to permit settlement of debts by annual hiring and to make breach of contract subject to criminal penalties. Thus, there was little incentive for US employers to use long-term contracts as the law was of little assistance in disciplining the workforce. Contracts were enforced by employers through industry blacklists and wage withholding.

Horace Wood's influential 1877 treatise on employment law was instrumental in establishing the employment-at-will doctrine. Wood's view was that, unlike in England, where the annual hiring presumption was accepted, there had never been an annual hiring presumption in the United States. Thus, Wood concluded that in the absence of evidence that the employment contract was for fixed duration, it was terminable at will by either party.

Overall, Jacoby argues that belief in the sanctity of the contract in combination with *laissez-faire* tendencies in the USA encouraged employment-at-will. Anti-unionism, in cases involving the right of employers to fire people for union activities, also supported employment-at-will. In Jacoby's view, courts were comfortable with the equality inherent in the notion of employees being able to quit and employers being able to dismiss. As will be seen, the principles developed in the one hundred years prior to the reconsideration of the employment-at-will doctrine in the 1980s are still operative in modern jurisprudence.

Exceptions to the Employment-at-will Doctrine

As noted, three exceptions to the employment-at-will doctrine have developed in the United States. They may be called the contractual exception, the good faith and fair dealing exception, and the public policy exception. Research by the Bureau of National Affairs indicates that, as of March 1994, 36 states had developed a contractual exception, 43 states a public policy exception, and 13 states a good faith and fair dealing exception. As regards the good faith and fair dealing exception, in most states the matter has never been litigated.[2]

The contractual exception

The basic principle of the contractual exception to the employment-at-will doctrine is quite simple – if the employer and the employee have agreed that the employment contract will not be terminated at will, then that contract should have force and effect. In the nineteenth century, such cases revolved around duration, that is whether the parties agreed that employment should be for a specified period of time.[3] The modern cases deal with the question of whether the parties agreed that the employment contract should not be terminable at will. In other words did the employer and the employee parties agree that the employee would be discharged only for just cause?

The courts have dealt with two categories of cases in this area. One category of cases may be called the implicit contract exception to the employment-at-will doctrine. The second category, the manual or handbook exception, addresses the implications of employee handbooks. This section of the chapter will examine each of these concepts, followed by an analysis.

Implied contract Foley v. Interactive Data Corporation (*IDC*), decided by the California Supreme Court in 1988,[4] represents an excellent illustration of the implicit contract exception. The employer, a wholly owned subsidiary of Chase Manhattan Bank, sold computer-based decision-support services to businesses. Foley had been hired by IDC in June 1976 as an assistant product manager at an initial salary of $18,500 per year. Between June of 1976 and his discharge in March 1983, Foley had consistently received promotions, awards, bonuses, and superior performance evaluations. He was consultant manager of the year in 1979 and was named manager of the Los Angeles branch office in 1981. At his termination, his salary was $56,164. In addition he received a merit bonus of $6,762 in March 1983, two days before he was terminated.

During 1982, Interactive named one RK to replace RE as Foley's immediate superior. Foley had reason to believe that RK was the subject of an investigation by the Federal Bureau of Investigation for embezzlement from his previous employer, a large bank in California, and he informed RE of what he knew. He claimed to have done this in the best interest of his employer, because Interactive worked with the financial community on a confidential basis, and he believed that his company would have a legitimate interest in knowing about allegations of criminal conduct against a high level executive. RE responded that Foley should not discuss "rumors" and that he should "forget what he heard" about RK's past.

In early March 1983, Foley was informed by RK, who had since taken the position as his superior, that Interactive had decided to replace him for reasons of "performance" and that he could transfer to a branch manager position in Waltham, Massachusetts. In Waltham, however, one week after he began, RK informed Foley that he was not performing well, later informing him that he could stay on as a branch manager if he went on a "performance plan." The next day, however, rather than presenting Foley with a performance plan, RK gave him the option of resigning or being fired. Foley was then terminated.

For our purposes, the major question in the case was straightforward — whether the employer's actions *vis-à-vis* Foley, over a period of years, gave rise to an implied contract that Foley would not be fired without just cause. The employer contended that there was a longstanding presumption that ordinary employment contracts were terminable at will by either party, and that the presumption should stand unless the employee could show an express written contract permitting discharge only for just cause, and that this contract was supported by independent consideration over and above the employee's normal work efforts.

The court addressed these differing contentions by first noting the primacy of traditional contract law. The court observed that

> We begin by acknowledging the fundamental principle of freedom of contract: employer and employee are free to agree to a contract terminable at will or subject to limitations. Their agreement will be enforced so long as it does not violate legal strictures external to the contract, such as laws affecting union membership and activity, prohibitions on indentured servitude, or the many other legal restrictions already described which place certain restraints on the employment arrangement. As we have discussed, [California law] establishes a presumption of at-will employment if the parties have made no express oral or written agreement specifying the length of employment or the grounds for termination.[5]

The court then went on to observe, however, that

> This presumption may . . . be overcome by evidence that despite the absence of a specified term, the parties agreed that the employer's power to terminate would be limited in some way, e.g. by a requirement that termination be based only on "good cause."[6]

In essence, the court stated that the parties could agree by contract to terminate the relationship only for just cause. Typically, one thinks of contracts as written documents, setting out the obligations of each party. In Foley, however, there was no written contract. As the court noted, however, the fact that there was no written contract did not mean that a contract to terminate only for just cause did not exist. The court observed:

> The absence of an express written or oral contract term concerning termination of employment does not necessarily indicate that the employment is actually intended by the parties to be "at will," because the presumption of at-will employment may be overcome by evidence of contrary intent. Generally, courts seek to enforce the actual understanding of the parties to a contract, and in so doing may inquire into the parties' conduct to determine if it demonstrates an implied contract. "It must be determined, as a question of fact, whether the parties acted in such a manner as to provide the necessary foundation for [an implied contract], and evidence may be introduced to rebut the inferences and show that there is another explanation for the conduct." . . . Such implied-in-fact contract terms ordinarily stand on equal footing with express terms. . . .
>
> At issue here is whether the foregoing principles apply to contract terms establishing employment security, so that the presumption of [employment-at-will in California law] may be overcome by evidence of contrary implied terms, or whether such agreements are subject to special substantive or evidentiary limitations.[7]

Thus the court rejected the argument of the employer that the presumption of employment-at-will was so strong that it could be overcome only on the basis of an express (written) agreement between the employer and the employee stating that the employee would not be discharged except for just cause. Rather, the court ruled that a contract could be created by methods other than an express agreement. Behavior during the employment relationship could also be used as evidence of a contract. Specifically, if the behavior and words of the employer were such as to create an understanding on the part of the employee that he or she would be terminated only for just cause, and the employee accepted that, then a contract existed.

The court also rejected the employer's argument that the implied contract exception to the employment-at-will rule was one-sided because an employer who was obligated to discharge employees only for just cause did not receive an equivalent guarantee that the employee would not quit. The court noted that employers would receive additional loyalty and productivity. More important, however, the court believed that the employment contract should be treated in the same manner as other contracts.

What evidence would suffice to create an implied contract? The court provided some guidance.

> [The employer] overemphasizes the fact that plaintiff was employed for "only" six years and nine months. Length of employment is a relevant consideration but six years and nine months is sufficient time for conduct to occur on which a trier of fact could find the existence of an implied contract. . . . As to establishing the requisite promises, "oblique language will not, standing alone, be sufficient to establish agreement;" instead, the totality of the circumstances determines the nature of the contract. Agreement may be "shown by the acts and conduct of the parties, interpreted in the light of the subject matter and of the surrounding circumstances." [citation omitted] Plaintiff here alleged

repeated oral assurances of job security and consistent promotions, salary increases and bonuses during the term of his employment contributing to his reasonable expectation that he would not be discharged except for good cause. . . .

Finally [Foley] alleges that he supplied the company valuable and separate consideration by signing an agreement whereby he promised not to compete or conceal any computer-related information from defendant for one year after termination. [This] non-competition agreement . . . may be probative evidence that "it is more probable that the parties intended a continuing relationship, with limitations upon the employer's dismissal authority [because the] employee has provided some benefit to the employer, or suffers some detriment, beyond the usual rendition of service" [citations omitted].

In sum [Foley] has pleaded facts which, if proved, may be sufficient for a jury to find an implied-in-fact contract limiting defendant's right to discharge him arbitrarily — facts sufficient to overcome the [employment-at-will] presumption of [California law]. . . . In other words, [Foley] has pleaded an implied-in-fact contract and its breach, and is entitled to his opportunity to prove those allegations.[8]

The *Foley* case, then, provides the basics of the implied contract exception to the employment-at-will doctrine. A contract need not be written; one may be implied by actions, behavior, and words during the employment relationship. If it can be shown that the employer promised that the employee would be discharged only for just cause, and the employee relied on that promise in the performance of his or her duties, an implied contract would be made out.

Also interesting is the principle of additional consideration. The basic argument of IDC was that a promise on its part to discharge only for just cause would require extra consideration from Foley to create a valid contract. The court seemed to accept the notion that extra consideration would be required, but found that extra consideration in the extra effort Foley would put forth on behalf of IDC because of the promise. Monetary consideration is not the only consideration a court will deem valid. We will return to this after examining the doctrine of employer handbooks.

Employer handbooks One of the best known cases on the contractual nature of employer handbooks is *Toussaint* v. *Blue Cross and Blue Shield of Michigan*, issued by the Michigan Supreme Court in 1980.[9] Toussaint was hired by Blue Cross on May 1, 1967 as an assistant to the company treasurer with responsibility for analyzing and preparing financial reports. When Toussaint was interviewing for the position, he inquired about job security. In response, he was given oral assurances of job security "as long as he did his job." In addition, he was handed a manual of Blue Cross personnel policies. The personnel policies contained disciplinary procedures, stating that the procedures applied to all Blue Cross employees who had completed their probationary period and that it was the "policy" of the company to release employees "for just cause only."[10]

In early 1971, Toussaint was assigned the responsibilities of administering Blue Cross's company car program. After Toussaint assumed these responsibilities, upper level management began to receive complaints regarding the administration of the program. One complaint involved an allegation that the odometer on several cars over which Toussaint had control had been "set back." After meeting with Toussaint and his supervisor, Blue Cross decided to terminate both men on May 7, 1972. On November 20, 1972, Toussaint filed a suit alleging wrongful discharge in violation of an employment contract. At trial, a jury found for Toussaint and awarded him $72,835.52 in damages.

The key question in this case was whether Blue Cross, through its representations to Toussaint in its handbook, had promised that it would not discharge him without just cause. The court found that, indeed, the employer's policies did constitute such a promise. In so doing, the court rejected Blue Cross's contention, based on Michigan law, that employment *must* be terminable at will. The court observed that the employer created personnel policies in its interest. The court noted:

> While an employer need not establish personnel policies or practices, where an employer chooses to establish such policies and practices and makes them known to its employees, the employment relationship is presumably enhanced. The employer secures an orderly, cooperative and loyal work force, and the employee the peace of mind associated with job security and the conviction that he will be treated fairly. No pre-employment negotiations need take place and the parties' minds need not meet on the subject, nor does it matter that the employee knows nothing of the particulars of the employers' policies and practices or that the employer may change them unilaterally. It is enough that the employer chooses, presumably in its own interest, to create an environment in which the employee believes that, whatever the personnel policies and practices, they are established and official at any given time, purport to be fair, and are applied consistently and uniformly to each employee. The employer has then created a situation "instinct with an obligation."[11]

The court then took the next step, essentially saying that if the employer creates personnel policies in its own interest, those policies should apply to all the covered employees. The court observed:

> Blue Cross offered no evidence that the manual and guidelines are not what they purport to be — statements of company policy on the subjects there addressed, including discipline and termination.
>
> The jury could properly conclude that the statements of policy on those subjects were applicable to Toussaint although the manual did not explicitly refer to him. The manual, by its terms, purports to apply to all employees who have completed a probationary period. The inference that the policies and procedures applied to Toussaint is supported by his testimony that he was handed the manual in the course of a conversation in which he inquired about job security.
>
> Although Toussaint's employment was for an indefinite term, the jury could find that the relationship was not terminable at the will of Blue Cross. Blue Cross had established a company policy to discharge for just cause only, pursuant to certain procedures, had made that policy known to Toussaint, and thereby had committed itself to discharge him only for just cause in

compliance with the procedures. There were, thus, on this separate basis alone, special circumstances sufficient to overcome the presumptive construction that the contract was terminable at will.

We hold that employer statements of policy, such as Blue Cross Supervisory Manual and Guidelines, can give rise to contractual rights in employees without evidence that the parties mutually agreed that the policy statements would create contractual rights in the employee, and, hence, although the statement of policy is signed by neither party, can be unilaterally amended by the employer without notice to the employee, and contains no reference to a specific employee, his job description or compensation, and although no reference was made to the policy statement in pre-employment interviews and the employee does not learn of its existence until after his hiring.[12]

The employer also argued its case based on practical grounds, claiming that the day-to-day administration of its human resources function would be impaired if it was legally held to what it wrote.

[It has been argued] that large organizations regularly distribute memoranda, bulletins and manuals reflecting established conditions and periodic changes in policy. These documents are drafted "for clarity and accuracy and to properly advise those subject to the policy memo of its contents." If such memoranda are held by this Court to form part of the employment contract, large employers will be severely hampered by the resultant inability to issue policy statements.

An employer who establishes no personnel policies instills no reasonable expectations of performance. Employers can make known to their employees that personnel policies are subject to unilateral changes by the employer. Employees would then have no legitimate expectation that any particular policy will continue to remain in force. Employees could, however, legitimately expect that policies in force at any given time will be uniformly applied to all. If there is in effect a policy to dismiss for cause only, the employer may not depart from that policy at whim simply because he was under no obligation to institute the policy in the first place. Having announced the policy, presumably with a view to obtaining the benefit of improved employee attitudes and behavior and improved quality of the work force, the employer may not treat its promise as illusory.[13]

Analysis Looked at from one perspective, these two cases can be interpreted as a substantial departure from the principle of employment-at-will. Both cases suggest that, under some circumstances, employees not covered by a collective bargaining agreement may have some protection against summary termination by their employer.

While this is the case, it is also true that these cases are both grounded in traditional notions of contract theory. Both cases stand for the proposition that the employer and the employee should be held to that which they promised to do. In essence, both cases state that if the employer promised to discharge an employee only for just cause, the employer should be held to that promise. There remains a presumption of employment-at-will. There is no general right to be free from summary termination. The employee must demonstrate that the contract entered into between himself or herself and the employee was one that does not incorporate the presumption of at-will employment.

The major change is the evidence that courts will use to find such a promise by the employer. The employer in Foley urges a very traditional standard for finding a promise. There must be independent consideration and an "express manifestation of mutual assent." In other words, only if the employee provides some extra consideration, over and above his or her labor, and only if the promise to discharge only for just cause is clearly expressed (in writing) can the at-will presumption be overcome.

The California Supreme Court was not willing to adopt such a narrow view of the contract. Rather, the court said, the entire relationship can be examined to see if a promise of just cause for termination was created. A promise could be *implied* as well as *expressed*. Length of service, promotions, bonuses, and oral assurances of job security could all be used to demonstrate a promise that discharge would only be for just cause.

This principle of examining the employment situation in its totality is illustrated in other cases. In *Coelho* v. *Posi-Seal International*,[14] the Connecticut Supreme Court ruled that a jury properly found that a quality control manager who was discharged after repeated conflicts with the manager of manufacturing was terminated in violation of an implied contract based on the statements of the company president at the time of hire that Coelho had a great future with the company and that he would be supported by top management in any conflicts with the manager of manufacturing.

In *Tonry* v. *Security Experts*,[15] the Ninth Circuit upheld a US District Court finding of an implied contract for discharge only for just cause where the plaintiff had been employed for eight years, had received an early promotion to a division manager position in San Francisco, had relocated to San Francisco at the company's request, had received a series of increases in his annual salary, had special benefits, including a company car, provided to him, had received no criticism of his work, and had acquired ownership interest in the corporation. The court also took into account the employer's practice of only discharging employees for just cause.

On the other hand, courts are reluctant to find an implied contract based on a single statement. In *Barber* v. *SMH (US) Inc.*,[16] the Michigan Court of Appeals upheld a trial court decision that the employer's pre-employment statement that Barber would have the job of sales representative "as long as [he] was profitable and doing the job"[17] did not constitute an implied contract where the employer's statement was not made in response to an inquiry regarding termination for cause.

Similarly, in *Anderson* v. *Post/Newsweek Stations*,[18] a US District Court ruled that statements by a company official that a discharged employee would have the "full support"[19] of his superiors were too vague to create an implied contract to be discharged only for just cause.

The foregoing cases involved the question of what constituted a contract when statements are not reduced to writing. *Toussaint* represented a different twist, addressing the question of the import of statements that were written. The interesting thing about *Toussaint* is that, fundamentally, it is a contract case that really breaks no new legal ground. According to the court, the typical employment contract is one for an indefinite period of time that is terminable at will by either party. The key question in *Toussaint* was whether employment contracts *must* be terminable at will.[20]

The court held that an employer and an employee may enter into such a contract. The court found that there was no public policy against discharge for just cause, as was indicated by inclusion of just cause provisions in collective agreements and limitation to just cause discharge in fixed duration contracts.

The court noted that Toussaint negotiated regarding job security. Toussaint inquired about job security and was told that he would be with the company as long as he did his job, and was handed a personnel manual that provided that discharge would be only for just cause. The manual stated that discharge would only occur for cause. This inquiry, and the employer's response with the personnel manual, constituted, the court said, a promise.

A question was also raised in *Toussaint* regarding the matter of additional consideration provided by Toussaint for the promise not to discharge except for cause. The court in *Toussaint* found such consideration in the employee's improved performance. In essence, the court viewed the employer as providing the promise of job security to obtain improved employee performance. This difference between employee performance absent the promise of job security and with the promise of job security is the employee consideration that creates the contract.

One of the points of *Toussaint* is that when an employer informs a prospective employee of a benefit or an employer policy that is favorable to the employees, the employer receives the benefits of that policy in terms of employee morale, extra effort, etc. (Indeed, is this not one of the reasons for informing the employee of that benefit?) Having received something from the employee, the employer is held to that promise.

Thus these benefits of improved employee attitudes, morale, etc., that come from written personnel policies come with an additional cost. Those polices become part of the contract that must be honored. In essence, the court tells employers, if you are going to encourage people to come to work for you through your personnel manual and procedural fairness, you are going to be held to that personnel manual and procedural fairness. The court notes that there is no requirement that the employer establish personnel policies. But if the employer chooses to establish them, they may create a contract.

The court also points out that a contract exists although pre-employment negotiations did not explicitly take place. As long as the policies exist and are made known to employees, the employment relationship is enhanced. The employer secures an orderly and cooperative workforce and the employee secures peace of mind. If an employer chooses, in its own interest, to create an environment in which personnel policies are believed by the employees to be official and in force, it has created an obligation. Since the manual applied to all employees, it applied to Toussaint, even though it did not refer to him personally.

There are two general employer responses to *Toussaint*. One response is to do nothing, to accept the principle that the employer is legally bound by its written policies and to live by that principle. The other is to make it clear in its policies that employment is at-will, and may be terminated at any time. In *Pratt* v. *Brown Machine Company*,[21] the court ruled that a "tear-sheet" at the end of an employee handbook, stating that "It is agreed that my employment with the Company, is at the will of the Company," was sufficient to demonstrate that the employee was at-will. Although Pratt claimed that he had not committed any of the acts listed in the handbook that would result in discharge, the court refused to accept the argument that these were exclusive, at least in the context of the "at-will" language.

The benefit of stating unequivocally that employment is at-will is that it provides legal protection to the employer and avoids the possibility of entering into an unwanted contract based on the handbook. The cost, however, is that it presents an obstacle to recruiting and hiring employees. No employer wishes to raise with a potential employee it is attempting to attract the possibility of dismissal.

Finally, it should be noted that handbooks and policies are open to interpretation. Thus, in *Martin* v. *Capital Cities Media, Inc.*,[22] the Pennsylvania Supreme Court upheld a lower court decision that a listing of offenses for which an employee may be disciplined did not constitute a promise to discharge only for just cause. This case suggest that not all employer policies will necessarily be contracts. Given the still existing presumption of employment-at-will, courts may also require clear and unequivocal proof of an agreement to modify the presumption.

Good faith and fair dealing exception

The second major basis for an exception to the employment-at-will doctrine, the principle of the covenant of good faith and fair dealing, is illustrated in the 1985 case of *Khanna* v. *Microdata Corp.*[23] Khanna, an experienced computer salesperson, was hired by Microdata, a computer manufacturer in the San Francisco area, on July 12, 1978. In order to attract Khanna to work for Microdata, the company offered him the Van Waters and Rogers (VWR) account and the commissions from sales to VWR. VWR was a large consulting firm which the company anticipated would make a substantial computer purchase from Microdata. This was confirmed in a July 12, 1978 letter to Khanna.

During the next several months, the sales relationship between Microdata and VWR changed. VWR decided to purchase the Microdata computers through a third party vendor (ESCOM) rather than directly from Microdata. Khanna, per instructions, stopped working on the VWR account, but continually inquired how he was to be compensated for the time he had spent on the VWR account. In November 1978, Microdata decided that Khanna would receive 60 percent of the normal commission for computers sold to and installed at VWR within the San Francisco branch territory. Khanna believed that this decision was inconsistent with the July 12 letter, which he believed gave him a right to a commission regardless of where the computers were installed.

Khanna and Microdata continued to dispute the amount he was owed. Finally, in December 1979, Khanna filed suit against Microdata, requesting $210,000 in compensatory damages and $500,000 in punitive damages. The figure of $210,000 was based on 12 percent of $1.75 million, which was the amount of a sale from Microdata to VWR that Khanna believed to be imminent.

While the suit was pending, Khanna continued to work for Mircrodata, once exceeding his sales quota by 49 percent. Meanwhile, "discovery" proceedings in the suit were unable to locate a sale of $1.75 million to VWR. The only sale to VWR was one that resulted in a late 1978 commission of approximately $4,800, which Microdata admitted owing but never paying.

On December 9, 1980, the same day that his attorney neglected to pay a jury fee and the court granted a continuance to permit Khanna to obtain new counsel, Khanna was discharged for disloyalty to Microdata. This disloyalty cited bringing suit against Microdata based on "unfounded" representations of Microdata personnel. At the time of his discharge, Khanna was owed approximately $250,000 in commissions for computers ordered but not yet installed or paid for. This was consistent with the standard company compensation that all salespersons had signed, which stated that if a salesperson was terminated, he or she had no right to collect a commission on sales that were not booked, installed, and paid for. The court noted that "The compensation plans were presented to the salesmen on a take it or leave it basis, with no opportunity to bargain or negotiate its terms."[24] Khanna then filed a suit alleging that he had been discharged for breach of an implied covenant of good faith and fair dealings in employment contracts.

In considering Khanna's allegation, the court agreed that an employer has an obligation for "good faith and fair dealing" *vis-à-vis* its employees. What did that constitute? The court defined the breach of this obligation as occurring "whenever the employer engages in 'bad faith' action, extraneous to the contract, combined with the [employer's] intent to frustrate the employee's enjoyment of contract rights."[25]

In other words, the good faith and fair dealing concept provides that an employer may not terminate an employee for the purpose of depriving that employee of benefits obtained from the employment relationship regardless of whether or not there is an employment contract. Thus, the employer may discharge an employee for dissatisfaction with services, but the discharge may not be to deprive the employee of a benefit, in this case commissions of nearly $250,000. The court found that there was substantial evidence to support the jury's inference that this was one of the reasons for the discharge.

The court also believed that a reason for the discharge was the filing of a lawsuit by Khanna to enforce his contract rights. The court also viewed this a breach of the obligation of good faith and fair dealing. Here again, the motive was to "frustrate [Khanna's] enjoyment of his contract rights."[26]

The *Khanna* case presents an excellent example of a discharge in violation of the covenant of good faith and fair dealing. A classic violation of the covenant differs from a violation of an agreement in that in the former, the employer, by its discharge action, attempts to deprive an employee of a previously earned benefit to which he or she would be entitled if he or she remained employed. In the latter, the employer has agreed not to terminate the employee except under certain conditions.

The good faith and fair dealing exception generally arises in situations in which employees are provided performance-based compensation at some point in the future based on criteria over a period of time. Typically, this performance-based compensation is commission, pay based on sales (performance) over a specified period of time, and bonuses, compensation based on past organizational performance over a period of time. As noted by the Arizona Supreme Court, "The covenant [of good faith and fair dealing] . . . protect[s] an employee from a discharge based on an employer's desire to avoid the payment of benefits already earned by the employee, such as sales commissions."[27]

In a 1985 case, *Wakefield* v. *Northern Telecom*, the second circuit found that, under New York or New Jersey law, a breach of the covenant of good faith and fair dealing could be found if the plaintiff demonstrated that the discharge was motivated by the desire to avoid paying him or her for commissions earned. On the other hand, a discharge for poor performance or some other reason would not fall under the good faith exception. As the court noted:

> Commission agreements are customarily used in circumstances in which agents or employees cannot be directly supervised and their performance cannot be effectively monitored or measured apart from concrete results. In such circumstances, an unfettered right to avoid payment of earned commissions in the principal or employer creates incentives counterproductive to the purpose of the contract itself in that the better the performance by the employee, the greater the temptation to terminate.[28]

In *Edwards* v. *Massachusetts Mutual Life Insurance Co.*,[29] the court did not find that the employer had breached the covenant in a case involving an employee who elected early retirement with a 25 percent reduction in retirement benefits because the company wished to terminate him and save money by hiring someone who could do the job for less. The employer's action did not constitute a breach of the duty of good faith and fair dealing since Edwards's only claim was for future compensation.

In *Frankina* v. *First National Bank of Boston*,[30] the court ruled that an employee could not make a claim under the covenant of good faith and fair dealing where the employer told the employee that his or her job had been eliminated, when, in fact, it had not been eliminated. The court said that the principle only applied when an employee was denied already earned compensation.

On occasion, however, courts have been willing to interpret the good faith and fair dealing exception more broadly than the right to earned compensation. In *Luedtke* v. *Nabors Alaska Drilling Co.*,[31] the Alaska Supreme Court ruled that the principle had been violated when an employee was suspended after failing a drug test because the test was administered without proper notice and no other employee was tested. There, the court noted that "the covenant of good faith and fair dealing also requires the parties to act in a manner which a reasonable person would regard as fair."[32]

In good faith and fair dealing cases, the employer is often accused of violating some social norm requiring good faith and fair dealing. A violation of the covenant, because it is a social norm, may be brought under tort law. If so brought, the employee may be eligible not only for compensatory damages, but also for punitive damages from the employer. The violation of tort law is thought to be a violation of a public duty, and thus warrants punishment.

Public policy exception

The public policy exception covers two distinct categories of acts, discharging an employee for refusing to violate a public policy, and discharging an employee for exercising an employment related right, such as filing a workers' compensation claim. The problem, and the solution, are illustrated in the 1985 case of *Watson* v. *Cleveland Chair Company.*[33]

> [Charles Howard Watson and Gilbert Garner Barnett] were employed as truck drivers by the Cleveland Chair Company. On January 17, 1983, they were fired for alleged insubordination and bad attitude. However, [Watson and Barnett] contend that they were fired because they refused to violate state speed laws and rest regulations of the Interstate Commerce Commission....
>
> [B]ased upon our review of this area of the law we are compelled to note that any substantial change in the "employee-at-will" rule should first be microscopically analyzed regarding its effect on the commerce of this state. There must be protection from substantial impairment of the very legitimate interests of an employer in hiring and retaining the most qualified personnel available or the very foundation of the free enterprise system could be jeopardized....
>
> Tennessee has made enormous strides in recent years in its attraction of new industry of high quality designed to increase the average per capita income of its citizens and thus, better the quality of their lives. The impact on the continuation of such influx of new businesses should be carefully considered before any substantial modification is made in the employee at-will rule.
>
> While we agree with this policy ... a strong argument could be made for the proposition that lawlessness thrives upon the ability of an employer to coerce employees at-will to join in criminal acts by threats of discharge. Conversely, the inability of an employer to discharge an employee for refusing to commit a crime would seriously curtail criminal fraud in business.
>
> Since the industry we seek to attract and retain are corporate citizens who will respect our laws, we do not believe the proposed exception would adversely affect the quality of the lives of our citizens. Instead, such an exception would remove the unfortunate employee from the untenable position of

either having to violate the law or lose the means of support for himself and his family. In addition, the adoption of this exception would promote the over-riding public policy that the people of this state should be encouraged to be law abiding citizens. . . .

Therefore, we find that a cause of action for retaliatory discharge arises when an at-will employee is terminated solely for refusing to participate, continue to participate, or remain silent about illegal activities.[34]

A more thorough analysis of the issue can be found in the 1980 decision of the California Supreme Court in *Tameny* v. *Atlantic Richfield Co.*[35] Gordon Tameny was discharged by Atlantic Richfield in 1975 for "incompetence" and "unsatisfactory performance." Tameny had been hired in 1960 as a relief clerk. By 1966, he had advanced to the position of retail sales representative, which was the position he held when he was discharged. Tameny sued, alleging that his discharge was not for incompetence, but due to his refusal to participate in a scheme to fix prices that was unlawful under the Sherman Anti-trust Act. Tameny claimed, and the employer did not dispute, that he was directed to pressure service stations selling Atlantic Richfield gasoline to price the gas at or below a level set by Arco. Tameny claimed that by discharging him for his refusal to participate in illegal activity, Arco had committed a tort, a harm to the public.

Atlantic Richfield did not deny the allegations, but claimed that Tameny had no contract of employment, and therefore could be discharged at any time. As there was no employment contract between Tameny and Atlantic Richfield that limited its right to discharge him, he could be terminated at the discretion of the employer. The trial court agreed with the employer, and dismissed the suit.

On appeal, the California Supreme Court overturned the trial judge's decision. The court noted that

Over the past several decades . . . judicial authorities in California and throughout the United States have established the rule that under both common law and the statute an employer does not enjoy an absolute or unfettered right to discharge even an at-will employee . . . courts have recognized that an employer's traditional broad authority to discharge an at-will employee "may be limited by statute or considerations of public policy."

. . . fundamental principles of public policy and adherence to objectives that underly the state's penal statutes require the recognition of a rule barring an employer from discharging an employee who simply complied with his legal duty and refused to commit an illegal act.[36]

But the issue of whether an employer could discharge an employee for refusing to violate the law went beyond simply the propriety of the discharge. It was the position of the employer that, if the discharge was improper, it was only because it violated the employment contract; therefore Tameny's remedy was limited to remedies under contract law and could not include punitive damages. The court rejected this employer contention, finding that a discharge in violation of public policy could be the basis of a tort action. The court, citing a leading authority on torts, explained the difference between contract suits and tort suits:

> Whereas contract actions are created to protect the interest in having promises performed . . . tort actions are created to protect the interest in freedom from various kinds of harm. The duties of conduct that give rise to them are imposed by law, and are based primarily upon social policy and not necessarily upon the intention or will of the parties.[37]

Thus, from the point of view of the court, a discharge in violation of public policy was more serious than a breach of contract. The latter was essentially only a broken promise; the former was a violation of community norms.

The court concluded

> that an employer's authority over its employees does not include the right to demand that the employee commit a criminal act to further its interests, and an employer may not coerce compliance with such unlawful directions by discharging an employee who refuses to follow such an order. An employer engaging in such conduct violates a basic duty imposed by law upon all employers, and thus an employee who has suffered damages as a result of such discharge may maintain a tort action for wrongful discharge against the employer.[38]

The fundamental principle implied in the public policy exception is simple and commonsensical — the employer should not be able to use its control over the employee to violate the law, and the employee should not be placed in the position of either losing his or her job or acting illegally.

A key question that often arises in such cases is what is meant by "public policy." How does one know what public policy is? In the *Foley* case, discussed earlier, the California Supreme Court ruled that Foley's attempt to inform his supervisor about the alleged embezzlement of a newly hired manager did not protect Foley from discharge under the public policy exception. Although Foley may have had a public policy-based duty to inform upper management, the court was unable to find the source of that duty in statute, law, or regulation. The public policy exception covers employees who refuse to commit a crime or who report a crime to the public authorities, but it does not cover activities meant to serve the private interest of the employer.

In *Sucholdolski* v. *Michigan Consolidated Gas Company*,[39] the employer was found not to have acted unlawfully when it discharged the employee, a senior auditor, for internally reporting and attempting to correct what he believed were improper accounting procedures. The improprieties that Sucholdolski claimed existed and that he reported included shifting losses from appliance sales to rate payers, defining certain accounts receivable as uncollectible, and selling company property, including office equipment and automobiles, to employees at very low prices.

Sucholdolski claimed that the company's practices violated the Code of Ethics of the Institute of Internal Auditors and could have resulted in interference with the ability of the Public Service Commission to regulate the company. Sucholdolski based his claim on a Michigan Court of Appeals ruling that an employer had acted unlawfully by discharging a worker for filing a workers' compensation claim.

The court in Suchóldolski, however, affirming the decision of the trial court and the Court of Appeals, ruled that the internal code of ethics of a private, professional association did not establish a public policy. In addition, the court ruled that the general fact that the employer was regulated did not, in and of itself, make the discharge a violation of public policy. The accounting regulations of the Michigan Public Service Commission did not confer rights on employees, and Sucholdolski was not asked to falsify reports or documents required by the Commission.

Such falsification, however, did occur in *Holmes* v. *General Dynamics*.[40] There, the employer was found to have unlawfully terminated an employee for notifying his supervisor that the corporation had made incorrect statements to the government on federal contracts, resulting in overcharges to the government. The statements were found to have violated the Federal False Statements Act. In *Holmes*, unlike *Sucholdolski*, a statute was involved. This suggests that public policy must be discerned from legislation, administrative rules, court decisions, and regulations.

Other Issues in Employment-at-will

Statutory protection from unjust discharge

Although almost all states have accepted one or more of the exceptions to the employment-at-will doctrine, only Montana has enacted legislation providing employees protection from unjust discharge. The Montana statute defines a "wrongful discharge" as a discharge in violation of public policy, in violation of the express provisions of a personnel policy, or that was not for "good cause" provided the employee has completed a probationary period. Remedies are limited to back pay and interest up to a maximum of four years from the date of discharge, although punitive damages are permitted if it can be shown that the discharge was motivated by fraud or malice. Discharges prohibited by any other state or federal statute or covered by a collective agreement are excluded. Prior to going to court, the employee must exhaust all internal remedies provided they do not take more than 90 days. Either party may offer to arbitrate according to statutory provisions. If arbitration is accepted, it becomes the exclusive remedy. If arbitration is refused and the party who declines to accept does not prevail, that party is responsible for attorney's fees.[41]

Several other states have considered legislation on unjust discharge, but have failed to enact it. The proposed legislation would have generally been patterned after the Montana statute, in essence greatly increasing the number of employees covered, but reducing the monetary amounts victims of unjust discharge may recover. Since such bills have generally been defeated with employer opposition, it can be presumed that employers would prefer to take their chances on large damage awards for law covering a small number of employees, rather than permit a large number of employees access to the legal system for dismissals, albeit with limitations on damage awards.[42]

Whistleblower statutes

Many states have passed specific statutes protecting employees from discharge for whistleblowing. Whistleblowing occurs when an employee discloses employer violations of law to the proper authorities. These laws generally prohibit employers from discharging or otherwise retaliating against employees because they report violations of state law. Usually, the laws require that the employees provide the employer an opportunity to correct the problem. Disclosures must be in good faith. Relief may be through the courts (some with injunctive relief) or through special boards, although some states require employees to exhaust internal administrative remedies. The standard remedy is reinstatement with back pay, although some states permit punitive damages or multiples of back pay. There may also be civil or criminal penalties imposed on employers.[43]

Unjust discharge and collective bargaining

The relationship between state law involving employment-at-will and collective bargaining was explored by the US Supreme Court in 1994 in *Hawaiian Airlines* v. *Norris*.[44] Norris, an aircraft mechanic covered by a collective agreement, refused, in good faith, to sign the maintenance record for a repair that he believed his supervisor required to be done unsatisfactorily. Norris's supervisor then terminated him for insubordination.

Norris filed a grievance, but his grievance was denied at the first step of the procedure. Norris then filed a suit in Hawaii state court alleging that his discharge was in violation of public policy and in violation of Hawaii's Whistleblower Protection Act. The employer argued that because Norris was covered by a collective agreement and the firm was covered by the Railway Labor Act, which included a procedure governing the resolution of disputes arising out of grievances or the interpretation or application of a collective agreement, his remedies were limited to those contractual procedures.

The court disagreed, saying that the Railway Labor Act, which governs labor relations in the airline and railroad industries, did not preempt state protection of labor conditions. In this case, the dispute involved employment protections that were independent of the Railway Labor Act. Based on the *Norris* case, then, an employee who is covered by a collective agreement, almost all of which prohibit discharge without just cause, still is entitled to whatever protection against unjust discharge the law in his or her state provides.

Summary and Conclusions

Although the incursions on the long-established doctrine of employment-at-will have received a great deal of attention, examining the doctrine and the cases in total, it can be seen that the cases have been decided based on well-established principles of law. Both the implied contract and personnel manual/handbook cases stand for the proposition that employers should be held to the promises they make. The major change was expanding the scope of sources of promises – from only express promises made for that purpose to a search for promises based on the totality of circumstances of the employment relationship. In all these cases, however, the employee continues to bear the burden of proof of showing a special promise.

The good faith and fair dealing exception is also a well-established tributary from contract law. It simply states that employers must act in good faith *vis-à-vis* their employees and not make decisions that deprive them of benefits they are promised under their employment contract, broadly defined. While in a sense broader than the implied contract and handbook doctrines, in that no promise to the employee need be shown, this is also a well-established doctrine, dictating that one party to a contract should not act so as to deprive the other party of the benefits of that contract. The good faith and fair dealing doctrine does not expand the scope of the written or oral promise.[45] Rather, it simply seeks to assure that employees reap the benefits they have been promised.

The public policy exception is rooted in tort law and in common sense. It basically states that the authority that employers have over employees in the employment relationship should not be used to require employees to violate the law or public policy or to prevent employees from exercising their rights under relevant statutes (e.g. workers' compensation).

What is also clear is that this small erosion of the employment-at-will doctrine is well-established and is unlikely to change. It is a situation that employers will be required to accept.

Questions for discussion

1 Discuss the differences between the "moral obligation" and "freedom of contract" views of employment. What are the underlying assumptions of each view as regards the nature of employers and employees? To what extent are these assumptions true?

2 The "implied contract" exception to the employment-at-will doctrine is based on the premise that a contract need not necessarily be written. Should all contracts be written? What are the advantages of placing all contracts in writing? What are the disadvantages?

3 In *Toussaint*, the employer argued that it would be hampered in the day-to-day operation of the business if the statements in its handbook were taken to be an enforceable contract. Discuss the purposes of employee handbooks. What are they designed to accomplish? Given *Toussaint*, would you advise against a written employee handbook or written employer policies? If so, what would be other options?

4 The *Watson* case raises the question of the factors that judges should consider in rendering decisions. Should judges consider the impact of their decisions on economic development and "business climate" or should decisions be made solely on the basis of the evidence and the law? As

an employer, would you make a decision on the location of a facility based on whether a state had judicial exceptions to the employment-at-will doctrine?

5 A key question regarding the "public policy" exception to the employment-at-will doctrine is the definition of "public policy." How would you define "public policy?"

NOTES

1 See Sanford Jacoby, "The duration of indefinite employment contracts in the United States and England: an historical analysis," *Comparative Labor Law*, 5 (No. 1, Winter 1982), pp. 85–128. See also Ellen Kossek and Richard N. Block, "The employer as social arbiter: considerations in limiting employer involvement in off-the-job behavior," *Employee Rights and Responsibilities Journal*, 6 (No. 2, 1993), pp. 139–55.

2 Bureau of National Affairs, *Individual Employment Rights Reference Manual*, 505 (March 1994), pp. 51–2.

3 Jacoby, supra, note 1.

4 3 IER Cases at 1729.

5 3 IER Cases at 1738.

6 Ibid.

7 Ibid.

8 3 IER Cases at 1740–1.

9 408 Mich 579.

10 408 Mich at 597–8.

11 408 Mich at 613.

12 408 Mich at 614–15.

13 408 Mich at 619.

14 3 IER Cases 821, 1988.

15 9 IER Cases 522, 1994.

16 9 IER Cases 244, Mich CA, 1993.

17 9 IER Cases at 245.

18 7 IER Cases 472 (DC Conn, 1992).

19 7 IER Cases at 474.

20 Contracts for a defined period of time are assumed to be for that period – thus the employee may not be discharged during that time period without cause (see, for example, *Toussaint*, 408 Mich at 611).

21 3 IER Cases 1211 (CA 6, 1988).

22 1 IER Cases 476, Pa SC, 1986.

23 1 IER Cases 1854, Cal CA, 1985.

24 1 IER Cases at 1857.

25 1 IER Cases at 1860.

26 Ibid.

27 *Wagenell* v. *Scottsdale Memorial Hospital*, 1 IER Cases 526, 538 (Ariz SC, 1985).

28 *Wakefield* v. *Northern Telecom*, 1 IER Cases 1762, 1765 (CA 2, 1985).

29 1 IER Cases 1046 (CA 7, 1991).

30 7 IER Cases 1440, 1447 (DC Mass, 1992).

31 7 IER Cases 834 (Alaska SC, 1992).

32 7 IER Cases at 837.

33 122 LRRM 2076 (Tenn CA, 1985).

34 122 LRRM at 2077–8.
35 1 IER Cases at 102.
36 1 IER Cases at 104.
37 1 IER Cases at 105–6.
38 1 IER Cases at 107.
39 115 LRRM 4449 (1982).
40 8 IER Cases 1249 (Cal CA 1993).
41 See Bureau of National Affairs, *Individual Employment Rights Manual*, 567 (September 1987), 4–7.
42 See Alan B. Krueger, "The evolution of unjust discharge legislation in the United States, *Industrial and Labor Relations Review*, 44 (No. 4, July 1991), pp. 644–60; Jack Stieber and Richard N. Block, "Comment on 'The evolution of unjust discharge legislation in the United States,' " *Industrial and Labor Relations Review*, 44 (No. 4, July 1992), pp. 792–6 and "Reply by Alan B. Krueger," *Industrial and Labor Relations Review*, 44 (No. 4, July 1992), pp. 796–9.
43 BNA, *Labor Relations Reporter*. The following states have whistleblowing statutes that cover public employees only: AL, AK, AZ, AR, CO, DE, GA, ID, KA, KY, MD, MA, MO, MS, NV, NY, OK, OR, PA, SC, UT, VA, WA, WV, WI. The following states have statutes that cover both public and private employees: CA, CT, DC, FL, HA, IL, IA, LA, IN (private employees under public contract only), ME, MI, MN, MT (incorporated in wrongful discharge statute), NE, NH, NJ, NM, NC, ND, OH, RI, TN.
44 114 SC 2239 (1994).
45 Thus, in *Khanna*, the court did not require the employer to pay Khanna anything above what it had promised to pay him.

Chapter 11
Employer Involvement in Employee Non-work Activities

Introduction

In recent years, there seems to have been an increase in employer involvement in what is often considered the non-work aspects of an employee's life. Many employers have become involved in such matters as employee fitness, child care, elder care, and assistance programs for troubled employees. Often employer involvement in these issues is associated with health care costs – employers claim that they have an interest in their employees' non-work lives because healthy employees result in lower insurance premiums.

This chapter explores the balance between matters of employee privacy interests and employer productivity interests as it has been struck by the courts. The first section of the chapter addresses general issues of privacy. The second section deals with the one aspect of employee privacy that has been addressed by the US Congress – polygraph testing.

General Issues of Employee Privacy

Employer involvement in the private lives of employees is based on the employer's belief that employee on-the-job performance may be affected by the employee's off-the-job behavior. It is believed that healthy employees with few personal problems are likely to have better attendance records than their counterparts, are likely to be more productive, and have a greater chance of reaching their full potential as employees, thereby maximizing their value to the organization.

On the other hand, there is a belief that there is some zone of privacy to which employees are entitled and which is unrelated to the employees' work situation. Under this view, as long as the employee does his or her job, the employer has no right to inquire into an employee's off-the-job activities.[1]

These issues have been addressed for many years by labor arbitrators under collective agreements. Such agreements generally permit discharge only for "just cause." In these cases, arbitrators have typically taken the view that an employer may discipline an employee for off-the-job behavior if it can be shown that the off-the-job behavior will adversely affect the employer. In other words, some linkage between the off-the-job behavior and the employer's interests must be demonstrated.[2]

The right to be free from discharge except for just cause is generally only available to employees under collective agreements or employees who have employment contracts, written or implied. Non-represented employees who believe they have privacy rights that have been violated have resorted to the courts for redress. On what grounds have such cases been brought? The answer differs as to whether the employee is in the private sector or public sector. Private sector employees have generally attempted to argue that an infringement of some aspect of personal behavior is a violation of some implied contract or public policy. Public employees have generally argued that the public employer, usually a government agency, has violated a constitutional right. It is more difficult for private employees than for public employees to prevail on the latter argument, as generally persons do not have a constitutional protection against the actions of private parties. The cases discussed below illustrate the issues in the private and public sectors, respectively.

Private sector

The cases discussed in this section focus primarily on questions involving romantic or sexual conduct. These cases are analyzed because they represent the conflict between employee privacy and employer interests in a stark way, while at the same time not involving illegal activity. While much has been written on sexual harassment, e.g. unwanted romantic or sexual overtures, this section explores the relationship between employment and romantic or sexual overtures that are welcome.

A straightforward but quite illustrative case is *Somers* v. *Westours*.[3] The *Somers* case involves a wrongful discharge suit by David and Judith Somers. Judith Somers, then Judith Allington, was hired by the Fairbanks, Alaska, Travellers' Inn in 1977. She eventually advanced to the position of general manager. David Somers was hired by the Fairbanks Travellers' Inn in 1980, eventually advancing to the position of executive chef. In early 1983, Somers and Allington became involved in a romantic relationship. Soon after their relationship began, the management of Westours, which had assumed the management of the Travellers' Inn in 1983, began to receive complaints from other employees and customers that the relationship between Allington and Somers was disruptive to the motel and was affecting employee morale. Specifically, Somers and Allington were accused of engaging in romantic horseplay during working hours, coming to work late, and neglecting their duties. Westours' management had also received a complaint that Allington's former husband had come to the motel and threatened Somers with a gun.

In response to these complaints, Mr Stephen Leonard, a representative of Westours' management, met separately with Allington and Somers in June 1983. Leonard informed each of them of the complaints the company had received and directed them to refrain from socializing at the motel over coffee, dinner, and cocktails.

In August 1983 Leonard again visited the Fairbanks Travellers', although for reasons unrelated to Somers and Allington. While there, he noticed Somers and Allington having a late night dinner together at the motel. Upon his return to company headquarters in Seattle, Leonard received another complaint about the conduct of Allington and Somers. As a result of this complaint and what he had observed on his visit, Leonard terminated them.

Somers and Allington sued, alleging that the discharge violated Alaska public policy; in essence claiming that they had a constitutional right to have a romantic relationship. The Alaska Court disagreed, deciding that an employer could lawfully discharge an employee whose romantic activities caused problems in the facility. Because neither Allington nor Somers had an employment contract with Westours, the court found that their discharge was lawful.

A more complex case involved Virginia Rulon-Miller and the IBM corporation.[4] Rulon-Miller had been hired in 1967 as receptionist at an IBM site in Philadelphia. At that time, she was told that career opportunities in IBM were available as long as she performed satisfactorily and was willing to accept new challenges. While working at the Philadelphia site, Rulon-Miller earned her bachelor's degree at night. She was promoted to equipment scheduler and received a merit award. She was then transferred to Atlanta, where she worked for 15 months as a data processor. She was then transferred to the office products division in San Francisco, where she became a marketing support representative, demonstrating to customers how to use the IBM products they had purchased.

In 1973, she became a product planner, in which she had oversight responsibility for new office products. This position required moves to Austin, Texas, and Lexington, Kentucky. At the urging of her managers, she went to IBM sales school in Dallas in the office products division, after which she was assigned to San Francisco. She was a very successful salesperson of typewriters and other office equipment in San Francisco. In 1978, she was named marketing manager in the office products branch.

In 1976, Rulon-Miller began to see socially one Matt Blum, who was an account manager for IBM. In 1977, however, Blum left IBM to join QYX, an IBM competitor, and moved to Philadelphia. In 1978, Blum returned to the

San Francisco area while still working for QYX, at which time he and Rulon-Miller resumed their relationship.

In 1979, Rulon-Miller's manager called Rulon-Miller into his office and told her to stop dating Blum on the grounds that their relationship represented a conflict of interest. The next day, Rulon-Miller was informed by her manager that she was being removed from her management position due to the conflict of interest. Rulon-Miller inferred a dismissal from this action, and her manager said that, in that case, she was dismissed.

IBM had two policies relevant to the case, one concerning employee rights of privacy, the other concerning conflicts of interest. Employee rights of privacy were outlined in the following excerpt of a memo to all IBM managers signed by Chairman Tom Watson:

> The line that separates an individual's on-the-job business life from his other life as a private citizen is at times well-defined and at other times indistinct. But the line does exist, and you and I, as managers in IBM must be able to recognize that line.
>
> I have seen instances where managers took disciplinary measures against employees for actions or conduct that are not rightfully the company's concern. These managers usually justified their decisions by citing their personal code of ethics and morals or by quoting some fragment of company policy that seemed to support their position. Both arguments proved unjust on close examination. What we need, in every case, is balanced judgment which weighs the needs of the business and the rights of the individual.
>
> Our primary objective as IBM managers is to further the business of this company by leading our people properly and measuring quantity and quality of work and effectiveness on the job against clearly set standards of responsibility and compensation. This is performance – and performance is, in the final analysis, the one thing that the company can insist on from everyone.
>
> We have concern with an employee's off-the-job behavior only when it reduces his ability to perform regular job assignments, interferes with the job performance of other employees, or if his outside behavior affects the reputation of the company in major way. When on-the-job performance is acceptable, I can think of few situations in which outside activities could result in disciplinary action or dismissal.
>
> When such situations do come to your attention, you should seek the advice and counsel of the next appropriate level of management and the personnel department in determining what action – if any – is called for. Action should be taken only when a legitimate interest of the company is injured or jeopardized. Furthermore the damage must be clear beyond reasonable doubt and not based on hasty decisions about what one person might think is good for the company.
>
> IBM's first basic belief is respect for the individual, and the essence of this belief is a strict regard for his right to personal privacy. This idea should never be compromised easily or quickly.
>
> s/Tom Watson, Jr.[5]

On the other hand, IBM also had a policy prohibiting employees from engaging in activities that placed them in a conflict of interest with the company. The relevant text of that policy was as follows:

> Obviously, you cannot solicit or perform in competition with IBM product or service offerings. Outside work cannot be performed on IBM time, including "personal" time off. You cannot use IBM equipment materials, resources, or "inside" information for outside work. Nor should you solicit business or clients or perform outside work on IBM premises.
>
> Employees must be free of any significant investment or association of their own or of their immediate family's [*sic*], in competitors or suppliers, which might interfere or be thought to interfere with the independent exercise of their judgment in the best interests of IBM.[6]

These IBM policies were crucial to the court's decision favoring Rulon-Miller and upholding the jury's decision. The court noted that IBM had a policy which stated that it had no interest in the outside activities of their employees if those activities did not interfere with their work. The court found that Rulon-Miller was entitled to the benefit of that policy. Thus, the court agreed with the jury that IBM had no right to inquire about the non-work activities of Rulon-Miller in the absence of evidence that it prevented her from doing her work. The court noted that there was no such evidence, and that she did not have access to IBM information which would be of any value to QYX.

An important aspect of these two cases is their use of legal theories developed in the unjust discharge cases to assert a privacy interest in the workplace. This is necessary because employees have no right of privacy *vis-à-vis* their *private* employer. If the supposed private conduct is not to be subject to employer sanctions, the employee must link the private conduct to some other legal theory.

Thus, in the *Somers* case, the discharged employees attempted to argue their case based on principles of good faith and fair dealing, essentially arguing that they had a right to have a private social relationship. Their claim failed, as the court found there was no employment contract in effect that limited the discharge to just cause; nor did the discharge violate the employer's obligation to deal fairly with the employees, since the employer would not gain financially from the dismissal. The court also did not find that Westours had violated any public policy by dismissing the employees, noting that the discharge reflected a business judgment as regards the effect of their relationship on the operation of the motel.

In the *Rulon-Miller* case, IBM was held to its stated policy regarding employee off-the-job behavior. This is consistent with the *Toussaint* decision discussed in chapter 10 – employer policies are, in essence, contracts between the employer and its employees. The court held that IBM had granted its employees certain privacy rights, and it held IBM to that standard.

The key seems to be a nexus between job performance and the social relationships. In the *Rulon-Miller* case, the employer had a policy that gave employees the right of privacy, in essence stating that private social relationships did not have a *per se* nexus with impaired job performance or harm to the employer. In *Rulon-Miller*, the employer was unable to show harm to the business that was sufficient to outweigh its policy. The employer was held to its policy. In *Somers*, on the other hand, the two employees were discharged because the employer believed, in good faith, that their open relationship at the workplace was disrupting the workplace and lowering morale.

In *Somers*, on-the-job romantic activity that disrupted the workplace was not viewed as a sufficiently strong privacy interest to invoke an exception to the employment-at-will doctrine. On the other hand, Rulon-Miller's privacy interest did invoke such an exception, because there was no link to the job and because of the policy of her employer.

Somewhat interesting in the *Rulon-Miller* case is the court's willingness, albeit in an ambiguous way, to refer to Rulon-Miller's constitutional right of privacy.

> In this case, there is a close question of whether those rules or regulations permit IBM to inquire into the purely personal life of the employee. If so, an attendant question is whether such a policy was applied consistently, particularly as between men and women. The distinction is important because the right of privacy, a constitutional right in California . . . [citation omitted] could be implicated by the IBM inquiry.[7]

Does this imply that IBM, a private entity, could have compromised that right of privacy? Although the notion that a private party can infringe upon the *constitutional* rights of another private party is not the dominant legal view, some courts seem willing to entertain the argument that state constitutional guarantees of privacy can be violated by a private employer. Thus, in *Somers*, the court cited with approval a case involving Frito-Lay, in which the court upheld a discharge because a social relationship adversely affected the plant, "not because he was attempting to exercise some statutorily guaranteed right or perform some public duty."[8]

Does this mean that if the discharge had been solely for engaging in a social relationship, it would have been unlawful? Does the public policy exception to the employment-at-will doctrine implicitly incorporate a constitutional right of privacy? To date, there are no definitive answers, but the public policy exception to the employment-at-will doctrine could be a path to providing private employees with a constitutional right of privacy.

Finally, in a 1989 Louisiana case, *Fayard* v. *Guardsmark*,[9] a former employee of a security agency sued the company for engaging in a surveillance of her home. The security agency believed that she was fraternizing with an employee of a client firm in violation of the security agency's policies. The court considered the case under the doctrine of tortious invasion of privacy, as opposed to a constitutional invasion of privacy. The court found, however, that because the agency observed her premises from public property, and did license plate checks of visitors to her home based on public information, no invasion of privacy was present.

In considering this case, the court stated: "The question is still open whether Louisiana's constitutional provision was intended to provide constitutional protection against private conduct."[10] This seems to be a succinct way of summarizing the cases. It is fair to say that courts have not adopted a right of privacy for private sector employees *vis-à-vis* their employer.

Rather, the cases that allege what might be termed infringements of privacy have been argued based on standard theories of employment law or tort law. Thus, the *Somers* and *Rulon-Miller* cases were argued based on accepted notions of unjust discharge. The *Schuerman* case was decided on a breach of contract basis. The *Fayard* case was decided on the basis of tort law. Thus, as of this writing, there is no generally accepted right of privacy *vis-à-vis* their employers for private employees in the United States.

Public sector

Unlike private employers, public employers are agencies of government. Since both federal and state constitutional provisions are designed to apply to the relationship between government and citizens, there are constitutional restraints on the relationship between public employers on the one hand, and public employees and job applicants on the other, that do not exist in the private sector. Notwithstanding these constitutional constraints, however, government, acting as an employer, must exercise some control over its employees and job applicants in order to legitimately carry out its public service function.

Thus courts have ruled that public employers may not violate the constitutional rights of employees or applicants. On the other hand, in carrying out its functions, a public agency may make inquiries of employees and applicants into activities that would otherwise be within the zone of privacy for non-employees. But such inquiries must be justified by some compelling state interest.

For example, in *Shawgo* v. *Spradlin*, decided in 1983,[11] male and female officers in the Amarillo, Texas, police department who had a romantic relationship were suspended for 12 days in late 1977 or early 1978. The basis of the suspension was an alleged violation of a provision of the General Rules and Regulations of the Amarillo Police Department that proscribed conduct that "if brought to the attention of the public, could result in justified unfavorable criticism of that member or the Department."[12]

The Fifth Circuit rejected the employees' argument that the department's suspension of them due to their relationship was an infringement on their constitutional right of privacy as the "state has more interest in regulating activities of its employees than the activities of the general population"[13] and there was a rational connection between department discipline in a quasi-military agency and a prohibition on officers of a different rank cohabiting. Thus, the court declined to find a violation of the employee's privacy rights where the city could make a link between the employee's otherwise private conduct and an organizational interest.

The balance between the interests of the government in carrying out its mandated missions and the interests of employees (current and prospective) in being free from invasions of privacy was explored in *Thorne* v. *City of El Segundo*[14] and *Walls* v. *City of St Petersburg*.[15] In *Thorne*, the employee, Deborah Thorne, had been hired as a secretary in 1973 by the El

Segundo, California, police department. In January 1978, Thorne took a closed (open only to employees of the department) examination for promotion to police officer. She was rated as an eligible applicant based on receipt of the second highest score on the oral and written tests. She also passed the physical agility test and the psychological screening.

In April 1978, Thorne submitted to the polygraph test required of all police officer candidates, also completing the required pre-examination questionnaire. In completing the questionnaire, Thorne reported that she had been pregnant and had a miscarriage. Upon further questioning from the polygraph examiner, Thorne revealed that the pregnancy was the result of a relationship with a married El Segundo police officer. She was then questioned further about her sexual relationships with other department personnel. Thorne claimed that she was also asked questions about other sexual activity in which she engaged involving persons outside the department, although the polygraph examiner claimed his questions were limited to her activities with department personnel.

The information in the questionnaire was reported to the Police Chief, who had earlier received a report from the polygraph examiner that Thorne lacked sufficient aggressiveness, self-confidence, and physical ability to be a police officer. The Police Chief warned Thorne that if she pursued her application, he could not guarantee the confidentiality of the information she had given the examiner. Thorne decided not to withdraw her application. A background investigation on Thorne resulted in a report that included a discussion of Thorne's affair with the police officer. Ultimately, Thorne was disqualified on the basis of excessive tardiness and sick leave use, deficiency in physical capabilities, and an insufficiently established interest in police work.

Thorne sued under federal law, claiming that the polygraph exam and the use of its results by the City of El Segundo violated her privacy rights under the US constitution. The Court of Appeals, overturning the ruling of the District Court, found in favor of Thorne. In so ruling, the court observed that the case involved two kinds of privacy interests protected by the constitution. In the context of the case, the court noted:

> The constitution protects two kinds of privacy interests. "One is the individual interest in avoiding disclosure of personal matters, and another is the interest in independence in making certain kinds of important decisions." Whalen v. Roe, 429 U.S. 589, 599 (1977). Both are implicated in this case. Thorne presented evidence that defendants invaded her right to privacy by forcing her to disclose information regarding personal sexual matters. She also showed that they refused to hire her as a police officer based in part on her prior sexual activities, thus interfering with her privacy interest and her freedom of association.
>
> The interests Thorne raises in the privacy of her sexual activities are within the zone protected by the constitution. This conclusion follows from the cases holding that such basic matters as contraception, abortion, marriage, and family life are protected by the constitution from unwarranted government intrusion.[16]

The court concluded that the city had conditioned Thorne's employment upon taking a polygraph examination and that the polygraph inquiry by the city bore "on those matters acknowledged to be at the core of the rights protected by the constitution's guarantees of privacy and free association — appellant's interest in family living arrangements, procreation, and marriage."[17] The court, however, did not state that the city, in its role as an employer, was absolutely barred from making all inquiries into the personal lives of job applicants. Rather, the court noted:

> the City must show that its inquiry into appellant's sex life was justified by the legitimate interests of the police department, that the inquiry was narrowly tailored to meet those legitimate interests, and that the department's use of the information it obtained about appellant's sexual history was proper in light of the state's interest.
>
> Defendants' own evidence shows a sufficient invasion of Thorne's privacy interests to require justification. The information about the polygraph examination given to Thorne indicated that questioning about sexual behavior would be a significant part of the overall examination.[18]

The city claimed that the purpose of the polygraph questions was to discover any sexual deviance that might impair Thorne's functioning as a police officer. The inquiry was also based on the department's view that sexual relationships among officers in a paramilitary organization compromised its functioning. The court, however, determined that the inquiry was directed toward discovering the identity of Thorne's sexual partners and whether she had ever had an abortion. These questions had nothing to do with sexual "deviancies." Indeed, the court noted that no sexual deviancies were found.

The court also observed that the relationship between Thorne and the El Segundo police officer had ended. Thus, any concern about impairment of the functioning of the police force was unjustified. More generally, the court stated that:

> We do not hold that the City is prohibited by the constitution from questioning or considering the sexual morality of its employees. If the City chooses to regulate its employees in this area or to set standards for job applicants it may do so only through regulations carefully tailored to meet the City's specified needs. The evidence established here that the City had no policy. Rather, the Police Chief testified that he simply applied the moral standards of the general society, as he saw them. Moreover, [the polygraph examiner's] questioning in the area of sexual activity was not regulated in any way. He was given free rein to inquire into any area he chose.
>
> The City set no standards, guidelines, definitions or limitations, other than the polygraph examiner's own personal opinion as to what might be relevant to job performance in a particular case. When the state's questions directly intrude on the core of a person's constitutionally protected privacy and associational interests, as the questioning of the polygraph examiner did in this case, an unbounded, standardless inquiry, even if founded upon a legitimate state interest, cannot withstand the heightened scrutiny with which we must view the state's action. We cannot even bestow legitimacy on the defendants'

search for "perverted deviancies" in this case because of the complete lack of standards for the inquiry. The risk that an infringement of an important constitutionally protected right might be justified on the basis of individual bias and disapproval of the protected conduct is too great. The very purpose of constitutional protection of individual liberties is to prevent such majoritarian or capricious coercion [citations omitted]. . . .

In the absence of any showing that private, off-duty, personal activities of the type protected by the constitutional guarantees of privacy and free association have an impact upon an applicant's on-the-job performance, and of specific policies with narrow, implementing regulations, we hold that reliance on these private non-job-related considerations by the state in rejecting an applicant for employment violates the applicant's protected constitutional interests and cannot be upheld under any level of scrutiny.[19]

In *Thorne*, the court went on to observe that the city had produced no evidence that Thorne's affair before becoming a police officer would affect her job performance or that it was likely to revive or cause morale problems. The incident was not a matter of public knowledge and had no effect on the department's standing in the community, Thorne's conduct would not be grounds for discipline, and the other police officer had not been disciplined.

The facts in *Walls* stand in contrast to those in *Thorne*. Walls had been hired by the City of St Petersburg, Virginia, in December 1985 as the administrator of the city's Community Diversion Incentive Program (CDI), which provided alternative sentencing for nonviolent criminals. In July 1986, administration of the CDI was transferred from the city manager's office to the police department. As a result of the change in administration, all CDI employees, including Walls, were required to undergo the same background check as other police department employees.

In March 1988, the department discovered that Walls had not completed the required questionnaire, and directed her to complete it. Walls refused, objecting to four questions: one dealing with the arrest and conviction records of members of her immediate family; one dealing with marriages, children to whom she had given birth, and divorce, if any; a third dealing with whether she had ever had a homosexual relationship; and a fourth inquiring about all outstanding debts and judgments against her or her spouse. Walls's objection was based on constitutional rights of privacy and freedom of association.

The district court had found in favor of the city, and the Court of Appeals agreed, ruling that those questions did not infringe upon Walls's constitutional rights of privacy. With respect to the question regarding homosexual conduct, the court cited a 1986 US Supreme Court decision, *Bowers* v. *Hardwick*, for the principle that the right of privacy did not extend to "homosexual sodomy."[20] Regarding the questionnaire item on marriages, divorces, and children, the court found that as most of this information was in the public record, Walls had no reasonable expectation that it would remain private, and that all information in the public record could be part of a background check. The analysis was the same for the item on arrests and convictions – it was all part of the public record. Finally, given Walls's position, the court believed that it was reasonable for the city to inquire into her financial position so as to guard against potential corruption.

In concluding, however, the court added a cautionary note:

> One other consideration in weighing the competing interests of the government and the individual is the possibility of unauthorized disclosure of information entitled to privacy protection. . . . When there are precautions to prevent unwarranted disclosure, an individual's privacy interest is weakened. . . . In this case, the information obtained from the background questionnaire is kept in a private filing cabinet that is locked at night, and only four persons would be authorized to have access to the information.
>
> We believe these precautions are reasonable and sufficient; however, if this type of information had been more widely distributed, our conclusions might have been different. In the past few decades, technological advances have provided society with the capability to collect, store, organize, and recall vast amounts of information about individuals in sophisticated computer files. This database capability is already being extensively used by the government, financial institutions, and marketing research firms to track our travels, interests, preferences, habits, and associates. Although some of this information can be useful and even necessary to maintain order and provide communication and convenience in a complex society, we need to be ever diligent to guard against misuse. Some information still needs to be private, disclosed to the public only if the person voluntarily chooses to disclose it.[21]

Both *Thorne* and *Walls* point out that there is a constitutional right of privacy that the government must honor, even when the government is acting as an employer. It is also the case, however, that when a citizen chooses to work for the government, or applies to the government for a position, then the citizen must be prepared to expect some invasion of the otherwise inviolate zone of privacy. In other words, the employee has legitimate privacy interests, and the government has interests in delivering public services efficiently and honestly.

Thus, in cases involving government employment, there are two basic questions that must be asked. First, is the information the government is seeking constitutionally protected? If not, the question is permissible. If so, the second question is: can government show a compelling interest in the information? That compelling interest will normally be shown by the government demonstrating a link between the information requested and the duties of the position. A speculative possibility is not sufficient to demonstrate this link. The linkage must be demonstrable and supported by evidence.

The city in *Thorne* did not make this link. Thorne demonstrated that she had constitutionally protected privacy interests in her sexual associations and activities. Once Thorne showed this, the city had the obligation to show a compelling need for the information. While the court may have been willing to accept the notion that the department should know about sexual activities among police officers in order to maintain discipline and morale in a paramilitary organization, it was unwilling to accept that with respect to an abortion she had. While the court was willing to accept the existence of a link between sexual relations between coworkers and job performance, as in *Shawgo*, the court would not go beyond *Shawgo* to permit a city to make broader inquiries. More generally, the court noted that the city had not demonstrated any relationship between future job performance and past sexual history that was unlikely to be revived.

The court in *Walls*, on the other hand, found for the city. What were the differences between *Walls* and *Thorne*? First, while all the information requested in *Thorne* was constitutionally protected, that was not the case in *Walls*. The court relied on a US Supreme Court decision to find that the question on homosexual relations was not part of the constitutional protection of privacy.[22] To the extent information on arrests, marriages, divorces, and children was available in public records, it was not constitutionally protected. Information not in public records, however, deserved constitutional protection. Thus, for at least some of the information in *Walls*, the answer to the first question – is the information the government is seeking constitutionally protected? – was "no."

As regards the question on financial information, however, the answer to this question was "yes" – it was constitutionally protected. Was there a "compelling governmental interest in the information"? Here the answer was also "yes." The court found that the city had an interest in deterring corruption, and that this was especially important in the job for which Walls was applying, since she was dealing with convicted criminals.

Overall, these two cases do a fairly good job of laying out the framework of privacy protection in public employment. There is privacy protection, in that there are matters that applicants for public sector jobs and public employees have a reasonable expectation will remain confidential. There is a "right to be let alone."[23] The more personal the information, the greater the privacy interest and the greater the expectation that it will not be subject to public scrutiny.

For the state to require disclosure of private information, there must be a compelling state interest and information sought must be narrowly drawn. Thus there seem to be three questions: (a) Is the information requested within that zone of privacy that is constitutionally protected? (b) If so, does the governmental agency have a compelling interest in the information? (c) If so, is the request for the protected information drawn to reflect only those interests and are there safeguards to prevent improper disclosure of the private information that has been collected?

Using this framework, the first question that must be asked is whether the information requested is within the zone of privacy. Outside that zone of privacy are such behaviors as homosexual activity[24] and adultery.[25] Personal information on the public record is also outside the zone of privacy (*Walls*).

The second question involves the matter of determining when a governmental interest is "compelling." What is meant by a compelling interest? Is the "compelling interest" standard met by any demonstrable link between information and job performance? The answer seems to be yes. If the public jurisdiction can show that job performance, morale, or integrity will likely be adversely affected by the otherwise private behavior, or by having the information that is within the zone of privacy, then the infringement on the employee's privacy rights will be upheld. On the other hand, speculation or very tenuous links between job performance or organizational interests and the information will usually result in a finding in favor of the employee or applicant.

Thus, in *Shawgo*, the city's interest in police discipline and morale was sufficient to warrant upholding discipline of two police officers who were involved in a sexual relationship. In *Walls*, the city's interest in the integrity of persons working with convicted criminals permitted them to ask a job applicant about her financial situation. In *Wilson* v. *Swing*, decided in 1978,[26] discipline was appropriate for a police officer who had an extra-marital, off-duty affair with another police officer and who thereby violated a departmental regulation that prohibited police officers from acting so as to bring the department into public disrepute. The court also agreed with the city that the behavior would lower department morale.

In *Fraternal Order of Police, Lodge No. 5* v. *City of Philadelphia*,[27] the court upheld questions seeking medical information (extended hospital stays, prescription drugs, and treatment for mental illness), financial information (debts and loans over $1,000, income received by employees, spouse, and children, property and investments, and gifts and honoraria over $100), and behavior information (arrest records of family members, gambling, alcohol use) from employees seeking positions in a newly created special investigations unit. The court determined that the city needed this information because of the long hours and stress associated with the job, and the potential for corruption.

In *Endsley* v. *Naes*,[28] the court ruled that a police department did not violate the constitutional rights of association of a female employee who was discharged because of rumors that she was involved in a homosexual relationship with another female police officer. The court relied on a judicial recognition of the "significant state interest in deterring the conduct of police officers which brings a police department in disrepute."[29] This is in contrast to *Thorne*, in which the city failed to demonstrate a linkage made between the information requested on Thorne's sexual activities and the job of police officer.

In *Shuman* v. *City of Philadelphia*,[30] the court found that the city violated a police officer's constitutional rights by discharging him for refusing to answer questions about his sexual relationship with a woman. Although the woman's mother had complained to the Chief of Police about the relationship, the city was unable to demonstrate that the relationship had any adverse effect on the police officer's job performance. The court observed:

> In the absence of a showing that a policeman's private, off-duty personal activities have an impact upon his on-the-job performance, we believe that inquiry into those activities violates the constitutionally mandated right of privacy.[31]

In *Briggs* v. *North Muskegon Police Department*,[32] the court found that the city's 1977 discharge of a married police officer for cohabiting with a women not his wife (and not a police officer) violated his constitutional right of privacy. Although the city had a legitimate interest in limiting employee behaviors that affect the department, there was no indication that such an adverse effect was occurring here. The relationship was not flaunted, was more than solely sexual, and was maintained through the time of the suit.

Unlike the *Swing* case, neither *Shuman* nor *Briggs* involved adultery, a married person engaging in sexual relations with a nonspouse. Thus, the charge of immoral conduct on the part of the police officer was much less compelling in the latter two cases than in the former case. Also in contrast to *Swing*, neither of the women with whom the plaintiffs in *Shuman* and *Briggs* were involved were employees of the police department or were in a position such as to bring the department into public; thus there was little adverse effect on the department.

The third question involves the precise nature of the question asked and the maintenance of records. Questions must be narrowly tailored. Thus, in *Thorne*, the city was scolded by the court for failing to adopt any standards for questioning employees about their off-duty activities. Similarly, in *Shuman*, the court found that the city had no standards as to when it would initiate investigations.

Use of the information is also relevant. In *Walls*, the City of St Petersburg was found not to be in violation of Walls's rights because the information collected was in a locked file cabinet to which only four persons had access; appropriate safeguards had been taken. On the other hand, in *Lodge No. 5*, the court continued in effect an injunction until the city had put into place procedures for preventing the unauthorized disclosure of the confidential information.

Privacy issues involving matters other than social relationships

Although social relationships present clear issues for analyzing the employer involvement in the personal lives of employees, the conflict between employer efficiency interests and employee privacy interests can occur in other contexts. In *Kurtz* v. *City of North Miami*,[33] the Florida Supreme Court upheld the City's requirement that, in order to reduce health insurance costs, job applicants refrain from smoking for one year prior to being considered for employment. The Court, after observing that persons must reveal whether they smoke when, for example, requesting a table in a restaurant or a hotel room, noted:

> Given that individuals must reveal whether they smoke in almost every aspect of life in today's society, we conclude that individuals have no reasonable expectation of privacy in the disclosure of that information when applying for a job and, consequently, that Florida's right of privacy is not implicated under these unique circumstances.[34]

Recently, in *National Treasury Employees Union* v. *US Treasury Dept*,[35] the court granted a preliminary injunction against the US Customs Service for requiring employees in non-law enforcement or drug interdiction positions (attorneys, paralegals, computer specialists, import specialists, etc.) to disclose extensive information about off-the-job alcohol and drug use, arrests and criminal charges regardless of whether they were convicted, financial situation, problems from "emotional or mental conditions," medical history, and educational records.[36] The court noted that there must be a "nexus (for the disclosure) to work responsibilities."[37] As these were positions that did not carry firearms or have access to sensitive information, there was no compelling governmental interest in disclosure.

Polygraph Testing

The Employee Polygraph Protection Act (EPPA) of 1988, which took effect on December 27, 1988,[38] prohibits most private employers in the United States from administering polygraph tests to employees or applicants, from inquiring about or otherwise using the results of such a test, and from taking any employment-related action, such as discharge or discipline, based on a polygraph test. Firms excepted from the prohibition include primarily security firms and firms working in national defense.

There is a key exemption, however. Private employers may use a polygraph test as part of an ongoing investigation of economic loss to the employer's business (specific economic loss), if the employee being tested had access to the property that is the subject of the investigation (employee access), the employer had a reasonable suspicion that the employee being tested was involved in the loss (reasonable suspicion), and the employer provides the employee with a written, signed statement at least 48 hours prior to the examination informing the employee of the specific loss, the access, and the basis of the reasonable suspicion. The employee must also be given a copy of the test results and the examiner's conclusions. It supersedes all state laws that are less stringent, but permits states to enact laws that are more restrictive.

Employers who conduct otherwise legal polygraph tests may take no adverse actions based solely on the test against employees who fail the test. There must be other corroborating evidence on which to base an adverse employment action. For the purposes of the EPPA, a refusal to take an otherwise exempted (permissible) test is considered to be a test failure; therefore an employer may not take an adverse action against an employee solely on the basis of the refusal to take the test.[39]

The EPPA incorporates both public and private enforcement measures. Public enforcement is through the Department of Labor, which is empowered to assess civil penalties and to sue in federal court to enforce the penalties. If the Administrator of the Wage and Hour Division believes the EPPA was violated, the Administrator may assess penalties of up to $10,000 per violation. Objections to the Administrator's decision are referred to a

Department of Labor Administrative Law Judge. Alternatively, the employee may sue the employer in federal court for reinstatement and back pay.

The key questions in EPPA cases are whether the testing is part of an ongoing investigation of a specific loss, whether the employee had access, and whether there was reasonable suspicion that the employee being tested was involved in the loss.

A recent Department of Labor case highlights the scope of the exemption requirements under the EPPA. In *Rapid Robert's Inc.*,[40] the employer, an operator of a small chain of convenience stores, initiated a polygraph testing of employees when inventory losses increased from 1 percent of total sales in 1988 to 12–15 percent of total sales in 1989, after the employer had ceased polygraph testing due to the passage of the EPPA. The judge ruled that a loss of this size met the "specific economic loss" criterion for a testing exemption. The parties stipulated that all employees had access, meeting that criterion. The judge also ruled that the following factors satisfied the "reasonable suspicion" criterion for one or more employees:

1 An unsupervised work situation, an "anti-company" attitude, driving a new car that was beyond the employee's means based on the employee's wage rate, and an expressed intent to leave.
2 Frequent presence of friends in the store which correlated with a practice by which an employee would ring up a price well below that of the product, an "anti-company" attitude, possession of a key and a security code.
3 A "high strung" personality and working closely with other suspected employees.
4 Possession of a security code and a demonstrated practice of re-entering the store to retrieve personal property.
5 "Running a tab" by taking store goods and paying for them at a later date.
6 A deteriorating attitude and poor financial condition.
7 Frequent presence of an employee's spouse in the store and personal handling of the spouse's transactions.
8 Deterioration of attitude and attendance (justifying a retest two and one-half months after the first test).
9 Excellent cash accounting skills and possession of a key.
10 Operation of the store alone for periods of the day, admission of theft from a previous employer, and admission of prior drug use.

All of these situations constituted an "observable, articulable basis related to the ongoing investigations of the inventory losses." The judge ruled, however, that retesting of three employees three months after the first test on the basis of no additional losses did not meet the specific loss criterion. Put differently, the judge suggested that only one test per loss would be permitted; a new test would only be justified by a new loss and new "observable articulable basis" for the test.

The judge also ruled that the required statement must be specific on the loss and suspicion. A statement that simply said "product loss" would not suffice. The statement should have informed the employees regarding which inventory was missing. The statement must also be specific on the suspicion. A statement that employees were suspected because they "work(ed) at the store" was not sufficient.

The employer was also found in violation of the Act where it threatened employees with discharge or suspension if they refused to take the test, and suspended employees based solely on that refusal. On the other hand, the employer did not violate the act by discharging an employee who failed the test and who had committed a serious violation of the company's check acceptance policy.

Regarding penalties, the judge ruled that the intent of the Act was to impose a maximum penalty of $10,000 per violation. The penalties were to be reduced by the seriousness of the offense, as violations were primarily violations of procedural requirements. The actual testing met the substantive criteria.

Conclusion

This review of the case law suggests that, while the private and public sectors have followed different legal paths, the two sectors have arrived at destinations very close to each other. Generally, the courts have permitted private employers to dismiss employees based on personal conduct that is believed to affect the workplace provided there is no employment contract present. The courts have been unwilling to find a public policy exception to the employment-at-will principle in these cases.

Public employers, although constrained by employees' constitutional rights, have been able to use the principle of compelling interest to make inquiries about private conduct of employees to the extent that it can be shown to adversely affect the functioning of the agency. Thus, making this link has given public employers much the same rights as private employers in this area.

Questions for discussion

1   Should employers be involved in the nonwork lives of their employees? If you believe they should not, how would you protect the employer's interest in a productive workforce. If you believe they should, how far would you go? Should employers be able to influence what employees eat (relationship between diet and health) and how much they exercise (relationship between exercise and health)? Is there anything an employee does that is not, in some way, related to performance on the job?
2   Do you believe that a friendship between two people who work for competing companies is necessarily a conflict of interest? If your answer is no, is there ever a situation in which such a friendship could become a conflict of interest? What factors would you consider in determining when a conflict of interest exists?

3 Should employers be permitted to consider for employment only non-smokers in order to reduce health insurance costs? If so, should a prospective employer also be permitted to inquire into an applicant's eating habits (hiring only employees with low cholesterol, low fat diets), exercise habits (hiring only employees who are in excellent physical condition), and genetic makeup/family health history (employees should not have a tendency toward heart disease)?

4 Should employees have constitutional protection from employer actions? Given the fact that most people depend on their jobs for their livelihood and are unlikely to have an incident involving law enforcement, is it not true that most people are far more likely to perceive their employer as a source of coercion than they are to perceive government as a source of coercion?

5 What kinds of employee activities would bring a public employer into disrepute? Should a right to engage in behavior depend on the nature of his or her employer's mission?

NOTES

1 Ellen Ernst Kossek and Richard N. Block, "The employer as social arbiter: considerations in limiting involvement in off-the-job behavior," *Employee Rights and Responsibilities Journal*, 6 (No. 2, 1993), pp. 139–55.

2 Frank Elkouri and Edna Asper Elkouri, *How Arbitration Works*, 4th edn (BNA, Washington, DC, 1985).

3 *Somers* v. *Westours, Inc.*, 1 IER Cases 1479 (Alaska SC, 1986).

4 *Rulon-Miller* v. *IBM*, 132 Cal. App. 3rd 241, 1 IER Cases 405 (Cal CA, 1984).

5 1 IER Cases at 409.

6 Ibid., at 409–10.

7 Ibid., at 409.

8 Ibid., at 1481.

9 *Fayard* v. *Guardsmark, Inc.*, 5 IER Cases 516 (DC ED La, 1989).

10 5 IER Cases at 517.

11 701 F.2d 470, 1 IER Cases 164 (CA 5, 1983).

12 1 IER Cases at 166.

13 Ibid., at 174.

14 *Thorne* v. *City of El Segundo*, 1 IER Cases 299 (9th Cir., 1983).

15 *Walls* v. *City of St Petersburg* (4th Cir., 1990).

16 1 IER Cases at 306.

17 Ibid.

18 Ibid., at 306–7.

19 Ibid., at 307–8.

20 5 IER Cases at 459.

21 1 IER Cases at 460.

22 *Bowers* v. *Hardwick*, 479 US 186 (1986), cited at 5 IER Cases 459.

23 1 IER Cases at 458.

24 *Dawson* v. *State Law Enforcement Division*, 7 IER Cases 629 (DC SC, 1992).

25 *Wilson* v. *Swing*, 463 F.Supp 555 (DC NC, 1978).

26 463 F.Supp. 555 (MD NC, 1978).

27 812 F.2d 195 (3rd Cir., 1987).

28 673 F.Supp 1032 (DC Kan, 1987).
29 673 F.Supp. at 1038.
30 470 F.Supp. 449 (DC ED Pa, 1979).
31 470 F.Supp. at 459.
32 1 IER Cases 195 (DC W Mich, 1983).
33 10 IER Cases 865 (Fla SC, 1995).
34 Ibid.
35 9 IER Cases 1 (DC DC, 1993).
36 In granting the preliminary injunction, the court determined that it was likely the union would win on the merits.
37 9 IER Cases at 5.
38 *In re Rapid Robert's Inc.*, 7 IER Cases 947, US Department of Labor, 1992.
39 Ibid., at 946, 955.
40 Ibid., at 946.

Chapter 12
Drug Testing and the Law

Introduction

The 1980s were marked by an increasing interest in drug testing among employers. Moreover, the belief arose among policy makers that drug use was a serious problem in the United States, often impairing productivity and safety. Thus, in the second half of the 1980s, the federal government began to manifest an interest in drug testing among employees. As it turned out, although only private employers in federally regulated industries are affected by federal regulation of drug and alcohol testing, the principles that have developed in court decisions involving federally mandated testing form the basis for the state regulation that affects private sector employers. Thus, we will first discuss federal regulation, with the discussion of state regulation to follow.

For the purposes of alcohol and drug testing, different legal domains apply depending on the sectoral location of the business. Within the private sector, there are differing legal rules depending upon whether the firm is in an industry that is regulated by the federal government, is unionized, or is a federal contractor. The law of drug and alcohol testing in the public sector is similar to the law in the private, regulated, sector, since the latter is viewed as being an agent of the government.

Federal Regulation of Drug and Alcohol Testing

Department of Transportation regulations

Since the late 1980s the federal government has used its authority to insure safety in regulated industries as a vehicle for requiring drug and alcohol testing in those industries. The most intensive government effort has been in the transportation industry – aviation, railroads, trucking, intercity buses, and mass transit. During the period 1987 to 1990, legislation to require drug and alcohol testing in safety-sensitive jobs in transportation was passed in the Senate on 11 occasions. All attempts through 1990 failed to reach the floor of the House of Representatives.[1]

During 1987 and 1988, however, the operating administrations (OAs) in the Department of Transportation used their rule making authority pursuant to various enabling statutes to promulgate rules on drug testing in safety-sensitive jobs.[2] These OAs included the Federal Aviation Authority (FAA) for aviation, the Federal Highway Administration (FHWA) for trucking and intercity buses, the Federal Railroad Authority (FRA) for the railroads, and the Federal Transit Authority (FTA), formerly the Urban Mass Transit Authority, for urban mass transit.

The structure of the rules was basically the same for all the OAs. They generally covered jobs considered to be "safety-sensitive" and required post-accident testing, pre-employment testing, random testing of a sample of employees in the safety-sensitive occupations, periodic testing, reasonable cause testing, and follow-up testing for employees who tested positive. Safeguards were required to assure privacy when taking the sample, chain of custody for the sample, accuracy of the test results, confidentiality, and no access to law enforcement authorities without the permission of the employee.

Once promulgated, the rules were challenged in court by unions representing employees in the industry. The basis of the challenge was that, because these tests were required by the government, they constituted governmental action that violated the employees' Fourth Amendment rights against unreasonable search and seizure. Although private parties are generally not subject to United States constitutional constraints,[3] when they act as an agent of government, or under governmental authority, constitutional constraints do apply to their actions.

In all cases, the challenges failed. In *Skinner* v. *Railway Labor Executives Association*,[4] the US Supreme Court upheld the constitutionality of the FRA regulations requiring blood and urine testing for drugs and alcohol for railroad employees after they were involved in a major train accident (defined as involving a fatality, the release of hazardous substances accompanied by an evacuation or reportable injury, or damage over $500,000), and permitting testing when a supervisor had a "reasonable suspicion" following a minor accident or when certain rule violations had occurred, such as missing a signal or excessive speeding. Although recognizing that the "physical intrusion (into the body to obtain a blood sample), penetrating beneath the skin, infringes an expectation of privacy that society is prepared to recognize as reasonable,"[5] and that "the collection and testing of urine intrudes upon expectations of privacy that society has long recognized as reasonable,"[6] the court ruled that the FRA regulations did not violate the fourth amendment.

In *Teamsters* v. *US Department of Transportation,*[7] the implications of the *Railway Labor Executives* case were explored. In the *Teamsters* case, the International Brotherhood of Teamsters, along with two other unions, petitioned the court for review of an order issued by the Federal Highway Administration on June 14, 1988 that mandated drug testing for commercial motor vehicle operators. The announced purpose of the FHA drug testing program was to detect and deter the use of drugs by truck and bus drivers. The order was challenged by the unions as violating the drivers' Fourth Amendment rights to be free from unreasonable search and seizure and as being promulgated arbitrarily and capriciously.

In adopting the rules after hearings, the FHA conceded that the evidence documenting actual drug use among truck and bus drivers and its role in highway accidents was scarce. The agency's rationale, however, was that this was due to the fact that drivers almost always worked without supervision and that drug studies were in their infancy. Rather, the agency relied on testimonial evidence at the hearings and the existence of a drug problem in the larger society.

The rules required the carriers to implement a drug testing program for drivers operating vehicles weighing more than 26,000 pounds, carrying at least 15 passengers, or carrying hazardous materials. Testing was required of all drivers who were employed for at least 90 days in a year. Testing would occur in six instances: (a) randomly, with the drivers chosen in a "scientifically acceptable manner;" (b) biennially; (c) prior to first employing new drivers; (d) after involvement in an accident that involved a fatality, medical treatment away from the scene, or at least $4,000 in property damage; (e) based on reasonable cause that the employee was using a controlled substance; and (f) follow-up testing for drivers who had previously tested positive.

The regulations also provided for procedures for conducting the drug tests. These included collection by urination in a private enclosure, supervision by a licensed medical professional, chain of custody procedures during collection and testing,[8] testing by laboratories approved by the Department of Health and Human Services, confirmatory tests when preliminary test results were positive, investigation of possible alternative explanations for a positive drug test, confidential treatment of employee records, and the establishment of an employee assistance program.

The fundamental question in the case was whether the testing violated the drivers' constitutional rights. Ordinarily, since the carriers were private employers, their treatment of employees could have no constitutional implications. This situation was an exception to that rule. The court noted:

It is now established beyond peradventure that drug tests constitute searches within the meaning of the fourth amendment. . . . Testing conducted by private employers under compulsion of governmental regulations amounts to governmental action subject to the fourth amendment's restrictions.[9]

Bringing the carriers under the governmental umbrella meant that a series of constitutional issues needed to be addressed. First, because the drug test was a search under the Fourth Amendment, there was the question of whether the employer was required to obtain a warrant before conducting the drug test. The court responded in the negative, observing that the rules provided administrators with minimal discretion regarding when the tests would be administered and to whom. Even the random testing did not give the employer the discretion to choose which employees would be tested. Because, in essence, the drug testing process was depersonalized, there was no need for a warrant.

The unions also argued that the random testing violated the constitutional rights of the employees because it was conducted without probable cause that drugs had been taken or reasonable suspicion that those tested had taken drugs. The court disagreed, observing that:

While a search must ordinarily be based on probable cause, in certain circumstances the government's interest "is sufficiently compelling to justify the intrusion on privacy entailed by conducting such searches without any measure of individualized suspicion." . . . We find that such circumstances exist in this case.[10]

The court conceded that the act of urination was a function traditionally accompanied by privacy. In this instance, however, general standards of privacy did not apply. The court noted:

the inquiry we undertake here asks not whether a particular search constitutes, in the abstract or in general, a substantial intrusion on personal privacy. Rather, we must assess the incremental decrease in privacy caused by the search relative to the existing privacy expectations of the drivers. . . .

The privacy expectations of commercial truck drivers are markedly less than those of the public in general. The trucking industry is highly regulated and drivers have long been subjected to federal regulation of their qualifications. See . . . 49 U.S.C. §3102(b) (authorizing Secretary of Transportation to prescribe qualifications of drivers in order to promote safety in the motor carrier industry); 49 C.F.R. §391.41 (regulating physical condition of drivers).

The regulation of drivers' qualifications already includes subjecting them to comprehensive biennial physical examinations. . . . These examinations include urinalysis to detect infections of the genito-urinary tract, a history of luetic infection, or latent syphilis. Drivers also must take road tests and written examinations. . . . Drivers' hours of service are strictly regulated in order to prevent fatigue. . . .

Accordingly, the intrusiveness of these drug-testing regulations, on their face, must be measured against the impositions on drivers' privacy already worked by the nature of their job and its attendant regulations. Indeed, drivers must maintain logs documenting when they are off-duty or in their sleeper berths. . . . In *Treasury Employees*, the Supreme Court specifically noted that employees' privacy expectations necessarily would be lowered if . . . their positions already entailed "background investigations, medical examinations or other [such] intrusions."[11]

Thus, the court found that drivers in the transportation industry had diminished privacy expectations. From the point of view of the court, the additional intrusion associated with the drug testing was minimal. But the diminished privacy interest of the drivers was insufficient, by itself, to permit the drug testing. The privacy interest, albeit diminished, was real. Thus, for the drug testing to pass constitutional muster, it must serve a compelling governmental interest.

What was that governmental interest? The court, in addressing the constitutionality of the random drug testing, noted that the

> FHWA cited enhanced transportation safety, accident avoidance, and deterrence of drug use as its primary motivation for enacting these regulations. . . . The unions argue that these reasons are not sufficiently compelling to justify an abridgement of the drivers' fourth amendment rights. They stress the lack of evidence of a serious drug problem among commercial drivers and the FHWA's failure to rely on less intrusive alternatives to drug-testing to achieve its goals. We reject both arguments and hold that the FHWA has enunciated a compelling governmental interest in conducting random drug tests of commercial drivers. . . .
>
> Given the enormous size of commercial trucks, relative to other vehicles on the road, a single mistake in judgment or momentary lapse in attention can have devastating consequences for other travelers. This is especially true for drivers who carry hazardous cargo. While a single accident may not imperil as many lives as a single airline or train crash, the vast number of drivers on the road at any given time multiplies the danger to motorists and raises the FHWA's concern for transportation safety to the level of a compelling governmental interest. . . .
>
> Furthermore, even assuming no evidence of substantial drug abuse among truck drivers existed, the FHWA's interest in deterring drug abuse and in "preventing an otherwise pervasive societal problem from spreading" to the trucking industry would "[furnish] an ample justification" for the testing program . . . "the deterrent purposes of the [FHWA's] program and the potential for serious harm" constitute a compelling justification for the regulations. . . .
>
> The Unions also contend that the governmental interest is not compelling because alternative, less intrusive means exist to promote transportation safety and drug deterrence. The Supreme Court, however, has explicitly rejected the notion that the constitutionality of a drug testing program turns upon the availability of less intrusive means to achieve the agency's goals. . . .
>
> Furthermore, it is not clear that alternative types of drug tests, such as reasonable suspicion testing, would accomplish the dual goals of safety and deterrence. The FHWA has enacted a comprehensive drug testing program involving a variety of different drug tests. In its considered judgment, such a thoroughgoing approach was necessary to ensure that commercial drivers abstain from drug use throughout their careers. Random drug testing has particular appeal because, due to its inherent element of surprise, complete abstinence from drug use is the drivers' only safeguard against failure. Temporary abstinence will often suffice to survive periodic or pre-employment drug

screens. Post-accident testing, although also containing an element of surprise, does not pack as powerful a deterrent punch because it is less frequent and less certain.

Random testing also responds to the "operational realities of the [drivers'] workplace.". . . Commercial drivers work alone and unsupervised for substantial periods of time. The opportunity for supervisors to detect drug usage, and thus have reasonable suspicion to conduct a test, is minimal. As a result, drivers could cause "great human loss before any signs of impairment become noticeable to supervisors or others.". . .

Having concluded that the incremental intrusion on drivers' privacy worked by random drug testing is minimal and that the FHWA's purpose for instituting the tests is compelling, we conclude that random drug testing of commercial drivers does not offend the fourth amendment despite the lack of a warrant or individualized suspicion.[12]

The court then applied the same analytical framework to the periodic testing, the pre-employment testing, and the post-accident testing, saying that the government's interest in highway safety was sufficient to overcome the drivers' somewhat diminished interest in privacy. The court also decided that the regulations were not arbitrary or capricious, concluding that their adoption was based on evidence.

The *Teamsters* case suggests that the courts have found that the constitution does not prevent the government from exercising broad authority, through regulated private employers, to require properly administered drug testing for safety purposes in industries which it has legal authority to regulate for safety purposes. Although such tests are viewed as governmentally imposed searches, and thereby subject to scrutiny under the Fourth Amendment, the constitutional standards that private employers subject to governmental regulations must meet to undertake drug tests are far more lenient than in the criminal situation normally associated with Fourth Amendment searches.

The court noted in *Railway Labor* that the constitution does not prohibit all searches, only "unreasonable" searches.[13] Although, in a criminal case, in which an individual may be deprived of his or her freedom, reasonableness is determined by the issuance of a warrant, a warrant is not necessary in government-mandated employment drug testing provided that the government is able to show a need for the drug testing and safeguards are included. The safeguards are designed to protect the tested employees' privacy, to insure test accuracy, and to avoid the possibility that the results of the test will be used in a criminal investigation without the employee's consent. A warrant is viewed as being inconsistent with the urgency of obtaining the test results at the workplace and too great a burden on supervisors, who are not accustomed to the legal intricacies of obtaining a warrant. Moreover, when the drug test is administered based on non-personal or objective criteria, with little or no supervisory discretion, there can be no bias for a neutral magistrate to determine and eliminate.

Ensuring safety has been considered a special need that justifies drug testing without a warrant. Importantly, the courts have not required that the government demonstrate a pre-existing serious drug problem that the testing is designed to ferret out and resolve. As can be seen from the *Teamsters* case, anecdotal evidence of a "special need" is sufficient. In a case involving a US Customs Service drug testing program for employees or job applicants for positions that involve carrying firearms and drug interdiction, the US Supreme Court said that it is not necessary to support a drug testing program with any evidence that a problem exists. A showing that drug use in a safety-sensitive job would likely compromise job performance was, by itself, sufficient to uphold a drug testing requirement.[14]

The courts have also made clear, however, that employee drug testing must be done carefully in order to be considered constitutional. It must be done on a depersonalized basis, with no supervisory discretion except where there is "reasonable cause" to believe an employee is using drugs. Thus, a random test, a post-accident test, or a test association with application to a safety-sensitive position are all considered non-discretionary, because the test is triggered by a discrete event that is outside the control of the employer.

Employee privacy when the urine sample is given must be guaranteed, taking into account the need to prevent the employee from submitting someone else's urine sample as his or her own. A positive on a preliminary test must be confirmed by a stricter test. The test results must be kept confidential. A rehabilitation program also seems to help the testing program to pass constitutional muster.

Also important in these cases has been the courts' perception of the privacy expectations of the employees. Because transportation and the physical condition of the employees in transportation had long been heavily regulated for safety reasons, the courts have found that the incremental invasion of the privacy of these employees caused by the drug tests was minimal.[15]

Despite these generally favorable court decisions, the Department of Transportation rules still left two major gaps that proponents of testing believed needed to be addressed. First, the rules generally applied only to testing for controlled substances (e.g. illegal drugs). They were not designed to deal with alcohol-related impairment. Second, the federal government lacked statutory authority to require drug testing in urban mass transit. This was the result of a 1990 court decision by the District of Columbia circuit in the case of *Amalgamated Transit Union* v. *Skinner*.[16] In that case, the court ruled that the Urban Mass Transit Act permitted the Urban Mass Transit Authority in the Department of Transportation only to direct local transportation bodies to submit implementation plans for insuring safety.

These perceived deficiencies, along with an August 1991 New York City subway accident that resulted in five deaths and 121 injuries and was due in part to driver intoxication, broke down House opposition to legislation. In October 1991, Congress enacted the Omnibus Transportation Employee Testing Act of 1991 (OTETA), a comprehensive attempt to eliminate substance abuse at the workplace in the industries and among employees regulated by the Department of Transportation.[17]

Pursuant to the requirements in the OTETA, in December 1993 each of the operating administrations issued proposed rules for alcohol testing.[18] The rules cover about approximately seven million employees in the interstate and intrastate transportation industry. They apply to persons who perform safety-sensitive functions in commercial transportation. The alcohol breath testing procedures act as screening devices for determining the presence of alcohol and need for further testing. The impairment level is 0.04 grams of alcohol per 210 liters of expired breath. Legal intoxication for purposes of driving is either 0.08 or 0.10 grams. The OTETA contains an express preemption of inconsistent state and local laws. Unlike drug testing, which is targeted whether use is on- or off-duty, the rules on alcohol testing cover on-duty use, as alcohol is a legal substance. The rules also prohibit an employee from refusing testing, as the consequences of a refusal are an inference of impairment. The OTETA required that the regulations must include provision for identification and opportunity for treatment for identified employees.

The rules provide for pre-employment/pre first-time sensitive duty testing and post-accident testing. The rules state that random testing be limited to the time period surrounding the performance of safety-related functions. The random testing may be done immediately preceding job performance, concurrently with performance, and immediately following job performance.[19]

The basic pattern for imposition of discipline based on an alcohol test is as follows:

1 Once there is determination that the employee has violated the rules prohibiting alcohol abuse, the employee must be removed from and cannot return to a safety sensitive function until, at a minimum
   (a) the employee undergoes evaluation and, where necessary, rehabilitation;
   (b) a substance abuse program has determined that the employee has been rehabilitated;
   (c) the employee tests at less than 0.02 (0.02 grams of alcohol per 210 liters of expired breath);
   (d) the employer determines that the employee can perform safety sensitive function.
2 An employee with an alcohol level of 0.02 to 0.04 is not permitted to perform a safety sensitive function for
   (a) at least eight hours;
   (b) or until a retest shows an alcohol concentration less than 0.02.

In general, the alcohol and drug testing promulgated pursuant to the OTETA follow the precedents of *Railway Labor* and related cases. Thus, they are likely to be upheld.

The Drug Free Workplace Act of 1988[20]

The OTETA was an attempt by the federal government to use its regulatory authority to oppose the use of drugs in the workplace. The Drug Free

Workplace Act of 1988 used the government's contracting authority to do the same thing. The Act covers all organizations receiving contracts or grants for $25,000 or more, all contracts awarded to individuals, and all recipients of federal grants. Employers who receive such grants must certify that they will meet certain requirements to keep their workplaces drug-free. The general implementing rules were promulgated on January 31, 1989 and cover all contracts or grants with an effective date on or after March 18, 1989.

Although each department in the federal government has its own variation of the rules, the Act did prescribe some basic characteristics each department must implement. Drug testing is not mentioned in the law. Rather, covered employers must: (a) publish and make employees aware of a policy prohibiting drugs in the workplace; (b) establish a drug-free awareness program which informs employees of the dangers of workplace drug abuse, informs employees of the employer's intent to maintain a drug-free workplace, makes employees aware of the availability of drug-related counseling, rehabilitation, and other assistance; (c) take appropriate action against employees convicted of a drug offense; and (d) report any criminal convictions to the federal government.

If an employer has an excessive number of convictions, it will be presumed to be out of compliance with the Act, which could result in disbarment from federal contracts. The number of convictions that is considered to be "excessive" will be decided by federal officials.

Other federal agencies

Although the Department of Transportation has been the most aggressive in addressing potential drug problems in the industry it regulates, other federal agencies have also established anti-drug programs and regulations.

Department of Defense[21] According to the Department of Defense anti-drug policy adopted in 1992, all defense contractors must establish a program to ensure that employees in "sensitive" positions do not use or possess illegal drugs. A sensitive position is defined as a position that has "access to classified information" or that has a "high degree of trust and confidence." In general, contractors must have an employee assistance plan for drug education, counseling, and rehabilitation, supervisory training to help managers to identify illegal substances, a procedure for employee self-referral and supervisory referral, and a drug-testing procedure for employees in sensitive positions based on safety, national security, and reasonable suspicion.

Nuclear Regulatory Commission[22] The Nuclear Regulatory Commission's Fitness for Duty Program requires licensees to adopt a policy that addresses the use of illegal drugs and the abuse of legal drugs, including alcohol. The program applies to all persons permitted unescorted access to protected areas, including employees and licensees, vendors, and contractors. Drug testing is required for all employees within 60 days after those employees are granted access to the area. The program also requires random unannounced tests, testing for cause (including after accidents), and removal only with confirmed positives (with the exception of initial positive findings for marijuana/THC or cocaine), employee confidentiality, and the establishment of an employee assistance plan.

Department of Energy [23] The Department of Energy has adopted a Workplace Substance Abuse Program for implementation at its sites. The final rule requires random testing for employees in designated positions and testing of all applicants for such positions. It also requires testing if there is an occurrence for which there is belief that drugs were a contributing factor and for reasonable suspicion. It also requires the establishment of an employee assistance plan at all sites to counsel and rehabilitate employees with drug problems.

National Aeronautics and Space Administration[24] The Civil Space Employee Drug/Alcohol Testing Act of 1991 (595: 891–4) directs administrator to establish a testing program applicable to all employees in safety-sensitive, security, or national security functions. The program is to provide for preemployment, reasonable suspicion, random, and post-accident testing for use of alcohol or illegal drugs ("controlled substance"). Violators are prohibited from performing these functions. The rules must provide for a rehabilitation program and privacy in testing. Rules within 18 months.

The National Labor Relations Act

Private employers that are unionized and covered by the National Labor Relations Act are not permitted to make changes in terms or conditions of employment without negotiating such changes with the union unless the union has waived its right to bargain over that change. In 1989, in *Johnson-Bateman Company*,[25] the NLRB ruled that drug and alcohol testing of current employees is a term or condition that cannot be implemented without first negotiating the implementation with the union, and that the management rights clause in the collective agreement did not constitute a union waiver of its right to bargain over the testing. In December 1986, Johnson-Bateman, a manufacturer of concrete pipe, unilaterally promulgated a work rule that required drug-and-alcohol testing for any employee who suffered an on-the-job injury. The purpose of the rule was to obtain information as to whether drug and alcohol use was the cause of a recent increase in on-the-job injuries. Local Lodge 147 of the International Association of Machinists, representing the employees of Johnson-Bateman, filed an unfair labor practice charging Johnson-Bateman with a violation of section 8(a)(5) of the NLRA, refusal to bargain collectively.

The board first ruled that the testing was a mandatory subject of bargaining as it was "plainly germane to the working environment."[26] It was a change in the method and mode of investigating employee misconduct that would affect an employee's job security. The board compared it to physical examinations and polygraph testing, which had been found to be mandatory subjects of bargaining in 1964 and 1975, respectively. The board also found that the drug-and-alcohol testing was not a decision that was so fundamental to the direction of the business as to take it outside the definition of terms and conditions of employment. Such decisions, the board said, normally involved capital investment.

The board declined to find in the management rights clause that gave the company the right to "issue, enforce, and change company rules" a waiver by the union of the right to bargain over the testing. The board said that such waivers must be clear and unmistakable. In this case, the company's right was expressed only in general terms, with no specific reference to particular rules.[27]

In *Star Tribune*,[28] on the same day as *Johnson-Bateman*, the board ruled that the employer had no obligation to negotiate with the union over a drug-testing program for job applicants. The board ruled that job applicants are not considered employees under the National Labor Relations Act, that there was no showing how drug testing for job applicants "vitally affects"[29] the interests of employees, and that it was among those decisions that lie at the "core of entrepreneurial control."[30]

State Regulation of Drug and Alcohol Testing

Overview

Unlike in the regulated private sector or the public sector, there is no overarching national statutory framework that is used to determine the legal right of non-regulated private sector employers and employees in the area of drug testing. The cases most often are heard in state courts, although federal courts have decided these cases, applying state law. The applicable precedents have derived from state and federal decisions. To the extent that the decisions are based on state statutes, common law, or state constitutions, there are likely to be differences among the states.

Court decisions and legal precedent

There seem to be two separate streams of decisions in the private sector cases: one applying a privacy framework and the other a very traditional employment framework. The first framework is more likely to result in constraints on employer drug testing than the second framework. Each of these will be discussed.

Privacy framework In cases decided under a privacy framework, the fundamental question is whether an employer violates an employee's privacy rights if it disciplines an employee for refusing to submit to a drug or alcohol test. Because the Fourth Amendment does not protect individuals from actions that are solely those of a private party, employee plaintiffs must find a source of privacy rights in some place other than the US constitution. Thus, the employee must argue and show that the intrusion on his or her property rights caused by the drug test brings the employer's discharge action within a recognized exception to the doctrine of employment-at-will. As would be expected, the privacy claim is based on both the procedure for taking the urine sample and the test itself.

Courts have been willing to consider arguments that such rights can be found in the state constitutions as well as public policy. The California courts seem to have been the most aggressive in finding such rights. In *Luck* v. *Southern Pacific Railroad Co.*,[31] the employer had terminated computer programmer Barbara Luck in July 1985 for refusing to submit to a urine sample as part of an unannounced test for illegal drugs administered by her employer. A jury had awarded Luck $485,042 based on her claim of wrongful discharge. Southern Pacific appealed, claiming that the state constitutional right of privacy did not prevent it from requiring its employees to submit to drug urinalysis and that it had not breached a covenant of implied good faith and fair dealing.

The court first found that the jury could reasonably find that a contract existed between Luck and Southern Pacific, and that Southern Pacific breached that contract. The court based this finding on Luck's promotion to a non-union position after two and one-half years, her receipt of grade and salary increase, and repeated compliments on the quality of her work. From the point of view of the court, all of this created an expectation on the part of Luck that she would not be terminated except for just cause. Thus, the jury could find a breach of a contract if she was terminated without just cause.

Clearly, however, the major issue in the case was the contention that Southern Pacific had violated Luck's right to privacy under the constitution of the state of California. In this regard, the court first ruled that the California constitution afforded all citizens a right of privacy, comparable to the right to defend life and to possess property. The court then observed that:

> the collection and testing of urine intrudes upon reasonable expectations of privacy. . . . This finding is consistent with that of the United States Supreme Court, which held that both the collection of a urine sample and its testing involve privacy interests and therefore constitute searches within the meaning of the Fourth Amendment. The "chemical analysis of urine . . . can reveal a host of private medical factors about an employee, including whether she is epileptic, pregnant, or diabetic. Nor can it be disputed that the process of collecting the sample to be tested, which may in some cases involve visual or aural monitoring of the act of urination, itself implicates privacy interests. As the Court of Appeals for the Fifth Circuit has stated: 'There are few activities in our society more personal or private than the passing of urine. Most people describe it by euphemisms if they talk about it at all. It is a function traditionally performed without public observation; indeed, its performance in public is generally prohibited by law as well as social custom . . . it' is clear that *the*

collection and testing of urine intrudes upon expectations of privacy that society has long recognized as reasonable." . . . Therefore, we are satisfied that urinalysis intrudes upon reasonable expectations of privacy. . . .

Nevertheless, Southern Pacific contends that the state constitutional right to privacy . . . does not apply to urinalysis. The constitutional amendment adopted in 1972 made explicit the right to privacy. . . . The "principal 'mischiefs'" at which the constitutional amendment was directed were the uncontrolled collection and use of personal information by government and business . . . the right to privacy has been held to protect a diverse range of personal freedoms. . . . The "constitutional right of privacy guarantees to the individual the freedom to choose to reject, or refuse to consent to, intrusions of his bodily integrity."[32]

Most importantly, the court rejected the employer's argument that, as a private employer, it was not required to observe the privacy guarantees in the state constitution. The court said the California Supreme Court had found that the ballot arguments in favor of the privacy amendment stated that it covered private business as well as governmental action. The court found that Luck's privacy interests were personal, involving zone of privacy, and therefore entitled to be given great deference. Based on these considerations, the court found that Southern Pacific was bound by the privacy provisions of the state constitution.

Given that the urinalysis infringed upon Luck's constitutionally protected privacy interests, the testing could still be justified if it met a compelling employer interest. The employer claimed that its interest was compelling in that it was directed toward safety. In considering this argument, the court examined Luck's job, describing it as follows:

> From 1981 until her 1985 termination, Luck worked at a computer terminal each day. She wore no safety equipment; high heels and a dress were her normal attire. Her job called for her to travel in order to install computers at other sites. Luck testified that in her last four years as a computer operator with Southern Pacific, she had nothing to do with the actual operation of trains and no responsibility for the operation of railroad equipment. A Southern Pacific official testified that at the time of her termination, Luck had no public safety duties.[33]

The court conceded that it was possible that a computer error could cause a safety problem, but the relationship between her duties and the actual rolling stock was too attenuated to infer that her job had safety implications. The court observed:

> While railroads clearly have an interest in the safe operation of their trains, it is not clear that testing Luck furthered this interest. When an employer asserts an interest that is not obviously applicable to the specific employee in question, federal decisions . . . have held that testing cannot be upheld absent a clear, direct nexus between the employee's duties and the nature of the feared harm. . . . Here, Southern Pacific suggested only indirect, potential safety ramifications that might result from an imprudent decision that an employee working as Luck did might make if her judgment were impaired by drugs. Under the federal authorities, Luck's job did not have sufficient safety aspects

to constitute a safety interest that might be balanced against the intrusion upon her privacy rights. When we also consider that the interest must be compelling in order to justify an intrusion of her privacy rights under our state Constitution – a higher showing than would be required under the Fourth Amendment analysis used by federal courts – it is clear that the trial court's implied ruling that Southern Pacific's safety interest did not justify the invasion of Luck's privacy was correct.

. . . Southern Pacific points out, safety is not the only possible employer interest that might be placed on the scale to balance against the employee's privacy right in order to determine whether urinalysis was justified. . . . However, the trial court correctly ruled that none of the non-safety interests asserted at trial are compelling. Even under the lower federal standard, workers may not be compelled to submit to urinalysis unless "a clear, direct nexus [can be shown between] the employee's duty and the nature of the feared violation."

. . . The trial court correctly ruled that Southern Pacific's other proffered justifications were not compelling. As Southern Pacific did not establish any compelling interest that might justify an intrusion of Luck's privacy rights, that intrusion was unjustified.[34]

Under the privacy framework, the employee is viewed as having a right of privacy and an interest in seclusion. A drug test is seen as intruding on that privacy. In order for an employer to be permitted to make such an intrusion, it must show a compelling interest. Based on the *Railway Labor* case as well as other cases arising out of the regulated sector, safety is such a compelling interest that it outweighs the employee's interest in privacy. But a mere assertion of safety without some link between the employee's duties and safety will not suffice to demonstrate a compelling interest. Thus, in *Luck*, although Southern Pacific had an interest in safety, and could legitimately test employees whose positions involved safety, they could not legitimately test Luck. Her position had only a tenuous relationship to safety, since she did not work with rolling stock.

The court ruled in *Luck* that the right of privacy in the California constitution could be violated by private parties. The court linked this constitutional right with the principle of good faith and fair dealing that was implicit in all contracts (including at-will employment contracts) in California, ruling that this principle encompassed employer compliance with rights of privacy afforded to employees by the California constitution. This did not mean that requiring employees to submit to a drug test was always bad faith. Rather, it meant that employers would be required to show a compelling interest in order to intrude upon the privacy interests of employees.[35]

Traditional private employment framework   As noted, the privacy framework used in *Luck* is one of two streams of legal theory that courts have used. The second stream may be called the traditional private employment framework. Under this theory, the employment relationship is viewed as a contract between two private parties. The contract is viewed as being entered into voluntarily. Government and the constitution are not involved. Thus, under this theory, a private employer can behave in any way it wishes *vis-à-vis* its employees provided that it does not violate a collective agreement, any other law or statute, or the terms of the employment contract. An example of a decision under this principle is the 1992 case *Baggs* v. *Eagle-Picher Industries, Inc.*[36] In *Baggs*, the company, a manufacturer of interior trim for the automobile industry in Kalkaska, Michigan, instituted a drug-free workplace policy in April 1989. This policy included drug testing under certain circumstances. The policy was adopted in response to complaints received by company management regarding employee drug use. As part of the drug program, the company notified local and county law enforcement officials, who placed an undercover agent in the plant. Based on surveillance, the agent informed the company that 60 percent of the workforce used illegal drugs.

Following this, the company strengthened its drug policy. Its new policy, distributed in a new employee handbook on August 7, 1989, stated that employee drug testing at management's request was a condition of employment. On August 10–11, 1989, the company carried out a surprise drug screening, in which all employees in the plant were required to provide a urine sample as a condition of continued employment. Nine employees, including seven of the plaintiffs, refused to submit a urine sample and left the plant. The company treated these refusals as voluntary resignations.

Twenty-nine employees[37] filed suit against Eagle-Picher, alleging breach of employment contract, defamation (for some public statements made by a company official), invasion of privacy, misrepresentation, negligence, and violation of Michigan state law prohibiting discrimination against disabled persons. The court found in favor of the company on all allegations. The plaintiffs appealed only the contract, defamation, and invasion of privacy claims.

The court dismissed the contract claim, stating that the employee handbook did not provide for progressive discipline in cases involving serious offenses, and that the company considered violation of the drug policy a serious offense. The court also dismissed the defamation claim on the grounds that the company official did not say that those who refused to take the tests were drug users; he simply stated that those who refused to take the tests would be forced to give up their jobs.

The court then turned to the difficult issue of invasion of privacy. The court first observed that Michigan did recognize a common law invasion-of-privacy tort that involved intrusion into a person's seclusion. This fact alone did not make it unlawful, however. The court explained its rationale:

> Although mandatory workplace urine testing may well be an intrusion that a reasonable person would find objectionable, our inquiry does not end there. The plaintiffs also must show that Eagle-Picher intruded into a matter that the plaintiffs had a right to keep private.
>
> The Michigan Court of Appeals has twice held that the relationship between the parties affects the right of a plaintiff to keep certain matters private. In [another case], the court stated that the right of privacy "does not extend so far as to subvert those rights which spring from social conditions, including business relations." ... The court affirmed summary judgment in favor of an employer who had obtained a copy of a confidential policy report of an

interview with an employee. The court held that the employee had no privacy right to keep the employer from obtaining the report because the interview concerned company business and because the employee had told the employer about the interview. . . .

More recently, the Michigan Court of Appeals affirmed a summary judgment for an employer who had undertaken extensive surveillance of an injured employee's home to determine if he was malingering. . . . The court conceded that the employer's use of a high-powered lens to observe the interior of the employee's home could be objectionable to a reasonable person. . . . The court found, however, that the intrusion was not a matter the employee had a right to keep private because the employer had a right to investigate the extent of the employee's disability. . . .

[The cases cited] compel us to conclude that Eagle-Picher's conduct did not invade a matter that the plaintiffs had a right to keep private under Michigan law. Both of those cases stand for the proposition that a Michigan employer may use intrusive and even objectionable means to obtain employment-related information about an employee. There is no dispute that the information Eagle-Picher sought, whether employees were reporting to work with drugs in their systems, was related to the plaintiffs' employment. Therefore, even accepting the plaintiffs' contention that Eagle-Picher's urine testing program may have been intrusive and objectionable to a reasonable person, summary judgment is still appropriate.[38]

The court's decision in *Baggs* proceeded from a traditional framework of contract law. Indeed, the constitution was not even mentioned. The court examined common law notions of privacy and found that it did not extend to matters related to employment, as these were not matters that an employee had a right to keep private from the employer. Thus, as long as there was an employment-related basis to the intrusion on the employee's privacy, and the employment contract was not otherwise violated, the employer had the right to invade the employee's privacy and require the test.

Decided along similar lines was *Mares* v. *Conagra Poultry Co.*, also decided in 1992.[39] In that case, the Tenth Circuit court of appeals ruled that the employer, pursuant to its drug testing policy, did not violate the employee's Colorado common law right of privacy by discharging her for a refusal to provide information about prescriptions and medicines she was using, the nature of the illness, the length of time she would be using medication, and the name of the physician. The court reasoned that the information was needed by the employer to insure the accuracy of its drug test results, and that it would keep the information confidential. Thus, the invasion of the employee's privacy was insignificant. Again, we see the court willing to defer to the employer's business judgment if it can show a legitimate need.

Job applicants Although one stream of legal theory appears to place some limitations on the right of private employers to test employees for drugs, employers seem to have very few constraints with respect to testing job applicants.[40]

Public sector

In general, the rights of public employers to test employees for drugs and alcohol are comparable to those that the government imposes on regulated private employers in transportation. Public employers can generally administer drug tests provided proper procedures are followed in terms of minimizing supervisor discretion and placing safeguards on the testing. There must also be some relationship between the potential use of drugs by the employee and the employee's job performance or safety. In *Treasury Employees* v. *Von Raab*,[41] the US Supreme Court upheld a urine testing program for Customs Service agents who carried firearms or were involved in drug interdiction, but found unconstitutional urine testing for all employees who handled classified material. The court reasoned that the government had a strong interest in preventing the impairment of individuals who were carrying firearms and avoiding susceptibility to bribery and blackmail that would result from drug users interdicting drugs. No warrant was necessary since the test results would not be used for criminal prosecution without the employee's consent.

The court, however, remanded to the Court of Appeals the question of the Custom Service's right to test all employees who had access to classified information. The court believed that the number of classifications covered made it unclear whether the testing would be limited to only those employees who truly had access to sensitive information. The court was concerned that the definition was overly broad.

In *NTEU* v. *Yeutter*,[42] the Court of Appeals found that testing of all workers in the United States Department of Agriculture Food and Nutrition Service (FNS) based on reasonable suspicion of off-duty drug use was an unconstitutional search, since not all employees were in jobs whose performance would be impaired by such off-duty use. The court, however, did uphold reasonable suspicion testing of all employees for on-duty drug use and random testing of all motor vehicle operators. In the latter situation, the court found that the FNS had a strong interest in safety, and that this could be compromised if motor vehicle operators were under the influence of drugs.

Technical and methodological issues[43]

The OTETA requires the use of scientifically recognized tests with confirmation. All labs used must show the capability of doing both screening and confirmatory tests. It requires the testing laboratory to insure the integrity of the test and to give the person an opportunity to take the sample tested for an independent confirmatory test.

General concerns   Among the key concerns associated with drug testing is the avoidance of false positives and false negatives. A false positive occurs when a test shows that the target drug is present when the drug is absent.

This can result from a cross-reaction. A false negative occurs when a drug is shown to be absent when it is present. This can result from poor testing techniques.

A second problem with urine tests results from large-scale consumption of liquids prior to the test. This can force the body to prematurely expel the drug through the urine or it can dilute the urine to the point where the drug or its metabolites (the substance that is created when the body metabolizes the drug) cannot be detected.

A third problem results from the inability of most tests to determine how long a substance has been in the body. Some substances metabolize slowly and may be in the body several days after use and after the effects have dissipated. Thus, a drug test on worktime may actually be finding off-duty use that has no impact on work. A related problem is that some substances, such as marijuana, can be ingested by passive inhalation. A test is unable to determine how the substances entered the body.

A final concern is the chain-of-custody for the test. The labs must be able to account for the handling of the sample at all times to assure that it was not tampere l with.

Screening Preliminary screening is generally done by immunoassay tests. These fast, inexpensive tests are useful for weeding out negatives. They are based on the drug or its metabolites in the urine (or other bodily fluid extracted, such as blood or saliva) acting as an antigen and combining with an antibody to form an antigen–antibody complex that can be easily detected by ordinary laboratory methods. A shortcoming of these tests is that they are non-specific and cross-reactive, as any number of drugs, legal and illegal, can form a complex. (For example, the over-the-counter drug ibuprofen can easily be mistaken for marijuana in an immunoassay test.) Thus, the likelihood of a false positive is quite high, and a positive screen requires confirmation.

Confirmatory tests When a drug shows positive on a screen, the Department of Transportation requires a confirmatory test to be done. A reliable confirmatory test is gas chromatography/mass spectrometry (GC/MS). GC is based on the known characteristics of certain substances to move through a solvent to a point on a chromatography plate. In GC, a sample to be tested is converted to a gas. The gas moves along a column with a coated packing. (Columns are typically 3 to 10 feet long and 0.01 to 2 inches in width.) The sample breaks down into components as the gas stream carries it along the tubing. Identification is made by the speed at which the components go through the column and are separated. As the components leave the tube, they enter a detector that records the presence of a component along a time line. Each substance produces a peak.

While GC does an excellent job of separating out substances, it is a poor technique for identifying substances, as any number of substances can break down at the same rate. MS is a useful method for identifying the substances. In MS, the separated substances are each given a positive charge with an electron beam that causes them to become ionized. The ionization causes the substances to form fragmentation patterns. Each fragment can be separated based on its mass. The fragments are then uncharged by a detector, with the loss of the charge activating a recorder. The result is a spectrum with peaks along a horizontal axis based on mass and a vertical axis based on concentration. These peaks are then compared with known patterns for a substance. For a substance to be proven, all the peaks should match the known pattern. The more peaks that are matched, the more accurate is the test.

Summary and Conclusions

Drug testing among safety-sensitive employees who work for the federal government or in industries regulated by the federal government has been declared constitutional. Although such tests may involve a search and seizure under the Fourteenth Amendment, they have been justified by the compelling interest of the government in insuring safety. The result is that many agencies of the federal government have adopted drug-testing rules for their contractors for employees working in safety-sensitive positions.

Although private employers are generally not subject to federal constitutional restrictions *vis-à-vis* employees' rights of privacy, they may be subject to state constitutional restrictions. On the other hand, where such state constitutional restrictions do not apply, it appears that employers may test for drugs. Employers whose employees are represented by a union, however, must first negotiate with that union over drug testing for current employees, although they may test new applicants.

In general, it appears that drug testing in appropriate circumstances has been accepted by the courts. Such circumstances include the testing of safety-sensitive employees or other employees on a random basis or with probable cause.

Questions for discussion

1   What evidence is there that drug use on the job is causing substantial harm to society? Assuming that there is some drug use on the job, is such use sufficient to randomly test employees, regardless of cause?
2   Does a person have a diminished expectation of privacy simply because he or she has a job in the transportation industry?
3   To what extent do you believe that political considerations, rather than efficiency or safety considerations, led to the regulations permitting drug testing in covered industries?
4   Discuss the reasons for using both a preliminary screening and a confirmatory test in drug testing.
5   Suppose that a high-performing employee tested positive for marijuana on a random drug test taken on a Tuesday, with the results confirmed by a preliminary screening and a confirmatory test. Upon confronting

the employee with the results, she informs you that, on Friday evening, she was at a get-together of old college friends from the late 1960s, and that one of her friends offered marijuana, "just like we used to do." The employee denies smoking any marijuana that evening, but says that several others in the room were smoking. She claims that the positive test must be the result of passive inhalation. How would you handle this situation?

NOTES

1 "House approves DOT Appropriations Bill that includes drug testing amendment," *BNA Daily Labor Report* (No. 197, October 10, 1991), A-5.
2 Bureau of National Affairs, *Individual Employment Rights Manual*, pp. 595:61–486. The OAs uniformly amended the rules in 1994.
3 As will be discussed later in the chapter, however, state constitutions may limit a broader range of private behaviors within the state than are limited by the federal constitution.
4 489 US 602, 4 IER Cases 224 (1989).
5 4 IER Cases at 224.
6 4 IER Cases at 231.
7 *International Brotherhood of Teamsters* v. *Department of Transportation*, 932 F.2d 1292, 6 IER Cases 647 (9th Cir., 1991).
8 Chain of custody procedures provide assurance that the whereabouts of the sample are always known to the testing agency, and that access to the sample is controlled, so there is no doubt that the urine sample has not been altered.
9 6 IER Cases at 652.
10 6 IER Cases at 653–4.
11 6 IER Cases at 654–5.
12 6 IER Cases at 656–8.
13 4 IER Cases at 232.
14 *National Treasury Employees Union* v. *Von Raab*, 489 US 656, 4 IER Cases 246 (1989).
15 In addition to the cases cited in the text, the following cases are also relevant: *Bluestein* v. *Department of Transportation*, 908 F.2d 451, 5 IER Cases 887 (CA 9, 1990), cert. den. 111 S.Ct 954, 6 IER Cases 288 (1990); *National Treasury Employees* v. *Yuetter*, 915 F.2d 1110, 5 IER Cases 1605 (CA DC, 1990); *Railway Labor Executives Association* v. *Skinner*, 6 IER Cases 833 (CA 9, 1991).
16 894 F.2d 1362, 5 IER Cases 1 (DC Cir., 1990).
17 Bureau of National Affairs, *Individual Employment Rights Manual*, Section 595 (hereinafter cited as IERM).
18 IERM, pp. 595:77, 73–100.
19 IERM, pp. 595:100f–100h.
20 IERM, 509:111–13; 509:801–79 (PL 100-690; Title V, Subtitle D, 102 Stat. 4181).
21 IERM, 509:113–14; 595:885–9.
22 IERM, 595:601–33.
23 IERM, 595:651–74.
24 IERM, 595:891–4.
25 *Johnson-Bateman Co.*, 295 NLRB No. 25, 131 LRRM 1393 (1989).
26 131 LRRM at 1396.

27 131 LRRM at 1398–9. On the other hand, in *Bath Iron Works*, 302 NLRB No. 143, 137 LRRM 1124 (1991), the NLRB deferred to an arbitrator's decision that upheld a drug testing procedure unilaterally adopted by the employer under a management rights clause, pursuant to which the employer had adopted rules prohibiting the use, possession, sale, or distribution of drugs or alcohol on company premises and being on company premises under the influence of drugs or alcohol. The board ruled that the arbitrator's decision was not "palpably wrong," or "repugnant to the Act," since the arbitrator found that the testing was an implantation of existing rules that had been consistently enforced between 1978 and 1986, when the drug and alcohol testing program was adopted.

28 *Star Tribune*, 295 NLRB No. 63, 131 LRRM 1404 (1989).

29 131 LRRM at 1409.

30 131 LRRM at 1396.

31 267 *Cal. Rptr* 618, 5 IER Cases 414 (Cal CA, 1990); rev. den. 5 IER Cases 672 (Cal SC, 1990); cert. den. 5 IER Cases (1991).

32 5 IER Cases at 420–1.

33 5 IER Cases at 423.

34 5 IER Cases at 424–5.

35 See also *Hennessey* v. *Coastal Eagle Point Oil Co.*, 7 IER Cases 1057 (SC NJ, 1992).

36 957 F.2d. 268, 7 IER Cases 318 (CA 6, 1992).

37 750 F.Supp. 264 (WD Mich, 1988).

38 7 IER Cases at 322–3.

39 971 F.2d 492, 7 IER Cases 997 (CA 10, 1992).

40 See, for example, *Jevic* v. *Coca Cola Bottling Co.*, 5 IER Cases 765 (DC NJ, 1990).

41 489 US 656, 4 IER Cases 246 (US SC, 1989).

42 915 F.2d 1110, 5 IER Cases 1605 (CA DC, 1990).

43 This section is based on Kevin B. Zeese, *Drug Testing Legal Manual: Guidelines and Alternatives* (Clark Boardman and Company, Ltd, New York, 1988), chapters 2 and 3. Readers interested in more detail on the technical aspects of testing should refer to Zeese and the references therein.

13
Conclusion

Historically, public policy towards employment in the United States has been characterized by a tension between two often conflicting principles: free markets and freedom of action on the one hand, and considerations of social justice and individual fairness on the other. As discussed in the chapter on employment-at-will, the United States came of age in the early nineteenth century, when ideas associated with freedom of contract and individual liberty (in both political and economic arenas) were displacing seventeenth- and eighteenth-century notions of the state as the protector of the commercial and economic interests of the nation.[1]

This enhanced freedom in the commercial marketplace was, in the context of employment, characterized by a view of complete freedom of contract. Employers and employees should be able to freely enter into contracts without government involvement. As a corollary to this, persons should be unconstrained by laws in decisions regarding hiring, pay, promotion, termination, and other conditions of employment. Employers should be able to hire or refuse to hire whomever they wished, determine their employment conditions on any basis they desired, and terminate their employees at will. Employees, by the same token, were viewed as having the corresponding right to accept employment with whomever they wished and to resign whenever they chose, perhaps because they could earn more elsewhere.

Constraints, if there were any, were provided by the operation of the market. An employer that treated its employees "poorly" would, in theory, have difficulty attracting workers, thus encouraging that employer to change its practices. An employee who demanded a wage that was "too high" would have difficulty finding a position, and would be forced to lower the wage he or she would accept. Thus, efficiency in the operation of the labor market would be obtained, maximizing productivity and the economic welfare of all labor force participants.

This system, although consistent with the accepted principle in the United States of freedom of contract, was imperfect, as it became clear that it often conflicted with other emerging values. With late nineteenth-century industrialization, conditions at work became a matter of social concern, as it became apparent that unlimited freedom of contract constrained only by the market could result in outcomes deemed undesirable by the larger society. Thus, when the result of freedom of contract was the widespread use of child labor, laws were passed in many states limiting the extent to which children could work.[2]

Laws limiting the use of child labor were accompanied or soon followed by laws restricting the extent to which women could work. These restrictions on the heretofore unlimited right to purchase and sell labor were justified as constraints on the labor market that were necessary to protect the public's health and safety.[3] Similar concerns influenced the passage of minimum wage statutes, social security, and unemployment insurance. These laws were in place by the late 1930s.

The legal issues discussed in this book represent modern incarnations of the continuing tension between freedom of contract, on the one hand, and desirable social outcomes and individual fairness, on the other. A standard value underlying the operation of the labor market in the United States is fairness through meritocracy – a person should be able to progress as far economically as his or her merit permits. Discrimination in the labor market on the basis of race, gender, religion, age, or disability prevents individuals from advancing economically on the basis of their skills and ability. Additionally, such discrimination injured the country's economic growth and prosperity by depriving a significant portion of the workforce of the opportunity to exploit their talents, skills, and intelligence. In essence, to the extent that freedom of contract was used to deny people opportunities, it was viewed as creating undesirable outcomes.

These considerations form the basis of much of our anti-discrimination law: Title VII of the Civil Rights Act of 1964, the Civil Rights Act of 1991, the Age Discrimination in Employment Act, the Equal Pay Act, the Rehabilitation Act, and the Americans with Disabilities Act. These statutes, therefore, reinforce considerations of meritocracy and social justice by assuring that all labor force participants are treated fairly. Thus, access to job opportunities is not invidiously denied based on a worker's personal characteristics which are unrelated to a person's ability to perform, as employers are barred from making decisions based on personal bias or stereotypes associated with an individual's membership in a protected group. As a result, it is likely that employer compliance will result in an expansion of the pool of available workers and enhance employer efficiency by eliminating nonmerit factors in the hiring process.

The core values of Title VII, the elimination of race, gender, religion, age, and national origin as factors in determining the allocation of employment opportunities, are generally endorsed by the larger US society. Thus, there has been little effort to modify them. Indeed, the effort to eliminate discrimination has resulted in the passage of legislation broadening the protection afforded minority groups; hence the passage of such legislation as the Age Discrimination in Employment Act, the Americans with Disabilities Act, and the Rehabilitation Act.

The OSHA represents a classic example of the tension between employer freedom of action and the law. The OSHA mandates certain practices that are designed to eliminate health and safety dangers at the workplace. The assumption behind the OSHA is that the market, operating by itself, cannot provide a safe workplace. By requiring that employers take specified actions, such as installing certain structures or determining the materials that can be used, the OSHA can involve itself in the production process and the nature of the employment relationship.

Anti-discrimination laws and the OSHA represent examples of statutory employment law enacted at the federal level. Originally, efforts by workers to be compensated for on-the-job injuries were determined by common law. But the application of common law doctrines of contributory negligence and assumption of risk meant that the common law often operated to deprive workers of appropriate relief. The objective of avoiding such harsh outcomes helped to trigger the enactment of workers' compensation laws in all states. While the scope of protection varies across states, a transcendent element of all statutes is the provision of benefits to employees who are hurt and some financial disincentives to employers whose employees are injured more frequently than would be expected based on experience ratings.

The history of workers' compensation law is a reminder that, in the absence of statutory law, the common law prevails. Moreover, as the cases involving alleged unjust discharge and employment-at-will, privacy, and drug-testing indicate, common law remains an important tool for defining employer and employee rights.

For almost 200 years, the employment-at-will doctrine was well accepted in the United States, essentially giving employers the absolute right to terminate employees when they saw fit, provided that no specific statute or written contract was violated. Exceptions to the employment-at-will doctrine have resulted from judicial determination of the existence of implied contracts, the contractual nature of employer handbooks, the application of the principle of good faith and fair dealing, and the prevention of unlawful conduct. The employment-at-will doctrine reflects a judicial willingness to curb employer actions grounded on freedom of contract when those actions conflict with principles of fairness or require employee conduct that may be contrary to public policy.

There seems to be little debate over the current status of employment-at-will. Only one state (Montana) has enacted legislation covering all employees. To our knowledge, no state has enacted legislation overturning a judicial decision on employment-at-will. Thus, although some states are likely to expand the exceptions, the basic structure of the law of employment-at-will is likely to remain stable.

Issues concerning employer involvement in the private lives of their employees and employee suits over invasions of privacy are also controlled by the common law. This conflict between employee demands for privacy and employer needs for freedom of action is illustrated by the cases addressing employer involvement in the non-work activities of employees. Consistent with the principle of freedom of contract, with some exceptions, private sector employers have been given wide latitude to base employment decisions on the non-work activities of employees. Thus, private sector employees have no constitutional protection against the actions of their private employers. At the same time, private sector employers must respect privacy rights that are protected by express or implied contracts. Within the public sector, government infringements on employee privacy interests would be viewed as unconstitutional unless justified by compelling interests of efficiency, safety, or productivity.

Drug and alcohol testing regulation arises from a combination of statutory law, common law, and constitutional law. Employees in industries that are regulated by federal statute are generally subject to drug-testing requirements based on government regulations (adopted pursuant to legislation) and the US Constitution. Other private employees may generally be tested for drugs at the will of the employer. Public employers, subject to constitutional constraints, must show some relationship between the drug-testing and considerations of efficiency, safety, and/or productivity. Where drug-testing is permitted by the regulations or the constitution, it must follow prescribed procedures to assure accuracy in test results.

Looking to the Future: Emerging Issues in Employment Law

While this examination of employment law is intended to clarify existing public policy, it is also true that law and policy are not static; they are subject to constant change and evolution. For example, while public policy attempts to strike a balance between the interests of workers and the legitimate concerns of employers for organizational efficiency, production, and competitiveness, reasonable people may differ at the point at which a balance should be struck. What is viewed by some as protection of workers' rights might be viewed by others as an excessive and onerous burden on management. Such issues require decision-makers to make difficult, and often value-laden, choices. The choices made may change over time as courts and administrative agencies modify policies on the basis of experience and reflection. Perhaps most immediately reflecting the changing political consensus, Congress may review public policy and amend existing legislation, or enact new laws. It is within this context that Congress enacted the Pregnancy Discrimination Act, the 1991 Civil Rights Act, and the Older Worker Benefit and Protection Act.

While, as noted, there seems to be broad acceptance of the core values associated with most of employment legislation in the USA, there will always be issues around which there is legitimate disagreement. What employment law issues are likely to arise in the near future? As this book goes to press, the United States is in the midst of an important debate over the legitimacy of governmentally mandated affirmative action plans used in the selection and promotion of workers.[4] Proponents view affirmative actions as an indispensable element for permitting minorities and women to overcome discriminatory barriers and to gain their fair share of job opportunities. On the other hand, opponents have argued that the use of affirmative action has unfairly given members of protected groups special preferences unrelated to merit and has discriminated against others not in these protected groups. The question of whether affirmative action is an important tool to prevent discrimination, or grants unfair preferences to certain groups, thus inhibiting meritocracy, is one that is likely to be debated for the rest of the decade.

A second key issue with respect to anti-discrimination laws is enforcement. When a law is passed, it must be enforced. In almost all cases, procedures under the law are triggered by an employee complaint, charge, or suit. The period coinciding with the enactment of these laws has resulted in a substantial increase in the number of employment law charges filed. For example, between 1971 and 1991, the number of employment law cases in the federal district courts increased from 4,331 to 22,968, an increase of 430 percent. Between 1981 and 1993, the number of complaints filed with the EEOC ranged from 54,000 to 88,000. In part this substantial increase reflected new charges that were filed in 1992 following passage of the ADA.

This apparent increase in litigation must be examined from three perspectives. From the employer perspective, this increase can be interpreted as a burden; employers are now subject to charges under an increased number of statutes, and the increasing volume of litigation lends support for their concerns.

On the other hand, it is also clear that, given the application of these laws to nearly every person employed in the United States, the number of cases as a percentage of the labor force is quite low. For example, in 1993, the number of employed persons in the United States was approximately 105 million.[5] Thus, if one uses the figure of 87,942, the number of EEOC complaints filed in 1993, and we assume that no employee filed more than one complaint, then roughly 0.08 percent of employees filed an EEOC complaint in 1993. Put differently, the probability of an individual employee filing an EEOC complaint in 1993 was roughly 8 in 10,000, or 1 in 1,250.

It is also true that these complaints, although representing but a small percentage of the US labor force, tax the resources of the EEOC and the legal system. This has caused a substantial backlog at the EEOC and impaired the agency's ability to carry out its compliance mission. Thus, charges can take a great deal of time and resources to resolve, creating uncertainty for both the employer and the employee. A deserving employee may be denied relief for a substantial period of time, and the employer may be subject to uncertainty concerning the legality of its personnel practices and to a large, and growing, financial liability. These concerns have influenced interest in arbitration and mediation as an efficient means of resolving these disputes.[6]

Another emerging issue is the enforcement structure for employment law. Enforcement authority for employment laws is divided among state agencies, the EEOC, the Department of Labor, and federal and state courts. Employers whose employees are covered by a collective agreement with an anti-discrimination clause are also subject to grievance and arbitration procedures. Employees may file a complaint over the same action with the EEOC, with the analogous state agency, with the labor department, and, if covered by a collective agreement, through the grievance procedure. Thus employers argue that they are subject to litigating the same complaint in multiple forums. One potential reform that addresses this concern is the establishment of a specialized labor court, wherein all employment disputes are resolved in a single forum.[7]

Another area of debate is occupational safety and health. The OSHA is structured around detailed regulations, complaints, and penalties. Does the OSHA take into account industry differences and the day-to-day realities of production? Are there less litigious methods of improving worker safety and health? Thus, one proposal has called for a special board to review OSHA safety standards. Another proposal attempts to encourage employers to work with OSHA and their employees to create safe workplaces without the threat of fines or penalties.[8] These proposals reflect the continuing debate over the level and nature of government intervention required to promote health and safety at the workplace.

Finally, the concurrent existence of federal and state (statutory and common) law governing employment could soon raise the more fundamental issue of the proper governmental level at which the regulation of employment should be placed. All federal legislation covering employment is grounded on the commerce clause of the United States constitution, the right of Congress to regulate interstate commerce. Since the late 1930s, the Supreme Court has interpreted the right of Congress to regulate interstate commerce as giving Congress broad authority to regulate many aspects of the economic life of the country, including employment. In April, 1995, in *United States* v. *Lopez*,[9] the Supreme Court struck down as unconstitutional a federal statute making it a federal offense for a person to possess a firearm in a designated "school zone" near a school. The court rejected as unconvincing the contention that the safety of children at school was necessary to a strong educational system, which, in turn, was important to the economic prosperity of the country. Rather, the court viewed the matter of firearms at school as an educational matter, and education was under local and state, not federal, control. In the court's view, there was little relationship between safety at school and interstate commerce.

A case such as this may lead to more challenges of federal regulation as outside the scope of federal authority under the commerce clause. Whether this case is limited to its facts, or is used as a building block for establishing additional limitations on the authority of Congress to act under the commerce clause, remains to be seen. To the extent that the latter situation occurs, the role of the federal government in the regulation of employment will shrink, and the role of the states may expand.

Currently, state courts, each applying the unique combination of common and statutory law within that state, may reach different legal conclusions when deciding employment-at-will, privacy, and drug-testing issues. A reduction of the federal role in employment law may exacerbate these differences, especially for national employers that must operate in multiple states, with different statutory and common employment law constraints.

We are authors, not seers, and have no way of determining what other issues may arise. The traditional conflicts between employers and employees/unions will continue to be played out in the political arena. For example, in many states in recent years employers have been able to use the increased concern about economic competitiveness to reduce their costs of workers' compensation through reducing the availability and/or the level of benefits available to employees.[10] Similarly, statutory (case) law and common law will continue to evolve as parties litigate to protect their interests. Whatever issues may arise, however, it is our hope that the knowledge in this book will prepare the reader for the expected and the unexpected in employment law. If so, we will have accomplished our purpose.

NOTES

1 See, for example, Ellen Ernst Kossek and Richard N. Block, "The employer as social arbiter: considerations in limiting involvement in off-the-job behavior," *Employee Rights and Responsibilities Journal*, 6 (no. 2, 1993), pp. 139–55.
2 See, for example, Carl Raushenbush and Emanuel Stein, eds, *Labor Cases and Materials: Readings on the Relations of Government to Labor* (F.S. Crofts, New York, 1941).
3 For example, in *West Coast Hotel Company* v. *Parrish*, 300 US 391 (1936), the Supreme Court noted, "The Constitution does not speak of freedom of contract. It speaks of liberty and prohibits the deprivation of liberty without due process of law. In prohibiting that deprivation the Constitution does not recognize an absolute and uncontrollable liberty. Liberty in each of its phases has its history and connotation. But the liberty safeguarded is liberty in social organization which requires the protection of law against the evils which menace the health, safety, morals and welfare of the people. Liberty under the Constitution is thus necessarily subject to the restraints of due process, and regulation which is reasonable in relation to its subject and is adopted in the interest of the community is due process" (300 US at 397).
4 See, for example, Bernard Mower, "Hearing on affirmative action debates possible amendment of Civil Rights Act," *BNA Daily Labor Report* (May 3, 1995), pp. AA-1 to AA-2; "Testimony on affirmative action before House Economic and Educational Opportunities Subcommittee on Employer–Employee Relations," *BNA Daily Labor Report* (May 3, 1995), pp. E-1 to E-13. For a mainstream press coverage of the controversy, see, for example, Howard Fineman, "Race and rage," *Newsweek* (April 3, 1995), pp. 22–34.
5 *BNA Daily Labor Report* (February 10, 1994), pp. B-1 to B-4.
6 For a possible response to these issues, see, for example, "ADR Task Force

approves prototype for arbitration of statutory rights," *BNA Daily Labor Report* (May 11, 1995), pp. A-8 to A-9; "Prototype agreement on job bias dispute resolution," *BNA Daily Labor Report* (May 11, 1995), pp. E-11 to E-13.

7 See, for example, Commission on the Future of Worker–Management Relations, *Fact-finding Report*, supra, note 5; *Report and Recommendations* (US Departments of Commerce and Labor, Washington, DC, December 1994).

8 See, for example, Dean Scott, "Ballenger proposal calls for OSHA Standards Board to issue, revoke rules," *BNA Daily Labor Report* (May 1, 1995), p. B-1; Dean Scott and Barbara Yuill, "Draft Bill attracts industry support; plan for review, Standards Board, debated," *BNA Daily Labor Report* (May 1, 1995), pp. B-1 to B-3; Jennifer Combs, "Clinton administration releases plan designed to create 'new' OSHA," *BNA Daily Labor Report* (May 17, 1995), pp. AA-1 to AA-2; and Dean Scott, "Clinton unveils OSHA reinvention, criticizes GOP efforts to cut agency," *BNA Daily Labor Report* (May 17, 1995), pp. AA-2 to AA-3.

9 US, no. 93-1260 (April 26, 1995).

10 See "Insurers post improved underwriting results," *1995 Issues Report* (National Council on Compensation Insurance, Boca Raton, FL, 1995), pp. 1–9.

Case Index

Case Index

Subject Index

Subject Index